Puerto Ricans
IN THE
United States

LATINOS/AS:
EXPLORING DIVERSITY AND CHANGE

SECOND EDITION

Puerto Ricans
IN THE
United States

A Contemporary Portrait

Edna Acosta-Belén
Carlos E. Santiago

LYNNE
RIENNER
PUBLISHERS

BOULDER
LONDON

Published in the United States of America in 2018 by
Lynne Rienner Publishers, Inc.
1800 30th Street, Boulder, Colorado 80301
www.rienner.com

and in the United Kingdom by
Lynne Rienner Publishers, Inc.
Gray's Inn House, 127 Clerkenwell Road, London EC1 5DB

Library of Congress Cataloging-in-Publication Data
Names: Acosta-Belén, Edna, author. | Santiago, Carlos E., 1952– author.
Title: Puerto Ricans in the United States : a contemporary portrait / Edna
  Acosta-Belén, Carlos E. Santiago.
Description: 2nd edition. | Boulder, Colorado : Lynne Rienner Publishers,
  Inc., [2018] | Includes bibliographical references and index.
Identifiers: LCCN 2018011259 | ISBN 9781626376755 (pbk. : alk. paper)
Subjects: LCSH: Puerto Ricans—United States—History. | Puerto
  Ricans—Emigration and immigration—History. | Puerto Rico--History. |
  Puerto Rico—Social conditions.
Classification: LCC E184.P85 A23 2018 | DDC 972.95—dc23
LC record available at https://lccn.loc.gov/2018011259

British Cataloguing in Publication Data
A Cataloguing in Publication record for this book
is available from the British Library.

Printed and bound in the United States of America

The paper used in this publication meets the requirements
of the American National Standard for Permanence of
Paper for Printed Library Materials Z39.48-1992.

5   4   3   2   1

To the loving memory of our parents,
David Acosta Ramírez & Marcolina Belén Vega
José Angel Santiago & Irma Luisa Pedrosa

Contents

Tables and Figures

Tables

Figures

Acknowledgments

The first edition of this book, published in 2006, was propelled by the need for a comprehensive source on the history of Puerto Ricans in the United States that included a portrait of the contemporary demographic and socioeconomic conditions faced by this population. Over a decade later, this second edition has been updated and revised: new chapters have been added and other chapters substantially rewritten to incorporate new research and perspectives on what is today one of the longest and largest continuing migrations in the history of the United States.

In various ways, the book summarizes many of the ideas and issues introduced in our previous individual research, adding new information and insights that we hope will inspire others to continue documenting Puerto Rican migration experiences and the communities they continue to shape throughout the United States. For us, this is a challenging, stimulating, and never-ending endeavor. But it also represents a labor of love and commitment to our island and stateside communities. Thus, we are hopeful that the book's merits and usefulness outweigh any shortcomings it may have. We recognize that there is still a great deal of work to be done to fully document Puerto Ricans' presence and their vast legacies in the United States. New generations of Puerto Rican studies scholars will undoubtedly rise to the challenge.

Whenever a book is completed, there are many people to thank who made things easier along the way. First, we acknowledge each other for being able to combine our respective scholarly interests with our enduring enthusiasm to work together, which we were able to do for almost two decades as department colleagues and friends at the University at Albany,

State University of New York (SUNY), and have continued to do in subsequent years. Next, we must express our gratitude to several individuals and institutions that greatly facilitated our archival research and compilation of statistical data. These include foremost the Center for Puerto Rican Studies at Hunter College, the leading institution and archival repository for documenting the history of Puerto Rican migration and the communities of the diaspora. Our appreciation goes to center director Edwin Meléndez for his leadership in strengthening the links between the stateside and island Puerto Rican communities and for fostering the ongoing publication of research data briefs and scholarly studies that keep us abreast of the most recent patterns of migration and the changing demographic profile of stateside Puerto Ricans. His scholarly work with center research associate Carlos Vargas-Ramos and research assistant Jennifer Hinojosa has been essential in defining current patterns of Puerto Rican migration during the course of the new millennium and in helping us project what lies ahead for Puerto Rico and the stateside Puerto Rican community.

Our gratitude also goes to the always attentive staff of the Center for Puerto Rican Studies Library and Archives for facilitating the availability of documents and photographs. Associate director Alberto Hernández-Banuchi's valuable insights and suggestions always made our visits to the library productive and enjoyable. Our thanks to senior archivist Pedro Juan Hernández for many years of supporting our work and multiple requests and to former library staff member Diego Valencia for helping us locate specific photographs for the book.

Data support was also provided by the Mauricio Gastón Institute for Latino Community Development and Public Policy of the University of Massachusetts–Boston. We appreciate the willingness of former director María Idalí Torres to deploy senior research associate Phillip Granberry and research associate Trevor Mattos to provide updated statistics.

As with the first edition, Ruby Wang of the Center for Social and Demographic Analysis at the University at Albany, SUNY, was also instrumental in providing more recent census data and information.

Our special thanks to the Juan Antonio Corretjer Puerto Rican Cultural Center (PRCC) in Chicago and its executive director, José E. López, for his generosity in giving us access to the center's collection of mural photo images; providing the image of the mural *Unidos para Triunfar* (Together We Overcome) by John Pitman Weber, displayed on the front cover of this edition; and assisting us in obtaining the artist's permission. PRCC also provided the photo of the mural *Sea of Flags* painted by Gamaliel Ramírez and Star Padilla, included in Chapter 8. We will always remember José's warm hospitality during our visit to PRCC and his personal tour of Paso Boricua and the various institutions created under his inspiring leadership. Our gratitude is also shared with Alejandro Luis Molina, secretary of PRCC's board of directors, for his warm welcome and subsequent assistance in locating photographs. We could not have included other photos of artwork in Chapter 8 without the support of visual artists Yasmín Hernández and Juan Sánchez and graphic artist Edgardo Miranda-Rodríguez. We very much appreciate their permission to include samples of their artwork in the book.

We are deeply grateful to Barbara R. Sjostrom for her always insightful content and editorial comments and to Susan Liberis-Hill for her valuable assistance with the English translations and for her editing suggestions.

This book is part of Lynne Rienner Publishers's series *Latinos/as: Exploring Diversity and Change*. We are very pleased to have the opportunity to work with this prominent Latin American and Caribbean studies publisher and contribute to the series. Our thanks to Lynne for supporting the publication of this new edition and for the helpful assistance of her staff throughout the stages of the publication process.

Last but not least, we want to thank our respective partners and families for their steady encouragement and patience during the time-consuming and occasionally trying process of updating, revising, and expanding the manuscript. Christine E. Bose and Azara Santiago-Rivera, especially, understand this process much too well, since they have experienced it so many times in their own research and writing. They also understand that the best creative sanctuary is found at home, surrounded by the people you love. Their many invaluable comments and suggestions account for a sharper and more polished product.

—*Edna Acosta-Belén*
and Carlos E. Santiago

1

Puerto Rico:
An Island at a
Critical Crossroads

The opening chapter of our book—in essence the framework for our comprehensive historical account of Puerto Rican migration and presence in US society and our analysis of the commuting circuit that, after many generations, keeps island and stateside Puerto Ricans interconnected through cultural, family, and personal relationships—has been unexpectedly shaped by the life-changing events of Hurricane Maria (September 20, 2017) and its aftermath. The landscape of widespread destruction and desolation left by the hurricane magnify in almost indescribable ways the island's decade-long debt crisis and current fiscal insolvency. Most Puerto Ricans would agree that at no other time in their modern history have they faced the critical predicaments and challenges they now confront. Nor have their current precarious state of affairs and relationship with the United States garnered as much sustained US national media coverage as in 2016 and 2017 (see Chapter 5).

Basic facts about Puerto Rico were not widely known among the US population until recently. The island has been an unincorporated colonial territory of the United States since it was ceded by Spain in the aftermath of the Spanish-Cuban-American War of 1898, and since 1917 island Puerto Ricans have been US citizens.[1] On September 26, 2017, nearly a week after Hurricane Maria struck the island, the *New York Times* reported that a Morning Consult poll of 2,200 people showed that only 54 percent of Americans knew that Puerto Ricans born in the Estado Libre Asociado de Puerto Rico, known in English as the Commonwealth of Puerto Rico, are fellow US citizens. The extensive media coverage of the devastating nature of the island's current conditions and struggles has, at least partially, brought to an end more than a century of Puerto Rico's virtual invisibility in US public discourse and national consciousness. Discussions surrounding Puerto Rico's long-standing debt and more recent hurricane-created

1

humanitarian crisis, along with its prospects for reconstruction and recovery, will be kept alive from here on by virtue of its being a nation of US citizens with a growing stateside diasporic population (which is larger than the island's), expanding its electoral presence and political and economic power in several US cities and states. These sobering realities make it harder for Congress and the current administration and its federal agencies to completely ignore Puerto Rico's most immediate needs. Nonetheless, US agencies and government officials' halfhearted initial hurricane emergency relief efforts and the absence so far of a clear fiscal commitment from the US Congress to the island's long-term recovery from widespread destruction and economic collapse only confirm for many Puerto Ricans their unequal treatment as US citizens and further expose the limitations of the island's subordinate colonial status. The traumatic circumstances created by the overlapping crises also have brought Puerto Ricans to a critical crossroads in dealing with the powerlessness and dependency inherent in their colonial condition. Due to Puerto Rico's decline in strategic military importance to the United States since the 1970s and, in more recent decades, its gradual loss of its status as a tax haven and source of low-wage labor to attract US industries, prompting many of these companies to leave the island, federal funding is no longer a priority and thus a lot less forthcoming than it was in the past.

Having to adjust, at least for the time being, to a less dependable relationship with the United States, Puerto Ricans are realizing that they must embrace a more pivotal role as self-reliant active agents in the rebuilding and renewal of their homeland. Central to achieving this particular goal is envisioning a sustainable path to forge ahead that is based, first and foremost, on providing the citizens of Puerto Rico with basic services, opportunities, and protections under a democratic government that strives to improve their present and future well-being and also safeguards the island's environment and natural resources, rather than on solutions and demands imposed by US officials, debt holders, disaster predators, or other external interests. In many different ways, numerous island and stateside voices are rising to the challenge by calling on the creative imagination and drive of island and stateside Puerto Ricans to join in dealing with the multiple challenges of what appears to be, up to this point, a rugged path to an "uncertain" future (see Chapters 5 and 9).

Migration and Its Repeating Cycles

Migration, a process that remains a central aspect of the island's normal course of life, is even more important in the present, considering the precarious socioeconomic conditions Puerto Rico faces and its low prospects for any swift or sustained recovery. The magnitude of different waves and cycles of migration to the United States is closely related to the specific socioeconomic and political conditions in Puerto Rico at different historical periods but also connected to its subordinate colonial condition and the enduring US stranglehold on the island's economy. Since the mid-twentieth century, the island's economy has become more integrated into the US economy and, therefore, highly dependent on its priorities and policies, susceptible to its fluctuations, and more intensely affected by its downturns. The continuing migration from Puerto Rico to the continental United States and the rising levels of the massive population exodus of recent decades— markedly accelerating after Hurricane Maria—are only comparable to those of the mid-twentieth-century Great Migration (mid-1940s to 1960s; see Chapters 4 and 5). The expanding range of geographic dispersion of Puerto Ricans to locations throughout the United States and the frequent back-and-forth displacements between the island and stateside communities allow one to see these mass movements and dislocations as defining the contemporary portrait of a diasporic nation of commuters and nomads.

Use of the often-contested term "diaspora" to refer to the deterritorialized communities of Puerto Ricans in the United States—an outcome of their colonial condition and US citizenship—offers a good example of the multiple connotations and boundaries of the word. Deviating from its former conventional usage, the widely used term is now more reflective of contemporary transnational migration practices. In our globalized world, the label is continuously applied in the present to almost "any formation of dispersion from a place" (Dufoix 2008, 2). It has been used numerous times in previous and contemporary scholarship on Puerto Ricans. The consciousness and proliferation of diasporic identities in our global societies, configured by the intersecting relationships among the homeland left behind, the host country, and carved nonterritorial spaces (Golubov 2011), give the actual term its own discursive sense of dispersion.

A cursory statistical portrait of the formation and evolution of the stateside Puerto Rican diaspora based only on census data immediately delineates the magnitude and significance of more than a century of sustained Puerto Rican migration and expanding presence in the United States. In the decennial US census of 2010, the US Puerto Rican population stood at 4.6 million, at the time a figure almost a million higher than that of Puerto Rico's 3.7 million residents. Five years later, the most recent data collected and made available by the US Census American Community Survey (ACS) estimate that the stateside Puerto Rican population has surged to 5.4 million, while Puerto Rico's population has declined to around 3.4 million. Thus, currently there are almost 2 million more Puerto Ricans living stateside than on the island. This significant increase in the US Puerto Rican population and concomitant decrease in Puerto Rico's population during the course of the new millennium is mostly attributed to migration and, to a lesser degree, declining birthrates on the island due to an aging population (see Chapters 4 and 5; Tables 4.1, 4.2, and 4.3).

Unquestionably, migration has been a fundamental aspect of Puerto Rican life since shortly after the United States invaded the island in 1898 as a result of the Spanish-Cuban-American War, a conflict that brought an end to over 400 years of Spanish colonial rule in the Americas and turned Puerto Ricans into US colonial subjects. Puerto Rican migration to the United States, however, did not show a pattern of sustained growth until the second decade of the twentieth century. Back in 1910, the US census only registered a total stateside Puerto Rican population of slightly over 1,500 people, but by 1920, the number had increased to 11,811, a figure that by 1930 was over five times larger, totaling 52,774 people (see Table 4.3).[2] Net out-migration from the island slowed down during the Great Depression years, amounting to only around 18,000 Puerto Ricans coming to the United States in the 1930s. The levels of out-migration increased dramatically in the 1940s, however, most notably after the conclusion of World War II, when the total number of migrants reached 151,000. Migration grew again in the 1950s, with a peak figure of 470,000 migrants during that particular decade. With these levels of migration, by 1960 the total stateside Puerto Rican population had reached 892,513 people, more than twice what it had been in 1950. It took until the late 1960s for net migration to experience a downward trend, with only 214,000 new migrants coming to the United States—still a considerable figure—before showing a more striking decline in the 1970s, surging once again in the 1980s and 1990s, and doing so even more dramatically in the twenty-first century (see Tables 4.1 and 4.2, Figure 4.1, and Chapter 5).

During the major decades of the postwar Puerto Rican Great Migration (mid-1940s to 1960s), an unprecedented number of island residents left to seek better employment opportunities and pursue the possibility of a more prosperous life in the United States, settling primarily in New York City and other cities in the Northeast and Midwest (see Table 4.2). Puerto Ricans became the first and largest airborne influx of migrants of a single nationality to the United States, and a great deal was written at the time about the impact of this still unmatched "invasion" on New York City (see Handlin 1959).

Despite the continuity of Puerto Rican migration since those years, researchers could not anticipate that in the first two decades of the twenty-first century, mass migration from Puerto Rico would occupy, once again, center stage and reach levels currently approaching those of the mid-twentieth-century Great Migration. In this study, we refer to the current migration cycle as the New Millennium Migration—also referred to by demographer Mario Marazzi-Santiago as the Second Great Migration or Second Great Exodus from Puerto Rico (see Acevedo 2016).[3]

The current wave of new migration comes at a time when the United States is dealing with the highly contested issue of immigration control—

enveloped by divisive xenophobic, racist, misogynist, and anti-LGBTQ hatred that fuels the fears and bigotry of the approximate third of the mostly white US population that constitutes the Donald Trump administration's "base" of support. The continued inflammatory rhetoric comes from an administration intent on deporting many of the estimated 11 million undocumented immigrants (mostly Mexicans and other Latinos/as) currently living and working inside the United States (López and Radford 2017)—including those known as the Dreamers, who had been protected by the Deferred Action for Childhood Arrivals program—and on banning the entrance into the country of Muslims from several targeted nations. The alarming intrusion of racist and anti-immigrant sentiments into the public discourse of various government officials, media pundits, and white supremacists is threatening the foundations of the nation's Constitution and democratic system and weakening the global standing of the United States as a free and open society.

Given their decreed status as US citizens, Puerto Ricans, however, are not immigrants; rather, they are migrants who do not need visas to reside or work in the United States. But regardless of their US citizenship, their stateside condition as an ethnic and racial minority exposes them, along with other Latinos/as, to experiences of racism, discrimination, and socioeconomic inequalities deeply embedded in US society. This has been so ever since the Puerto Rican migrant pioneers of the late nineteenth and early twentieth centuries first arrived in pursuit of freedom or the American dream of socioeconomic prosperity and mobility (see Chapter 3).

Today, about 69 percent of the stateside Puerto Rican population is US born, an indication of the several generations who grew up and forged their lives in this nation. Increasingly, their long-standing historical presence in US society is being unveiled and documented. Yet knowledge about the histories of Puerto Ricans and most of the other non-Anglo populations—namely, those of color—is still overwhelmingly inadequate in most mainstream historical narratives of the nation or in the public consciousness of the majority population. Island Puerto Ricans tend to fare better in this regard, in part because of the vigorous transnational connections that persist between island and stateside Puerto Rican communities and the multiple endeavors of scholars, writers, artists, musicians, politicians, and those engaged in the worlds of business, finance, and trade who navigate and bridge both shores, in addition to the numerous families, relatives, and friends of those who migrate. Overall, new generations of island Puerto Ricans in particular are increasingly more informed about the history and experiences of their fellow compatriots of the diaspora than they were half a century ago.

Because of the long history and experience of migration of Puerto Ricans and the declining socioeconomic conditions in Puerto Rico since the last few decades of the twentieth century, which took a turn for the worse in the first two decades of the new millennium, large-scale migration is, once again, a pivotal factor in the lives and survival struggles of Puerto Ricans. The high levels of migration are mainly the result of over a decade of negative economic growth and escalating debt accumulation that plunged the island into the previously mentioned fiscal crisis that began a decade ago and has led to Puerto Rico's current portrayal as an island "adrift in debt" (Brown et al. 2017).

In turn, the high levels of migration and rapid decline of the island's population during the course of the new millennium are contributing to a serious decrease in the island's tax revenues, forcing the government to enact vast budgetary cuts in key areas during the last few years, such as civil service employment, education, health services, and the upkeep of the country's infrastructure. These conditions are also having a notable impact on the exodus of many Puerto Rican professionals and members of the middle class, along with larger numbers of lower-income citizens. Although the loss of many professionals does not yet represent a "brain drain" (see Chapter 5), it is, for instance, already affecting the island's pool of available physicians in certain areas of expertise, as well as of science, technology, engineering, and math specialists and teachers. The migration impact is also being felt in those US cities and states that have become preferred destinations for large numbers of Puerto Rican migrants (see Tables 4.4–4.7, Figures 4.2–4.4, and Chapters 4 and 5), particularly by those institutions and agencies that offer a variety of support services to the stateside communities. In some areas, it is also adding to overcrowded urban public schools, increasing a need for bilingual teachers, and reducing the availability of low-cost housing and health services for new migrants. Most recent data show that migration from Puerto Rico is moving at a faster pace in the 2010s and reaching levels that will likely surpass those of the mid-twentieth-century Great Migration.

What, therefore, are some of the key conditions that account for an unabated migratory process unleashed over the course of the island's 120-year colonial relationship with the United States? Throughout this book we address the evolving nature of Puerto Rican migration by examining past and present circumstances and government policies that, at various historical moments, brought waves of Puerto Ricans to the US colonial metropole. Setting aside the specific socioeconomic or political conditions and government-sponsored migration policies, Puerto Ricans' limited control of their territory, economy, trade, and other government affairs by definition facilitates migration. These conditions also provide the fundamental framework for our comprehensive analysis of the factors that historically have contributed to migration and, at different times, have compelled island Puerto Ricans to uproot themselves in mass numbers. In what he calls state "sponsored migration" policies that gave impetus to the post–World War II Great Migration, Edgardo Meléndez (2017) cogently argues, "Puerto Rican migration to the United States must be understood as a colonial migration—that is, a migration of U.S. citizens coming from a colonial (unincorporated) territory of the United States" (10). Thus the colonial realities make the particular migration circumstances and experiences of Puerto Ricans comparatively different from those of other US Latinos/as, despite many other similarities and conditions that both immigrants and migrants of multiracial backgrounds confront in US society.

From the beginning of colonial rule, US officials clearly proclaimed that the inhabitants of the island they called "Porto Rico" (its official name was changed from the onset and remained so until 1932; see illustrations in Chapter 3) were to be instructed in the art of democratic self-government under "the advantages and blessings of enlightened civilization" and the benevolent guidance of the United States.[4] The condescending nature of this initial proclamation by the imperial power set the boundaries of its relationship with its new colonial subjects and revealed the nature of the discourses that would reinforce its domination of them. Soon after the invasion, numerous photographic books written by US journalists, researchers, travelers, and public officials about Puerto Rico and the other invaded "insular possessions" were published. These publications were the first to introduce an American public to the conquered colonial subjects to be blessed with "enlightened civilization."[5] The cumulative effect of recycled multiple visual and textual colonial discourses was that they propagated and reinforced what were deemed to be the essentialized traits and attributes for constructing the subordinate "otherness" of Puerto Rico and its people (Thompson 1995; G. García 2000). Thompson's critical analysis of these books in *Imperial Archipelago* (2010) underscores that it is those "representations, comprised of symbols, meanings, and propositions that create subject peoples and justify imperial rule over them" (3). Those early constructions of Puerto Rican subordinate "otherness" resurface repeatedly in most matters and issues that pertain to past and present relationships and interactions between Puerto Rico and the United States. In fact, similar representations have been used in the past to describe the populations of all US colonial subjects and those of other western European imperial powers.

After the US takeover, the island's civil government was placed in the hands of a series of US-appointed governors and cabinet members—a situation that lasted for almost five decades—restricting the political power and participation of Puerto Ricans in managing their own affairs. Through the early years of the US regime, the governor and members of his Executive Council were all US-appointed officials. Island Puerto Ricans were only able to elect representatives to a legislative House of Delegates.

Puerto Ricans were endowed with US citizenship by the Jones-Shafroth Act of 1917 (generally known as the Jones Act). According to Venator-Santiago (2017), this citizenship was based on a form of parental *blood right* that was later transformed into a *birthright* citizenship by the Nationality Act of 1940, available to island Puerto Ricans born after 1941; he also argues that "today, being born in Puerto Rico is tantamount to being born in the United States" (13).[6] Although the factual basis behind this statement is correct, it does not prevent island Puerto Ricans from being treated as "second-class citizens"; nor does it spare stateside Puerto Ricans from experiencing racial and ethnic discrimination and unequal treatment.

A second Jones Act, until recently less known to many Puerto Ricans, specifically refers to the Merchant Marine Act of 1920, which defines the federal cabotage laws that regulate commerce between US ports. This Jones Act requires Puerto Rico to use US-flagged ships and US sailors to transport all island exported and imported goods. Because of the trade limitations imposed by the act, island Puerto Ricans end up paying about 20 percent more for these imported products than other consumers pay in the continental US market. The island is also restricted from engaging in trade with foreign countries without explicit US approval. For a nation that imports about 85 percent of its consumer products from the United States, maintaining the archaic Jones Act is both very profitable for US shipping companies and very costly for Puerto Rico's residents.[7]

The aforementioned Jones Act is only one way in which being US citizens did not accord island Puerto Ricans the same "inalienable rights" and equal treatment afforded to stateside citizens under the US Constitution. After the US citizenship decree, Puerto Ricans were able to also have a bicameral legislative system composed of a newly added elective Senate, and the existing House of Delegates became the current House of Representatives. Nevertheless, their representation in the US Congress was still restricted to an island-elected nonvoting resident commissioner, a position created in 1904 that continues to limit any effective congressional representation of island Puerto Ricans.[8] Additionally, island Puerto Ricans are not allowed to vote in US presidential elections.[9] They are, however, exempt from paying federal income taxes, although they make federal contributions to programs such as Social Security, Medicare, and other applicable areas of federal taxation.

Shortly after the implementation of a US civil government on the island under the Foraker Act of 1900, two years after the invasion, Puerto Rico's colonial status quandary was further complicated by several federal court decisions, known as the Insular Cases.[10] Some of these legal challenges regarding the status of US territories acquired in the aftermath of the Spanish-Cuban-American War and the inhabitants of the new "island possessions" (i.e., Cuba, Puerto Rico, the Philippines, and Guam)—now the stateless citizens of US territories—reached the US Supreme Court. In *Downes v. Bidwell* (1901), a closely divided Supreme Court ruled that the islands seized by the United States from Spain in 1898 were "unincorporated territories," not part of the United States, and their inhabitants therefore would not have the same constitutional protections provided to other US citizens unless they achieved incorporation. For Puerto Rico, this particular Supreme Court ruling sent a signal that Congress had no plans for incorporation that eventually would lead to statehood for the island, at least not in any foreseeable future. Thus, as an unincorporated territory, Puerto Rico was to be governed under the "plenary powers" of the US Congress. This was a different path from that taken by the territories in the Southwest United States annexed after the conclusion of the Mexican-American War (1846–1848), which became states of the union in subsequent decades. The *Downes v. Bidwell* ruling also stated that "in an international sense Porto Rico was not a foreign country, since it was owned by the United States, it was foreign to the United States in a domestic sense because the island had not been incorporated by the United States," and it was merely "a possession" (quoted in Duffy Burnett and Marshall 2001, 13).[11] Torruella (2007) and other scholars (Trías Monge 1999a, 1999b; Cabán 1999; Duffy Burnett and Marshall 2001) agree that this was the most important case in establishing the constitutional limitations of Puerto Rico's territorial status. A few years after *Downes v. Bidwell*, the Supreme Court ruled in another insular case (*Gonzales v. Williams*, 1904) that for immigration purposes, Puerto Ricans were not to be treated as "immigrant aliens" but rather placed under the ambiguous status of "noncitizen nationals." In one of the most comprehensive historical retrospectives and analyses of these legal cases, Torruella (2007) characterizes them as establishing "a regime of political apartheid" and as "some of the most notable examples in the history of the Supreme Court in which its decisions interpreting the Constitution evidence an unabashed reflection of contemporaneous politics, rather than the pursuit of legal doctrine" (285); he concludes that "the present legitimacy of the *Insular Cases* is untenable" (286) and "can no longer be reconciled with a rule of law in which all citizens are entitled to equality" (287). Even after Congress made island Puerto Ricans US citizens in 1917, they were still treated as holders of a "separate and unequal" and thus "second-class" citizenship devoid of some of the equal protections afforded by the US Constitution to stateside US citizens. The decision in *Balzac v. People of Porto Rico* (1922) consented to this "unequal" treatment by ratifying the notion that some provisions in the US Constitution indeed did not apply to US "unincorporated" territories—meaning territories not part of the federal union of states. Consequently, the long-lasting legal consequences of the Insular Cases allow for the perpetuation of the subordinate colonial status of the US citizens of Puerto Rico (see Torruella 2007).

Ambiguity surrounds the US citizenship status of island Puerto Ricans and the enduring congressional control over the island's land, economy, financial institutions and currency (the US dollar), shipping and trade, military installations and forces on the island, social services programs, and federal courts, as well as which federal laws ultimately do or do not apply to Puerto Rico. This means that despite Puerto Rico's professed autonomy or self-government, the federal courts and the US Congress can easily overrule the authority of its island-elected government.

Under the US regime, Puerto Rico's public school system was central to the implementation of colonialist Americanization policies that made English the primary language of instruction, a policy that was initially implemented in 1902 and lasted until 1947, along with a curriculum that hailed the virtues of American civilization, democracy, and exceptionalism, as well as the benevolent US role in introducing Puerto Ricans to these values (see Chapter 3). The Americanization process also diminished the importance of Puerto Rican historical, cultural, and racial legacies in an attempt to legitimize US colonial authority and curtail nationalist sentiments among Puerto Ricans or political claims for the island's independence (Negrón de Montilla 1971; Méndez 1980; del Moral 2013). Protestant missionaries also made their way to the primarily Catholic island to spread their gospel, another step in the process of immersing Puerto Ricans in white Anglo-Protestant values and ways of life (Silva Gotay 1997).

As US citizens, island Puerto Ricans are also subject to military service in the US armed forces. For many decades, up to the Korean War, Puerto Rican servicemen were assigned to segregated units—an experience also shared by African American and Mexican American soldiers. Over a century later, the 65th Infantry Regiment, also known as the Borinqueneers, was awarded a Congressional Gold Medal in 2016 in recognition of its members' service to the US armed forces and their courage and sacrifices in combat.[12] Many Puerto Ricans were drafted into or volunteered to join the military during World War I (1914–1918). Since the United States did not enter this conflict until 1917, in the past some scholars have argued that the main motivation for Congress's decision to extend US citizenship to Puerto Ricans was the inclusion of the military draft in the Jones-Shafroth Act. However, more recently, other scholars have contended that it was rather an attempt to convey some sense of "US permanence in Puerto Rico" by solidifying US control of the island and strengthening its "bond" with Puerto Ricans (Venator-Santiago and Meléndez 2017) or that granting US citizenship was also aimed at maintaining the "socio-political stability" of an island territory that was of strategic military value to the United States (Franqui-Rivera 2017). Setting aside the various motivations of US officials and island political leaders in supporting the citizenship decree, Edgardo Meléndez (2013) has shown that US citizenship for island Puerto Ricans was envisioned by Congress as "colonial citizenship," since it maintained the "alien exclusion" status endorsed in the Insular Cases that excluded them from the same US citizenship rights afforded to citizens of the fifty states of the union under the Fourteenth Amendment to the US Constitution. Notwithstanding, whether through compulsory or volunteer military service, Puerto Ricans have served in the US armed forces since World War I through all subsequent wars waged by the United States.

The extensive militarization of Puerto Rico reflected the United States' territorial control and the island's strategic military importance to expansionist efforts in consolidating US hegemony in the Caribbean and the rest of the hemisphere. This military presence began with the US invasion but grew considerably during the World War II years (1939–1945) (Rodríguez Beruff 1988; Estades Font 1988). The numerous US military installations built throughout an island with a territory of 3,500 square miles included bases in the adjacent smaller island municipalities of Vieques and Culebra, which are part of Puerto Rico's archipelago. This massive buildup started a few years before the United States finally entered World War II in 1941, after the Japanese attack on the Pearl Harbor naval base in Hawaii. The military expansion involved all branches of the US armed forces and made Puerto Rico the most strategic territory in the United States' expanding sphere of power and long history of military interventions in the Americas (see Rodríguez Beruff 1988; Rodríguez Beruff and Bolívar Fresneda 2015; Estades Font 1988). Needless to say, for most of the twentieth century the value of the island as a post to protect US geopolitical interests in the hemisphere was immeasurable. But as early as 1973, the US military started a cycle of closing or relocating most of Puerto Rico's military installations, with the closing of Ramey Air Force Base in Aguadilla and Culebra's naval base a year later. After the US Navy's withdrawal from Vieques in 2003 and the closing of Roosevelt Roads, the remaining and largest military naval installation on the island, it became clear that Puerto Rico's key strategic military role in the Americas had ended.[13]

Paradoxically, the significant post–World War II population exodus from Puerto Rico that came to be known as the Great Migration happened at a time when the island was experiencing a heavy influx of US capital investment to support a widely hailed export-led industrialization and modernization project. Both US and island political leaders viewed this economic overhaul, which rapidly transformed Puerto Rico from a traditional agrarian into a modern industrial society, as a magic formula to deal with "a broken pledge" to what was, up to that point, a largely neglected colony (Diffie and Diffie 1931) or a "stricken island" (Tugwell 1947). After decades of US rule, the Puerto Rico of the 1930s and 1940s was still overrun with rampant unemployment, widespread poverty, malnutrition, disease, high levels of illiteracy, precarious living conditions, and what most government officials and policymakers diagnosed as an "overpopulation problem" that served to justify mass migration to the United States as well as population-control policies that encouraged the mass sterilization of Puerto Rican women (see Chapter 3).

Almost half a century after the US invasion, US and Puerto Rican government officials were marketing the celebrated industrial development project—suitably named Operation Bootstrap (Operación Manos a la Obra, which means "putting hands to work")—as an alternative democratic model for developing countries to achieve socioeconomic prosperity without resorting to socialist revolution, a path followed by neighboring Cuba in 1959. Hence, as a proclaimed "showcase of democracy," Puerto Rico could not escape being ensnared in the regional and hemispheric Cold War geopolitics of the time (Underhill 1961).

From the 1940s to the 1960s, an array of US capital investors and manufacturing industries descended upon Puerto Rico, mostly driven by the availability of low-wage labor and generous tax-exemption incentives for new industries granted by the island's government. Under this massive industrial development project Puerto Rico became one of the first global models of capitalist development based on the considerable levels of outsourcing of US manufacturing production for export. In this particular case, however, the chosen nation also happened to be an unincorporated territory of the United States.

The industrial free trade zones (*zonas libres*) created by Puerto Rico's Operation Bootstrap were precursors to the numerous export processing zones that decades later swelled in numerous Latin American and Asian countries. Ironically, the promise of industrial development and modernization for Puerto Rico gradually devastated its agricultural economic base, then dominated by sugar production controlled by absentee US sugar trusts and members of the island's landowning elite (Ayala and Bernabe 2007). This dramatic shift in Puerto Rico's economy displaced massive numbers of already impoverished workers living in rural areas and small towns. Migration from rural to more urbanized areas of the island and also to the United States turned into a government tool to deal with rampant unemployment and a socioeconomically disenfranchised population, despite the occasional public disclaimer from Puerto Rico's government that it was "neither encouraging or discouraging" migration. However, Meléndez (2017) examines and documents the multiple ways in which the island government did play an extensive role in formulating and implementing the policies and planning strategies that impelled the Great Migration. The establishment of Migration Division Offices in San Juan, New York, and other US cities under the jurisdiction of the US Department of Labor facilitated this management of mass migration (Meléndez 2017; Cabán 2005). The most significant socioeconomic and political changes on the island that propelled the Great Migration will be discussed in more detail in Chapters 4 and 5.

A Changing Portrait in the New Millennium

This revised and expanded second edition of *Puerto Ricans in the United States: A Contemporary Portrait* introduces a fresh and updated analysis of the current status of the stateside Puerto Rican population. Along with this new introductory chapter (Chapter 1), Chapters 5 and 9 are also new for this second edition. The remaining chapters have been updated to discuss new scholarship, cultural and artistic creativity, and institution building endeavors that bring more recent perspectives and enhance our understanding of the changing realities of stateside Puerto Ricans.

As in the previous edition, this inquiry into the origins and evolution of the Puerto Rican diaspora is connected to prevailing conditions and socioeconomic and political processes in Puerto Rico that drive mass migration. It therefore entails a partial revisiting of the island's colonial relationship with the United States: subordinate ties that began in 1898 and endure. Our multiple analyses incorporate the most recent available data from the US census and other sources to provide a comprehensive portrait of what is currently the second-largest group among US Latinos/as. We also pay attention to the historical and cultural legacies stateside Puerto Ricans have forged as US citizens and as part of a wider population of Latinos/as and other people of color. With an estimated total population of 55.4 million (US Bureau of the Census 2014), US Latinos/as are currently the largest minority group, and stateside Puerto Ricans represent 9.5 percent of that total (5.4 million). Among all US Latinos/as in individual states, Puerto Ricans are also the largest single nationality in the states of Connecticut (55.7 percent), Pennsylvania (50.6 percent), Massachusetts (42.2 percent), New York (29.9 percent), and New Jersey (27.1 percent). They also are closing the gap in the state of Florida (21 percent), where Cubans still outnumber them (29.1 percent) (Hinojosa and Vargas-Ramos 2017).

In order to expand our understanding of the main factors that draw Puerto Ricans to specific geographic areas within the United States, we examine the historical formation and contours of some of the larger communities that are part of the Puerto Rican diaspora. We focus on the changing migration and settlement patterns of Puerto Ricans and their physical mobility to an expanding and more diverse array of US cities, states, and regions (Chapters 4 and 5). Additionally, we provide a socioeconomic and educational profile of the latest waves of migrants compared to those of prior generations (Chapter 6). As a whole, this study addresses the conditions and challenges Puerto Ricans face as they continue to leave their homeland in their quest for better employment possibilities and socioeconomic mobility in old and new geographic destinations and in pursuing the prospects of building what most migrants perceive to be a more promising way of life in US society.

Since the mid-twentieth-century Great Migration, researchers have portrayed Puerto Ricans as "a commuter nation" (Torre, Rodríguez Vecchini, and Burgos 1994) or "a nation on the move" (Duany 2002), characterizations that stem mainly from their back-and-forth migration patterns between the island and the United States. Others have mentioned their "revolving door" or "circular" migration patterns. The metaphor of a *guagua aérea* (airbus or flying bus), introduced in an essay by Luis Rafael Sánchez (1994), one of Puerto Rico's most prominent writers, came to represent the ease with which large numbers of Puerto Ricans routinely board a plane to cross the ocean that separates the island from the continental United States. The idiomatic phrase *brincar el charco* (literally, to jump over the puddle) was coined in popular lore to refer to the continuity and, by now, almost habitual nature of the constant and enduring experience of migration among Puerto Ricans. Bearing in mind their most recent patterns of internal migration and relocation within and throughout the United States and the incessant influx of new migrants from the island, Puerto Ricans are now also viewed as "nomads," a term that both captures and illustrates their considerable degree of physical mobility from place to place and the nature of the geographic diffusion and patterns of settlement that now characterize their diasporic experiences (see Meléndez and Vargas-Ramos 2014, 2017; Hinojosa and Vargas-Ramos 2017).

The current decline in Puerto Rico's population, mostly driven by the startling levels of mass migration during the early decades of the new millennium, should not detract from recognition of the presence of several generations of Puerto Ricans born or raised in the United States. These individuals, for the most part, tend to see the United States as their permanent home. In 2015, US-born Puerto Ricans represented about 69 percent of the total stateside Puerto Rican population. Consequently, for several generations, they have been contributing to the US economy with their labor and as taxpayers, consumers, and voters. Many are still striving to overcome poverty and improve their underprivileged socioeconomic and educational profile, but there has been notable progress in these areas; their collective status also has improved compared to the 1970s (see Chapter 6). As part of an expanding US population of color, Puerto Ricans confront similar experiences of racism, segregation, and socioeconomic inequalities shared by other groups included in this category. Widespread racial mixing is present in Puerto Rican history, an outcome of the violent encounters prompted by the Spanish conquest and colonization of the island that decimated the indigenous Tainos and replaced their forced labor with that of enslaved Africans (see Chapter 2). Hence, Puerto Rican culture evolved from the amalgamation of these three populations during the Spanish colonial period, which also accounts for the wide range of racial mixture and spectrum of skin colors among Puerto Ricans.

Following in the footsteps of Puerto Rican migrant pioneers who arrived in the United States in small numbers in the second half of the nineteenth century and early decades of the twentieth—and grappled with economic survival, discrimination, exclusion, and unequal treatment—new generations of stateside Puerto Ricans continue to face these challenges, build their legacies of survival, and make enduring contributions to the United States. They have actively engaged in the battles for social, political, and civil rights, fighting for equality and the empowerment of their communities, and created their own institutions and organizations to advance those goals. Equally resilient is their lasting and vibrant creative spirit, which now enriches US cultural and artistic life. These are some significant ways in which Puerto Ricans have become an integral part of the intricate mosaic of productive and engaged colonial migrants and immigrants of all races, colors, and origins that for many centuries have inhabited the vast territory that is today the United States. Although high levels of poverty, racial discrimination, and unequal treatment still curtail their social mobility in some states and regions, collectively their socioeconomic indicators have improved since the 1970s (see Chapter 6).

Puerto Ricans have solidified their presence and upheld their identities among the industrious medley of settlers and newcomers who continue to weave the social and cultural fabric of this nation. This book gives proper recognition to their multiple endeavors in becoming part of US society and offers an up-to-date comprehensive portrait of a productive and lasting historical record of labor output, civic and community activism, institution building, and cultural and artistic expression. In general, prevailing disparaging assessments and preconceptions about underprivileged and disempowered communities of color ingrained in the white Anglo-American mainstream often tend to draw more attention than Puerto Ricans' legacies and invaluable contributions.

Strong and mutually beneficial transnational ties between island and stateside Puerto Ricans increasingly have made these two communities more interdependent. The vitality of these connections and interchanges is expected to persist and become even more visible in the future as the stateside Puerto Rican population continues to grow in significant numbers. As of 2015, there were almost 2 million more Puerto Ricans living in the United States than in Puerto Rico, and a consistent pattern of population growth within the diaspora was evident throughout most of the twentieth century and continues at a faster pace in the new millennium. By implication, one can anticipate that political participation and representation of stateside Puerto Ricans also will continue to grow in the US Congress and at state and local levels—especially in those cities with the largest concentrations of Puerto Ricans (e.g., New York City, Philadelphia, Chicago, Springfield, Hartford, and Orlando). So far, relatively low voter turnout in US elections, as compared to those on the island, is hindering Puerto Rican political power (see J. Cruz 2017; Meléndez and Vargas-Ramos 2014, 2017).

The lyrics of a classic Puerto Rican *plena* capture the significance and durability of the ties that bind *boricuas de la banda acá* (Puerto Ricans from this shore) and *boricuas de la banda allá* (Puerto Ricans from that other shore), bonds of solidarity that in some instances allow differences in political ideologies to be set aside on behalf of the common good.[14] These mutual expressions of solidarity have been nurtured and given continuity by past and present generations of Puerto Ricans. In more recent times, collaborations between *los de aquí y los de allá* (those from here and those from there—a reference to island and stateside Puerto Ricans) were quite evident on several fronts at different times. Periodically, the island government and press would come out in defense of Puerto Rican migrants, especially in cases of racism and discrimination, labor exploitation by US companies, abuse by the police or slumlords, school segregation in less-than-adequate city schools, vilification in public statements, and the trampling of civil rights. They were equally proud to acknowledge the accomplishments of their organizations, community leaders, writers, artists, and musicians. Notwithstanding, island Puerto Ricans were not exempt from replicating common stereotypes and negative appraisals about the conditions of poverty and other problems that afflicted the lives of stateside Puerto Ricans. In fact, until recent decades the history and contributions of the diaspora remained a neglected chapter in Puerto Rico's historiography and school textbooks, and there was a generalized lack of knowledge among island Puerto Ricans about the generations of Puerto Ricans who built their lives in the United States.

Since the late 1960s, there have been visible instances of the diaspora engaging in the campaigns to free Puerto Rican political prisoners—nationalists and other militant members of organizations working toward the island's liberation and incarcerated for decades in federal prisons. Stateside Puerto Ricans have done so by supporting organizations working on their release and participating in mass demonstrations and rallies. Both island and stateside Puerto Rican writers, artists, and musicians also have lent their creativity to the cause, along with students and other community activists. These joint campaigns to free prominent patriots such as Lolita Lebrón and other nationalists have continued for decades, including the most recent successful efforts for the release of Oscar López Rivera in 2017, and are fresh in the memory of Puerto Rican activists of the late 1960s and beyond.[15]

The Peace for Vieques solidarity movement of the late 1990s and early 2000s gave national visibility to the joining together of island and stateside Puerto Ricans from different social and political sectors in a common cause. For many decades, with the help of pro-independence sectors and grassroots activists and little support from Puerto Rico's government, the people of Vieques struggled to get the US Navy to cease bombing-training practices and withdraw from the small island municipality, before it finally did so in 2003. The combined activism is manifesting, once again, in how Puerto Ricans from both shores are pressing the US Congress to provide the necessary assistance to allow Puerto Rico's government to deal more effectively with the island's current fiscal crisis and the widespread destruction and desolation left behind by Hurricane Maria. These high-profile contemporary issues show that island and stateside Puerto Ricans are ready to join forces around specific struggles that impact the lives of their compatriots. The fast-growing stateside Puerto Rican population is showing increased awareness of its realistic potential to expand its political power in supporting issues related to the welfare and advancement of its communities and also to persuade Congress and the administration to develop a comprehensive federal aid plan that facilitates the swift reconstruction of the island and that treats the US citizens of Puerto Rico in a similar way to those living in other stateside disaster areas.

In the early years of the US colonial regime in Puerto Rico, authorities began to use migration as a policy tool to deal with the widespread poverty and unemployment that afflicted the majority of the island's population. The new government played a central role in facilitating and managing labor migration to the United States and other overseas destinations—such as to the Hawaiian Islands, the Dominican Republic, and Cuba—places that attracted large US corporate investments during those years, mainly in the sugar and tobacco industries. It also became common practice for US-based companies to send their agents to the island to recruit Puerto Rican workers for employment in stateside farms, manufacturing industries, domestic work, and other service-sector jobs. These early practices foreshadowed the continuous use of migration as social policy in dealing with impoverished and unemployed island Puerto Ricans. The growth of organized labor on the island during the early decades of the twentieth century contributed to increased levels of activism and demands for better wages and other labor protections. It also fostered interconnections with unionized labor in the United States (especially the American Federation of Labor) and other international labor movements and their broad regional networks. These networks included labor organizations and workers from other Caribbean (most notably, Cuba) and Latin American countries, as well as western and eastern Europe. These transnational ties among workers were quite evident between island Puerto Rican workers, many of them anarchists or socialists, and those migrating to the United States (Quintero Rivera 1976a, 1976b, 1988; García and Quintero Rivera 1982; Shaffer 2013). Individual workers and labor groups and organizations from both sides nurtured these alliances and solidarity networks through active participation in international labor congresses and, with their subscriptions and donations, supported a radical labor press that circulated the articles, news items, creative literature, and letters that artisans and other workers contributed to these

Spanish-language newspapers (B. Vega 1977, 1984; García and Quintero Rivera 1982). In addition, since those early years, prominent island and stateside Puerto Ricans from the political, civic, labor, intellectual, cultural, and artistic sectors were drawn into many of the critical issues confronting their mutual communities (B. Vega 1977, 1984; Colón [1961] 1982; Sánchez Korrol [1983] 1994; Acosta-Belén and Sánchez Korrol 1993). Long-standing economic remittances from stateside Puerto Ricans to their families back on the island and the continuing cultural, artistic, and musical endeavors and exchanges between the two communities also have played a significant role in nurturing these vigorous transnational connections (Glasser 1995; Torruella Leval 1998).

It is within the context outlined above that we approach this interdisciplinary portrait of Puerto Ricans in the United States as a nation of commuters and nomads. Accessible low-cost air travel and innovative communication technologies facilitate back-and-forth transnational migration and make the relations between island and stateside Puerto Ricans more vital and mutually strategic than they were in the past.

Since the 1990s both stateside Puerto Ricans and new migrants from the island are showing persisting patterns of geographic mobility, settlement, and dispersal throughout the United States. The most recent demographic data illustrates the significant growth of the Puerto Rican population in a wider range of US cities, states, and regions. It also shows that large numbers of stateside Puerto Ricans are moving from some of the oldest urban centers of population concentration in the Northeast and Midwest to new urban areas and to smaller cities in the South (see Chapter 4).

About the Book's Scope and Contents

This comprehensive introductory chapter is followed in Chapter 2 by an overview of the historical and cultural roots of the Puerto Rican people, with special emphasis on their colonial experience under both Spanish and US regimes. The chapter begins by summarizing the experiences of conquest and colonization of the Taino indigenous population after the Spanish first arrived on the island in 1493 and the racial, cultural, and linguistic legacies of this population for the historical formation of the Puerto Rican people. An indigenous culture devastated by conquest has nevertheless continued to influence and inspire the creative imagination of writers, artists, and researchers of past and present generations. The rapid loss of the aboriginal population impelled the transport of large numbers of enslaved Africans to the island. They replaced the vanishing indigenous labor in agricultural, mining, and domestic tasks during the first century of colonization and, in larger numbers, during the late eighteenth century and throughout a good portion of the nineteenth century, when they were brought to the island to support the Spanish Crown's efforts to expand the colony's agricultural economy centered on sugar production. The vast array of their past and present contributions is being increasingly recognized since a new Puerto Rican historiography flourished in the 1970s and inspired new generations of scholars, writers, and artists to continue expanding knowledge about the vital but historically neglected Afro–Puerto Rican heritage (Baerga 2015; Rodríguez-Silva 2012; Géliga-Vargas 2011; Géliga-Vargas, Nazario, and Delgado Hernández 2007–2008; Godreau 2006, 2015; Jiménez Román and Flores 2010; Figueroa 2005; Scarano 1984; Sued-Badillo and López Cantos 1986; Valdés 2017; Zenón 1974, 1975). The violent encounter of these three culturally and racially different populations, two of them casualties of a rapacious Spanish colonizing enterprise, unleashed a process of racial, cultural, and linguistic mixture that led to the formation of the Puerto Rican people.

In succeeding chapters, we provide a framework for analyzing migration in terms of the dynamics of colonialism, capitalist development in Puerto Rico, the structural and political conditions that impel migration in a given period, and the social and political struggles that arose among different sectors of the island's population. Control of Puerto Rico's economy by North American capitalist interests intensified after the US occupation, bringing about new social and political antagonisms among colonial authorities, the creole and peninsular elites, and a Puerto Rican working class of peasants, artisans, and other workers. The landless majority of Puerto Rican laborers represented a low-cost and mobile workforce available to serve the employment needs of foreign and creole landowners; it had been so during the last century of the Spanish colonial period and continued as such for almost half a century of US rule. Under the new colonial regime, this workforce became a source of low-wage labor for US companies on the island and stateside. Moreover, for a large portion of the twentieth century, these companies actively recruited island laborers to work primarily in stateside agricultural fields, factories, and service jobs (History Task Force 1979; Edgardo Meléndez 2017).

Early migrations to the United States are the focus of Chapter 3. This chapter deals specifically with the pioneer settlements, or *colonias*, established in New York City and a few other US localities during the second half of the nineteenth century and first three decades of the twentieth. Migration continued to grow throughout the twentieth century, most markedly in the post–World War II decades (1950s–1960s), unleashing a process that is now central to Puerto Rican historical development.

The bulk of Chapters 4 and 5 are dedicated to a discussion of the historical, socioeconomic, and political factors that contributed to the various migratory waves to the United States, including a comparative analysis of different stages and patterns of migration. Chapter 4 focuses on the Great

Migration and the migratory trends that followed in subsequent decades. Contemporary patterns during the New Millennium Migration are the main focus of the newly added Chapter 5. A detailed analysis of this migration period accentuates the conditions contributing to the ongoing waves of large-scale migration from Puerto Rico and underscores the effects of the ongoing debt crisis and the new crisis created by Hurricane Maria in accelerating the pace and scale of migration. This chapter also examines patterns of settlement of both more recent island migrants and stateside Puerto Rican residents in a broader range of US geographic destinations, comparing and contrasting the current New Millennium Migration to the mid-twentieth-century Great Migration. An obvious population decline in Puerto Rico driven by an aging population, increasing death rates, lower fertility rates, and the current accelerated pace of the New Millennium Migration has given rise to "a demographic winter," also discussed in this chapter.

A comprehensive demographic portrait of stateside Puerto Ricans is the main focus of Chapter 6. Data from the 2010 US decennial census, more recent ACS population report estimates for 2014 to 2017, and other reports provide the basis for assessing their current collective status. Relying on the most recent data and that from previous censuses, we analyze close to two decades' worth (2000–2017) of changes in the overall status of Puerto Ricans in US society. Our comprehensive analysis emphasizes population increases, geographic settlement and dispersal, labor-force participation rates, income and education levels, and other socioeconomic indicators. We also examine some major differences in the demographic profile of stateside and island Puerto Ricans.

Chapter 7 provides a detailed account of the diaspora's social, political, and educational struggles during the pivotal years of the US civil rights movement (1960s–1970s), inserting Puerto Ricans into a movement that is still largely identified with the African American population, despite the fact that Puerto Ricans, Chicanos/as, and Native Americans also were active participants in these struggles. The chapter offers a synopsis of the issues that mobilized stateside Puerto Ricans into collective action, as well as the emergence of vigorous and influential Puerto Rican community institutions and organizations of the Puerto Rican movement (Torres and Velázquez 1998) during the civil rights period and in subsequent decades, emphasizing their main goals and range of activities. Organizations and institutions that endured and those that emerged in more recent years illustrate the collective civic and political engagement and institution-building endeavors of stateside Puerto Ricans. They additionally reflect their multifaceted and continuous synergies in empowering their communities in their battles against unequal treatment and in striving for their socioeconomic, educational, and political advancement (see Meléndez 2005; Enck-Wanzer and Morales 2010; Young Lords Party and Abramson [1971] 2011; Acosta-Belén 2011–2012;

Wanzer-Serrano 2015; Morales 2016). The chapter also includes the work being done by numerous researchers to unveil and examine the history and legacies of other stateside communities. More recent scholarship shifts the New York focus of most previous research on Puerto Rican migration and the diaspora to other US cities and to groundbreaking studies that will encourage more comparative work on the different experiences and outcomes of living in other geographic locations.

The diaspora's creativity, manifested through literature, the visual arts, and music, is featured in Chapter 8. These individual and collective endeavors have contributed to build and expand distinctive Puerto Rican cultural legacies and traditions throughout the United States. The voices and images of many writers and artists represent another dimension of the contemporary portrait of US Puerto Rican life captured in this volume. In updating this chapter, we go beyond the creative expressions and cultural movements that dominated the period between the 1970s and 1990s to include those of the most recent generations. Observations about what lies ahead for Puerto Ricans in charting a course that transcends the current "crisis mode" of fiscal insolvency, the traumatic devastation left behind by Hurricane Maria, and a migration exodus that continues to grow in leaps and bounds are at the core of the concluding Chapter 9, which addresses some of the most pressing issues and challenges that lie ahead for both island and stateside Puerto Ricans.

Notes

1. Some scholars have argued that when the United States invaded Cuba in 1898, sparking what is generally known as the Spanish-American War, there was already a war going on between the Spanish army and the Cuban rebels that had started in 1895. Thus the Spanish-Cuban-American War is a more accurate name for this historical event. This conflict also has been called the War of 1898 by other historians (see Foner 1972; L. Pérez 1998).

2. In his memoirs, Bernardo Vega (1984; Spanish edition, 1977) provides New York City population figures that are much higher than those provided by the 1900–1930 US censuses. Several scholars argue that the census generally undercounted members of poor ethnic neighborhoods. The accuracy of the US census data on the Puerto Rican population of New York City during the first half of the twentieth century is discussed by Sánchez Korrol ([1983] 1994), Haslip-Viera ([1996] 2017), and Thomas (2010).

3. Mario Marazzi-Santiago, executive director of the Instituto de Estadísticas de Puerto Rico, described the ongoing Puerto Rican New Millennium Migration to the United States as the Second Great Migration or the Second Great Exodus of Puerto Rico in an online interview with CNN reporter Jeffrey Acevedo, May 2, 2016, www.cnn.com/2016/05/02/americas/puerto-rico-exodus/index.html.

4. Right after the invasion of the island, the US military regime (1898–1900) changed the official Spanish name of Puerto Rico to "Porto Rico." The quoted excerpt in this paragraph is from the public declaration made by General Nelson Miles, who was in command of the invading US troops.

5. Some of these photographic books include Bryan (1899), which according to Thompson (2010, 34) sold 400,000 copies in its first edition; Baldwin (1899); Church (1898); Dinwiddie (1899); Neely (1898, 1899a, 1899b); and White (1898). Acosta-Belén (1992b) provides a critical review of some of the scholarly and journalistic literature on Puerto Ricans published by North Americans during the first half of the twentieth century. These studies tend to disparage an essentialized Puerto Rican national character and diminish the importance of Puerto Rico's history and cultural heritage. Some of these characterizations were often internalized and recycled by a number of Puerto Rican intellectuals prior to the emergence of what is known as the new Puerto Rican historiography in the early 1970s.

6. For a detailed discussion of the legal and political aspects of island Puerto Ricans' US citizenship and its present limitations, see Venator-Santiago and Meléndez (2017).

7. A week after Hurricane Maria, the Trump administration was pressured by several members of the US Congress and Puerto Rican government officials, community leaders, and activist groups to eliminate the Jones Act or suspend it for an extended period in order to provide much needed posthurricane relief to Puerto Rico by reducing the transportation costs that make all US imports transported to the island by US shipping companies at least 20 percent more expensive than they are in the fifty states. The requested suspension was also aimed at allowing direct shipments of disaster aid offered to Puerto Rico by other nations. Instead, the US administration capitulated to pressures exerted by US shipping companies, since eliminating the act would affect their profit margins. Despite the state of emergency and need for disaster relief and an uninterrupted flow of imported goods to Puerto Rico, the Trump administration suspended the Jones Act for only ten days—a meaningless gesture, considering the magnitude of the destruction caused by the hurricane and the island's urgent need for food, water, medicine, and other essential supplies.

8. A nonvoting "resident commissioner," elected by the voting residents of Puerto Rico, has represented Puerto Rico in the US Congress since 1900. Between 1993 and 1995, under the Democratic Party administration of President Bill Clinton, the resident commissioner was given voting rights in the US House of Representatives. This practice was rescinded when the Republican Party won the congressional elections of 1994 and took control of both the Senate and the House of Representatives.

9. Although island Puerto Ricans are not allowed to vote in US presidential or congressional elections, presidential primaries are held in Puerto Rico and both Democratic and Republican candidates actively campaign on the island for party convention delegates, who are able to cast a vote at the nominating presidential conventions. Island Puerto Ricans can only vote in US elections if they become residents of any of the fifty states and register to vote.

10. Cuba was under US military rule until it was granted independence in 1902. Nine of the Insular Cases deal only with Puerto Rico. Legal experts and scholars disagree on the number of legal cases that should fall under this category. The total number ranges from six to sixteen court decisions.

11. The phrase "foreign to the United States in a domestic sense" is part of the Foraker Act, passed by the US Congress in 1900. This act ended two years of North American military occupation and established a civil government in Puerto Rico (Duffy Burnett and Marshall 2001). A more detailed discussion appears in Chapter 3 of this book.

12. A one-hour version of the documentary film (2011) by Raquel Ortiz/Pozo Productions was first shown by PBS stations in 2007. Since then, the documentary has received multiple recognitions at film festivals and from several organizations.

13. As of 2018, only three US Army installations remain in Puerto Rico: Fort Buchanan, Fort Allen, and Camp Santiago, in addition to the Sector San Juan US Coast Guard station.

14. The expression *Boricuas de la banda allá, Boricuas de la banda acá* comes from the lyrics of the song "A los boricuas ausentes" (To the Boricuas who left) popularized by César Concepción and His Orchestra. *Boricua*, a word of Taino indigenous origin, was used during the Spanish colonial period to refer to the native inhabitants of Puerto Rico and later to identify all Puerto Ricans.

15. Oscar Collazo, Lolita Lebrón, Rafael Cancel Miranda, and Irving Flores, Nationalist Party members in federal prisons since the 1950s, were not released until their sentences were commuted by President Jimmy Carter in 1979. Another Nationalist political prisoner, Andrés Figueroa Cordero, was released in 1977 after being diagnosed with terminal cancer. The most recent campaign demanded the release of Oscar López Rivera. Associated with the clandestine group Los Macheteros, he was incarcerated for thirty-five years. His sentence was commuted by President Barack Obama in 2016.

2

Historical Roots of
the Puerto Rican People

The Spanish accounts of the indigenous "people who discovered Columbus" (Keegan 1992) during his voyages to the Caribbean
islands, later to be known as the West Indies or the Antilles,[1] distinguish
between the peaceful Taino native inhabitants with whom colonists first came
into contact and the reputedly warlike and cannibalistic Caribs, who frequently came to their coasts and raided their villages. However, some anthropologists have argued that the widespread dichotomy between the two
Amerindian groups is the result of the colonizers' imagination and that the dis-
tinction they made between the two indigenous groups mostly reflected Spanish self-interests, their less successful attempts at conquering and converting
the Caribs in comparison to the Tainos, and the Caribs' fierce resistance to the
European invaders (Sued-Badillo 1978). Notwithstanding, the questionable
origin of the names attributed to each of the first two aboriginal groups mentioned in the European chronicles of the Spanish Conquest reaffirms the
Manichean binary nature of their initial characterization: the indigenous word
Taino, said to mean "noble" or "good" (Keegan 1992), and *Carib*, standing
for great warrior or referring to the group's alleged cannibalistic practices
(Boucher 1992). Some anthropologists have rejected the original Taino/Carib
dichotomy altogether and maintain that despite the conflictive relationship
between these two aboriginal groups, they did not differ significantly from one
another, at least not ethnically (Sued-Badillo 1978; Hulme 1986).

Two unfortunate circumstances limit our knowledge of these indigenous populations and their cultural practices. The first is that aside from the
symbols that appear in their stone carvings, or petroglyphs, and the remains
of stone and clay ceramics and constructions found at archeological sites,
they did not leave a written historical record to rely upon. Second, their
rapid extinction after their encounter with the Spaniards meant relatively

25

little of their oral traditions or historical memory remained on the island. Moreover, a great deal about what was written about them during the colonial period was written by Spanish officials, conquistadors, and missionaries and not from their own perspectives about the devasting impact of conquest and colonization on their homeland and collective lives.

Most anthropologists of the pre-Columbian era, however, have agreed that the Taino indigenous population that inhabited Puerto Rico and much of the West Indies at the time of the Spanish Conquest migrated from the northern shores of the South American continent.[2] They have traced the origins of the Tainos to the Orinoco Valley in Venezuela. Despite the very different methodologies employed in these studies, Rouse (1986) argued that the following consensus emerged:

> From a geographical point of view, the ancestors of the *Tainos* could have entered the West Indies via either the east coast of Venezuela, Trinidad, or the Guianas. The historic evidence favors Trinidad and the Guianas; Arawakan speakers were concentrated there during the Historic Age. Nevertheless, archeologists and, to a lesser extent, linguists have focused upon Trinidad and the east coast of Venezuela in tracing the ancestors of the *Tainos* back to the mainland. Having failed in this endeavor, they are now turning their attention to the Guianas. (154–155)

There seems to be little doubt that Amerindians traveled frequently across the chain of islands that make up the West Indies and that significant movement occurred between continent and islands, within the Caribbean island chain, and in the circum-Caribbean area. Indigenous groups settled the islands of the West Indies and traversed the Caribbean Sea with considerable regularity, as indicated by the dispersion of their archeological sites and cultural remains. For them, territory was limited only by the technology of sea transport at the time. Anthropologists have even found evidence of Mesoamerican influence on West Indian aboriginal cultures, suggesting contacts by sea among different groups from more distant regions (Fernández Méndez 1972).

There has been a tendency to refer to Tainos also as Arawaks, which is the name of an indigenous language family of South American origin, but some anthropologists (Rouse 1986, 1992; Keegan 1992) have contended that although there were linguistic similarities between Tainos and Caribs, they spoke a different language and exhibited some cultural differences from South American Arawaks. Thus Rouse (1986) suggested that the inhabitants of the West Indies at the time of contact with the Europeans are more correctly referred to as Tainos than as Arawaks. In any event, sufficient evidence establishes that the Tainos occupied the islands of the Greater Antilles and the Caribs settled in the Lesser Antilles and that the latter were legendary for their frequent and belligerent incursions into the other islands, including Puerto Rico.

The Spanish wrote the rudimentary descriptions and accounts that we have of the lives of the Tainos, leaving us with a portrait of the conquered provided by the conqueror. One of these accounts, *Brevísima relación de la destrucción de las Indias* (A brief account of the destruction of the Indies), written by Spanish missionary Fray Bartolomé de las Casas in 1552 (see Casas [1552] 1992, 1951, 2:356), mentions the daily visits of inhabitants of the eastern tip of the island Columbus named Española (Hispaniola), where he first landed, to Puerto Rico, across the Mona passage, a route frequently traveled for decades by Dominicans seeking entry, albeit on an undocumented basis, into Puerto Rico. Even today, it is not uncommon for overturned *yolas* (small wooden boats) to wash up on Puerto Rico's western shores with little evidence of any occupants. The Dominican population of Puerto Rico was about 68,000 in 2010, further evidence of a migratory route through Puerto Rico that often ends in the continental United States.[3]

The Tainos' legacy in contemporary Puerto Rico is best represented in the remains of their pottery, stone artifacts, and symbols found at archeological sites, in the names of numerous towns and places, and in many commonly used words adapted from their native language into Spanish (Malaret 1955; Hernández Aquino 1969; Fernández Méndez 1972; Alvarez Nazario 1977). The physical appearance of a small percentage of the racially mixed Puerto Rican population still reflects the indigenous influence. Legends and myths about the Tainos, including their rebellions and subjugation by the Spaniards, also appear in the chronicles of the colonial era and have been re-created in the writings of Puerto Rican creoles, particularly throughout the nineteenth century, although they have continued to inspire many contemporary writers as well.[4] The symbols from Taino stone carvings, found largely in some of the towns around Puerto Rico's Cordillera Central mountain range, coastal areas, and other parts of the island, usually find their way into its visual arts, popular crafts, and tourist souvenirs. The island's Taino heritage is frequently celebrated in local festivities, such as the annual Festival Indígena (indigenous festival) in Jayuya and the Festival Areyto (indigenous ceremonial dance festival) in Villalba.

The original Taino villages were headed by *caciques* (chieftains). Their social and political structure is interesting because of their matrilineal traditions. Some women inherited land and political power, and the Spanish chronicles referred to a few as *cacicas*. According to Puerto Rican anthropologist Jalil Sued-Badillo (1979, 41), Taino women from the upper social strata played a significant role in the community's political life, and there was a collective approach among Tainos for incorporating women into many of their rituals and activities.

Colonial writers described rituals such as the *areyto* as a mixture of dancing and oral recitation, a way of preserving and passing along the native population's history and traditions. Taino religion focused on worshipping nature and atmospheric phenomena: Guabancex (also called Atabex), the great goddess of the earth; Yocahú, the god of heaven and father of life and death; and Juracán or Huracán, who controlled the seasonal hurricanes so common in the Caribbean region.[5] The mountains of Puerto Rico inspired the religious *cemíes*, the small stone idols that guarded the spirits of tribal ancestors. These religious relics and other artifacts have been recovered in large numbers from archeological sites.

The myth of the Tainos' docility contributed to their "noble savage" image, which the Europeans frequently contrasted with that of the "barbaric" Caribs. Whether the Tainos were deserving of their peaceful reputation is subject to dispute, since historical documentation indicates that they resisted and held major rebellions on the islands of the region against the Spanish invaders, as most Amerindians did at some point. In fact, although colonization of Puerto Rico began in 1508, the Spanish could not establish control of the island until 1511, after subduing a major indigenous rebellion under the leadership of chieftain Agueybaná II. Spanish colonial chronicles also attest to the rapid decline of the Taino population of the West Indies, which was almost extinct by the late 1500s.

Even though the Spanish Conquest brought about the extermination of the indigenous Tainos, a Taino revival movement gained popularity among Puerto Ricans during the 1990s. The creation of Taino imaginaries and recovery of the memories of an indigenous past, an important component of Puerto Rican national identity since the nineteenth century, have taken on new life in contemporary Puerto Rico, as well as among a segment of the stateside Puerto Rican population. An important part of the early stages of creole Puerto Rican historiography on the island, this is still a significant component of Puerto Rican cultural heritage and nationalism celebrated and propagated through state institutions, the media and advertising, local festivities, arts and crafts, and educational curricula and textbooks. The re-creation of Taino images, symbols, and traditions is also a vibrant aspect of cultural expression and activity in the Puerto Rican diaspora in the United States. Haslip-Viera (1999) claimed that the contemporary Taino revival movement should be seen in a broader context as "part of a much larger phenomenon in which disaffected or alienated individuals are attracted to alternative cultures and lifestyles because of prejudice, discrimination, poor living conditions, and severely limited economic and social opportunities" (6). Those critical of this revival movement have argued that the mythifying of a long past Taino heritage tends to undermine the stronger and more marked African roots of Puerto Rican culture and is another manifestation of the underlying racism and reluctance on the part of the Hispanophilic cultural elites to accept the mulatto character of the Puerto Rican nation (Jiménez Román 1999). Other scholars validate the notion that emphasizing the indigenous Taino heritage is in itself a sign of cultural resistance and a way of counterbalancing the harmful effects of Spanish and US colonialism on Puerto Rican history and culture.[6] Regardless of the arguments and debates, even more than five centuries since the Spanish arrival in Puerto Rico, the influence of the Taino cultural roots clearly remains a vital component of Puerto Rican national imaginaries and of any definitions of the Puerto Rican nation put forth by the intellectual elites and other sectors of the population.

The Beginnings of Spanish Colonial Rule

The first encounter between the Spanish and the Taino indigenous population took place on November 19, 1493, during Christopher Columbus's second voyage to what became known as the New World, after Florentine explorer Amerigo Vespucci's voyages and a version of one of the letters he wrote about them was published in the pamphlet *Mundus novus* (1503). According to Spanish chronicles, the island's Taino name, Boriquén, meant *tierra del altivo señor* (land of the valiant warrior), an indication of the gallantry and respect conveyed by the native *caciques*. Columbus named the island Isla de San Juan Bautista in honor of St. John the Baptist, who became its patron saint. The indigenous name was eventually adapted into Spanish as Borinquen, another name commonly used to refer to Puerto Rico. The terms *borinqueños/as*, *borincanos/as*, and *boricuas* date back to the Spanish colonial period when many Taino names and words were Hispanicized. These terms are still used interchangeably to identify Puerto Ricans (Hernández Aquino 1969).

The territory of the island of Puerto Rico is only around 3,500 square miles. Nearby are a few even smaller islands that are part of this archipelago; two of them—Vieques and Culebra—are populated municipalities. The Spaniards therefore focused their early colonizing efforts on the larger neighboring islands of Hispaniola (present-day Dominican Republic and Haiti) and Cuba. Serious efforts to colonize Puerto Rico did not begin until 1508, more than a decade and a half after Columbus's arrival. It was then that Juan Ponce de León, who had accompanied Columbus during his second voyage, was sent to the island to lead the colonizing enterprise. In 1509 he was appointed governor and established the island's first settlement, the Villa de Caparra, not far from the country's largest port, soon to be known as Puerto Rico. After a few years, the settlement was moved to the port's location, and with the passing of time, the Spanish name of the island and that of its main port were interchanged, making San Juan the colony's administrative center and capital and Puerto Rico the name of the island.

Spanish colonization of the Caribbean islands brought about the rapid decimation of the indigenous population; it had almost vanished a century after the first contact. The effects of the Spanish *encomienda* system of land concessions to colonists relied on forced indigenous labor. These exploitative conditions, along with warfare, new diseases, physical abuses, and suicides, all contributed to what Fray Bartolomé de las Casas ([1552] 1992) described as "the devastation of the Indies." By 1594, just over a century after the Spanish arrival, Puerto Rico's indigenous population was down to only 1,545 inhabitants (Sued-Badillo and López Cantos 1986, 85). According to estimates, this population figure represents only about 3 percent of the total indigenous population at the time of the conquest.

The African Heritage

For about four centuries the transatlantic slave trade, one of the most shameful and profitable commercial enterprises in human history, extracted millions of Africans from their homelands. Africans, mostly from the West Sudan and the Bantu regions, were brought to Puerto Rico beginning in the early years of colonization and in larger numbers in later years, as the colonizers needed to replace the rapidly declining Taino forced labor initially used to support the settlement process and perform agricultural and mining tasks (Alvarez Nazario 1974). Enslaved Africans were also used in the construction of roads, buildings, and military fortifications and in domestic service. The population of African origin, however, did not surpass that of the indigenous Tainos until the 1590s, when it rose to around 2,281 (Sued-Badillo and López Cantos 1986, 85). This figure was not to increase significantly until the late eighteenth and early nineteenth centuries, when Spain fostered the immigration of Spaniards and other Europeans to Puerto Rico in order to promote economic development based on the expansion of sugar production. The growing economic activity increased the demand for enslaved labor. Thus, there was enough growth in the African-origin population throughout a good portion of the nineteenth century to begin altering the island's overall racial balance and profile. Largely the outcome of subjugation, miscegenation was common in most of the Spanish colonies, and Puerto Rico was no exception. The widespread sexual abuse and violence toward Taino and African women by the Spanish colonists, along with other consensual relationships and a few marriages, produced a significant degree of racial mixing. The Spanish mixed with the indigenous Tainos and enslaved Africans, producing through the years new generations of creole mestizos and mulattos.[7] By the early nineteenth century, the African racial roots were more evident than the indigenous ones in the general profile of the island's creole population.

The African heritage is often referred to as "the third root" (CEREP 1992) in the cultural and racial composition of the Puerto Rican nation. This important component of the island's heritage was essentially understated in the initial nineteenth-century historical narratives written by the peninsular and creole intellectual elites. These early attempts at documenting the history of an emerging Puerto Rican nation tended to give preponderance to the Spanish European heritage. Even after the abolition of slavery in Puerto Rico in 1873, the Spanish peninsular and creole elites were far from seeing blacks and mulattoes as equal; therefore racial prejudice, labor exploitation, and the tendency to criminalize the black population were part of their real conditions (Rodríguez-Silva 2012). Through the years a handful of segregated black communities developed on the island around some coastal areas and barrios of the larger cities. During the course of the nineteenth century Puerto Rico unquestionably became more Africanized, both racially and culturally. But the Spanish rulers and the creole intellectual and political elites, mostly educated in Europe, for the most part did not view African heritage or the disenfranchised Afro-descendant population as significant components of an emerging Puerto Rican nation. Although not totally oblivious to the folklore and traditions of the racially mixed peasant population, which at the time represented the majority of the island's inhabitants, nineteenth-century creole intellectuals conceptualized the Puerto Rican nation from a Hispanophilic perspective, one that regarded the dominant white Spanish European civilization as the essence of the island's creole culture. This long-standing view prompted one of the most prominent Puerto Rican writers of the Generation of 1950, José Luis González, to argue in his provocative 1980 essay "El país de cuatro pisos" (The four-storied country) that in the formation and coalescence of a Puerto Rican national identity, the first Puerto Ricans were actually black Puerto Ricans.

Besides the obvious black and mulatto racial influence upon a substantial portion of Puerto Rico's population, indicators of the African heritage are quite evident in many of the island's cultural expressions—music, dance, literature, visual arts, cuisine, and local festivities. The famous annual carnivals of the municipalities of Loíza, Ponce, San Juan, and Guayama recreate the traditional display of *vejigante* customs and masks,[8] as does Hatillo's Festival de las Máscaras (Festival of the Masks). Puerto Rican Spanish also reflects African linguistic roots in some of its vocabulary and in the names of places and people (Alvarez Nazario 1974). The syncretism that took place between Catholicism and African religious traditions can be seen in the practices of Santería and Espiritismo among some Puerto Ricans. Santería rituals and invocations to Changó, the powerful god of fire, thunder, and lightning; Oshún, the goddess of love; Yemayá, the goddess of the moon and seas; and many other African-origin deities still provide an expedient way of dealing with negative influences or evil spirits or of ameliorating the whole gamut of human physical and spiritual ailments (González-Wippler 1973). Some researchers have documented the therapeutic psychological functions of the religious practices of Espiritismo, which has absorbed influences from Santería and other religions in the Caribbean and Latin America (Rogler 1985; Rogler and Hollingshead 1961).

After the Spanish Conquest of the Indies, Puerto Rico remained an island with important connections to a continent or "mainland," in this case the European continent and the mainland of Spain.[9] Increased migration of Spaniards to other parts of the Americas when the scant gold deposits in Puerto Rico, Hispaniola, and Cuba were depleted meant that enslaved Africans eventually represented a significant segment of the local labor force.

Racial mixture and cultural hybridity and syncretism between the Spanish, Tainos, and Africans form the core of Puerto Rico's creole population. These three groups make up the basic racial and cultural profile of the Puerto Rican people, with the subsequent incorporation of new immigrant groups (with few exceptions, from western Europe) that came to the island at different times. These immigrant groups included French, Corsicans, Italians, Germans, Dutch, British, Scottish, and North Americans, among others (Scarano 1981, 1993). For a long period Puerto Rican cultural nationalism tended to emphasize the superiority and dominance of the Spanish European heritage, but since the final decades of the twentieth century, more attention has been given to the island's African roots and its connections with other Hispanic and non-Hispanic Caribbean nations.

Prominent anthropologist Sidney Mintz (1974) once noted that "a search for Africa in the Caribbean is among other things, an exploration of the nature of cultural disguise" (25). Without question, this statement applies to Puerto Rico, a nation where racism historically has been "camouflaged" by the myth of a racially harmonious society devoid of racism (Blanco 1948). In his pioneering work on blacks in Puerto Rican culture, Isabelo Zenón (1974) exposed the long-standing historical erasure of blacks and persistent denial of racism in Puerto Rico: "El dato más original y omnipresente del racismo puertorriqueño es la negación absurda y obstinada de su existencia" (The most original and omnipresent fact about Puerto Rican racism is the absurd and obstinate negation of its existence). Because of the prevalence of the generalized myths about the absence of racism in Puerto Rico, a stateside Puerto Rican scholar emphatically noted that many Puerto Ricans tend to whitewash racism by believing in "the prejudice of having no prejudice" (Betances 1972, 1973).

Puerto Ricans are not by any means immune to racial prejudice, but it is also fair to say that racial conflict has not manifested itself in modern or contemporary Puerto Rico in the same polarizing ways that it has in the United States or other countries torn by a widespread or deeply ingrained system of apartheid and a long history of racial tensions, violence, and racially based civil wars. This statement does not in any way minimize the abuses and killings of many enslaved Africans by their owners or overseers, especially when they attempted to escape or to rebel for their freedom. The insidious violence, abuse, and exploitation borne by enslaved Africans and their Afro-descendants on the island persisted after the abolition of slavery in 1873 (see Rodríguez-Silva 2012; Godreau 2015; Baerga 2015). Even after their emancipation, they were often criminalized or degraded by the racism embedded in white privilege and the subordination of blackness.

Racial definitions and perceptions among Puerto Ricans are not strictly determined by biological factors, as they tend to be in the United States, where the notion that one drop of nonwhite blood makes someone a person of color. Among most Caribbean, Latin American, and US Latino/a populations, social status, multiple gradations of skin color, and other physical features influence racial perceptions (see C. Rodríguez 2000a; Vargas-Ramos 2017). The popular expression *mejorar la raza*, meaning to improve the race by whitening it, conveys the desirability and privilege attributed to whiteness and the subordination of blackness, but there is a wider spectrum of physical and social factors embedded in the way Puerto Ricans and other Latinos/as perceive racial differences and mixing and how they define themselves racially. These multiple factors differ from the hypodescent perspective that dominates US racial definitions, regards any racial mixture as inferior to whiteness, and categorizes individuals of mixed race as "people of color." For populations of color, their own racialized experiences often shape their internalized notions of blackness and whiteness.[10]

For the growing number of Puerto Ricans born or raised in the United States, the persistent open forms of racism and discrimination they encounter as migrants, together with the continuous back-and-forth migration between the island and stateside communities, have contributed to an increased awareness of race and racism in Puerto Rico. This includes a wider recognition of the historical suppression of blackness, or the "silencing" of race (Rodríguez-Silva 2012), and the underlying manifestations of racial prejudice that for a long time perpetuated the historical invisibility of the lives and contributions of Africans and Afro-descendant populations to the development of the Puerto Rican nation. Simultaneously, the expanding presence of Puerto Ricans and other Latinos/as in US society is changing its dichotomized black-and-white constructions of race. It has introduced new perspectives rooted in the racially mixed profile of Latinos/as and that of other multiracial groups frequently lumped into the "people of color" category and furthered a broader and more nuanced understanding of the social, racial, and cultural dynamics that shape constructions of race.

The Strategic but Neglected Spanish Colony

Despite its strategic geographic location as the "entrance and key to the Antilles,"[11] for almost three centuries Puerto Rico remained a neglected part of the vast Spanish New World empire. More attention was given to the larger colonies that could supply the precious mineral wealth and raw materials to support Spain's imperial hegemony, mercantile economy, and competition with other European monarchies. The larger colonies sustained the mercantile trade that helped finance the religious and military ventures of the Spanish Crown. Until the latter decades of the eighteenth century, Puerto Rico was not heavily populated, and the island's Spanish military government received subsidies from the Viceroyalty of New Spain in Mexico to administer the colony. The island's creoles relied mostly on subsistence agriculture and contraband trade with neighboring non-Hispanic Caribbean islands to satisfy some of their basic needs (Morales-Carrión 1971). The population of Puerto Rico remained very small during the first three centuries of Spanish colonization; the subsistence nature of most of the island's agricultural productivity also reflected this stagnant population growth.

The initial neglect by Spanish authorities did not alter the significance of Puerto Rico's geographic location. In Spain's quest to hold on to its imperial glory, Puerto Rico was strategically important to counteract the growing commercial interests of the British, French, and Dutch in the Caribbean region. Competing European powers also recognized the island's strategic value and attempted to take it away from Spain. Puerto Rico was subjected to unsuccessful attacks from the British in 1595 and 1598 and the Dutch in 1625. The threat of foreign invasion motivated the Spaniards to build imposing military fortifications on the island and in its other Caribbean colonies. San Juan, the center of Puerto Rico's colonial administration and site of the country's major port, was eventually converted into a walled city. The fortifications surrounding the capital contributed to a sharp separation between the locus of colonial administration, where most of the Spanish civilian population and the army resided, and a large portion of the sparse creole population, scattered throughout the island and mostly disconnected from the ruling authorities. As late as 1797, the Spanish once again fended off another unsuccessful British attempt to take over Puerto Rico.

Life in the colonies began to change after the modernizing French Bourbon dynasty came to occupy the Spanish throne in the early eighteenth century. Reforms were gradually introduced to foster economic development and commerce throughout the colonial empire. These reforms reached Puerto Rico in 1765, when the Spanish Crown sent Field Marshall Alejandro O'Reilly to assess the island's socioeconomic conditions and potential for economic growth. O'Reilly's visit led to the implementation of wide-ranging reforms, which included relaxing the monopolistic Spanish trade, discouraging contraband, and promoting European immigration to increase Puerto Rico's population base. In the late 1700s and early 1800s, Puerto Rico was to witness a large influx of immigrants from Spain (primarily from the Balearic and Canary Islands and the provinces of Cataluña and Valencia), French Corsica, Germany, Italy, Holland, England,

Scotland, and the United States. Most of these immigrants were attracted by land grants and other Spanish colonial government incentives given to individuals with enough capital to invest in agricultural development in different parts of the country (see Cifre de Loubriel 1964, 1975, 1989, 1995; Scarano 1981). Other immigrants, especially from Venezuela, Haiti, and the Dominican Republic, sought refuge in Puerto Rico in the early 1800s after the political turmoil generated by those colonies' respective wars of independence from Spain.

In addition to building Puerto Rico's defenses, the Spanish colonial government actively encouraged commercial agriculture, focusing on production of sugar and its derivatives for export and, to a lesser degree, on coffee and tobacco crops. These products became the island's main exports to Spain, and sugar would be central to Puerto Rico's agricultural economy until the mid-twentieth century.

More substantial progress in Puerto Rico's conditions did not occur until the Spanish metropolis introduced the Real Cédula de Gracias (Royal Decree of Concessions) of 1815, aimed at further expanding commerce and economic activity. Concurrently, it brought about the implementation of additional reforms to create an environment more favorable for cultural and social development and less inviting for revolutionary insurgency at a time when the spirit of revolution was engulfing most of the European colonies in the Americas. Among the most significant economic changes were the introduction of new industrial machinery and the opening of trade between Puerto Rico and the United States.

An increase in the importation of enslaved African labor also supported this period of economic development. The combined factors account for a striking pattern of population growth on the island that began in the late 1700s and continued into the 1800s. Puerto Rico's population almost tripled, from only 44,883 in 1765 to 129,758 in 1795. Another significant population increase came about after the reforms implemented by the Real Cédula de Gracias. The island's population grew from 183,211 in 1807 to 185,000 in 1812, to 235,157 in 1824, to 302,672 in 1828, and to 443,000 in 1846 (Silvestrini and Luque de Sánchez 1988, 240; Scarano 1993, 412).

The majority of the Spanish New World colonies secured their independence in the years between 1808 and 1824, but the repressive policies and authoritarian rule of the Spanish Crown's appointed governors largely discouraged revolutionary activity in Puerto Rico. In 1809, Puerto Ricans were for the first time allowed to send a representative to the Spanish Cortes, the main parliamentary body under the ruling monarchy, but this representation completely ceased in 1837 and was not restored until 1870, over three decades later. Political conditions in Spain had been in turmoil since the Napoleonic invasion of 1808, which had forced the Spanish people to take up arms against the French invaders and produced the liberal

Cádiz Constitution of 1812. However, the return of King Ferdinand VII to the Spanish throne two years later nullified the progressive constitutional reforms, restored absolutist rule, and set the stage for a political confrontation between conservative supporters of the monarchy and liberals seeking representative government and the establishment of a Spanish republic. During this politically unstable period, there was an outbreak of wars of independence in the New World colonies, and Spain lost most of its empire. Conditions in the Spanish metropolis deteriorated even further after the death of King Ferdinand VII in 1833, which put an end to decades of Spanish monarchical absolutism. Serious divisions regarding the succession to the Spanish throne gave impetus to several wars (*guerras carlistas*) between conservative royalists and liberals, and these struggles dominated Spain's political landscape throughout the remainder of the nineteenth century.

Left with only the colonies of Cuba and Puerto Rico in the Americas, Spanish officials ruled them with an iron hand.[12] Freedom of expression was limited or, at different times, completely suppressed. Most nongovernment newspapers were regularly censored to discourage growing creole claims for liberal reforms, autonomy, or independence. For many decades it was common practice for the Spanish colonial government to censor journalists, send them to prison, or force them into exile. A few clandestine revolutionary cells operated in Puerto Rico, trying to keep alive the separatist struggle and end slavery, but the suppression of freedom of expression and other political rights did not provide the necessary environment inside the island to incite a prolonged, effective insurrection against the Spanish colonial regime.

On September 23, 1868, Puerto Rico claimed its independence with the Grito de Lares armed revolt, but the Spanish army crushed the insurrection only a few days after it began. In contrast, the rebellion that started in Cuba with the Grito de Yara, only a few weeks after the Grito de Lares, signaled the beginning of the neighboring island's Ten Years' War (1868–1878) for independence. The outbreak of war in Cuba and the movement to liberate the two islands was sustained by the activities of Antillean political expatriates living in cities in Europe, the United States, and other Latin American countries that already had achieved independence from Spain. Mounting a revolution in Puerto Rico, however, was a daunting and dangerous endeavor. First, local political and social divisions did not facilitate the development of a strong and unified creole revolutionary movement, similar to those that emerged in other larger Spanish colonies, that could incite and organize a large sector of the scattered island population to take up arms against the Spaniards. Second, the repressive practices of the Spanish colonial government meant that any supporters of the revolutionary cause had to operate in underground cells or secret societies. Thus, while other Spanish colonies carried out wars of independence and most had become sovereign republics by the 1830s, Puerto Rico remained under Spanish control throughout the nineteenth century. This was also the case with Cuba, although the Cubans were able to keep their armed resistance alive during two separate wars of independence—the already mentioned Ten Years' War and the Spanish-Cuban War that began with the Grito de Baire of 1895 and was disrupted in 1898 by the US invasion of Cuba and, shortly thereafter, Puerto Rico.

By the 1860s, liberals in Spain had again gained some political ground against supporters of the monarchy, which translated into a more open political climate in the colonies. In 1870, for the first time, Puerto Rico was given the right to form its own political parties, and nongovernment newspapers began to appear (Pedreira [1941] 1969). The first Spanish Republic was finally created in 1873, and one significant outcome of this short-lived political change in Spain was the abolition of slavery in Puerto Rico and Cuba that same year. The liberalizing political environment quickly came to an end with the restoration of the Spanish monarchy less than a year later and the gradual return to authoritarian rule for the colonies during the decades that followed. Political instability once again engulfed the Spanish metropolis as the remaining two island colonies continued to state their claims for more civil liberties and control of their own affairs.

The political conditions described herein made it more difficult for the Puerto Rican creole propertied class to fulfill its ruling-class aspirations, which, in the case of other colonies, had been a key factor in galvanizing their respective struggles to rid themselves of Spanish colonial rule and secure their independence. Puerto Rico's creole propertied class was largely composed of hacendados (hacienda owners) involved in export trade mainly to Spain and the United States. By the mid-1800s the United States had become the island's main trade partner. The growing trade between Puerto Rico and the United States was mostly based on the exportation of sugar and its derivatives, such as rum and molasses, and, to a lesser degree, coffee, tobacco, and other island agricultural products. At the same time, Puerto Ricans began to rely on the importation of manufactured goods from an expanding US economy seeking new foreign markets. The sugar industry boomed between 1815 and 1870, while coffee produced by creole and immigrant hacendados began to take over as the main export product during the decades between 1870 and 1900 (Quintero Rivera 1976a; Scarano 1993). Peninsular control of commerce and banking, however, severely limited the economic influence of the hacendado propertied class in this export-oriented agricultural economy. Although the hacendados owned most of Puerto Rico's land, control of commercial transportation and financing was in the hands of Spaniards, who had the support of the colonial administrative structures. Acute class, racial, and political divisions within Puerto Rican society additionally impeded the emergence of a cohesive creole bourgeoisie and of a revolutionary consciousness capable of nourishing any claims for independence or of challenging the control of the ruling peninsular elites (see Quintero Rivera 1988; Picó 1990).

The influx of new immigrant entrepreneurs in the late 1700s and early 1800s has been considered another obstacle to the development of a strong creole bourgeoisie on the island. In the first place, this foreign population did not share strong nationalist sentiments or loyalties toward Puerto Rico. Additionally, the new immigrant investors and proprietors began to erode the already limited economic power of the creole propertied class. Immigrant newcomers gained more access than creoles to certain sectors of Puerto Rico's economy, such as banking and financing, and even came to dominate the economic activity of certain regions of the island. These combined factors contributed to thwarting the development of a strong creole national consciousness in nineteenth-century Puerto Rico.

The growth of the economic relationship between Puerto Rico and the United States during the course of the nineteenth century was another factor in shaping the propertied class's political views regarding the future of the island. It has been argued that the expanding commercial relationship between the two countries introduced Puerto Rico's propertied class to the "bourgeois" values of their North American neighbors and fueled aspirations among some members of this class for a possible future annexation of the island to the United States. According to Quintero Rivera (1976a):

> The golden dream of Puerto Rican landowners regarding commercial expansion was access to the expansive North American market. That was the case not only for those whose commercial production was fundamentally based on sugar, a product that at the time found its main export market in the United States, but also among coffee producers yearning to penetrate that market; the main one for coffee around the world. The evidence tends to demonstrate that a considerable part of the nineteenth-century anti-Spanish struggle involved a desire for a future annexation to the United States. (25, author's translation)

This environment of expanding commercial connections between Puerto Rico and the United States was conducive to increased travel between the two countries. Businessmen, professionals, skilled and semiskilled artisans, students, white-collar workers, and their families were drawn to the modernity and progress associated with the thriving United States (Haslip-Viera 1996). Another important factor to consider is that during this initial period of contact between Puerto Rico and the United States, the prevailing view of the United States in the hemisphere was that of a republic firmly grounded in democratic principles and a successful free enterprise capitalist system. The United States was regarded as a model of the kind of democracy and industrial innovation that the former colonies in the Americas envisioned for their own countries after securing their independence. The intellectual and political elites and the entrepreneurial sectors of the emerging Latin American nations also were particularly drawn to the United States. The perception of a threat of US imperialism over the hemisphere did not really enter Latin American discourses until the latter decades of the nineteenth century.

North American democracy contrasted with the more repressive environment that was found again in the Puerto Rico of the late 1880s during the infamous administration of Spanish governor Romualdo Palacio. Reacting to the growing support for political autonomy among island creoles and to a series of boycotts they organized against the businesses of peninsular merchants, the colonial government decided to crack down on any challenges to its authority or the interests of the Spanish ruling class. Due to the abuses in 1887 Governor Palacio's administration came to be known as the *régimen del componte* (the "behave yourself" regime). Most of the prior modest gains in civil liberties, especially freedom of expression, were suspended. Nongovernment newspapers were closed, illegal searches became routine, and prominent liberal political leaders were arrested. The return to these despotic measures limited the political options of Puerto Rico's creole propertied class. Even with the more liberal environment found again in the 1890s, the unpredictable and unstable nature of the political situation in Spain, along with the authoritarian rule practiced by most colonial governors, forced creole political leaders to seek a moderate course of action for getting some political and economic concessions from the Spanish metropolis. Creole leaders chose to fight for reforms that would eventually allow the island to achieve a considerable degree of self-rule without a total separation from Spain.

The Partido Liberal Reformista (Liberal Reformist Party) had represented creole reform aspirations since its founding in 1870. Frustrations with the unpredictable and limited nature of Spanish colonial reforms eventually moved liberal creoles to claim political autonomy rather than independence. Under the leadership of Román Baldorioty de Castro, in 1887 the Partido Autonomista Puertorriqueño (Puerto Rican Autonomist Party) replaced the Liberal Reformist Party. The new political entity sought a larger degree of administrative and economic decentralization from a distant Spanish colonial metropolis. Two years later, after Baldorioty's death, Luis Muñoz Rivera, a prominent politician and journalist of the creole propertied class, took the reins of the Autonomist Party. Puerto Rico's autonomists made a pact with Spain's Liberal Party members to merge with them if they managed to win control of the metropolitan government. In exchange, Spanish liberals promised to grant political autonomy to the island. When the Liberal Party came to power in Spain in 1897, Puerto Rico was finally granted the Carta Autonómica (Autonomic Charter). This new government endowed Puerto Rican creoles with the right to elect a governing cabinet and enjoy the political autonomy experienced by other Spanish provinces. The autonomist cabinet, headed by Muñoz Rivera, included prominent members of the creole propertied class and its political and intellectual elites. Autonomy was a welcome experiment in self-government for Puerto Rico, but also short-lived. The new government lasted less than a year and came to an end with the US invasion of 1898.

The US military occupation liberated Puerto Rico from Spanish rule, but it also ended the brief autonomous government that Puerto Rican creoles had claimed and marked the beginning of a new but also restrictive colonial relationship for the island. The creole propertied class's economic dependence on the United States and admiration of its modern industrial achievements were major factors in this class's initial welcoming response to the arrival of the invading North American troops. However, the creole elites did not anticipate that the new regime would immediately open the doors to US investors, weakening the position of both Puerto Rico's creole propertied class and peninsular businessmen. US companies not only took control of Puerto Rico's agricultural economic production in a very short period but also shifted its focus. Most of the new US capital was invested in the establishment of modern, larger, and more technically advanced sugar mills, or *centrales*, numerous cigar factories, and the needle industries. Control of shipping, the setting of trade tariffs, and the devaluation and replacement of the Spanish national currency with the dollar were some of the immediate changes introduced by the new colonial rulers that mostly benefited US investors and had a devastating effect on the island's creole propertied class and peninsular business sectors.

At the time of the US invasion, coffee dominated agricultural production in the haciendas. With the new focus on expanding sugar production and control of the land in the hands of US absentee corporations, the local haciendas entered a stage of decline accelerated by a reduction in the demand for coffee exports and a drop in the price of this product in the international market. The effects of Hurricane San Ciriaco in 1899, which destroyed most of that year's coffee crop, only worsened the economic predicament of hacienda owners. Clearly Puerto Rico's economy would once again serve the interests of a new colonial metropolis at the expense of the island's own interests and those of its creole propertied class and the larger sector of artisans, factory workers, and peasant laborers.

Notes

1. When Columbus first arrived in the New World islands in 1492, he believed he had reached parts of Asia or the Orient, then known as the Indies. Thus the term "Indies" has been used since Columbus's first voyage. Later, the word "West" was added to the name to differentiate the New World islands from those of East Asia. The name "Antilles" also was used early in the colonial period to refer to the islands. The name was taken from the classical myth of the lost cities of Antillia. During the colonial period the name "Caribbean" was used to identify the sea where the islands were located and then adopted to describe the whole region. The name derived from the indigenous Carib tribes that inhabited the Lesser Antilles at the time of the conquest.

2. Rouse argued that many of the islands in the Caribbean were settled by 5000 BC (1986, 108). The movement of the ocean currents dictated the direction of the migratory flow, in a northwesterly direction from the Lesser Antilles to the Greater Antilles.

3. For more information about Dominican migration to Puerto Rico, see Jorge Duany, ed., *Los dominicanos en Puerto Rico: Migración en la semi-periferia* (Río Piedras, PR: Ediciones Huracán, 1990).

4. Nineteenth-century authors such as Alejandro Tapia y Rivera and Cayetano Coll y Toste frequently incorporated indigenous legends, myths, and historical events into their writings. For a compilation of these legends, see Cayetano Coll y Toste, *Leyendas y tradiciones puertorriqueñas* (Río Piedras, PR: Editorial Cultural, 1975). Alejandro Tapia y Rivera's legend *La palma del cacique*, his poem "El último borincano," and his opera script *Guarionex*, centered on the legendary *cacique* Taino, all deal with indigenous themes. See Alejandro Tapia y Rivera, *Obras completas* (San Juan: Instituto de Cultura Puertorriqueña, 1968).

5. Anthropologist Eugenio Fernández Méndez (1972) argued that Yocahú and Huracán might have been the same god. Sued-Badillo (1979, 25–26), however, believed that Huracán referred to the terrible storms and winds unleashed by the earth mother Guabancex as punishment for some violations of social norms.

6. The most complete analysis of different aspects of the Taino revival movement can be found in Haslip-Viera (1999).

7. The term "mestizo/a" has been used since the early years of the Spanish colonial period to refer to the racial mixture between white Europeans and Indians. The term "mulatto" refers to the mixture between white Europeans and Africans. In its broader sense, the term *mestizaje* is used in the Caribbean and Latin America to signify the continent's mixing of races.

8. *Vejigantes* are the folkloric characters wearing colorful masks and ornate costumes in Puerto Rican carnivals and festivals. The mischievous characters they represent often carry *vejigas*, or symbolic animal bladders, to strike anyone who annoys them or whom they want to make the target of their playful pranks.

9. While the geographical relationship between island and mainland can be fairly straightforward, the conception of the relationship on cultural, political, social, and economic grounds is more relevant in terms of the colony-metropolis connection.

10. The label "people of color" is used mostly in the United States to refer to nonwhite or racially mixed Afro-descendant and indigenous populations from what were in past decades characterized as Third World countries. This term is strongly contested, since, for instance, Latinos/as can be white, black, Indian, or any racially mixed combination of these races. See Mörner (1967), Peter Wade, *Race and Ethnicity in Latin America* (New York: Pluto Press, 1997), C. Rodríguez (2000a), and Vargas-Ramos (2017).

11. The island's Spanish governor, Fernando de Lando, described Puerto Rico as the "entrance and key to the Antilles" in a 1534 letter to Emperor Charles V (King Charles I of Spain). See Eugenio Fernández Méndez, ed., *Crónicas de Puerto Rico desde la conquista hasta nuestros días*, 2 vols. (San Juan: Ediciones del Gobierno, 1957).

12. The Philippines and Guam in the Pacific region were also Spanish colonies ceded to the United States in the aftermath of the Spanish-Cuban-American War of 1898.

3

Early Migrations
to the United States

The island of Puerto Rico has long served as a crossroads— between the North and the South American continents, between the Old and New Worlds, between memory and opportunity, and between native and new-comer. Puerto Ricans have always represented the emerging newness that arises from the blending and synergy that occurs at a crossroads. This blend-ing can be social, political, cultural, and racial—a blending of Amerindian, African, and Spaniard that is manifested in language, old and changing tra-ditions, religion, and civil society—and shows up in the ways some Puerto Ricans "code switch" (switch languages) between Spanish and English and oscillate between the traditions, styles, and values of Puerto Rico and those of the United States. Political life is also part of this crossroads, as reflected by the back-and-forth swing of electoral mandates, from support for the current Commonwealth colonial status to advocacy for statehood, and by the inability to develop a consensus about the viability of independence and decolonization or other possible alternatives that put an end to the country's colonial dilemma. Scholars and creative writers have produced many metaphors that allude to the tenuous condition of, and ambivalence inher-ent in, being at the crossroads: "un barco a la deriva" (a ship adrift) (Pedreira 1934), a nation suffering from "cultural schizophrenia" (Seda Bonilla 1972; R. Carr 1984), a nation in "limbo" (Méndez 1997), and "la nación en vaivén" (the wavering or straddling nation) (Duany 2002). This crossroads also can be characterized by borders—borders that are some-times easily traversed and other times serve as obstacles, borders that may be exclusionary and defensive or welcoming and encompassing.

The concept of "island," as land surrounded by water, can elicit thoughts of isolation. It can also give way to insular perceptions of events. In the 1930s, the prominent intellectual Antonio S. Pedreira (1934) wrote a

43

classic treatise about the sense of *insularismo* (insularity) that he believed engulfed Puerto Rican life. But the notion that Puerto Rico has simply been an island disconnected or isolated from the rest of the world is a misconception. At different times, Puerto Ricans have left their homeland to seek a more prosperous life elsewhere, but, similarly, Puerto Rico has served as a refuge for immigrants with similar socioeconomic aspirations and for those escaping political repression. It is also a homeland to return to for those Puerto Ricans who have lived afar for much of their working lives and a transitory stay for others who continue to periodically move between the island and the United States.

Additionally, the conception of Puerto Rico and Puerto Ricans, from the perspective of an outsider, particularly one unfamiliar with the Caribbean and its milieu, is fraught with contradictions and is, in some sense, unfathomable. The island's ambiguous and unresolved colonial relationship with the United States and its uncertain path toward decolonization leaves most non–Puerto Ricans puzzled. Though not a sovereign nation, Puerto Rico displays deeply rooted attributes of nationhood and a strong collective sense of national identity. For stateside Puerto Ricans, these are reflected in the murals on the walls of New York City's barrios, subway stations, and other public spaces, in those of Boston's Villa Victoria and Philadelphia's Taller Puertorriqueño; in the monumental Puerto Rican steel flags and murals of Chicago's Paseo Boricua and the exhibits and collections of the National Museum of Puerto Rican Arts and Culture; in the numerous institutions and organizations established to provide a wide range of services to Puerto Rican communities; in the over fifty parades and festivals of varying sizes held annually in numerous US cities with concentrations of Puerto Ricans; in the bodegas (small grocery stores) and other small businesses of Lorain, Ohio, and Kissimmee, Florida; in the enticing aromas of the typical *cuchifritos* (fried foods) stands on the streets of most barrios; and in the bumper stickers and flag-bearing pennants that hang from the rearview mirrors of newer or well-worn automobiles in cities throughout the United States. They are also at the core of Puerto Rican cultural expressions (see Chapter 8).

As stated in Chapter 1, the experience of migration has been and continues to be one of Puerto Rico's most constant and changing historical realities. In pre-Columbian times the indigenous Taino population migrated to the island from the northern shores of the South American continent, and during the Spanish colonial period, many Puerto Ricans left their homeland, while numerous foreigners came to the island's shores and made it their home, for political or socioeconomic reasons. But not until the US occupation of Puerto Rico did migration become such a useful government policy tool to fulfill the cheap labor needs of stateside US corporations and for displacing the impoverished surplus population of workers from their homeland. By the 1920s, migration was turning into a more frequent and persistent occurrence in the lives of island Puerto Ricans. This chapter provides a synthesis and analysis of the historical, socioeconomic, and political factors that contributed to the first waves of Puerto Rican migration to the United States, which began even before the US invasion of the island from Spain.

The Pilgrims of Freedom

The first indications of a Puerto Rican presence in the United States came in the second half of the nineteenth century, when many individuals were forced to abandon the island to escape the tyrannical rule of the Spanish colonial authorities. As noted in Chapter 2, political persecution and exile were a common destiny for those Puerto Ricans advocating liberal reforms or independence from Spain. These political émigrés have been appropriately named "the pilgrims of freedom" (Ojeda Reyes 1992) since some of them spent a portion of their lives in exile in different countries in Latin America, the Caribbean, and western Europe and many ended their lives away from their beloved homeland. Among them were leading members of the creole propertied class and the intellectual and political elites, as well as self-educated artisans, most notably *tabaqueros/as* (cigar rollers and other tobacco industry workers) and typographers. The majority of cigar rollers were men, although occasionally, in smaller family workshops, women learned the trade. In the larger cigar factories, most women were employed as *despalilladoras*, performing the labor-intensive task of stripping the tobacco leaves from the stalk by hand.

Puerto Rican political émigrés settled mostly in New York, although other cities like Philadelphia, Boston, New Orleans, Tampa, and Key West developed neighborhoods or settlements, called *colonias*, that attracted Cubans, Puerto Ricans, Spaniards, and other Latin American and European immigrants. Expatriates from the Caribbean and Latin America (e.g., Haitians, Dominicans, Venezuelans) started coming to the United States during the early 1800s when the creole elites, in what were then the Spanish New World colonies, began to stake their claims for independence from Spain and revolutionary wars broke out in some of these territories.

Most creole liberals in Puerto Rico at the time were seeking political reforms, hoping to achieve more participation in the island's government, representation in the Spanish Cortes (Spain's legislative parliament), and increased civil liberties, especially freedom of expression and of the press. Others espoused more radical positions by supporting the abolition of slavery and complete separation from Spain. As early as the 1820s, many Puerto Rican separatists, who supported independence, were forced into exile by the Spanish colonial regime, a practice that intensified during the last few decades of the nineteenth century. They mostly settled in cities in Spain, such as Madrid and Barcelona, or in those of other European and Latin American republics. In 1824 the Spanish Crown authorized foreign trade with the colonies of Cuba and Puerto Rico, the first step in the development of a commercial relationship with the United States that significantly expanded and continued for most of the nineteenth century. The trade decree opened up new markets and a reciprocal export-import relationship between the United States and the two remaining Spanish colonies in the Americas. These commercial bonds also allowed some political émigrés from Puerto Rico to shift their point of destination from Europe to the United States.

Such was the case of Puerto Rican liberal journalist Julio Vizcarrondo, publisher of the newspaper *El mercurio* (The mercury), who was forced to leave the island in 1850 because of his abolitionist views. He settled in Boston, married a North American woman, and lived there for four years. Shortly after returning to Puerto Rico, Vizcarrondo had to endure a second exile. This time he went to Madrid and continued his political activities there, creating the Sociedad Abolicionista Española (Spanish Abolitionist Society), collaborating with the newspaper *El abolicionista español* (The Spanish abolitionist), and supporting the political efforts that led to the Revolution of 1868, which removed the Spanish monarch from the throne and eventually led to the establishment of the First Spanish Republic in 1873. Vizcarrondo kept defending the abolition of slavery in Puerto Rico from the Spanish capital until it was finally granted by the new republican government that same year.

Vizcarrondo's journey offers an early example of the back-and-forth pilgrimage undertaken by many Puerto Rican creoles during those years. In nineteenth-century Puerto Rico the Spanish ruling authorities had little tolerance for political dissent, and those who promoted liberal political ideas or incited revolution were censored, fined, incarcerated, or forced into exile. Hence, many of the most outspoken supporters of either reforms or independence for the island who, for the most part, were journalists and writers often endured a lifetime in exile. These expatriates continued advocating political change from abroad, and Puerto Rican separatists, in particular, created their own organizations to carry on the fight for complete freedom from Spanish rule. Some separatists came through New York City in the course of their exile and settled there for many years; others had briefer sojourns and later moved back to Puerto Rico or to other major Latin American or European cities. More than a few were never able to return to the island.

Collaborations between Cuban and Puerto Rican separatists provided the impetus for the 1865 founding in New York of the Sociedad Republicana de Cuba y Puerto Rico (Republican Society of Cuba and Puerto Rico) to gather support for armed revolutions from those sympathetic to their cause in the United States and throughout the continent. The leading figure among Puerto Rican separatist émigrés was Ramón Emeterio Betances, a physician and fervent abolitionist.[1] He and friend and fellow abolitionist

Segundo Ruiz Belvis sought refuge in New York after barely escaping from arrest by Spanish authorities back home. In the New York metropolis the two expatriates joined José Francisco Basora, another Puerto Rican separatist and abolitionist physician and one of the original founders of the Sociedad Republicana, in forming the new Comité Revolucionario de Puerto Rico (Revolutionary Committee of Puerto Rico). Basora was also one of the editors of New York's Spanish-language newspaper, *La voz de la América* (The voice of America), published between 1865 and 1867 and aimed at advancing the separatist cause. This newspaper was a major source of information for reporting on revolutionary activities and events back on the islands and in the former Spanish colonies that became the independent nations of Latin America.

With the support of the growing Antillean separatist movement in exile, Betances and his comrades designed a plan to back up an armed rebellion in Puerto Rico. This plan included raising funds to bring weapons to the island with the hope that the few clandestine revolutionary cells able to operate in Puerto Rico could mount a successful insurrection that would eventually spread to other parts of the island. The first steps were taken when Betances left New York for the Caribbean in 1867 to make arrangements for a shipment of armaments and supplies to Puerto Rico's insurgents. In November of that year, he issued from St. Thomas "Los diez mandamientos de los hombres libres" (The ten commandments of free men), calling for the Puerto Rican people to take up arms against the Spaniards in the name of freedom. Around the same time, he received news of the death of Segundo Ruiz Belvis, who had gone to Chile to garner support for the Antillean separatist cause and died there of illness shortly after his arrival. In a published tribute to him, Betances wrote, "His venerated shadow wanders from one end of the island to the other, inviting us to break away from the chains of servitude that hold our homeland bent over at the feet of its own oppressors" (Ojeda Reyes 2001, 113, author's translation).

Enduring exile along with many other patriots and losing his loyal comrade in the struggle for the abolition of slavery and independence only strengthened Betances's resolve. He moved forward with his plans to have a ship deliver weapons for the planned uprising in Puerto Rico, but an informer thwarted the revolutionary plot, and St. Thomas authorities confiscated the shipment before it left port, forcing Betances to escape to the Dominican Republic. He then left for Paris, where he had lived as a medical student in the 1840s and 1850s. He spent a good portion of his exile there practicing medicine, but his decades of involvement in the separatist movement never wavered. From Paris, in the 1890s he accepted a diplomatic post representing the expatriate Cuban provisional government, a position that also facilitated his efforts on behalf of Puerto Rico's independence. For more than four decades Betances lived in exile, although he was in continuous contact with other Puerto Rican and Cuban patriots in New York and other cities. Their correspondence was essential to keeping the flame of freedom burning within the various expatriate communities (see Ojeda Reyes 2001).

Betances's "Los diez mandamientos de los hombres libres" inspired, less than a year later, Puerto Rico's Grito de Lares separatist revolt of September 23, 1868, a cry for freedom from Spanish colonial rule. Rebels took control of the mountain town of Lares and declared Puerto Rico an independent republic. However, Spanish troops were mobilized and within a few days stopped the insurgency from spreading to other towns.[2] More than two weeks later, on October 10, rebels in Cuba also proclaimed a free republic with the Grito de Yara, marking the beginning of Cuba's Ten Years' War (1868–1878) of independence against the Spanish.

The arrival of Eugenio María de Hostos in New York in 1869 added another important Puerto Rican voice to the expatriate Antillean separatist movement. Hostos had come from Madrid, where he studied law and began a career as a journalist. A man of impressive intellectual acumen, during his student years in Spain Hostos had been critical of Spanish colonialism and was a strong advocate of the abolition of slavery and other liberal reforms for Puerto Rico. His political beliefs became more radicalized after the unsuccessful Grito de Lares insurrection, so he left Spain for New York and joined the émigré separatist movement there. Shortly after his arrival in the city, Hostos was named editor of the Spanish-language newspaper *La revolución* (The revolution), published from 1869 to 1876 by the Junta Central Republicana de Cuba y Puerto Rico (Republican Central Council of Cuba and Puerto Rico). Before long the ideological differences began to surface between Hostos and Anglophilic Cuban and Puerto Rican separatists wanting to end Spanish colonial rule, but also promoting the islands' annexation to the United States. Because of his anti-annexationist views and the newspaper's refusal to declare itself against this particular political course, Hostos eventually decided to leave New York for South America. He spent the next decade living in Venezuela, Colombia, Peru, Argentina, and Brazil before finally settling down in the Dominican Republic in 1879. During his long pilgrimage in Latin America, Hostos wrote his best-known essays about the future of the Caribbean islands, continuing to defend their liberation and promoting the idea of an Antillean federation of independent republics. He returned to New York for the last time in 1898, after the US invasion of Cuba and Puerto Rico, with the objective of creating the Liga de Patriotas Puertorriqueños (League of Puerto Rican Patriots).[3] This organization was aimed at pressuring the US government to allow Puerto Ricans to hold a plebiscite to decide the nature of their future political relationship with the United States and assert the island's right to self-determination. But Hostos and his collaborators were unable to persuade US authorities to allow Puerto Ricans to participate in this process. The Liga also wanted to educate Puerto Rican citizens in understanding and defending their civil liberties in other aspects of their public and private lives (see Auffant Vázquez 2012).

José Martí, Cuban independence patriot and writer, was the central figure of the émigré Antillean separatist movement (Poyo 1989; López Mesa 2002). Also an exile, he lived in New York from 1881 to 1895. At the time of his arrival he was twenty-eight years old, so his New York years represented a significant portion of his adult life. Being "in the belly of the beast," as he once said, inspired Martí to write his most important essays about what he called *nuestra América* (our America), referring to the new Latin American nations that had emerged from the demise of Spanish colonialism.[4] Living in the United States enhanced Martí's understanding of US imperialism, and he foresaw its imminent threat to the young Latin American nations in the rest of the continent. He also called for the new Latin American nations to promote a unity and progress based not on European or Anglo-American models but on an understanding of the multiplicity of cultures, races, and classes endemic to each country (Acosta-Belén 1999). Thus the experiences of exile for Antillean patriots and thinkers like Martí, Betances, and Hostos shaped their visions for their respective homelands' emancipation, including the process of building their own free societies and nations, and their future relationship with the United States. Their regional and hemispheric concerns placed them among the most prominent voices in warning Latin Americans about the threat of US hegemonic aspirations and interventionist policies for consolidating US dominance in the Americas.

The émigré Puerto Rican separatist movement included members of the creole elite as well as members of the working class. Both groups put out Spanish-language newspapers to advocate their ideals and outline a vision for the future of their respective countries after independence. *Tabaquero* and labor activist Flor Baerga arrived in New York in the 1880s, after participating for many years in labor organizing in Puerto Rico.[5] In New York, Baerga, together with Cuban cigar rollers Juan Fraga, Rafael Serra, and others, founded the Club Los Independientes (The Independents Club) in 1881. This particular organization was aimed at promoting the separatist cause among workers. The founding of multiple separatist clubs reflected existing political, national, class, and racial differences and internal divisions among New York's Antillean separatists, but all supported the fundamental notion of ending Spanish domination over the two islands. Nonetheless, they often had their own separate clubs and newspapers and expressed their commitment in different ways. Some focused on proselytizing and fund-raising activities; others started newspapers or wrote about their ideals; more than a few eventually took up arms and joined the fighting rebel army in Cuba. Puerto Rican expatriate pharmacist Gerardo Forrest, for instance, started the separatist publication *Cuba y Puerto Rico* (1897) in New York before leaving to join the Cuban insurgency.

The alliance between Cuban and Puerto Rican separatists in New York City, which started in the 1860s, continued for several decades. The presence of José Martí strengthened those collaborations. Martí worked tenaciously to bridge existing class, racial, and ideological divisions within the movement and, in addition, nurtured relations between Cubans and Puerto Ricans. The founding of the Partido Revolucionario Cubano (Cuban Revolutionary Party, PRC) in New York in 1892 was a significant moment, since its platform included support for Puerto Rico's independence. Puerto Rican separatists created the Club Borinquen that same year to mark their official involvement in the PRC. This revolutionary club was headed by Sotero Figueroa, a mulatto artisan typographer and journalist who had emigrated to New York in the late 1880s. Back in Puerto Rico, he had worked for and been mentored by the abolitionist patrician José Julián Acosta. Figueroa's *Ensayo biográfico de los que más han contribuído al progreso de Puerto Rico* (Biographic essay of those who have contributed to the development of Puerto Rico, 1888) had won a prize in an island writing contest and been published by Acosta's printing press. An expression of a national consciousness that separated creole Puerto Ricans from their peninsular Spanish rulers, it was a pioneering contribution to Puerto Rico's historiography.

After settling in New York, Figueroa started the Imprenta América, the press that from 1892 to 1898 printed the separatist newspaper *Patria* (Motherland), founded by Martí. The role of Figueroa, who developed a close friendship with the Cuban leader, rapidly expanded beyond the newspaper's typographical production. He was named to the post of administrative editor and wrote many of the newspaper's editorials during Martí's frequent travels to Cuban communities outside New York, especially those in Florida, to continue the flow of financial and political support for the independence struggle.[6]

Another prominent member of the Club Borinquen was Puerto Rican typographer, journalist, and poet Francisco Gonzalo "Pachín" Marín. Marín had been exiled from the island because of the publication of his liberal newspaper, *El postillón* (The courier, 1887). He arrived in New York in 1891 and a year later started publishing *El postillón* from there, but this time the newspaper described itself in more radical terms as "an unconditional voice of revolution." Pachín Marín also befriended Martí and other separatists. Although Martí left for Cuba in 1895 to fight in the Spanish-Cuban War and was killed during a skirmish with Spanish troops shortly after arriving in his homeland, his death inspired other émigré separatists to join the rebel army. Marín's brother, Wenceslao, also had lived in New York for a few years before deciding to follow in Martí's footsteps and leave for Cuba. He was killed on the battlefield in 1896. This personal loss persuaded Pachín Marín to trade his pen for a rifle and also go to Cuba. Less than a year later, he died of illness in the Cuban jungle, adding his name to the long list of separatists giving their lives in the struggle for Antillean freedom.

Also included among the many Puerto Ricans going to New York during this period was Arturo Alfonso Schomburg, a working-class Puerto Rican mulatto who had migrated in the early 1890s. Born and raised in Puerto Rico, Schomburg claimed that his mother was from St. Croix and his father, the son of German immigrants, was born in Puerto Rico. Since his parents never married, Schomburg was closer to his mother's relatives who lived in St. Croix and St. Thomas, islands where he spent some of his youth with relatives. However, he received most of his primary education in Puerto Rico, where he was living before he decided to migrate to New York City. In his *Memoirs* (1984, 195), Bernardo Vega claims that Schomburg was mostly self-educated and learned his ABCs from being around the *tabaqueros* (cigarmakers), although records show that he enrolled in public school (Des Verney Sinnette 1989). There is plenty of evidence to show that Schomburg was, indeed, drawn to the world of artisans, known for being avid autodidacts and one the most socially and politically conscious sectors of the working class. For a period, he worked as an apprentice typographer in an Old San Juan stationery shop and made friends with other artisans, especially typographers and cigarmakers.After saving enough money for the trip, Schomburg left the island for New York, bringing with him a letter of introduction to cigarmakers Baerga and Serra, and they helped him in his initial efforts to settle and find employment in the city. It was Schomburg's friendships with New York's Puerto Rican artisans that also drew him into the separatist movement. He collaborated with Serra and others in the founding of the Club Las Dos Antillas (The Two Antilles Club) in 1892. He served as secretary of the club for four years.[7]

Baerga was an avid collector of newspaper clippings and photographs that documented the presence and history of Puerto Ricans in New York City. His dedication to this endeavor influenced a young Arturo Schomburg to develop a greater interest in history and pay tribute to those individuals who had given their lives fighting for freedom (Ortiz 1986; Des Verney Sinnette 1989; Valdés 2017). Years later, Schomburg decided to dedicate his life to collecting books and other materials that documented the history and experiences of peoples of African descent around the world (see Chapter 8).

Puerto Rican poet Lola Rodríguez de Tió and her journalist husband, Aurelio Tió, also lived in New York during their several exiles. They came to the city first in 1892 and then again in 1895, returning to Cuba in 1898 after the US invasion. In New York, the poet and other women separatists engaged in fund-raising to support the rebel army and the cause of freedom. Women separatists gathered around the Club Mercedes Varona (Mercedes Varona Club), founded in 1892 and named for a Cuban patriot who supported the Ten Year's War of independence and was imprisoned and exiled by Spanish authorities. Inocencia Martínez de Figueroa, Sotero Figueroa's wife, presided over this first women's club of the PRC. Another important women's club, the Hermanas de Ríus Rivera (Sisters of Ríus Rivera), was founded in 1897 and named for a Puerto Rican general who had distinguished himself fighting in both Cuban wars of independence. This other club was established by Juan Ríus Rivera's Honduran wife, Aurora Fonts, along with Rodríguez de Tió, Martínez de Figueroa, and a few other women committed to advancing the independence cause.[8]

Rodríguez de Tió first published some of her best-known patriotic poems in the newspaper *Patria*. Her revolutionary poetry was a source of inspiration for the independence struggles. Some of her poems also promoted Antillean unity. The famous verses of her classic poem "A Cuba" (To Cuba) celebrate this ideal: "Cuba y Puerto Rico son / de un pájaro las dos alas / reciben flores o balas / sobre el mismo corazón" (Cuba and Puerto Rico are / the two wings of one bird / they receive flowers or bullets / in the very same heart).[9]

In 1895, only a few months after Martí's death on the Cuban battle-field, a Sección de Puerto Rico (Puerto Rico Section) of the PRC was established. But the absence of the fallen separatist leader gave other Cuban leaders who succeeded him the opening to set a different course to end the Spanish-Cuban War. The idea of US intervention in the conflict and the possibility of US annexation of the islands had been supported by a sector of the separatist movement since the 1860s but intensified after Martí's death. The more Anglophile and conservative commercial and professional sectors of the Antillean separatist movement began to dominate the PRC and set a new course for bringing to an end the Spanish-Cuban War. Tomás Estrada Palma succeeded Martí in taking the reins of the PRC. As a former general during the Ten Years' War (1868–1878) and provisional president of the Cuban Republic in Arms (1875), he was captured by Spanish soldiers in Cuba two years later and forced into exile. He lived in upstate New York (Orange County) and for over a decade was the leader of the émigré Cuban revolutionary junta that preceded the founding of the PRC in 1892. Along with Martí, he was part of the top leadership of the PRC. Although some Cuban and Puerto Rican separatists took the US imperialist threat seriously, Estrada Palma and his supporters also viewed the United States as a symbol of democracy and modernity. They saw the promise of a future for Cuba and Puerto Rico without the political instability and socioeconomic hardship by then afflicting most of the new Latin American republics after their independence. However, behind their support for US intervention in the Cuban War in 1898 was also an agreement that the United States would ultimately grant independence to the island. This finally happened in 1902 with the inauguration of the Cuban Republic and the election of Estrada Palma as the first president of the new nation.

The Sección de Puerto Rico of the PRC to some extent also reflected the increased support among separatists for US intervention in the Spanish-Cuban War and the annexation of the islands. The sección was headed then by Julio Henna, a Puerto Rican physician and supporter of annexation. Other members included annexationist physicians Roberto H. Todd and Manuel Besosa, as well as anti-annexationists Sotero Figueroa, Pachín Marín, Antonio Vélez Alvarado, Juan de Mata Terreforte, and Gerardo Forrest. For a brief period, the sección published the separatist newspapers *Cuba y Puerto Rico* (1897) and *Borinquen* (1898). After the outbreak of the Spanish-Cuban-American War, Todd and Henna played a key role in encouraging US officials to invade Puerto Rico, providing them with information about the location of Spanish military installations and troops around the island.[10]

From Paris, Ramón Emeterio Betances kept writing articles in Spanish- and French-language newspapers and sending letters to comrades laying out his revolutionary agenda, including his vision for the creation of a post-independence Antillean federation of sovereign republics. He also expressed his opposition to those separatists favoring US intervention in the Spanish-Cuban War and the possible annexation of Cuba and Puerto Rico by the United States. For many years, Betances's pronouncement "Las Antillas para los antillanos" (the Antilles for the Antilleans) alerted the world to US imperialist ambitions in the Caribbean and affirmed the islands' right to become independent nations.[11] Little did Betances know that only several weeks before his death in 1898 his worst fears would become a reality with the outbreak of the Spanish-Cuban-American War and the US invasion of Cuba and Puerto Rico.

The "Splendid Little War"

The Spanish-Cuban-American War broke out after the mysterious explosion of the battleship *Maine*, a US naval vessel stationed at the port of Havana. Claiming that the explosion was an act of sabotage, the North American yellow press accused the Spanish government of responsibility and rapidly promoted a "Remember the *Maine*" mentality aimed at galvanizing public opinion to demand retribution for what was described as "an act of aggression" and encouraging US intervention in Cuba's ongoing war against Spain. The "Remember the *Maine*" battle cry evoked the "Remember the Alamo" frenzy that half a century earlier prompted a declaration of war against Mexico and the subsequent annexation of almost half of Mexico's territory by the United States after the conclusion of the Mexican-American War (1846–1848). In response to mounting public pressures and its own expansionist designs, the US Congress used the sinking of the *Maine* to declare war against Spain and invade its colonies of Cuba and Puerto Rico.

The Spanish-Cuban-American War ended with the Treaty of Paris, which forced Spain to relinquish the remainder of its overseas colonial empire. While Cubans were promised independence, Puerto Rico, along with Spain's Pacific island colonies of the Philippines and Guam, were ceded to the United States. After the treaty was signed, Cuba remained under the protection of the United States until it was officially granted independence in 1902. However, the Platt Amendment to the Constitution of the Republic of Cuba gave the United States authority to intervene in the affairs of the new nation whenever it deemed necessary. Thus, for more than half a century, Cuba remained within the US sphere of influence until the triumph of the Cuban Revolution in 1959.

The Spanish-Cuban-American War brought the Antillean separatist movement to an end. Few of the most militant separatists returned to Puerto Rico. Schomburg stayed in New York and eventually diverted his attention to his bibliophilic and historical interests. He developed close ties with leading African American and Afro-Caribbean intellectuals of the Pan-African movement of the early twentieth century. He moved to Harlem and married an African American woman. Some scholars argue that his adoption of Pan-Africanism made him more aware of the racism he often felt within his own native culture and may have contributed to his distancing from the Puerto Rican community. A sign of this estrangement was his anglicizing of his first name to Arthur and moving to the African American section of Harlem.

In 1911, Schomburg was among the founders of the Negro Society for Historical Research, and in later years he presided over the American Negro Academy. He amassed an extensive collection of books and materials about the histories and experiences of African populations around the world. Schomburg sold his collection to the New York Public Library in later years. The collection was the nucleus of the Schomburg Center for Research on Black Culture of the New York Public Library. Opened to the public in 1927, the center and its vast collection became focal points during the years of the Harlem Renaissance and attracted numerous US and foreign researchers interested in the diverse African diasporas. From 1930 to 1932, Schomburg had a brief academic career as a lecturer and bibliographer at Fisk University, helping this institution develop its black archival collection, but he eventually left to accept the post of curator of his own collection at the New York Public Library. Two years before his death, he wrote the column "Our Pioneers" for the New York newspaper *Amsterdam News*, which gave him the opportunity to celebrate the achievements of notable black personalities from various parts of the world, including Hispanic countries. In this regard, he played a pioneering role in documenting the experiences and contributions of African peoples in many different countries.

The US invasion of Cuba brought an end to the Spanish-Cuban War, which most scholars agree the rebels were close to winning (Foner 1972; L.

Pérez 1998). Nonetheless, the international press focused its attention on glorifying the battlefield histrionics of Colonel Theodore Roosevelt and his Rough Riders in the liberation of Cuba and in putting an end to Spanish tyrannical rule in the Americas. The Cuban rebel army received little credit at the time for its considerable battlefield accomplishments in weakening the Spanish army during almost three years of fighting prior to the US intervention. In a letter to Roosevelt, US ambassador to England John Hay characterized the US invasion as "a splendid little war."[12] After all, it had made the United States an imperial power and more determined than ever to replace its European counterparts and consolidate its hegemony in the American hemisphere. The war also made Teddy Roosevelt a legendary military hero and facilitated his winning the US presidency in the 1904 election.

Puerto Rican general Juan Ríus Rivera, a Cuban rebel army commander, was appointed civil governor of Cuba during the US occupation but resigned from the post after the United States introduced the Platt Amendment to Cuba's new constitution, affirming its power to intervene

"Will wear the Stars and Stripes"
Uncle Sam: "Here, sonny, put on these duds." (*Source: Minneapolis Journal.*)

in the island's affairs. While Cuba was finally granted its independence in 1902, Puerto Rico was kept as "an unincorporated territory" of the United States, establishing a colonial political status examined in more detail in later sections of this chapter.

The US–Puerto Rico connection intensified after the Spanish-Cuban-American War of 1898. The US invasion immediately ended the autonomous government that Spain had granted Puerto Rico less than a year before. Some island leaders had regarded the charter of autonomy as an important step

"Americanization": A cartoon by Puerto Rican artist Mario Brau Zuzuárregui meant to criticize the thwarted policies of the US colonial regime in Puerto Rico, such as the imposition of English as the main language of instruction in the public school system. The twisted spike bears the word "Americanization"; Uncle Sam is pounding the spike with a sledge hammer that reads "Idioma Inglés" (English language). (*Source:* Colección Puertorriqueña del Sistema de Bibliotecas de la Universidad de Puerto Rico.)

toward Puerto Rico eventually becoming a sovereign republic. Nonetheless, the new regime disbanded the governing autonomic cabinet. Hence, most of the initial US colonial policies stemmed from North American military and economic interests, with limited involvement of creole political leaders and often promulgating patronizing and disparaging views of the Puerto Rican people and their former Spanish rulers. These new policies also aimed at Americanizing the island and manufacturing the necessary consent among the population to legitimize the new US colonial regime.

Among the most controversial Americanization policies were the implementation of English as the official language of Puerto Rico and its school system; the use of island schools to inculcate US values and accelerate the adoption of English; the undermining of Puerto Rican history, culture, and the Spanish language; and religious proselytizing by Protestant missionaries among a primarily Catholic population (see Negrón de Montilla 1971; Silva Gotay 1997; Méndez 1980). The new colonial government even changed the official name of the island to "Porto Rico."[13] The push to implement these policies generated strong opposition from some sectors of Puerto Rican society, particularly the creole intellectual elite, who viewed them as a concerted attempt to "denationalize" Puerto Ricans by diminishing the importance of their native language and cultural patrimony and espousing the superiority of the Anglo-American way of life. But segments of the population believed that the US presence was bringing democracy, economic prosperity, and modernity to Puerto Rico and that the island was better off under the new US colonial regime than under the previous Spanish rule.

From the beginning, military officials with little knowledge of island affairs headed the US colonial administration. Soon it became evident that creole political leaders were not expected to play any prominent role in shaping most of the policies and decisions initially implemented. Puerto Rico and Cuba were becoming pawns in a larger plan to consolidate the United States' military and geopolitical interests and advance its expansionist goals in the Caribbean and the rest of the hemisphere. These Manifest Destiny aspirations superseded any local considerations. The United States allowed Cuba to become an independent republic but used its Platt Amendment prerogatives to dictate the course of Cuba's affairs several times in the decades that followed and even after the triumph of the Cuban Revolution. But independence was not an alternative offered to Puerto Rico. Its designation as "an unincorporated territory" relegated the island to a powerless colonial status under the jurisdiction of the US Congress.

The Beginnings of Labor Migration
The history and evolution of Puerto Rican migration to the continent is closely related to the complex subordinate colonial relationship that developed

"New Porto Rico": This postcard image, also used on a cigar box, publicizes Puerto Rico's new status as a US possession. The colonial government used the name "Porto Rico" rather than the official Spanish name on all its documents until the 1930s. (*Source:* Postcards Collection, Center for Puerto Rican Studies Library and Archives.)

between Puerto Rico and the United States once the latter took possession of the island. But a wider context must also be considered in dealing with all transnational migratory movements of workers. This context is directly related to the development of capitalism as a mode of production and the power relations it engenders, particularly among the more industrialized capitalist nations and the less developed nations.

Bonilla and Campos (1986) provide a useful summary of the evolving patterns of Puerto Rican migration before and after the US invasion, pointing to the shifts that occurred in the capitalist mode of production and how they affected the island's labor force. Their study divides the migratory process into three major phases, each responding to the international dynamics of capitalist development that produced a displacement and reshuffling of workers throughout the world, which in turn influenced the specific local factors and conditions leading to Puerto Rican migration. The colonial relationship between Puerto Rico and the United States and the status of Puerto Ricans as colonial migrants generated a unique set of circumstances because of the island's inherent subordinate condition, which is key to understanding the early patterns of migration to the United States.

According to Bonilla and Campos (1986), the first phase of Puerto Rican migration ran from 1873 to 1898, dates that refer to two main events in the island's history: the abolition of slavery and the US invasion of the island. The years between these two events marked the expansion of hacienda-based production in Puerto Rico and a significant increase in export trade and commercial ties between the island and the United States. This commercial relationship had shifted to sugar production by the 1880s. The US occupation of Puerto Rico in 1898 initiated a second migration cycle, which ended in 1929 with the US stock market crash that prompted the Great Depression and an unprecedented worldwide downturn of the capitalist industrial economies. During this period, the island's economy witnessed the transition from hacienda-based production to US-controlled agricultural plantation capitalism focused on sugar production. An agricultural economy controlled by large and technologically advanced sugar trusts prompted the decline of economic activity in the local coffee haciendas of creole landowners. The third phase, known as the Great Migration, developed during the post–World War II period and encompasses Puerto Rico's transition from an agricultural to an industrial manufacturing economy also dominated by US capital investments. This latter cycle continued throughout the 1950s and 1960s.

During the post–Great Migration decades (1970s–1980s), the socioeconomic effects caused by the collapse of New York City's manufacturing sector and the financial crisis that overwhelmed its government affected stateside Puerto Ricans, since at the time, the large majority of them were living there or in nearby areas. For the first time, there was a high level of return migration to the island. By the 1990s, however, scholars were noticing some gains in the socioeconomic profile of the stateside community. Rivera-Batiz and Santiago (1994) extensively documented and analyzed these "changing realities"in relation to the geographic dispersion of Puerto Ricans to other cities and states (see Chapters 4 and 6). The progress became more defined in the 1990s and has continued during the New Millennium Migration years. The next three chapters provide, respectively, a review of the post–World War II Great Migration, a discussion of the New Millennium Migration, and an up-to-date contemporary demographic and socioeconomic portrait of stateside Puerto Ricans.

As we have seen, early migrations of Puerto Ricans to other neighboring Caribbean islands, propelled by socioeconomic conditions and changes and government decisions in Puerto Rico, date back to the last few decades of the eighteenth and the early part of the nineteenth centuries, when the island was still under Spanish colonial rule. During this period the island began to move away from subsistence agriculture, a pervasive contraband economy, and the stagnant Spanish mercantile monopoly that characterized the initial three centuries of the colonial regime and adopted the hacienda economy that came to dominate most of nineteenth-century Puerto Rico. Hacienda production was largely in the hands of creole and immigrant landowners (Scarano 1981). Sugar was the dominant export product from the mid-1820s to the mid-1870s, and the United States was the main market. But coffee took sugar's place in the island's economy for the remainder of the nineteenth century. Tobacco was also among the main export products. The largest portion of the coffee and tobacco exports, however, went to Spain and Cuba rather than the United States.

Puerto Rico's hacienda mode of production relied on the labor of *agregados* (tenant farmers), day laborers, and, before the abolition of slavery in 1873, enslaved Africans. The demand for workers in the expanding agricultural sector had prompted the colonial government to implement in 1849 the Reglamento de Jornaleros (Day Workers' Regulations), professed anti-vagrancy measures that forced large numbers of peasants to work for the meager wages that the hacendados were willing to pay them. Nontenant and landless peasant workers were compelled to carry an official *libreta de jornaleros* (worker's journal) as a record of their daily employment in order to avoid heavy fines imposed by the ruling colonial authorities. This system was in effect for twenty-four years before it was ended in 1873.

Economic activity on the haciendas intensified in the nineteenth century with the growing demand for agricultural products for export to the US market. The expanding trade relationship with the United States exposed the island's hacendados, merchants, other professionals, and students to North American ways and to the expanding world of bourgeois capitalism (Quintero Rivera 1980). However, Puerto Rican emigration was still relatively low during those years. According to the US census, between 1900 and 1910 the US Puerto Rican population was less than 2,000 people (see Chapter 4, Table 4.3).

The US takeover of Puerto Rico immediately generated several official reports and books about the island and the other new North American possessions. The bulk of the early publications describing the territories acquired in the aftermath of the Spanish-Cuban-American War tend to glorify the benevolent expansionist role of the United States in spreading its democratic values and civilized progress in the American hemisphere and other parts of the world. Titles such as *Our New Possessions* (Baldwin 1899; T. White 1898), *Our Islands and Their People* (Wheeler and Olivares 1899), *Our Island Empire* (Morris 1899), and *America's Insular Possessions* (Forbes-Lindsay 1906) began to set the tone for the colonial discourses that introduced Puerto Ricans, Cubans, Filipinos, and Guam's Chamorros to a US audience. These books contained the first photographic images and descriptions of the Puerto Rican people to become embedded in the minds of the US public, portraying them as a destitute, racially inferior island population redeemed from Spanish tyrannical rule and thus in need of introduction to democracy, enlightened civilization, and prosperity by the magnanimous guiding hand of the United States. These publications take a paternalistic tone and propagate a disparaging portrait of the subservient nature, character traits, and way of life of the aforementioned populations as seen through the eyes of the US colonizer (see Thompson 1995; García 2000).

According to an 1899 report by military governor General George W. Davis, the following conditions prevailed in Puerto Rico at the time of the US occupation: "Nearly 800,000 of the 960,000 population (260 to the square mile) could neither read nor write. Most of these lived in bark huts and were, in effect, the personal property of the landed proprietors. . . . They were poor beyond the possibility of our understanding and if they were so fortunate as to have enough for the current hour, they were content" (War Department 1902, 669). These first impressions of the island's population were accompanied by descriptions of early efforts by the US regime to build better roads and more schools and to deal with the numerous health problems afflicting Puerto Rican peasants, at the time the largest segment of the island's population. Among the most pressing problems were numerous tropical diseases, widespread malnutrition, and a high mortality rate. The presence of US enterprises with business interests throughout the Caribbean and Latin American regions was also immediately felt, as many companies began to send recruitment agents to Puerto Rico to hire low-wage contract laborers. This practice soon turned into the main conduit for the migration of workers.

After two years of military rule, Charles Allen was appointed as the first US civil governor of Puerto Rico under the new colonial regime. Governor Allen made reference to the emigration of Puerto Rican workers in his first report about the state of island affairs, submitted to Congress in 1901. In this document he noted that "emigration [had] been almost unknown" on the island and that Puerto Ricans seemed to be "essentially home-loving people, and remarkably attached to their native land" (History Task Force 1982, 14). The North American governor then referred to the widespread devastation of 1899's Hurricane San Ciriaco, which caused many deaths and destroyed the island's agricultural economy and the livelihoods of the great majority of its peasant population. He viewed these conditions as favorable for emigration agents to induce Puerto Rican peasants to work in the sugarcane fields of Hawaii or the iron mines of Cuba, places where US companies had an immediate demand for low-wage labor. He also believed that the island could easily dispense with these workers:

"Most of the emigrants are of the very poorest class of laborers, many of them without a box or a bundle or anything whatever more than the scanty apparel in which they stand upon the wharves. Very few of them have the least rudiments of education. In other words, these emigrants comprise the least desirable elements of this people" (History Task Force 1982, 15).

Clearly, the US colonial government was using the emigration of Puerto Rican workers as a policy device to alleviate extreme poverty and high unemployment among the destitute peasant population and in this way get rid of "the least desirable elements" of Puerto Rican society. This initial migration strategy coincided with a strong demand by US investors for cheap labor for their companies located in the acquired territories, on other Caribbean islands, and in other countries in the Americas, as well as in the expanding industrial sector in the continental United States. Thus US companies were encouraged to recruit workers from Puerto Rico to work in agricultural fields or in manufacturing and service industries.

Migration of Puerto Rican workers to other countries, as mentioned, had occurred at a much slower pace and scale under the Spanish colonial administration and only began to show a perceptible growth pattern after the US takeover. Desperate conditions of poverty and the lack of employment opportunities for many peasants, artisans, and other day laborers had prompted the former Spanish rulers to foster emigration, especially after the abolition of slavery, which created a surplus of unemployed workers (History Task Force 1982). During those years, Puerto Rican workers were encouraged to leave the island for the Dominican Republic, Cuba, Panama, and Venezuela, countries needing agricultural workers or other forms of manual labor.

Not only working-class laborers left during this early period. The limited educational opportunities for Puerto Ricans under Spanish rule motivated the island's most affluent families to send their male offspring to Spain or other European countries to receive an advanced education. Given the expanding commercial connections between Puerto Rico and the United States, the focus began to shift toward the end of the nineteenth century to North American universities, with the trend increasing after the island became a US territory. Since then, many island Puerto Ricans have sought professional training abroad, coming into contact with the various Puerto Rican or Latino/a communities in several US cities.

There is no question that US control over Puerto Rico propelled the second migration phase described by Bonilla and Campos (1986). The rapid flow of investment capital from the United States into Puerto Rico after the invasion was the main catalyst for the development of full-fledged agrarian capitalism under the control of large sugar trusts that purchased large portions of the island's available land to support expanded harvesting of the commodity and all its derivative products (e.g., molasses, rum). Large-scale sugar production not only shifted the focus of but also monopolized the island's agricultural economy. More than half the available agricultural land was soon concentrated in the hands of a few US corporations, which built large, more technologically advanced sugar mills, or *centrales*. This land concentration reduced the number of smaller farms owned by the local hacendado propertied class. The shift from coffee production, which was the heart of the hacienda economy, to sugar production further debilitated the economic power and social position of the hacendados and increased unemployment among peasant workers.

According to Quintero Rivera (1980), the consolidation of US-led agrarian capitalism had multiple effects in reshaping social and political relations in Puerto Rican society, including the emergence of "a dependent anti-national bourgeoisie" (14) whose main role was to fulfill the island's needs for importing consumer products from the United States; the concomitant growth of a sector of "intermediary professionals" (17) who saw the United States as the conduit for bringing progress and modernity to Puerto Rico; and the proletarianization of the island's labor force, which faced the trials and tribulations of "wage-labor capitalist relations" (22) and endured labor exploitation by US companies. This new proletariat was also caught in the contradictions stemming from their rejection of the seignorial and paternalistic relations of the hacienda economy and the old Spanish colonial order, on the one hand, and their admiration for North American liberal democracy, with its promise of more civil liberties and worker protections than they had experienced before, on the other. Thus, Quintero Rivera (1976a, 1976b, 1980) has emphasized that the Puerto Rican workers' movement developed an internationalist socialist outlook rather than assuming anti-American positions or subscribing to the Hispanophilic nationalistic stance of the creole propertied class being stripped of its limited economic power by the US corporations.

The desperate economic conditions that developed during the latter years of Spanish rule and the early years of the US occupation motivated workers to organize. Numerous workers, especially from the artisan sector, joined the Federación Libre de los Trabajadores de Puerto Rico (FLT, Free Federation of Puerto Rico's Workers), the island's largest labor union, which had been founded in 1899. However, only two years after its founding, the FLT became an affiliate of the American Federation of Labor (AFL). For the next four decades the FLT was led by Santiago Iglesias Pantín, a Spanish émigré carpenter who had come to Puerto Rico from Cuba in 1896. He traveled to New York in 1900 and developed ties with US workers affiliated with the AFL. He became an AFL labor organizer and was instrumental in getting the FLT to affiliate with the larger and stronger North American union that would advocate for better wages and worker protections for Puerto Ricans. The connections between the FLT and the

AFL, both seen to represent the interest of workers, along with prevailing class antagonisms between Puerto Rican workers and the creole hacendado class, which had been exploiting their labor since the years of Spanish colonial rule, contributed to the labor sector's support for the US presence in Puerto Rico and for the possibility of future statehood for the island.

In 1915 the FLT founded the Partido Socialista (PS, Socialist Party), which became the FLT's political arm in challenging the control of local politics by creole landowners. The *tabaqueros/as*, men and women who worked in the island's tobacco factories and shops, were the largest and most vocal group among the artisans and within the wider Puerto Rican labor movement. Men concentrated on cigar making while women were largely relegated to stripping the tobacco leaves. The needle industries, another active sector in the labor movement, employed mostly women. In addition to working in *talleres* (workshops), women engaged in commissioned home-based needlework.[14]

Growing numbers of workers migrated to the United States during these early decades of US domination. In 1910 the total US Puerto Rican population was 1,513; it had increased to 11,811 by 1920 and to 52,774 by 1930 (see Chapter 4, Table 4.3; Wagenheim 1975). Because of its affiliation with the AFL, Puerto Rico's FLT actually encouraged workers to migrate to the United States rather than to other countries with lower wages and fewer labor protections.

The economic debacle produced by the Great Depression slowed down Puerto Rican migration, but a growth pattern continued. By 1940 the US migrant population had increased to 69,967, which was 33 percent higher than the previous decade. This increase, however, was much lower than the larger annual percentage increases of the 1910s and 1920s.

Another economic change characterized this second phase of Puerto Rican migration. Puerto Rico was exporting a few agricultural products needed in the metropolis but was becoming a major consumer of US manufactured goods. A noted scholar captured this dependent relationship in simpler terms when he stated decades later that Puerto Rico "produces what she does not consume and consumes what she does not produce" (G. Lewis 1963). The ultimate result of this pattern was an enduring condition of economic dependency that evolved throughout the twentieth century but, in a broader sense, would remain unchanged in some concrete ways. The consistency of the pattern is clear: under US rule, Puerto Rico was to serve the specific economic interests of US investors and corporations, initially in the agricultural sector and later in labor- and capital-intensive industries during the Operation Bootstrap years. Additionally, because of the persistent levels of unemployment, the island's workers would serve as a source of cheap labor to satisfy shortages in the colonial metropolis and find themselves compelled to migrate in order to make a living. A major consequence of this manipulation of Puerto Rico's labor force has been the increased dependency of the local government on the influx of federal funds from the US Congress to provide essential social services to the poor and unemployed and to support public agencies and other aspects of the island's infrastructure. Although many island workers contribute to Social Security and Medicare, Puerto Rico is not treated on a par with other states since, proportionally, its government does not receive from Congress federal transfers for these programs comparable to those allocated to the fifty states.

Economic dependency lay side by side with political subordination and the limited political power for self-government granted to Puerto Ricans by the US Congress. Two major congressional acts have guided Puerto Rico's relationship with the United States: the Foraker Act of 1900 and the Jones-Shafroth Act of 1917.[15] The Foraker Act provided a civil government for the island after the initial two years of military occupation, establishing a government headed by a North American governor and an Executive Council composed of North American officials appointed by the president of the United States. Puerto Rican participation in the ruling structures was limited to an elective House of Delegates. The Jones-Shafroth Act granted US citizenship to Puerto Ricans and eliminated the US-appointed Executive Council. In its stead, the act introduced an elective Senate, which provided Puerto Ricans with a bicameral legislative system that increased their level of participation in running the insular government. The citizenship decree also introduced compulsory military service. This meant that before the draft was abolished in the 1970s, Puerto Rican men were compelled to serve in the US armed forces. They were drafted for the first time during World War I and thereafter in all subsequent US armed conflicts.

The changes in the island's political and socioeconomic conditions engendered by US colonial control of its economy, along with other global economic forces and labor needs that propelled migration, must be examined in more detail in order to better illustrate the specific characteristics and differences between each of the major Puerto Rican migratory phases outlined by Bonilla and Campos (1986) and discussed earlier in this chapter. It is important to also consider that in making Puerto Rico a territorial possession, the United States initially acquired a country confronting severe conditions of poverty, widespread malnutrition and tropical diseases, and pervasive unemployment. Politically, the island was just beginning to develop in the latter decades of the nineteenth century, after languishing as a neglected colony for the first three centuries of the Spanish colonial period, then enduring the burden of authoritarian rule, before finally receiving autonomy from Spain in 1897. The autonomic government that made Puerto Rico a self-governing "overseas province" of Spain was inaugurated in February 1898 and lasted less than six months before it came to end with the US invasion of Puerto Rico.

The socioeconomic and political dislocations produced by the initial occupation of Puerto Rico and subsequent control of the local government by US officials, together with the US Congress's overarching powers over island affairs, can be correlated with the pace and magnitude of the various migratory waves. As the United States came out of the Great Depression and entered World War II, migration began to intensify. This was due, on the one hand, to the increasing demand for labor during wartime and, on the other, to the mass industrialization and modernization project that changed Puerto Rican society and shifted the focus of its agricultural economy. This significant shift explains why the great majority of Puerto Rican migration studies have focused on the postwar Great Migration period (1940s–1960s), the third phase in Bonilla and Campos's (1986) periodization.

A shortcoming of many of the bulk of migration studies is a tendency to emphasize push-pull socioeconomic factors that caused Puerto Ricans to leave their homeland and settle in the United States, without enough attention to the fundamental dynamics and contradictions of the island's subordinate colonial relationship and Puerto Ricans' basic condition as colonial migrants and US citizens. These key factors made migration such a viable, unrestrained, and expeditious policy tool for dealing with economic problems. At many different times, both US authorities and the island's political leadership consented to this manipulation of workers without officially acknowledging their role in sponsoring migration.

Early arguments to explain migration showed a propensity to overemphasize Puerto Rico's extreme poverty, high unemployment, and overpopulation problems, a situation that US colonial and island officials also dealt with by introducing new population-control and family-planning policies that became a significant component of the development discourse of the 1940s and 1950s (Ramírez de Arellano and Seipp 1983). In fact, the overpopulation argument was at the forefront of all explanations about the island's widespread poverty, and migration and population control were seen as the two most expedient solutions to this problem.

Unsurprisingly, then, population pressure on the island has been commonly cited as the main rationale for the drive to foster Puerto Rican migration. The idea generally emphasized the dual objectives of economic development and growth. Most of the early migration studies reiterated the notion of an "overpopulated," impoverished island lacking in natural resources. Mills, Senior, and Goldsen dramatized this perspective in the opening line of *The Puerto Rican Journey* (1950): "If the United States were as crowded as Puerto Rico, it would almost contain all the people in the world" (3). In an earlier study, Chenault (1938) had expressed a similar view by stating, "One important factor which can cause migration from a country as crowded as Puerto Rico is the lack of natural resources to support its growing population" (12). The irony is that while these assertions were being made to justify migration, especially by US researchers and public officials, Puerto Ricans were migrating in large numbers to New York City, which had a population density almost 150 times higher than that of Puerto Rico at the time (History Task Force 1979, 20). The stress on an overpopulation problem implied that Puerto Rico had neither the natural nor the human resources to sustain its growing population and thus migration was the most logical alternative to alleviate these conditions. This particular view, however, obfuscated the real structural socioeconomic and political factors that created the conditions that impelled the migration of island workers. In Puerto Rico's case, these conditions were inherent in the development of US-controlled capitalism on the island and the ways in which colonialism shifted the balance of power and social and economic relations within Puerto Rican society and hindered the ability of the island's government to control the country's economy.

Other common explanations for increased migration to the United States during the postwar period were the island's persistent high rates of unemployment and illiteracy. At the time of the US invasion, about 60 percent of Puerto Rico's population could not read or write, although illiteracy rates went down considerably in later decades. An additional factor frequently cited to explain a pattern of increased migration during the early decades of the twentieth century (see Table 4.2) is the granting of US citizenship to Puerto Ricans in 1917, since this allowed island workers to move without restriction to the colonial metropole, although it had been relatively easy for Puerto Ricans to do so since 1898. The geographic proximity of the island to the United States and, since the 1940s, the availability of air travel and inexpensive airfares between Puerto Rico and several major US cities also facilitated the Great Migration.

A fixation on the various migration push-pull factors summarized above, said to have a causal effect on Puerto Rican migration, often understates the weight of the planning efforts of US and Puerto Rican policymakers and government agencies. At different times they used migration as a safety valve to deal with some of the island's harsh socioeconomic conditions and to provide a source of low-wage labor for US manufacturing and agricultural employers and those in the service sector.

Migration, however, was not the only tool for dealing with Puerto Rican poverty and population growth. Some government policies aimed at population control and reducing the birthrate relied on the use of various contraceptive methods. The introduction of oral contraceptives to the island facilitated the push for population control. Moreover, US pharmaceutical companies used Puerto Rican women as guinea pigs for testing "the pill" before it was introduced to the US market (Ramírez de Arellano and Seipp 1983). Another popular method fostered by the government was the mass sterilization of women through the surgical procedure that became known as *la operación*.[16]

These population-control practices intensified during the rapid industrialization period of the 1950s, when Puerto Rico developed one of the highest women's sterilization rates in the world. A couple of decades after the beginning of Operation Bootstrap, about 35 percent of all Puerto Rican women were sterilized, compared to 30 percent in the United States (Vázquez Calzada 1973; Presser 1980). Between 1950 and 1970 the fertility rate on the island declined by 48 percent, from 5.2 to 2.7 children per woman.

Puerto Rican migration continued at a steady pace and reached one of its highest levels during the Great Migration years, a direct consequence of the impact of industrialization on the island's economy, as the new manufacturing industries could not absorb a substantive portion of the displaced agricultural workforce. These conditions are analyzed in greater detail in Chapter 4.

Migration to Hawaii

The 1900–1901 migration of agricultural workers to the sugarcane plantations of Hawaii was the first large exodus of contract labor out of Puerto Rico, but Hawaii was not the only destination. During the first decade of US occupation, workers also were recruited to labor in the Dominican Republic and Cuba to support the expansion of North American sugar trusts on the two neighboring islands (History Task Force 1982).

Puerto Ricans leaving for Hawaii were desperately searching for any source of employment following the aforementioned destruction caused by Hurricane San Ciriaco in 1899. Laborers were recruited for the sugarcane fields of the Hawaiian Islands, and entire families traveled there in the course of eleven expeditions beginning in November 1900 and ending a year later. There, Puerto Ricans joined other groups of immigrant workers mostly from Portugal, China, Japan, Korea, and the Philippines.

The journey from Puerto Rico to the Hawaiian Islands was long and onerous, since it involved going to the port of New Orleans by ship and then by train to San Francisco in order to board another ship to the final destination. Many agricultural workers were uninformed about the ordeal they would face on their journey to Hawaii, but changing their minds was not an option, since they were constantly under the surveillance of the employing company's agents. A description of the initial voyage summarizes some of the hardships:

> The first group of 114 men, women and children came on the S.S. Arkadia to New Orleans where they were loaded onto two tourist cars of the Southern Pacific Railway and began a slow and eventful journey via a southwest route across the United States to San Francisco. Overcrowding in the cars led to much discomfort. The lightweight clothing worn by the people, while suitable for Puerto Rico and Hawaii, was not warm enough for the winter trip. The trip was a slow one as the agents wanted to time the arrival

of the train to San Francisco to coincide with the departure of the S.S. City of Rio de Janeiro for Honolulu, so that the passengers could be put on the ship immediately and be on their way to Hawaii. (Camacho Souza 1986, 27)

Even with the watchful attention of the agents of the Hawaii Sugar Planters' Association, which paid for workers' transportation, defections did occur, as only fifty-six Puerto Ricans landed in Hawaii on the first voyage. Some of the dropouts managed to stay in New Orleans or San Francisco, leading to small concentrations of Puerto Ricans in these localities.

The working conditions of Puerto Rican workers in the sugar fields were harsh indeed, whether in Puerto Rico or Hawaii. A 1903 government report spoke disparagingly about the Puerto Ricans workers transported to Hawaii:

> They have brought with them a criminal element which may take time to eliminate, but will find the islands a decidedly discouraging field of operations, and they have faults and weaknesses which it may require a generation or two fully to correct. They are somewhat given to drinking, gambling, and carrying concealed weapons, and are more quarrelsome and vindictive than the other inhabitants. (US Department of Labor 1903, 361)

The report went on to minimize the potential contributions of Puerto Ricans to Hawaiian society by stating, "The ultimate effect of the Porto Rican immigration upon the islands will probably be unimportant. Those who remain will doubtless amalgamate more or less with the Portuguese during their transition into Hawaiian Americans. They and their descendants will in all probability be vastly better off than they had any prospect of being in their own country" (361).

The conditions of Puerto Rican laborers were significantly less idyllic than those described by US officials in Hawaii, and the tone of the discourse was consistent with US colonial policies and practices at the time. That entire families were transported halfway across the globe under deplorable conditions to work in a society and culture that was alien to them, particularly linguistically, can explain some of the defiant behavior of Puerto Ricans in their new environment. What US officials described as indolence was most likely a form of resistance to deplorable working conditions and the abusive behavior of company employees toward foreign contract workers. The experience of Puerto Ricans in Hawaii represents the first coordinated migration following the Spanish-Cuban-American War.

Succeeding generations of Puerto Ricans shared the basic motivation to leave their homeland in search of employment or better economic opportunities in the United States. Economic necessity propelled another small contract-labor wave of Puerto Rican migration to Hawaii in 1921, but by then most migration was to New York City. Puerto Ricans have integrated into the larger Hawaiian society through intermarriage with native Hawaiians, Japanese, and other ethnic groups on the islands, yet maintain important aspects of their own island culture. Through the years, various civil associations have emerged to sustain Puerto Rican culture, language, and traditions. Moreover, many of the features of these early migrations foreshadowed the wider Puerto Rican experience in the United States: the underlying economic motivation for the risky journey, the need to maintain community and cultural heritage, the desire to cling to one's native language, openness to interaction with the surrounding society, and celebration of the homeland's heritage.

Research into the early migrations of Puerto Ricans to certain US localities like Hawaii, before it became a state in 1959, only began in the 1970s. Some of the descendants of Hawaii's *Borinkis* (a name for Puerto Rican Hawaiians) started the Puerto Rican Heritage Society of Hawaii in 1980 to promote the documentation of their presence in and contributions to the islands. Several important studies released in the 1980s detailed the formation and evolution of this particular community (Rosario Natal 1983; Camacho Souza 1986; N. Carr 1989). The number of self-identified Puerto Ricans residing in the state of Hawaii was 44,116 in 2010, according to the US census. This figure constitutes 2.5 percent of the total population of the islands and less than 1 percent of the total Puerto Rican population in the continental United States.

The existence of community organizations such as the Club Puertorriqueño de San Francisco (Puerto Rican Club of San Francisco), founded in 1912, reveals the presence of those Puerto Ricans who stayed in San Francisco on their way to Hawaii or settled there on their way back from the islands. Contract workers from Puerto Rico also were recruited to work on farms and factories in California and nearby states during those years, although more sporadically than in other areas of the country. The influx of Puerto Ricans to other parts of California expanded over the decades as they settled in relative small numbers in cities such as San José, Los Angeles, San Diego, and Union City (see Chapter 4). Another community organization, the Liga Puertorriqueña de California (Puerto Rican League of California), was established in 1922. More than half a century later, in 1973, the Western Region Puerto Rican Council was founded to draw attention to the needs of Puerto Ricans in that part of the country and to their presence there since the early decades of the twentieth century. These organizations served important social and cultural functions and, in addition, gave the community a voice in dealing with pressing collective needs and civil rights issues.

A pattern of Puerto Rican labor migration to closer destinations, most notably to the neighboring Caribbean islands, developed after the United States purchased the Virgin Islands from Denmark in 1917. A preferred destination was the island of St. Croix, where Puerto Ricans were hired to work in agriculture and on stock farms. This exodus intensified after 1927, but an exchange of agricultural workers between Puerto Rico's eastern island municipality of Vieques and St. Croix had existed since the nineteenth century. With the large expropriation of almost two-thirds of Vieques's territory by the US Navy in 1941, migration of *viequenses* from Puerto Rico to St. Croix sharpened. Migration from other Puerto Rican towns to St. Croix augmented in later years. In 2010 about 20,000 Puerto Ricans lived in St. Croix, representing a notable portion of the island's total population.

The Growth of the New York Community

The New York Puerto Rican community was the largest and fastest-growing one during the early decades of the twentieth century, but according to the US census, it numbered less than 2,000 in 1910 (Table 4.3). A notable growth began during the World War I years, since many of the war industries relied on immigrant contract labor and Puerto Rican migrants were one group that fulfilled this demand. Puerto Ricans also were recruited for industries in New Orleans, Louisiana; Wilmington, North Carolina; Charleston, South Carolina; and Brunswick and Savannah, Georgia. Some of the contract labor was gender specific, as illustrated by the recruitment of Puerto Rican men for agricultural work in upstate New York and New Jersey and women for work in the cordage factories of St. Louis, Missouri, and New York's garment industry (Centro History Task Force 1982).

The granting of US citizenship to Puerto Ricans in 1917 encouraged the island's largest labor union, the FLT, to point out the advantages and protections that Puerto Rican workers would gain if they sought employment in the United States rather than going to other countries. But despite the linkages between the FLT and the AFL, North American companies were not deterred from exploiting Puerto Rican contract workers or forcing them to work in conditions less favorable than those afforded other US workers. Thus, in the United States, Puerto Ricans became part of an underprivileged working class and a major source of low-wage labor for the country's manufacturing, agricultural, and service sectors.

Census data from the 1920s and 1930s showed that New York City was becoming the preferred point of destination for Puerto Rican migrants. The first Puerto Rican barrios were forming in Manhattan and Brooklyn, and others emerged through the years in greater New York City. At the time, most Latinos/as in the city were of Spanish, Cuban, and Puerto Rican origin, although there were others from a wider range of Latin American nationalities. The Chelsea area was the site of more than 500 Hispanic-owned tobacco factories and shops (Sánchez Korrol [1983] 1994). The socialist *tabaqueros/as* were an important sector of the community, since they tended to be active in grassroots organizing, which translated into the creation of organizations and publications aimed at empowering community members

Early 1900s advertising for steamship travel from San Juan to New York and San Juan to New Orleans, a first destination for Puerto Rican contract workers going to Hawaii. (*Source*: Center for Puerto Rican Studies, Library and Archives.)

to speak out and denounce the injustices endured by migrants in the workplace or in the society at large. The largest concentration of Puerto Ricans was in the eastern section of Harlem—which soon became known as Spanish Harlem, or El Barrio. After the postwar Great Migration years, Puerto Ricans began to spread out to the Lower East Side, Upper West Side, the South Bronx, and the Williamsburg section of Brooklyn, later known as Los Sures (the southern section).

The migrants included numerous displaced agricultural workers, as well as factory workers and skilled artisans, with fewer businessmen, professionals, students, writers, and artists. Regarding the various types of occupations held by Puerto Rican migrants during the early stages of migration, Clara Rodríguez (1989) stressed the importance of recognizing "the diversity and richness of the migrant population" (2) and noted that "migrants brought non-transferable skills" and "transferable skills that were not transferred" (2), statements that underscored the predicament for newcomers: they had "to accept whatever jobs were available" (Handlin 1959, 70). The working-class nature of Puerto Rican migration was therefore unquestionable, with a large representation in the manufacturing, agricultural, and service sectors. The overrepresentation of Puerto Rican workers in semiskilled, low-wage manufacturing and agricultural employment was not to change until the 1980s (see Rivera-Batiz and Santiago 1994; Chapter 4 in this volume).

Women migrants were a major source of labor for New York's garment industry. This particular industry not only reflected a gendered division of labor but also historically had relied on various immigrant groups, such as Jewish and Eastern European women, and mirrored the prevalent ethnic and racial pecking order in US society at a given period. White workers, in particular, were resistant to letting Puerto Rican women into the International Ladies' Garment Workers' Union, and when they did, they denied them equal access to work in the best shops or leadership positions (Ortiz 1996). Other sectors of women's employment were meatpacking, tobacco stripping, confectionery work, domestic service, clerical work, and other kinds of manufacturing and service industry jobs. Puerto Rican women who did not work outside the home frequently engaged in child care, did home-based needlework, or took in boarders to contribute to the household income. The few migrants with higher levels of education held positions as teachers, librarians, nuns, and social and health workers and frequently wrote for community publications or the city's Spanish-language press. Sánchez Korrol ([1983] 1994) emphasizes the diversity and importance of women's "informal networks" to the early community, since they facilitated the exchange of vital information about finding housing, employment, schools for their children, medical and social services, and places to shop or find cultural enrichment or social entertainment.

Important Puerto Rican organizations that emerged during the 1920s fostered a sense of community cohesiveness and facilitated the early migrants' incorporation into the host society. The Hermandad Puertorriqueña en América (Porto Rican Brotherhood of America) was founded in New York City in 1923 to promote "unity, brotherhood and mutual aid among Puerto Ricans" (Sánchez Korrol [1983] 1994, 147). This organization gave rise to the idea of establishing an umbrella federation for different Latino nationalities to combine their goals and activism into a unified front. In this way, they could have a more effective voice in addressing pressing community issues, such as the negative image and coverage of Puerto Ricans in the mainstream press. Promoting this kind of unity also was important in dealing with civil rights violations and other injustices perpetrated against community members. These concerns also lay behind the 1927 creation of the Liga Puertorriqueña e Hispana (Puerto Rican and Hispanic League), which published a biweekly bulletin for six years. The bulletin was an informative educational tool and included social commentary on a variety of community-related issues.

A few workers' organizations also emerged during this period. Two of the most active were the Alianza Obrera (Workers' Alliance) and the Ateneo Obrero (Workers' Atheneum). Many hometown clubs were established in New York City and other cities with large concentrations of Puerto Ricans as another way of strengthening communal ties. The New York City clubs included the Club Caborrojeño, Mayagüezanos Ausentes, and Hijos de Camuy, among several others, all bearing the name of a Puerto Rican town (see Sánchez Korrol [1983] 1994). These clubs provided a social and cultural atmosphere for migrants to feel at home and share their experiences. In addition, they helped Puerto Ricans sustain their connections with the homeland. To this day, the city halls of all municipalities in Puerto Rico hold celebratory activities during their respective annual *fiestas patronales* (patron saint festivities) to welcome *los puertorriqueños ausentes*, those Puerto Ricans who have left the island and live abroad, mostly in the United States.

The proliferation of small businesses, a characteristic of New York City's ethnic enclaves, also occurred in Puerto Rican neighborhoods. The Puerto Rican Merchants' Association was founded in the 1940s to promote and protect the interests of these small businesses. Small entrepreneurs started bodegas (grocery stores), restaurants, travel agencies, banks and finance companies, record stores, beauty parlors, barber shops, auto dealerships, dry cleaners, clothing stores, moving companies, and traditional *botánicas* (shops that sold herbal remedies). The latter are very common in Puerto Rico, so their presence in the US barrios made available to migrants popular herbal remedies and other traditional concoctions and recipes to deal with physical or emotional ailments.

As discussed in Chapter 8, the writings of grassroots activists and journalists Bernardo Vega and Jesús Colón, who migrated to New York in 1916 and 1918, respectively, provide a detailed record of this earlier stage of community formation. Vega (1977, 1984) and Colón (1961, 1983; Acosta-Belén and Sánchez Korrol 1993) described the many pioneer organizations and newspapers created during those years, the array of functions they served, and their most prominent leaders. These outlets facilitated the process of a primarily working-class migrant community's settlement in and adaptation to a culturally and linguistically different and largely unwelcoming urban environment. They also contributed to enriching migrants' cultural and social lives, engaging them in issues that influenced their collective well-being, and helped strengthen communal ties. Along similar lines, the writings of Joaquín Colón López (2002), Jesús Colón's older brother, collected and published posthumously, have been indispensable for unveiling the early history of New York's Puerto Rican community.

The Poverty-Stricken Island

Conditions in Puerto Rico during the years before and after the Great Depression were precarious, to say the least, in both economic and social terms. The sugar plantation economy that developed during the early years of the US regime significantly changed the lives of the Puerto Rican working class. The decline of production in the coffee haciendas, in particular, created a surplus of unemployed rural workers that the jobs generated by the US-controlled sugar industry or the new tobacco and needle factories established on the island could not absorb. The seasonal nature of work in the monopolizing sugar industry intensified the precariousness of employment for agricultural workers and was also a major catalyst for internal migration from mountain to coastal and urban areas, to the slums or other working-class neighborhoods of the capital of San Juan, and to the barrios of New York City or other urban areas (e.g., Chicago, Philadelphia, Newark). The situation deteriorated even further when sugar and tobacco production continued to decline in the early 1920s, as the prices of these products in the international market began to plummet. The downturn in local agricultural production foreshadowed the broader economic crisis that was to come in 1929 with the Great Depression and lasted for most of the 1930s. As if dreadful economic conditions were not enough, the forces of nature brought added desolation to Puerto Rico with two devastating hurricanes: San Felipe in 1928 and San Ciprián in 1932.

The island's socioeconomic plight during the Great Depression years was captured in the song "Lamento borincano" (A Puerto Rican peasant's lament, also known as "El jibarito"), written by Puerto Rico's most famous composer, Rafael Hernández. The song, which dramatizes the dismal conditions of the composer's poverty-stricken homeland, touched the hearts and souls of the Puerto Rican people. It recounts the tale of a peasant riding his mare to the city's market, hopeful that he can sell his scant agricultural produce to support his family. But the *jibarito* (peasant) finds no buyers and is forced to return home empty-handed, overwhelmed by sadness and hopelessness, lamenting his fate and wondering what the future will bring to the island, to his children, and to his home. The sense of hopelessness in the song's lyrics "todo está desierto y el pueblo está muerto de necesidad [everything is barren and the people are dying of deprivation]," accompanied by the poignant image of the destitute Puerto Rican peasant, was forever ingrained in the minds of the generations of Puerto Ricans who witnessed the wretched socioeconomic conditions and despair that engulfed the island during those years. Perhaps even more so, it was meaningful to those who migrated in the hope of a better future in the United States. Rafael Hernández was one of those migrants (see Chapter 8).

Once again, after three decades of US rule, Puerto Rico found itself a neglected colony, just like it had been during the first three centuries of

Spanish rule. The capitalist economic collapse that shattered the lives of so many workers in the United States and other parts of the world during the Great Depression years was only magnified in the deplorable socioeconomic conditions that prevailed in the Puerto Rico of the 1930s and 1940s. *Porto Rico: A Broken Pledge* (1931), by Bailey W. Diffie and Justine Whitfield Diffie, captured the realities that burdened the majority of Puerto Ricans during that period. In this study, Diffie and Diffie searched for answers to explain why, after more than three decades of US rule, the government had failed to reduce poverty or significantly change the standard of living of the impoverished masses. They concluded that the answers were rooted in the conditions created by colonialism and imperialist rule:

> The problem of the United States in Porto Rico, in the opinion of the authors, revolves itself into one question: can we govern the Island for its own best interests? As long as the United States Government has the ultimate word in policies, the Island will be governed for the good of those interests considered "American." Porto Rico is at once the perfect example of what economic imperialism does for a country and of the attitude of the imperialist towards that country. . . . Its land owned by absentee capital; its political rights resting in the hands of the United States Government; its people in the depths of deprivation, it has been told to help itself. That is the "remedy" which the President [Herbert Hoover] prescribes—imperialism's answer to problems of its own creation! No solution further than a policy followed for the last thirty-three years—a policy which has not solved Porto Rico's problems. Porto Rico can hope for no relief under the existing system. (220)

The Diffies' scolding assessment of the island's state of affairs contradicted President Herbert Hoover's statement to the press about being "well satisfied" with the conditions he found in Puerto Rico after a brief visit in 1931. That the US president said this in the midst of the Great Depression, which was having severe socioeconomic consequences in his own country, is an indication of the neglect and indifference that most US officials have shown toward Puerto Rico through the years. A decade after Hoover's visit, prosperity was still an elusive dream for most Puerto Ricans. The island's last appointed North American governor, Rexford Guy Tugwell, was a trusted and influential member of President Franklin Delano Roosevelt's New Deal Brain Trust. He occupied the post from 1941 to 1946. A year after the end of his term, he published a book in which he referred to the island as "the stricken land." Tugwell's study underscored Puerto Rico's socioeconomic and political predicament during those years and recounted the efforts of his administration to turn things around (Tugwell 1947).

But turning things around on an island engulfed by poverty was also a daunting challenge for a new generation of liberal Puerto Rican leaders, most of them educated in the United States, who made their presence felt on the island's political scene. They shared the view that relying on short-term federal emergency assistance was not sufficient to deal with the dire economic conditions faced by the majority of the population and the hold of US corporations over Puerto Rico's land and its overall agricultural economy. Instead, this younger generation of Puerto Rican leaders envisioned a wide-ranging project of national reconstruction. Governor Tugwell, the first North American governor of Puerto Rico to openly acknowledge that several decades of US presence had had little effect in changing the dismal conditions of poverty afflicting the island's population, reached out to this new generation of Puerto Rican political leaders and technocrats in seeking solutions to some of the country's major problems. Poverty was still rampant, unemployment and underemployment remained unchecked, malnutrition and tropical diseases had deleterious consequences for the population's welfare and kept mortality rates high, schools, hospitals, and other service institutions were limited and inadequate, and most agricultural land was concentrated in the hands of a few US corporations and creole landowners.

On his first visit to Puerto Rico in 1934, seven years before his appointment to the island's governorship, Tugwell was an assistant secretary of agriculture. This visit allowed him to learn firsthand about prevailing conditions and to engage in discussions with Puerto Rican political leaders with progressive views who were pushing for social and political reforms. Some of the New Deal emergency measures directed at getting the United States out of the Depression had been transferred to Puerto Rico, where the Puerto Rico Emergency Relief Administration (PRERA), a federal agency popularly known as "la Prera," was established in 1933. The PRERA offered food and other essentials to the most indigent Puerto Ricans but represented just a provisional response to serious conditions requiring more permanent solutions.

Among the Puerto Rican leaders was Carlos Chardón, an outspoken advocate of radical reforms, including the government's taking land away from large absentee corporate landowners to redistribute among small Puerto Rican farmers and workers. At the time, Chardón was chancellor of the University of Puerto Rico, the country's largest public university. In order to develop a comprehensive reconstruction plan, Chardón enlisted the collaboration of other local leaders, among them Luis Muñoz Marín, son of prominent political leader Luis Muñoz Rivera. Muñoz Marín had lived in Washington, DC, for many years, where he went to college and started a journalistic career and began to write poetry. He then moved to New York with his North American wife, Muna Lee, a poet and suffragist. He returned to the island in 1926 to become editor of the newspaper *La democracia*, originally founded by his late father in 1890, but was drawn into the world of politics shortly thereafter. By 1932, he was serving in the island's Senate as a member of the Liberal Party (former Unionists) and had some access to members of the US Congress and of the Roosevelt administration.[17] Chardón, Muñoz Marín, and others articulated a plan for getting the country out of its economic crisis and accelerating the process of national reconstruction. In 1934, the year of Tugwell's first visit to Puerto Rico, the Plan Chardón (Chardón Project) was being formulated.

The Plan Chardón was the first major initiative coming out of a generation of native politicians, policymakers, and technocrats clearly committed to bringing significant social and economic changes to the island. It stated, "The economic problem of Puerto Rico, in so far as the bulk of the people is concerned, may be reduced to the simple term of progressive landlessness, chronic unemployment and implacable growth of the population" (Maldonado 1997, 36). The plan called for land reform and economic reconstruction and, subscribing to neo-Malthusian "overpopulation" claims promoted by scholars, policymakers, and government officials in the 1940s and 1950s, stressed the need to reduce population growth on the island. Similar arguments had been made in the past, without yielding significant changes. Some of the new plan's proposed measures relied on the active involvement and support of the colonial state, meaning Congress and the Roosevelt administration, to carry on the massive reconstruction initiative. The measures proposed included the government's expropriation and purchase of lands from large landowners, to be parceled out among small farmers. Other proposals included creating a state-owned cement company to build government buildings and public housing and controlling sugar production, the prices corporations paid sugar growers, and the salaries of sugar industry workers. As a result of these proposals, in 1935 the Roosevelt administration authorized the creation of the federal Puerto Rico Reconstruction Administration (PRRA) and placed at its helm another North American New Deal liberal, Ernest Gruening. Prior to this appointment, Gruening had been in charge of the US Department of the Interior's Territories and Insular Possessions Division, so he was quite familiar with Puerto Rico's problems. PRRA tried to implement some of Plan Chardón's proposals and stimulate the economy by expanding employment in the public sector. This project provided the initial steps for the process of change that was to overtake the island during the 1940s and 1950s.

Between Reform and Revolution
While the majority of Puerto Rico's population was dealing with basic survival issues, two major developments were overtaking the political arena. Political realignments in Puerto Rico during the 1930s were to influence US policies and shift the balance of power among the major local political parties during the decades that followed. Since the early years of the US occupation, island politics had been controlled by opportunistic alliances between

the three major parties—Unionists, Republicans, and Socialists—and the political personalism and patronage practices of their longtime leaders. But the island's political landscape was about to take a major turn.[18]

First, under the leadership of Pedro Albizu Campos, a charismatic Harvard-educated mulatto lawyer, the Partido Nacionalista Puertorriqueño (Puerto Rican Nationalist Party), originally founded in 1922 after the Unionist Party drifted away from supporting independence, was revitalized in 1930 as the main front of local opposition to US colonialism. Second, a populist political movement was also taking shape; it presented itself as a new and more viable political option for change, offering the poverty-stricken peasant and working-class masses and a smaller middle class "Pan, Tierra y Libertad" (bread, land, and liberty). Luis Muñoz Marín led what became, in 1938, the Partido Popular Democrático (PPD, Popular Democratic Party), also known as the Populares. The PPD had been formed after Muñoz Marín and the left wing of the Partido Liberal were expelled from the latter organization because of their strong opposition to its decision to eliminate the independence option from its platform.

Puerto Rican Nationalists began to gain visibility by denouncing the US imperialist presence in Puerto Rico; they found a receptive audience among some members of the island's intellectual elite and the struggling working class. Albizu's political rhetoric denounced the illegality of the Treaty of Paris that had forced Spain to cede an autonomous Puerto Rico to the United States. He also condemned the large US sugar corporations' usurpation of the island's land and exploitation of its workers and lamented the decline of the creole propertied class. The leader called for the liberation of Puerto Rico through any means, including armed struggle. The Nationalists' main credo was "La patria es valor y sacrificio" (The motherland signifies courage and sacrifice). The party organized the paramilitary group Cadetes de la República (Cadets of the Republic), whose members marched in political rallies dressed in military garb. The group was inspired by the Sinn Féin (meaning "we ourselves") Irish nationalist liberation movement (see J. A. Silén 1996), which fought against British colonialism and eventually secured the creation of the Irish Free State dominion of the British Commonwealth in 1922. The new status put an end to the Irish War for Independence but provided only a limited form of governance. After many years of turmoil and violence the British finally granted sovereign status with the establishment of the Republic of Ireland in 1949.[19]

Despite its initial growing appeal, the Nationalist Party had a conservative and essentialist vision of Puerto Rico as a Catholic Hispanic country struggling against the colonizing forces of Americanization and seeking to recover "the nation of proprietors" that existed prior to the US invasion. This particular vision did not necessarily resonate with the impoverished Puerto Rican masses, who believed that the Spanish past, with all

its social and political divisions—including those between the landowning
hacendado class and the landless peasants—was not a utopia to return to.
The Nationalist movement, however, was more successful in planting the
roots of the strong cultural nationalism, subsequently reaffirmed by Puerto
Rico's intellectual elite, that ultimately spilled over into other sectors of the
population intent on resisting colonialism and the forces of Americanization. Even those Puerto Ricans favoring statehood for the island, often
referred to pejoratively as *pitiyanquis* (a Spanish adaptation from the
French *petit yankée*, meaning "little Yankee"), eventually came to endorse
a form of *estadidad jíbara* (literally peasant-like statehood, meaning creole statehood), rejecting assimilation into Anglo-American culture, affirming their belief that Puerto Rico's cultural and linguistic distinctiveness and
patrimony must be preserved under this status, and arguing that Puerto Rico
could be a bilingual state of the American union. That the US Congress
would consider, much less accept, such a proposition is hard to imagine.

The insurgent activities of the island's Nationalist Party from the 1930s to
the 1950s posed a threat to the United States. Because of the poverty in Puerto
Rico, any political unrest could potentially reach the levels of violence that
characterized British efforts to suppress the Irish nationalist movement a few
decades earlier, and the United States was also facing resistance to its colonial
domination in the Philippines. These liberation movements and Puerto Rico's
strategic military value to the United States in the region and hemisphere contributed to the determination of both federal and local authorities to destroy
the emerging Nationalist movement and its leaders.

A sustained repressive campaign of persecution, blacklisting, and violent confrontation between Nationalists and the local authorities in the
1930s began to seal the fate of the movement. The killing of four Nationalist University of Puerto Rico students by the Río Piedras police in October 1935 pushed members of the party to seek retribution in the month of
February 1936 by assassinating the North American chief of the island's
police force, Colonel Francis Riggs. Two Nationalists, Hiram Rosado and
Elías Beauchamp, were arrested for the murder, taken to police headquar-
ters, and, in retaliation, shot to death while in police custody.

Colonel Riggs was an old friend of Blanton Winship, the island's US-
appointed governor at the time. Without hesitation, Governor Winship
immediately unleashed a series of repressive measures carried out systematically by US and Puerto Rican officials and government agencies, all
aimed at eradicating the Nationalist Party. Albizu and some of his followers
were arrested and accused of conspiring against the United States. His first
trial, which had a majority of Puerto Rican jurors, ended with a hung jury.
A new jury, composed mostly of North Americans, was picked for his second trial and found Albizu guilty of sedition. He was to spend the next
decade of his life in a federal prison in Atlanta, Georgia.

Albizu's imprisonment did not deter the Nationalists from continuing their political activities. In 1937, the Puerto Rican police denied the party permission to hold a rally in the southern city of Ponce, Albizu's birthplace. The event, organized to commemorate the abolition of slavery, was to be on Palm Sunday. Nationalists refused to cancel the rally, and government authorities mobilized the police. During the scheduled demonstration, shooting broke out, leaving 19 Nationalists and 2 policemen dead and close to 100 people injured. This incident was later to be known as la Masacre de Ponce (Ponce Massacre).

The escalating political violence in Puerto Rico and the international denunciations of colonial oppression against the United States even prompted the US Congress to consider granting independence to Puerto Rico. The title of an incendiary popular book written by a North American elementary school teacher who went to Puerto Rico in 1936 to teach English characterized the political violence of those years as "dynamite on our doorstep." The book also offered a disparaging view of the island and its people (Brown 1945). US Senator Willard Tydings enlisted Ernest Gruening's help in introducing a bill to let Puerto Ricans decide if they wanted independence from the United States. The proposed Tydings Bill, however, included no economic plans for Puerto Rico during the transition to independence and eventually faded, although not without causing serious divisions and realignments within the local political parties.[20]

The politically charged environment made it easier for the reform movement initiated by Muñoz Marín and his followers to gain wider popular support. The Populares' proposals would indeed "revolutionize" the country but were couched as a "peaceful revolution," in stark contrast to the anticolonial armed struggle espoused by the Nationalists.

Muñoz Marín's charismatic and populist style of campaigning brought him to the desolate Puerto Rican countryside, where he was in direct contact with the poor peasantry and learned about their conditions and needs. He emphasized his connection with the impoverished peasant by choosing the image of a *jíbaro* with a straw hat as the symbol of his new party and the catchy and upbeat musical slogan *Jalda arriba va avanzando el Popular* (The Populares are moving uphill and forging ahead), which captured the energy and impetus for meaningful social, economic, and political change. The charismatic leader persuaded peasants not to "sell" their vote to the old political parties and to believe that each vote, even the votes of people who could not read or write, was important and could give the PPD the opportunity to transform Puerto Rican society.

The PPD campaigned vigorously for land reform by limiting to 500 acres the amount of land that any corporation or landowner could own and by distributing free *parcelas* (land parcels) to the poor. The party also made a pledge to bring running water and electricity to every home, even those in isolated rural areas, as well as to make food and health services available for the indigent, reduce illiteracy by building more public schools, provide better access to higher education, and improve the country's infrastructure to support economic development. All of these promises resonated with the impoverished popular masses, tired of the political alliances among the old political parties that mostly benefited their leaders and the privileged elites.

Many of Muñoz Marín's early proposals reflected the socialist and pro-independence ideals of his youth and were characteristic of the social policies behind the concept of a welfare state—a government plays a key role in promoting and protecting the socioeconomic well-being of its citizens. However, he modified his views because of the political compromises he had to make in order to secure the support of the US Congress and other officials to carry out the socioeconomic and political reforms envisioned by the Populares (see García Passalacqua 1996). More than anything else, this meant accepting that without the continuation of US federal assistance and private investment capital, the party would not be able to execute its ambitious agenda to achieve progress by modernizing and transforming Puerto Rican society.

The PPD did not gain an outright win in the first election in which it participated, in 1940, but the close results gave the Populares enough legislative power to start trampling over the opposition and take control of Puerto Rico's politics. Their victory placed Muñoz Marín at the head of the Puerto Rican Senate and dealt a mortal blow to the grip that the old parties had had on island politics for over two decades and to their shady coalitions. President Roosevelt's 1941 appointment of Rexford Tugwell to the island's governorship allowed the younger generation of local politicians to push their reform proposals and feel hopeful about securing changes in Puerto Rico's relationship with the United States. But Governor Tugwell's term was not devoid of controversy. The local political opposition perceived him to be a supporter of the PPD's agenda. Some members of Congress considered his reform proposals too socialistic because of their heavy reliance on state support. Clearly the period of Tugwell's administration was important for Puerto Rican society, although there is no doubt that the bulk of the reforms enacted during his term could not have happened without the major role played by the new PPD's political leadership. Decades later, Tugwell's governorship was hailed as "the administration of a revolution" (Goodsell 1965), and he was commended for his role in providing a "turning point from colonial misery and decay to self-government and astounding economic progress," which perhaps would not have come to fruition without his efforts "in breaking through established routines and his willingness to foster native forces that were ready to take over" (Friedrich 1965, vii–viii). Unquestionably, Tugwell was the most receptive and successful of a long line of US-appointed governors of Puerto Rico, but the driving forces that eventually carried out the country's socioeconomic and political transformation of the 1940s and 1950s were in the hands of Muñoz Marín and his inner circle of policy advisers and technocrats.

Toward the end of his tenure, Tugwell recommended to President Harry Truman that he appoint a Puerto Rican to succeed him as governor. The president accepted the recommendation and in 1946 appointed Jesús T. Piñeiro, a member of the PPD, as the island's first Puerto Rican governor. Another major US concession was the passage of a law allowing Puerto Rico's voters to elect their own governor for the first time in 1948. As the PPD's candidate for the governorship, Muñoz Marín was elected to the post by an overwhelming 61.2 percent of the vote.

By the end of the 1940s, Muñoz Marín's position regarding Puerto Rico's political status had shifted considerably from that of his younger years, when he was an ardent defender of independence. After graduating from Georgetown University, he worked as a journalist, wrote poetry, and moved to New York's Greenwich Village with his wife, Muna Lee. During those years, Muñoz Marín wrote for various US newspapers and was critical of North American colonialism.[21] He shuttled between New York, Washington, DC, and Puerto Rico for most of the 1920s, but he finally settled on the island in 1930 in order to follow in his father's footsteps and pursue a career in politics. Less than a decade after his return, Muñoz Marín began to publicly modify his views about Puerto Rico's relationship with the United States. He continued to defend his socially progressive positions but started to question the feasibility of achieving his social and economic goals for the island without the financial support of the United States. Thus, from its inception, the PPD did not attempt to challenge US jurisdiction over Puerto Rico, as the Nationalists did. Instead, the Populares advanced a vision for a new political arrangement that would guarantee self-government but allow the United States to maintain territorial and military control over Puerto Rico and, in exchange, allow Puerto Rico to receive increasing amounts of federal assistance and create the conditions to attract more US capital investments in manufacturing and other sectors of the island's economy.

Since the early years of occupation, island political leaders had been lobbying the US Congress to give Puerto Rico a larger degree of self-government. The idea for a new political status, labeled the "Estado Libre Asociado de Puerto Rico" and modeled after the Irish Free State, had floated around island political circles and congressional corridors since the early 1920s.[22] The Populares, seeking an innovative solution to the denunciations of colonialism against the United States made by Nationalists and other independence supporters, revived this old political formula. As an *estado libre asociado*, officially known as a commonwealth in English, Puerto Rico would be granted the right to enact its own constitution but would remain a territory "in permanent union with the United States," rather than a sovereign nation. This meant that the US Congress and the Pentagon were not willing to relinquish their territorial control over the island, and Puerto Ricans would continue to be US citizens and thus only able to travel to foreign countries with a US passport. Thus, when applied to Puerto Rico, the term "commonwealth" may be considered a misnomer, since it bears little resemblance to the commonwealth agreement established by the British government with some of its former colonies.

Several decades earlier, Pedro Albizu Campos, the main leader of the Nationalist movement, had been found guilty of conspiring to overthrow the US government in Puerto Rico and, along with many of his closest allies, condemned to a federal prison in 1936. It has been well documented that during his long incarceration in Atlanta, he was subjected to mistreatment and torture, including radiation experiments (Maldonado-Denis 1972; J. A. Silén 1976; Ferrao 1990). These caused Albizu to develop severe health problems, including the strokes that eventually would end his life. Because of his deteriorating health he was transferred to Columbus Hospital in New York City, where he was held until close to his release from his eleven-year sentence. He was able finally to return to Puerto Rico in 1947.

The sensationalist media coverage of the violent incidents involving clashes between Puerto Rican Nationalists and government authorities in Puerto Rico and the United States reached its peak during the 1950s. On October 30, 1950, a Nationalist revolt began in Puerto Rico's mountain town of Jayuya and spread to a few other island municipalities, prompting Governor Muñoz Marín to mobilize the national guard. That same day a shooting at the entrance to La Fortaleza, the governor's official residence in Old San Juan, ended with the death of five Nationalists. Two days later, there was an attempt to assassinate President Harry Truman when two party members tried to shoot their way into Blair House, his Washington, DC, temporary residence. One of the perpetrators, Oscar Collazo, was arrested, and the other, Griselio Torresola, was killed. A North American security guard was also killed during this attempt. Albizu was arrested, accused of fomenting subversive activities against the government, and, for the second time, sentenced to a long prison term. He was pardoned by Governor Muñoz Marín in 1953 but arrested and sent to prison again the following year after three armed Nationalists entered the chambers of the US House of Representatives and started shooting. Five members of Congress were injured. Nationalists Lolita Lebrón, Andrés Figueroa Cordero, and Irving Collazo were arrested for the attack and spent the next three decades in a federal prison. Albizu, who was already imprisoned in Puerto Rico, suffered a second stroke, which caused him some paralysis. However, because of his failing health, Muñoz Marín pardoned him again, in 1965, and he died in an island hospital a few months later.

The incidents involving Puerto Rican Nationalists not only drew international attention to Puerto Rico's colonial condition but also increased negative feelings among the wider US population toward the growing presence of Puerto Ricans in New York and other cities during the peak years of the Great Migration. In order to deal with the backlash produced by these incidents, US and Puerto Rican authorities engaged in an all-out offensive to discredit and crush the Nationalist movement. Puerto Rican Nationalists were summarily labeled fanatics or terrorists by the media, and US officials and Puerto Rico's Commonwealth government swiftly condemned their use of violence. Officially sanctioned surveillance and blacklisting against Puerto Rican Nationalists intensified as a result of these incidents, and these practices were also applied indiscriminately to other independence advocates. The Ley de la Mordaza (Gag Law or Law 53), enacted by the Puerto Rican legislature in 1948, basically prohibited any expression of dissent challenging US authority over Puerto Rico or perceived as a threat to the stability of the insular government. This law was used primarily to justify Albizu's incarceration and that of his supporters (Acosta 1987, 1993).

The US desire to keep territorial jurisdiction over Puerto Rico was directly linked to the island's strategic military importance in the Caribbean and the rest of the hemisphere, which had intensified during World War II, the subsequent Cold War period, and the post–Cuban Revolution years. In simpler terms this meant that the various branches of the US armed forces infamously interfered with any congressional proposals for granting more autonomy to Puerto Rico or putting an end to its colonial territorial status. By settling for the limited commonwealth arrangement, the leadership of the PPD remained hopeful that this status would eventually lead to the creation of a real "free state" without the need to sever the island's economic and military "association" with the United States. Those critical of the arrangement argued that the purported "new" status was nothing new. Its most ardent critics described it as a fiction, a farce, or a meaningless cosmetic makeover of the colonial relationship that did not remove some of the basic stipulations or limitations of the Foraker Act (1900), the Jones-Shafroth Act (1917), and the Jones Act (1920) or mitigate the overriding power of the US Congress over Puerto Rico (Géigel Polanco 1972; Maldonado-Denis 1972). Although a large majority of Puerto Ricans now acknowledge the colonial nature of the Commonwealth, that was not the case for many decades after its creation.

A retrospective analysis of this outcome raises a fundamental question: Why did Luis Muñoz Marín accept such an imperfect political status compromise when his party had the overwhelming support of the great majority of Puerto Ricans, the only time in the island's history when any politician or political party has commanded such a popular mandate? The answer lies, at least partially, in the weight of family history. Just like his father, Luis Muñoz Rivera, half a century earlier, Muñoz Marín believed that the benefits of maintaining the links with the colonial metropolis outweighed those of Puerto Rico's becoming a sovereign state. Thus he did not use his populist movement to challenge or denounce US colonial authority. Instead, he practiced the politics of *posibilismo*, that is, striving to achieve only those goals perceived to be within the realm of real possibility or settling for more pragmatic alternatives to the colonial condition that presumably would contribute to economic development, political stability and the socioeconomic advancement of the island's population. With his vision for the political future of Puerto Rico, Muñoz Marín indeed chose the ambiguity of autonomy and preserved ties with the United States over the unknown and more disconcerting consequences and irrevocability of independence without US federal assistance. Once again, the Puerto Rican political elites settled for a limited share of political power that maintained the country's dependence on the colonial metropole rather than pursuing a national sustainable development project that responded, first and foremost, to the needs and interests of the Puerto Rican people, promoted their self-reliance, or envisioned the island's independence.

This snapshot of Puerto Rico's socioeconomic and political conditions sets the stage for the events that accelerated the pace of migration to the United States during the 1940s and 1950s. Most of the studies about the early community have focused on New York City, but new historical studies about other communities in the pre–Great Migration years are emerging. A recent example is Víctor Vázquez-Hernández's 2017 study *Before the Wave: Puerto Ricans in Philadelphia, 1910–1945*. Regarding this new study, Carmen Teresa Whalen, whose pioneering work on documenting the presence and history of Puerto Ricans in Philadelphia during the Great Migration has become essential reading, noted in this book's back cover that because of its focus on migration during the pre–World War II period, Vázquez-Hernández's contribution will stimulate scholars to "begin to think more comparatively about what we know about the early Puerto Rican diaspora." We address what can be learned from studies documenting the migration experiences of Puerto Ricans to diverse stateside geographic locations (besides New York) at different historical periods in Chapter 7.

From the Steamship Embarcados to the Transnational Guagua Aérea

Until the 1940s, the principal mode of transportation for Puerto Ricans to travel to the United States was the steamship. A few were given familiar Puerto Rican names, including those of island towns: *Borinquen, San Juan, Ponce, Coamo*. The steamship *Marine Tiger* was so identified with transporting Puerto Rican migrants during the early years that for a while Puerto Ricans were often called "Marine Tigers." The Puerto Rican expression *se embarcó* (s/he took a ship) was commonly used to refer to someone who had left the island for the United States. The expression continued to be used even after air travel became the primary mode of transportation.

Earlier in this chapter we documented the largely neglected pioneer migrations of Puerto Ricans to the United States prior to the mid-twentieth-century Great Migration. In truth, for many decades Puerto Rican migration was primarily identified with the mass exodus to the United States in the aftermath of World War II, in part because Puerto Ricans were the first and, to this date, the largest airborne group of migrants to come to the United States. As air travel became available in the 1940s and the jet engine was introduced in the early 1960s, the character of the migratory movements of workers from developing countries seeking employment in highly industrialized societies like the United States began to change. In Puerto Rico's case, the island government encouraged US airline carriers to introduce special low-fare flights from San Juan to New York. One airline commercial luring Puerto Ricans to the city in the 1960s coined the slogan *En el Jet 55, a Nueva York en un brinco* (Board Flight 55 and take a leap to New York) for a low fare of $55. Fifty-five referred to both the flight number and the low fare. As the Puerto Rican migrant population continued to spread to other major US cities like Chicago, Philadelphia, and Newark, low fares were extended to those airport destinations as well.

Puerto Ricans came from a country in the Americas, and historical events and relations connected the United States with their homeland, as was the case with immigrant Mexicans and other Latinos/as. This was a major deviation from the patterns established by prior immigrants, the vast majority of whom had come to North American shores from a distant Europe or Asia, leaving behind their native countries and facing limited possibility of ever going back again. US citizenship status, the geographic proximity between the island and the continental United States, and access to low-cost air travel created a transnational bridge that fostered bidirectional cultural, socioeconomic, and political exchanges between island and continent. This uninterrupted *ir y venir* (back-and-forth movement) that stateside Puerto Ricans have with their homeland has introduced a new model of im/migrant assimilation and relationship to Anglo-American society that differs from the traditional "melting pot" ideology. During the past few decades, a more flexible multicultural perspective has been taking hold; it is based on an individual's capacity to function in more than one culture and language and hold a sense of identity that straddles different cultural locations and affiliations. As mentioned in the introductory chapter, stateside Puerto Ricans share a strong sense of ethnic identity, whether they are first-generation migrants or were born or raised in the United States. But whether symbolic or actual, this connection to the homeland does not preclude different generations of stateside Puerto Ricans from valuing their rights as US citizens, having a sense of affiliation with North American society, or being Americans of Puerto Rican descent (see Chapter 7).

Puerto Ricans often use the popular phrase *brincando el charco* (jumping over the puddle) to reflect the normality of a people constantly transcending their island's borders *para buscárselas* (to seek fortune) in numerous US cities and localities. Similarly, some Puerto Ricans continue to return to the island after spending some portion of their lives in the United States, although, except during a few years in the late 1960s and early 1970s, the rate of reverse migration to the island has been much lower than that for emigration (Hernández Alvarez 1967; see also Chapter 4).

Prominent Puerto Rican author Luis Rafael Sánchez (1994), who spent several years living between Puerto Rico and New York, invented the metaphor *la guagua aérea* (the airbus or flying bus) to describe Puerto Rico as a nation "flotante entre dos puertos de contrabandear esperanzas [floating and smuggling hopes between two ports]" (22). Others have referred to Puerto Ricans as straddling two cultures and languages (Flores 2000) or as constantly on the move or caught up in a *vaivén* (coming and going, oscillating) (Duany 2002). (The latter term is a double entendre in Spanish: *va y ven* indicates back-and-forth movement, and *vaivén* indicates fluidity or wavering.)

There is no disagreement that the commuting relationship between the island and the US metropolis constantly introduces changing realities and migration patterns; some are now quite evident, others are in flux, and some, as we will see in later chapters, cannot be predicted with any comfortable degree of certainty.

Notes

1. For one of the most complete sources of biographical information about Betances, see Ojeda Reyes (2001); Betances (2008).

2. One of the best-documented accounts of the events surrounding the Grito de Lares is found in Olga Jiménez de Wagenheim, *Puerto Rico's Revolt for Independence: El Grito de Lares* (Boulder, CO: Westview, 1985).

3. See Eugenio María de Hostos, "Manifiesto de la Liga de Patriotas Puertorriqueños," *Patria*, September 10, 1898. Most of Hostos's writings about the struggle for independence have been collected in Eugenio María de Hostos, *América: La lucha por la libertad*, ed. Manuel Maldonado-Denis (México: Siglo Ventiuno, 1980).

4. For an extensive analysis of Martí's writings about *nuestra América*, see Phillip S. Foner, *Our America by José Martí* (New York: Monthly Review Press, 1977); Andrés Sorel, ed., *José Martí en los Estados Unidos* (Madrid: Alianza Editorial, 1968); Jeffrey Belnap and Raúl Fernández, eds., *José Martí's "Our America": From National to Hemispheric Cultural Studies* (Durham, NC: Duke University Press, 1998).

5. For a detailed discussion of the activities of the *tabaqueros/as* in Puerto Rico, see Angel Quintero Rivera, "Socialista y tabaquero: La proletarización de los artesanos," *Sin nombre* 8, no. 4 (1978); García and Quintero Rivera (1982); Shaffer (2013). Bernardo Vega (1984) mentioned the involvement of Flor Baerga and

other *tabaqueros/as* in the separatist movement in his memoirs, first published in Spanish in 1977.

6. Some of Figueroa's writings in *Patria* include the six-part essay "La verdad de la historia," *Patria*, March 19, April 3, April 16, May 21, June 11, and July 2, 1892. Also see Josefina Toledo, *Sotero Figueroa, Editor de Patria: Apuntes para una biografía* (La Habana: Editorial Letras Cubanas, 1985); Edgardo Meléndez, *Puerto Rico en Patria* (Río Piedras, PR: Editorial Edil, 1996).

7. For a biography of Schomburg, see Ortiz, (1986); Des Verney Sinnette (1989); Flor Piñeiro de Rivera, *Arturo Schomburg: Un puertorriqueño descubre el legado histórico del negro* (San Juan: Centro de Estudios Avanzados de Puerto Rico y el Caribe, 1989). The intersections of Schomburg's blackness and *latinidad* are examined in Valdés (2017).

8. For a more detailed account of Inocencia Martínez de Figueroa's contributions to the separatist movement and to the founding of the Club Mercedes Varona, see "Síntesis biográfica de Inocencia Martínez Santaella," in Toledo, *Sotero Figueroa*, 119–151.

9. For a complete collection, see Rodríguez de Tió (1968b).

10. Roberto H. Todd (1939) made this claim in *La invasión americana: Cómo surgió la idea de traer la guerra a Puerto Rico*. Todd also wrote a long essay about Henna. See Roberto H. Todd, *José Julio Henna, 1848–1924* (San Juan: Cantero Fernández, 1930).

11. For a collection of Betances's writings, see Carlos M. Rama, ed., *Las Antillas para los antillanos* (San Juan: Instituto de Cultura Puertorriqueña, 1975); Betances (2008).

12. See Frank Freidel, *The Splendid Little War* (Boston: Little, Brown, 1958).

13. The name "Porto Rico" was adopted by the US colonial government as the official name for the island and had been used as such in world maps of earlier periods. The official name was not changed back to Puerto Rico until the late 1930s.

14. For detailed information about women's employment during this period, see Caroline Manning, *The Employment of Women in Porto Rico* (Washington, DC: Government Printing Office, 1934). For a focus on employment in the needle industries, see María del Carmen Baerga, ed., *Género y trabajo: La industria de la aguja en Puerto Rico y el Caribe* (San Juan: Editorial de la Universidad de Puerto Rico, 1993).

15. The Foraker Act was named for Joseph Foraker, the US senator from Ohio who introduced the bill in Congress on January 9, 1900. The Jones-Shafroth Act was named for Representatives William Jones and John Shafroth. A more detailed discussion of the Foraker and Jones acts can be found in Benjamin B. Ringer, *"We the People" and Others: Duality in America's Treatment of Its Racial Minorities* (New York: Tavistock Publications, 1983).

16. The documentary film *La operación* (1982), directed by Ana María García, focused on how government policies for population control and economic development in Puerto Rico relied on the massive sterilization of women, especially between the 1930s and the 1960s.

17. Muñoz Marín's contacts in Washington's power circles during the Franklin Roosevelt administration were facilitated by a prominent North American journalist, Ruby Black, a close friend of his first wife, Muna Lee, and First Lady Eleanor Roosevelt. See Teresita Santini, *Luis Muñoz Marín 1898–1998* (San Juan: Universidad Interamericana and Fundación Francisco Carvajal, 1998).

18. In 1924 the Partido Unión Puertorriqueña (Puerto Rican Union Party), also known as the Unionistas (Unionists), who advocated either autonomy or independence for Puerto Rico, and the pro-statehood Partido Unión Republicana (Republican

Union Party), or Republicanos (Republicans), formed a coalition known as La Alianza for that year's legislative elections. La Alianza aimed to counteract the electoral strength of the workers' Partido Socialista (Socialist Party). In response, the pro-statehood Partido Socialista joined a dissident group of pro-statehood Republicanos to form La Coalición. These arrangements lasted until 1932. The Unionistas dissolved that year and reconstituted as the Partido Liberal (Liberal Party). A new electoral coalition aimed at defeating the Partido Liberal was formed by the Partido Socialista and Partido Unión Republicana that same year. See Bolívar Pagán, *Historia de los partidos politicos puertorriqueños* (San Juan: M. Pareja, 1972); Robert W. Anderson, *Party Politics in Puerto Rico* (Stanford, CA: Stanford University Press, 1965).

19. The establishment of the Republic of Ireland, however, did not end British control of Northern Ireland, which has a primarily Protestant population. Many Protestants left the Republic of Ireland and moved to Northern Ireland after Irish Free State status was granted. Conflicts and violence between Protestants and Catholics have been going on for centuries and continued to manifest in Northern Ireland throughout the twentieth century, since Catholics resented their unequal treatment in the British-controlled area. In recent decades a peace process was successful in reducing the violence and getting the British to at least end their military presence in Northern Ireland.

20. Disagreements about the status issue and the Tydings Bill produced a split in Puerto Rico's Partido Liberal between its elderly leader, Antonio R. Barceló, who represented the more conservative wing of the party, and a young Luis Muñoz Marín and his more progressive followers. The Muñoz Marín faction supported Puerto Rico's independence with some economic guarantees from the United States. This faction split from the Partido Liberal in 1937 and founded the PPD.

21. In the 1920s, Muñoz Marín published some articles critical of US colonialism in the *Nation, New Republic,* and *American Mercury.*

22. In 1922 Representative Philip Campbell and Senator William King introduced a bill to Congress seeking to provide an autonomous government to be known as the Associated Free State of Puerto Rico, but the bill never made it to the floor of the House or Senate. See Ringer, *"We the People" and Others,* 1030–1036. The original idea was revived decades later, and under a new constitution, the island officially adopted the name Estado Libre Asociado de Puerto Rico (Commonwealth of Puerto Rico) in 1952.

4

The Great Migration
and Other Postwar Patterns

The conspicuous presence of Puerto Ricans in New York City during the late 1940s and 1950s led some observers to refer to them as "newcomers" (Handlin 1959), but as we have seen, the massive postwar influx was a continuation of a process that had started over half a century before. What is known as the Great Migration marks the period when mainstream US society became more aware than before of the Puerto Rican presence in New York, its surrounding urban areas, and a few other parts of the country. But the most obvious contradiction about this massive migration influx to the United States is that it occurred at a time when Puerto Rico was being showcased as a successful model of industrial capitalist development, modernization, and democratic rule. The island became an example for the rest of the Caribbean, Latin America, and other developing countries of what an undeveloped country could achieve with the assistance and tutelage of the United States. In order to understand this basic contradiction, we must examine the interplay of the political conditions and colonial power relations under which Puerto Rico's mid-twentieth-century socioeconomic transformation took place.

After their 1948 electoral victory, the Populares took over the reins of the island's government with the overwhelming support of the large majority of the population, making Luis Muñoz Marín the first Puerto Rican governor elected by popular mandate. Allowing Puerto Ricans to elect their own governor was the most significant political concession that the United States had made to the island since the 1917 Jones-Shafroth Act granted US citizenship to Puerto Ricans, and it served as a major catalyst for the inauguration of the constitution of the Estado Libre Asociado (ELA), or Commonwealth of Puerto Rico, on July 25, 1952. Paradoxically, the date commemorated the US invasion of Puerto Rico half a century earlier, perhaps indicating the ambivalent and problematic nature of the new status. Supporters called the new ELA a celebration of freedom, but it was "freedom with a long chain," as Muñoz Marín himself once said in private (Maldonado-Denis 1972). The ELA far from freed Puerto Rico from the territorial jurisdiction of the US Congress, but it at least allowed Puerto Ricans an acceptable degree of self-government.

After the Partido Popular Democrático (PPD, Popular Democratic Party) took over the insular government, debates within the party revolved around, among other issues, whether to place emphasis first on alleviating social ills and enhancing the island's political status or on a strong program of industrialization.[1] Teodoro Moscoso, a member of the party's upper echelon, championed an "industrialization-first" perspective. Shortly thereafter, he was named chief administrator of Fomento (to foster), the government's main agency to promote industrial economic development. Moscoso became the chief architect and driving force behind the Operation Bootstrap industrialization initiative that would modernize Puerto Rico.[2] One landmark document that promoted the determination to move toward an "industrialization-first" development strategy was the Plan Chardón (see Chapter 3).

Several crucial elements were required to achieve the increases in per capita income that the massive industrialization process of Operation Bootstrap was intended to produce. First, population growth had to be reduced. Second, goods manufactured in Puerto Rico needed a substantial market abroad. Third, US manufacturers needed an incentive to locate their operations on the island. Fourth, a stable political environment was necessary. Finally, island wages had to remain competitive and flexible.

The new Muñoz Marín administration rapidly met all those conditions in Puerto Rico. Family-planning and population-control initiatives to reduce births on the island and accelerated migration to the United States received high priority. Access to the US domestic market was key to achieving economies of scale. Thus a corporate federal tax exemption program was introduced and became a powerful instrument to attract US industrial capital. With the repression of the Nationalist movement and the imprisonment of most of the party's high-profile leadership, the Puerto Rican–US political relationship provided a stable and welcoming environment for North American businesses. Added to all of these was the incentive of having Puerto Rico supply a steady source of low-wage labor, so minimum wage boards were established on the island to set up industry-wide minima below the US statutory minimum wage level.[3] Moreover, the Muñoz Marín administration negotiated with the leaders of the island's major labor unions to foster an environment of "industrial peace" in order to attract more US investors. This meant avoiding strikes and settling for Fomento's policies for the new industrial labor force.

Capable hands can be flown to your plant from Puerto Rico U.S.A.
This ad highlights routes from Puerto Rico to Miami (1,000 miles)
and New York (1,600 miles) (Publicaciones 1949–1953). (*Source:
Centro Journal 22*, no. 1 [2010]: 12.)

The debate over the need for a comprehensive migration policy to forestall population pressure had strong proponents and detractors. Given the
Catholic Church's opposition to a state-sponsored plan of birth control on
the island, many policymakers felt that large-scale migration was the best
mechanism to control population growth. However, opponents argued that
Puerto Rico would experience a brain drain and that the migrants would
return when economic conditions improved, further exacerbating population pressure. Maldonado (1997) summarized the outcome of these debates
in the following manner:

Like so much in island politics, the debate over migration became a question of semantics. Muñoz insisted that the government's migration policy was neutral. But when a government makes it as easy as possible for its people to migrate, when it trains them, gives instructions in new living conditions, provides basic English classes, battles the airlines to keep the fares low, and establishes employment offices at their destination, isn't it in effect sponsoring a policy that encourages migration? (146)

The use of migration as an instrument of economic development and, more specifically, of industrialization was becoming fashionable in intellectual circles as well. Development economists were gradually more interested in the transition from agriculturally based societies to industrial ones as they scanned the international development landscape in the aftermath of World War II. Moreover, labor migration from rural to urban areas in the less-developed countries was to serve as a low-cost impetus to the early stages of rapid industrialization. Thus, development models with such labels as "surplus labor," "disguised unemployment," and "underemployment" were in vogue (W. A. Lewis 1954; Jorgenson 1961; Fei and Ranis 1964; Sen 1966). These intellectual currents simply confirmed the development strategy that had already been launched by policymakers in Puerto Rico and Washington, DC: industrialization was to be based on the migration of labor from rural to urban parts of the island and, subsequently, to the United States.

The first official recognition that migration was to be part of the social and political reforms and policies designed by the new Muñoz Marín administration was the establishment by the island's Department of Labor of the Oficina de Puerto Rico en Nueva York (Office of Puerto Rico in New York) in 1948, later known as the Migration Division, or Commonwealth Office in New York City. The main purpose of this agency was to facilitate the migrant's transition into US society. Because promoting contract labor was among the new administration's development strategies and there was a significant demand for low-wage labor coming from many industries in the continental United States, it was logical for the Puerto Rican government to try to manage the migration process through an agency that provided employment and housing information, job training, and referral services to potential workers. The Migration Division also promoted cultural activities, and its services especially targeted recent arrivals. Branches of this agency were started in other US cities with large concentrations of Puerto Ricans, such as Chicago and Philadelphia (see Chapter 7; Cabán 2005; and Meléndez 2017). However, the office frequently reflected the priorities of island-based planners and policymakers or US Puerto Rican professionals, without paying enough attention to the views of grassroots organizations that existed in the various Puerto Rican barrios or to their leadership.

In Puerto Rico, it was clear that population growth was viewed as a real constraint on economic development. High fertility rates, particularly in rural areas, kept productivity and hence per capita income very low. At the time, it seemed obvious that the number of jobs being created under Operation Bootstrap would never keep pace with the employment needs of the growing population. The general view was that both unemployment and underemployment would continue to rise in the absence of a population "safety valve" in the form of migration and birth control. Many influential figures in the Puerto Rican government as well as US policymakers supported this perspective.

These concerns led to the government-sponsored policy of migration from Puerto Rico to the United States. Its proponents failed, however, to imagine the extent to which migration would lead to massive numbers of people moving from the island's countryside to urban areas and later to the continental United States. Maldonado (1997) described the events in the following terms:

> The hope of industrialization had ignited a full-fledged "revolution of rising expectations" throughout Puerto Rico, setting into motion a massive migration from the country to the cities and grotesquely inflating the horrid slums that had appalled the Roosevelt New Dealers fifteen years earlier; the migration grew so huge that it spilled over the Atlantic to the slums of New York City. (75)

The process that would fundamentally transform the island and lead to the emergence and growth of Puerto Rican communities throughout the United States had been unleashed.

The determinant of the size of the US Puerto Rican population is the size and growth of the Puerto Rican population on the island. In this respect, the population of Puerto Rico grew substantially over the twentieth century (see Table 4.1), with an average annual growth rate of approximately 10 percent (from 1899 to 2015). But this statistic conceals the fact that population growth on the island was especially high during the period before the Great Migration.[4] During the first half of the twentieth century, birthrates were extremely high on the island, while mortality rates were declining slowly, thus producing dramatic increases in population. Mortality dropped because of key interventions such as inoculations, improved sanitary conditions, a more expansive health delivery system, and the extension of potable water to most communities. Although such declines in mortality generally precede declines in fertility, planners were not willing to wait for this change. Rivera-Batiz and Santiago (1996) describe this process of population growth and change in the following terms:

> Mortality rates started to drop precipitously in Puerto Rico in the 1930s. Between 1930 and 1950, the number of persons who died each year dropped from 20 per thousand to fewer than 10 per thousand. This reduced death rate was linked to improved health conditions and better nutrition. During the

Table 4.1   Population and Population Growth in Puerto Rico,
1899–2015

Year	Total Population	Increase in Population from Preceding Census	
		Number	Percentage Change
1899	953,243	154,678	19.4
1910	1,118,012	164,769	17.3
1920	1,299,809	181,797	16.3
1930	1,543,913	244,104	18.8
1940	1,869,255	325,342	21.1
1950	2,210,703	341,448	18.3
1960	2,349,544	138,841	6.3
1970	2,712,033	362,489	15.4
1980	3,196,500	484,487	17.9
1990	3,522,037	325,537	10.2
2000	3,808,610	286,573	8.1
2010	3,727,789	−82,821	−2.2
2015	3,474,182	−251,607	−6.8

*Sources: 1980 U.S. Census of Population and Housing: Characteristics of the Population,
"Number of Inhabitants: Puerto Rico," Table 1; 1990 U.S. Census of Population and Housing:
Summary Social, Economic, and Housing Characteristics*, Table 1; Census 2000 Summary File
1 (SF1): *Profile of General Demographic Characteristics; American Community Survey, 1-
Year Estimates 2000, 2015*, Table DP-1.

same time period, the birth rate stayed more or less constant, fluctuating
around 40 births per thousand. The stable birth rate, combined with the
sharply declining death rate, led to booming population growth. (24)

All the conditions described above set the stage for the perception, both in
Washington, DC, and in San Juan, that migration was a major component of
any economic strategy aimed at remedying the impoverished conditions
many Puerto Ricans faced on the island during those years.

There is little doubt that Puerto Rican emigration to the United States
during the 1950s represents one of the largest outflows of people relative to
the size of the island's population base.[5] An estimated net figure of 470,000
people, out of a population of approximately 2.2 million, left the island during
the decade of the 1950s, a loss of slightly over one-fifth of the island's population during a ten-year period (see Table 4.2). This represents a remarkable 21
percent emigration rate, one of the highest in modern times. Although net emigration has remained sizable since 1960, there was little conception after the
Great Migration that it would ever be repeated.

This issue also brings up an interesting perspective on the relative
numbers of Puerto Ricans residing in the United States vis-à-vis the island's
total population.[6] The 2000 US census indicated that just over 3.4 million

Table 4.2   Net Emigration from Puerto Rico, 1900–2015

Year	Net Number of Out-Migrants
1900–1910	2,000
1910–1920	11,000
1920–1930	42,000
1930–1940	18,000
1940–1950	151,000
1950–1960	470,000
1960–1970	214,000
1970–1980	65,817
1980–1990	116,571
1990–2000	96,327
2005–2015	443,443

Sources: The data for 1900 to 1970 are from Vázquez Calzada (1988); the data for 1970 to 2000 are derived from the 1980, 1990, and 2000 U.S. *Census of Population and Housing: Puerto Rico; American Community Survey*, 1-Year Estimates 2010, ACS PUMS.

Puerto Ricans were residing in the United States (see Table 4.3). At the time, less than half that number (40.3 percent) were born outside the continental United States. According to Table 4.1, just over 3.8 million people were residing in Puerto Rico in 2000. Although fewer Puerto Ricans resided in the United States than on the island at the turn of the twenty-first century, the former figure was growing at a faster rate than the latter. Projections suggested that by the first decade of the new millennium there would likely be more Puerto Ricans residing in the United States than the total population of Puerto Rico (see Figure 4.1). This change was driven, in good measure, by the relatively younger age of Puerto Rican migrants compared to the average age of residents of the island, even in the absence of the extraordinary migratory changes that occurred at the onset of the twenty-first century. The fact is that the Puerto Rican population in the United States is younger than the population residing in Puerto Rico and more likely to be of childbearing age.

Early writings by Kal Wagenheim (1975) suggested that the US Puerto Rican population would surpass the island population by 2000. Part of the reason for Wagenheim's estimate was the assumption that migration from the island would continue at an accelerated rate, as it had in the past. This proved incorrect. Net migration, which responds to so many different forces, is always a difficult variable to forecast; nonetheless, given that Wagenheim made his prediction about twenty-five years before he expected the stateside Puerto Rican population to exceed the population of Puerto Rico, he really was quite close to the mark. As shown in the next chapter, Wagenheim could never have anticipated the dramatic changes in emigration in the first decade of the twenty-first century.

Table 4.3   **Puerto Rican Population Residing in the Continental United States and Percentage Born Outside the United States, 1910–2015**

Year	Total Population	Percentage Change (Ann. Avg.)	Number Born Outside US	Percentage Born Outside US
1910	1,513	—		
1920	11,811	22.8	—	—
1930	52,774	16.1	—	—
1940	69,967	2.8	—	—
1950	301,375	15.7	—	—
1960	892,513	11.5	—	—
1970	1,442,774	4.9	777,881	53.9
1980	2,036,411	3.5	1,031,054	50.6
1990	2,620,352	2.6	1,210,352	46.2
2000	3,406,178	2.7	1,369,205	40.3
2010	4,623,716	3.1	1,500,773	32.0
2015	5,372,759	3.0	1,703,195	31.7

Sources: 1960 U.S. Census of Population and Housing, Puerto Ricans in the United States, subject report PC(2)-1D, Table A, p. viii; 1970 U.S. Census of Population and Housing, Puerto Ricans in the United States.

A study by Falcón (2004) suggests that the number of Puerto Ricans residing in the United States has already surpassed the number of Puerto Ricans residing on the island. Falcón applied the percentage of Puerto Ricans living on the island based on the 2000 US census to the annual estimate of the Current Population Survey (CPS) (US Bureau of the Census 2003) and compared his estimate to the CPS count of Puerto Ricans in the United States. Whereas the decennial census provided a more accurate count than the CPS, one could reasonably conclude that the 2010 census count would show that the number of Puerto Ricans residing in the United States surpasses both the total Puerto Rican population of Puerto Rico and the total island population, which also includes a large contingent of Dominicans and Cubans. This is exactly what transpired.

Chapter 5 discusses the economic and structural conditions that led to this unforeseen massive outflow. Clearly the magnitude of recent Puerto Rican migration is reminiscent of the Great Migration of the 1950s. From 2005 to 2015 net emigration from Puerto Rico surpassed 400,000 people, and while it did not reach the same 21 percent level of the total population as in the 1950s, it represents a significant change with substantive ramifications for both the island and the recipient communities in the United States.

The implications of this change in the US–Puerto Rican population balance are potentially significant (see Figure 4.1). For example, if US Puerto Ricans were to have a political voice in the periodic plebiscites conducted

Figure 4.1 **Projections of Puerto Rican and US Puerto Rican Populations, 1910–2050**

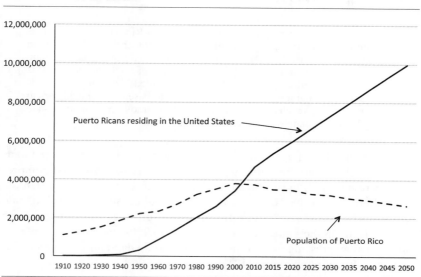

on Puerto Rico's future political status and its economic relationship with the United States, their votes could determine the outcome. Numerous writers, both on the island and stateside, have commented on how US Puerto Ricans continue to identify with their geographic, cultural, and linguistic roots despite their dispersion across the fifty states. These writers have argued as to the importance of seeing them as part of a single Puerto Rican nation. Indeed, if we combine the counts of the island- and US-based Puerto Rican populations from the Census Bureau's 2015 American Community Survey (ACS), the percentage of Puerto Ricans would reach 16 percent of the total US Latino/a population (the US census gives a figure of 9.5 percent, which does not include the island's population), far outnumbering other groups, with the exception of the Mexican/Chicano/a population, which in that year represented over two-thirds of all US Latinos/as.

The Growing Geographic Dispersion

Puerto Ricans are an extremely mobile population. Rivera-Batiz and Santiago (1994) claimed, based on the 1990 census, that 33.8 percent of Puerto Ricans residing in the United States had moved from one residence to another in the previous five years. This compares with 25.9 percent for the population at large. Little recent evidence suggests that this significant degree of geographic mobility has diminished. To the contrary, Meléndez and Vargas-Ramos (2014) argue,

> In the last decade over a million stateside Puerto Ricans migrated across state lines. This extraordinary rate of mobility is higher than the rate of the population of the United Sates as a whole or for any other major ethnic group. More stunning is the fact that this pattern of migratory behavior is fueled by movement among those born in the United States, not by island-born or recent migrants as one might speculate based on prior historical patterns. In fact, seven out of ten Puerto Ricans moving to another state during the last decade were born in the United States. (vii)

The Puerto Rican population in the United States is often referred to as resilient, a characteristic initially pointed out in 1994 in the first comprehensive review of Puerto Rican socioeconomic progress in the United States. In this work, based on the 1990 decennial census, Rivera-Batiz and Santiago (1994) write, "Given the dramatic changes occurring among Puerto Ricans in the United States during the 1980s, the authors can only conclude by expressing awe at the resiliency and adaptability to change of the Puerto Rican population" (121).

This resiliency is due, in large measure, to the mobility of the population. Whether leaving Puerto Rico to escape rural poverty in the 1950s, or dispersing from New York City during its default in the mid-1970s, or searching for employment in the midst of the Great Recession of 2007, Puerto Ricans have utilized "mobility" as a means to stabilize their life circumstances. The most recent volume on the socioeconomic progress of Puerto Ricans in the United States draws precisely the same conclusion: "The Puerto Rican story is one of resiliency. This is a community that despite facing difficult challenges in finding employment and staving off poverty has been especially proactive in taking steps to overcome dire circumstances" (Meléndez and Vargas-Ramos 2014, viii).

The Puerto Rican experience is unique not solely in the volume of mobility—the number of people who move frequently—but also in the pattern of that mobility. There is not only continuous migration between the island and the United States—often referred to as commuter, back-and-forth, or circular migration—but also a growing geographic dispersion of the Puerto Rican population throughout the continental United States.[7]

Historically, New York City has been the primary destination for Puerto Ricans. Even before the mid-twentieth-century Great Migration, 80 percent of the Puerto Rican population residing in the United States lived there (A. López 1980). New York City is certainly not the closest in geographic distance between San Juan and the continental United States. Miami, for instance, is closer. But New York City is an urban center that has historically absorbed wave after wave of immigrants from different parts of the world—western, eastern, and southern Europe, the Caribbean, Latin America, Asia, and so on. It was also "closer" to Puerto Rico in terms of people's ability to travel (costs of migration) from San Juan.

As Puerto Ricans settled in New York, families became concentrated in specific areas and communities that arose in various parts of the city. In the 1930s Puerto Ricans settled into the Upper East Side of Manhattan in East Harlem, which became known as Spanish Harlem, or El Barrio (A. López 1980, 321; C. Rodríguez 1989). Dispersion and subsequent concentration then occurred throughout the metropolitan area, so that by 1970 Puerto Ricans were a majority of the population in Washington Heights, East Harlem, and the Lower East Side in Manhattan, Williamsburg and Greenpoint in Brooklyn, and the South Bronx. These communities also had a high percentage of economically disadvantaged families.[8]

Another component of the Puerto Rican migration stream that has received much less attention is the seasonal workers coming from the island to work on farms in the Northeast. This work was transitory, and both the working and living conditions were precarious at best. Between the 1940s and the 1960s the Puerto Rican government facilitated the movement of this labor force between the island and agricultural areas of New Jersey, upstate New York, Connecticut, Pennsylvania, and Massachusetts. Pay was low, housing was often substandard, and these workers had fewer rights and benefits than other workers since unionization was almost nonexistent.

Given the roots established in New York City, Puerto Ricans have traditionally been concentrated in the US Northeast, where over 82 percent of the population resided in 1970. Another 9 percent lived in the Midwest at the time, mostly in Chicago and parts of Ohio. This settlement pattern changed dramatically between 1970 and 2015 (see Figure 4.2). A major rupture from earlier patterns of settlement occurred during the 1970s in the aftermath of New York City's fiscal crisis. New York City's default in 1975 had a devastating impact on the socioeconomic status of the Puerto Rican and African American populations, especially because of the simultaneous decline in the city's manufacturing sector.

By the 2010–2014 period, the percentage of Puerto Ricans residing in the Northeast had fallen thirty percentage points to 52 percent compared to forty years earlier. Over the same time, the population also showed significant growth in the Southeast, where now 28 percent of the Puerto Rican population resides. As pointed out in the first edition of this book (2006), between 1970 and 2000 there was a pronounced increase in the movement of US-born Puerto Ricans along the Northeast-Southeast corridor, with Puerto Rican migrants moving from the island to similar points of destination.

Between 1970 and 2015 Puerto Ricans increasingly gravitated to the South, moved within the Northeast, maintained their presence in the Midwest, and were found in every state of the union (see Figure 4.3). Migration

Figure 4.2   Distribution of the Puerto Rican Population in the United States, by Region, 1970 and 2014

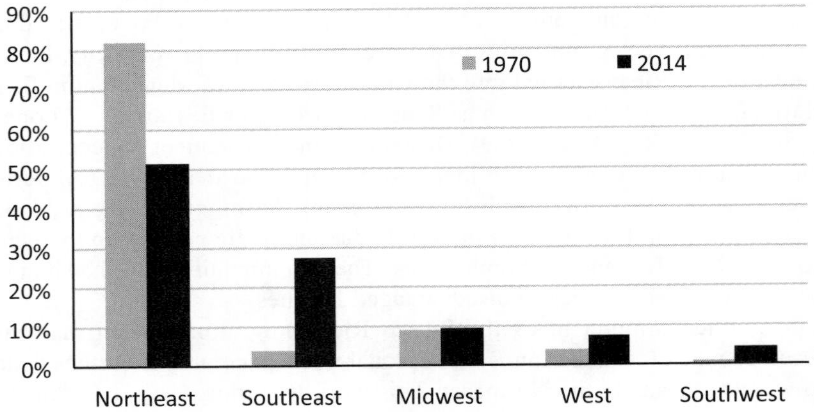

from Puerto Rico, once primarily aimed at New York City, now flows directly to other parts of the country. The traditional San Juan–New York City and back migratory route has become a multidestination one, with individuals staying in two or more locales and sometimes not returning to the point of origin. Puerto Ricans are not, however, a homogeneous group of people who travel for identical reasons. The character of the movement to the Southeast often differs from the movement of Puerto Ricans within the Northeast. In the former case, more educated individuals tend to be seeking employment within Florida's growing economy.

Throughout the Northeast we often see Puerto Ricans moving from large cities with more expensive housing to midsize cities with a more affordable housing stock. Rivera-Batiz and Santiago (1994) first highlighted this differentiated process of dispersion when they claimed that Puerto Rican mobility and its socioeconomic character "is not necessarily based on the traditional urban-suburban patterns observed among other groups in the population. Rather, a number of Puerto Rican communities are plagued with poverty and joblessness in midsize urban areas of the Northeast, while at the same time there exist many affluent, booming communities in the Southern and Western United States" (viii).

In 1970, over 80 percent of the Puerto Rican population in the United States was concentrated in only three states: New York, New Jersey, and Illinois (see Figure 4.4). By 2014, only a slightly lower proportion (77 percent) of the Puerto Rican population resided in New York, Florida, New Jersey, Pennsylvania, Massachusetts, Connecticut, Illinois, California, Texas, and

103

Figure 4.3 US Puerto Rican Population, by State, 2011–2015

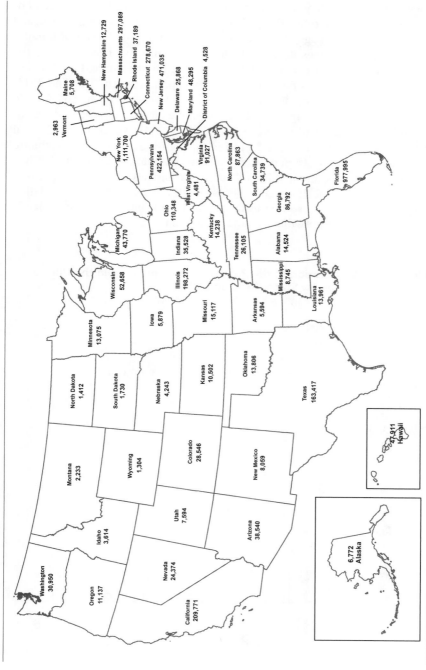

Source: Data from US Census Bureau, 2011–2015, ACS five-year estimates; map created by the Center for Social and Demographic Analysis, University at Albany, SUNY.

Ohio. Most noteworthy was the growing percentage of the Puerto Rican population residing in Florida, Pennsylvania, Massachusetts, and Connecticut and the declining percentage of the population residing in New York and Illinois.

But these changes do not tell the whole story. We need to place the change in Puerto Rican population by state in the context of broader changes in each state's population. For example, between 2010 and 2015, the Puerto Rican population of Florida increased from 864,577 to 1,069,446, a surge of slightly over 200,000, the largest increase in the number of Puerto Ricans of any state (see Table 4.4). However, Florida's total population grew by nearly 1.5 million during the same period, so Puerto Ricans made up only 14 percent of Florida's population growth during that period. In contrast, the number of Puerto Ricans in Connecticut increased by 15,362 during the 2010–2015 period; yet Connecticut's total population grew by only 13,813, so Puerto Ricans' net contribution to Connecticut's overall population growth was quite significant.

Figure 4.4   Distribution of the Puerto Rican Population in the United States, by State, 1970 and 2014

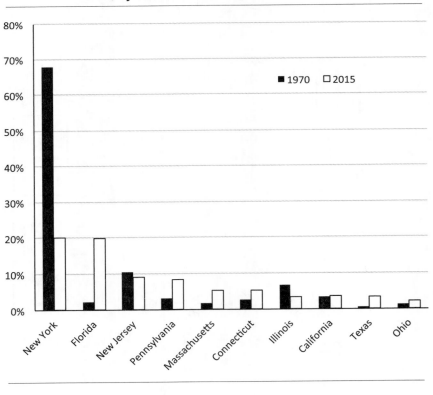

Table 4.4 Contribution of Puerto Ricans to State Population Growth, 1980–2015

State	Change in Total State Population (1)				Change in Puerto Rican Population (2)				Percentage Puerto Rican Contribution to State Population Growth (2) Divided by (1)			
	1980–1990	1990–2000	2000–2010	2010–2015	1980–1990	1990–2000	2000–2010	2010–2015	1980–1990	1990–2000	2000–2010	2010–2015
New York	432,383	986,002	401,645	417,689	100,212	−36,308	20,265	−435	23.2	−3.6823	5.0455	−0.1
Florida	3,191,602	3,044,452	2,818,932	1,469,962	152,235	235,017	365,523	204,869	4.8	7.7195	12.9667	13.94
New Jersey	365,365	684,162	377,544	166,119	76,593	46,655	67,304	57,109	21	6.8193	17.8268	34.38
Pennsylvania	17,748	399,411	421,325	100,124	57,186	79,569	137,525	68,820	322.2	19.9216	32.6411	68.73
Massachusetts	279,388	332,672	198,532	246,793	74,743	48,014	66,918	15,362	26.8	14.4328	33.7064	6.22
Connecticut	179,540	118,449	168,532	13,813	58,481	47,601	58,529	15,362	32.6	40.1869	34.7287	111.21
Illinois	4,084	988,691	411,339	16,829	16,894	11,792	25,138	−6,937	413.7	1.1927	6.1113	−41.22
California	6,092,119	4,111,627	3,382,308	1,890,862	33,379	14,153	49,375	954	0.5	0.3442	1.4598	0.05
Texas	2,757,319	3,865,310	4,293,741	20,043	20,043	26,523	61,072	45,522	0.7	0.6862	1.4223	1.96
Ohio	49,485	506,025	183,364	13,411	13,411	20,416	28,696	34,183	27.1	4.0346	15.6497	44.44

Source: US Census Bureau, *Census 2000;* . *American Community Survey,* "5-Year Estimates, 2006–2010, 2011–2015," Table DP05.

While the growth of the Puerto Rican population in Florida has received significant attention in the media because of its sheer size compared to Puerto Rican population growth elsewhere, the real story is the impact of this population growth in some areas of the Northeast. Although the West and the Southeast continue to attract large numbers of people, the Northeast has been a net loser of population. Thus, since general population growth has been relatively slow in the Northeast, Puerto Ricans have become an important contributor to population growth in these states.

Since the 1970s the states that have benefited most from Puerto Rican population growth have been in the Northeast. Connecticut, Pennsylvania, Massachusetts, and New Jersey stand out. Connecticut, in particular, has seen Puerto Ricans become important contributors to its population growth. As we will see, much of this growth occurred in midsize urban centers such as Hartford, Bridgeport, Waterbury, New Haven, and New Britain. But even in the states of Massachusetts, Rhode Island, New Jersey, and Pennsylvania, Puerto Ricans have become an important contributor to total state population growth over the last four decades.

The growing concentration of Puerto Ricans in states where overall population growth has been slow is an important consideration. For example, during the 2016 presidential election some believed that the large-scale Puerto Rican migration to Florida might tip the scales to turn the state "blue," given the proclivity of Puerto Ricans to vote for the Democratic Party. Although parts of central and southeastern Florida did vote Democratic, the state went for Donald Trump by a small margin, but enough to garner its twenty-nine electoral votes. At the same time, Darren Soto, a Puerto Rican from Florida's 9th Congressional District (eastern Orlando, Kissimmee, and St. Cloud), was elected to the US House of Representatives. It will be interesting to see whether Puerto Ricans' concentration in northeastern states where population growth is more modest will translate into greater political representation. If so, this will manifest in urban centers and other gateway cities.

The Urban Character of the Communities

Puerto Ricans in the United States have, by and large, resided in urban areas. This concentration would be expected in light of the significant and directed migration that occurred right after World War II. For several decades New York City was the primary destination. As relative newcomers to the New York City immigrant population, Puerto Ricans generally lived in the more economically depressed parts of the city, often residing in substandard housing. Differences in language, culture, and climate, unfamiliar surroundings, and an uncertain economic environment all posed real challenges for them.

As a racially mixed population, Puerto Ricans not only found themselves in a disadvantaged position with respect to housing in New York
City but also made up the growing low-wage labor force in the city. They
began filling the ranks of the city's workers in the service sector and also
increasingly in the light-manufacturing sector, especially in the Garment
District. The early large-scale migration of Puerto Ricans to New York City,
Chicago, and the Northeast coincided with a sustained period of economic
change in these industrial urban areas. Increasing evidence indicated that
the United States was embarking on a process of economic structural
change, later to be referred to as "deindustrialization," which culminated in
New York City's fiscal default in the mid-1970s. For Puerto Ricans this
played out in very unfortunate ways.

Despite a steady exit of Puerto Ricans during the 1970s, to this day New
York City still has the greatest concentration of this group. According to the
2015 ACS, 728,947 Puerto Ricans resided there (see Table 4.5). By 2010,
however, Philadelphia (with 121,643 Puerto Ricans) overtook Chicago (with
102,703 Puerto Ricans) as the second-largest concentration of Puerto Ricans.
It is noteworthy that the dramatic increase in Puerto Rican migration between
2010 and 2015 enhanced existing Puerto Rican populations in the United
States almost across the board. The relative growth of the Puerto Rican population in Philadelphia in particular, even while New York City and Chicago
declined between 2000 and 2010, is significant. Philadelphia's Puerto Rican
population practically doubled between 1990 and 2015 (from 67,857 to
133,968 people). Other large metropolitan cities that have experienced substantial Puerto Rican population growth over the past two and a half decades
are Boston, Orlando, Tampa Bay, Cleveland, and Milwaukee. Clearly, the
largest urban centers that historically served as the prime destinations for
Puerto Rican migrants, such as New York City and Chicago, are no longer filling that role, but this does not imply that the fundamentally urban character of
Puerto Rican settlement in the United States has changed.

Demographic data confirm that the initial concentration of Puerto
Ricans in urban centers has changed and that the population has become
more dispersed over time. The thirty-two cities with the highest concentrations of Puerto Ricans contained 63 percent of the total US Puerto Rican
population in 1980 (Table 4.6). But in 2015, these same cities contained
only 33 percent of the total. This phenomenon was particularly driven by
the fortunes of New York City and the decline in its Puerto Rican population base. By 2015, New York City was home to only 14 percent of the total
US Puerto Rican population. This contrasts sharply with the nearly 43 percent of the Puerto Rican population that resided in New York City in 1980
(and even more sharply with the nearly 60 percent in 1970).

Another important observation is that many midsize US cities with a
relatively small Puerto Rican population in 1980 showed considerable growth

Table 4.5 US Cities with Largest Concentrations of Puerto Ricans, 1980–2015

City and State	Puerto Rican Population					Growth Rate (Ann. Avg.)			
	1980	1990	2000	2010	2015	1980–1990	1990–2000	2000–2010	2010–2015
New York City, NY	860,552	896,763	789,172	723,621	728,947	0.4	−1.3	−0.83	0.15
Chicago, IL	112,074	119,866	113,055	102,703	104,325	0.7	−0.6	−0.92	0.32
Philadelphia, PA	46,587	67,857	91,527	121,643	133,968	3.8	3	3.29	2.03
Newark, NJ	39,732	41,545	39,650	35,993	37,129	0.4	−0.5	−0.92	0.63
Hartford, CT	24,615	38,176	39,586	41,995	42,495	4.4	0.4	0.61	0.24
Springfield, MA	12,298	23,729	35,251	50,798	54,141	6.6	4	4.41	1.32
Bridgeport, CT	22,146	30,250	32,177	31,881	30,922	3.1	0.6	−0.09	−0.60
Jersey City, NJ	26,830	30,950	29,777	25,677	27,575	1.4	−0.4	−1.38	1.48
Boston, MA	18,899	25,767	27,442	30,506	34,280	3.1	0.6	1.12	2.47
Cleveland, OH	12,267	17,829	25,385	29,286	30,240	3.7	3.5	1.54	0.65
Paterson, NJ	24,326	27,580	24,013	21,015	20,547	–	−1.4	−1.25	−0.45
Camden, NJ	a	22,984	23,051	23,759	24,198	–	0	0.31	0.37
Rochester, NY	10,545	16,383	21,897	27,734	24,198	4.4	2.9	2.67	−2.55
Milwaukee, WI	a	14,028	19,613	24,672	27,084	–	3.4	2.58	1.96
Reading, PA	6,957	11,612	19,054	28,160	29,185	5.1	5	4.78	0.73
Waterbury, CT	5,819	12,080	18,149	24,947	28,238	7.3	4.1	3.75	2.64
Yonkers, NY	a	14,420	18,097	19,875	21,999	–	2.3	0.98	2.14
New Haven, CT	a	13,866	17,683	20,505	20,939	–	2.4	1.60	0.42
Allentown, PA	4,279	9,670	17,682	29,640	33,128	8.2	6	6.76	2.35
Tampa, FL	4,038	9,863	17,527	24,057	26,068	8.9	5.7	3.73	1.67
Buffalo, NY	6,865	12,798	17,250	22,076	22,562	6.2	3	2.80	0.44
Worcester, MA	5,433	12,166	17,091	23,074	22,588	8.1	3.4	3.50	−0.42
Orlando, FL	a	7,035	17,029	31,201	39,392	–	8.8	8.32	5.25
Lawrence, MA	5,726	14,661	15,816	16,953	18,549	9.4	0.8	0.72	1.88
New Britain, CT	5,358	10,325	15,693	21,914	23,654	6.6	4.2	3.96	1.59
Holyoke, MA	a	12,687	14,539	17,825	18,497	–	1.4	2.26	0.75
Lancaster, PA	5,967	10,305	13,717	17,341	17,656	5.5	2.9	2.64	0.36
Los Angeles, CA	13,835	14,367	13,427	15,565	18,662	0.4	−0.7	1.59	3.98
Vineland, NJ	a	11,672	13,284	16,236	14,857	–	1.3	2.22	−1.70
Perth Amboy, NJ	a	13,531	13,145	12,090	14,127	–	−0.3	−0.80	3.37
Miami, FL	12,320	12,004	10,257	12,789	14,243	−0.3	−1.6	2.47	2.27
Ft. Lauderdale, FL	1,218	2,209	2,801	3,821	5,013	6	2.4	3.64	6.24

Source: US Census Bureau, *Census 2000;* American Community Survey 5-Year Estimates 2006–2010, 2011–2015, Table DP05.
Note: a. Data not available for the geographic designation or locale not among the top cities for 1980.

over the three and a half decades that followed. Most noteworthy are Hartford, Bridgeport, Waterbury, and New Haven, Connecticut; Springfield, Lawrence, and Holyoke, Massachusetts; and Reading, Allentown, and Lancaster, Pennsylvania. Puerto Rican population growth in these cities can be directly attributed to the movement of people from New York City and New Jersey to outlying areas. In addition, new areas of settlement that are not confined to a particular part of the country have become quite pronounced since the 1980s. These newer Puerto Rican communities include those within

Table 4.6 Total Puerto Rican Population in the United States by City, 1980–2015 (percentage)

City and State	1980	1990	2000	2010	2015
New York City, NY	42.729	32.876	23.169	15.65	14.09
Chicago, IL	5.565	4.394	3.319	2.22	2.02
Philadelphia, PA	2.313	2.488	2.687	2.63	2.59
Newark, NJ	1.973	1.523	1.164	0.78	0.72
Hartford, CT	1.222	1.4	1.162	0.91	0.82
Springfield, MA	0.611	0.87	1.035	1.10	1.05
Bridgeport, CT	1.1	1.109	0.945	0.69	0.60
Jersey City, NJ	1.332	1.135	0.874	0.56	0.53
Boston, MA	0.938	0.945	0.806	0.66	0.66
Cleveland, OH	0.609	0.654	0.745	0.63	0.58
Paterson, NJ	a	1.011	0.705	0.45	0.40
Camden, NJ	a	0.843	0.677	0.50	0.47
Rochester, NY	0.524	0.601	0.643	0.60	0.47
Milwaukee, WI	a	0.514	0.576	0.53	0.52
Reading, PA	0.345	0.426	0.559	0.61	0.56
Waterbury, CT	0.289	0.443	0.533	0.54	0.55
Yonkers, NY	a	0.529	0.531	0.43	0.43
New Haven, CT	a	0.508	0.519	0.44	0.40
Allentown, PA	0.212	0.355	0.519	0.64	0.64
Tampa, FL	0.2	0.362	0.515	0.52	0.50
Buffalo, NY	0.341	0.469	0.506	0.48	0.44
Worcester, MA	0.27	0.446	0.502	0.50	0.44
Orlando, FL	a	0.258	0.5	0.67	0.76
Lawrence, MA	0.284	0.538	0.464	0.37	0.36
New Britain, CT	0.266	0.379	0.461	0.47	0.46
Holyoke, MA	a	0.465	0.427	0.39	0.36
Lancaster, PA	0.296	0.378	0.403	0.38	0.34
Los Angeles, CA	0.687	0.527	0.394	0.34	0.36
Vineland, NJ	a	0.428	0.39	0.35	0.29
Perth Amboy, NJ	a	0.496	0.386	0.26	0.27
Miami, FL	0.612	0.004	0.003	0.28	0.28
Ft. Lauderdale, FL	0.06	0.001	0.001	0.08	0.10

Source: US Census Bureau, *Census 2000;* American Community Survey 5-Year Estimates 2006–2010, 2011–2015, Table DP05.
Note: a. Data not available for the geographic designation or locale not among the top cities for 1980.

the general proximity of New York City such as Yonkers and Buffalo, New York; and Camden, Vineland, and Perth Amboy, New Jersey. The Puerto Rican populations in Orlando and Tampa Bay, Florida, have also experienced phenomenal growth.

While decline in the New York City resident Puerto Rican population during the last few decades certainly fueled some of the population growth in surrounding cities, little evidence suggests that Puerto Ricans simply moved from the largest metropolis in the country to a nearby smaller city. The ring of sizable Puerto Rican communities within a 100-mile radius of New York City grew proportionately larger between 1980 and 2015 than the overall decline in the numbers of Puerto Ricans residing in New York City. One might argue that, by and large, migration to those cities from the island and the natural increase in the existing population fueled the growth of the Puerto Rican population. This does not mean that Puerto Ricans from New York City were not moving into these communities; rather, the growth of the Puerto Rican population in these cities was proportional to the growth of the Puerto Rican population overall. This also suggests that, despite the influx and outflow of people, these communities exhibited considerable stability in terms of population.

It also seems clear that Puerto Ricans with the economic means have been opting for a more suburban lifestyle. Whether they seek better housing, better schools, more affordable communities, or simply a change in lifestyle, there is little doubt that Puerto Ricans are following the path of earlier immigrant groups in New York City. Puerto Ricans have also been moving from the Northeast to parts of Florida. In Chapter 6, we explore how these migratory patterns relate to a growing Puerto Rican middle class, which is associated with a rising standard of living.

Finally, with respect to the mobility of Puerto Ricans, in certain communities where their numbers have been growing rapidly, their percentage of the city's total population has increased, in effect significantly increasing the Puerto Rican presence in these communities. This is particularly so in the Northeast, where population growth overall has slowed. The rather dramatic changes mean that Puerto Ricans now constitute over 20 percent of the total population in fifteen different midsize cities (see Table 4.7). This is all the more remarkable in that thirty-five years ago the Puerto Rican presence did not reach 20 percent in any of these cities. In 2015 over 40 percent of the population of Holyoke, Massachusetts, was Puerto Rican. Now Puerto Ricans comprise over 30 percent of the population in six different northeastern cities. This change raises the question of whether the increased presence of Puerto Ricans in midsize cities has translated into their greater political participation and representation in these communities. Much of the cursory evidence suggests that it has not yet, but the potential remains for greater influence in these communities as their numbers increase.

Table 4.7   Puerto Rican Presence in Cities with Greatest Concentrations of Puerto Ricans, 1980–2015 (percentage)

City and State	1980	1990	2000	2010	2015
Holyoke, MA	a	29.0294	36.4953	44.70	45.85
Hartford, CT	18.08	27.3195	32.5602	33.70	34.05
Camden, NJ	a	26.2698	28.8484	30.70	31.47
Perth Amboy, NJ	a	32.242	27.7889	26.80	27.07
Lancaster, PA	10.9	18.5505	24.3434	29.20	29.75
Kissimmee, FL	a	8.579	23.6583	33.10	31.30
Vineland, NJ	a	21.307	23.6072	26.70	24.36
Reading, PA	8.84	14.815	23.4635	32.00	33.14
Springfield, MA	8.07	15.1156	23.1789	33.20	35.17
Bridgeport, CT	15.54	21.35	23.0612	22.10	20.99
Lawrence, MA	9.06	20.8825	21.9536	22.20	23.54
New Britain, CT	a	13.6771	21.9366	29.90	32.41
Waterbury, CT	5.63	11.0865	16.9188	22.60	25.78
Allentown, PA	4.12	9.2016	16.5823	14.40	27.78
Paterson, NJ	17.63	19.5754	16.0921	14.40	13.98
Lorain, OH	10.65	13.1686	15.347	19.40	21.66
Newark, NJ	12.07	15.0951	14.4948	13.00	13.27
New Haven, CT	a	10.6274	14.3036	15.80	16.03
Bethlehem, PA	a	10.8137	14.1541	18.30	19.09
Jersey City, NJ	12	13.5427	12.4042	10.40	10.62
Elizabeth, NJ	a	10.9653	10.7732	10.80	11.05
Rochester, NY	4.36	7.0727	9.9635	13.20	11.48
Worcester, MA	3.36	7.1666	9.8993	12.70	12.32
New York City, NY	12.17	12.2466	9.8545	8.90	8.65
Yonkers, NY	a	7.6669	9.2291	10.10	11.03
Orlando, FL	a	4.2716	9.1578	13.10	15.34
Providence, RI	a	4.4529	7.3218	8.30	7.79
Philadelphia, PA	2.78	4.2796	6.0312	8.00	8.61
Buffalo, NYk	1.92	3.9004	5.8945	8.40	8.69
Tampa, FL	1.49	3.5223	5.776	7.20	7.33
Miami, FL	0.006	0.004	0.003	3.20	3.35
Ft. Lauderdale, FL	0.001	0.001	0.001	2.30	2.89

Source: US Census Bureau, Census 2000; American Community Survey 5-Year Estimates 2006–2010, 2011–2015, Table DP05.

Note: a. Data not available for the geographic designation or locale not among the top cities for 1980.

A Tale of Three Cities:
New York City, Hartford, and Orlando

New York City, Hartford, and Orlando are very different cities with considerably different historical origins. They vary in size, with over 8 million inhabitants in the immediate New York City area and over 20 million in the wider metropolitan area; Hartford has over 125,000 people residing in the city and over 1.2 million in its metropolitan area; and Orlando has nearly 260,000 people in its city and over 2 million in the metropolitan area (all data as of the 2015 ACS). These three cities also represent different facets of the Puerto Rican experience in the United States. The establishment of Puerto Rican communities in these cities occurred at different times and was motivated by different socioeconomic forces. In many respects, they also represent different phases of expansion in a long-term process of Puerto Rican population concentration and dispersion.

New York City's Puerto Rican population expanded dramatically via direct migration from the island in the 1950s. During the 1960s, net migration from Puerto Rico to the United States declined compared to the previous decade. Although the net migration flow was still in the direction of New York City, return-migration patterns were already emerging, thus reducing the rate of growth of the Puerto Rican population in New York City compared to the 1950s (Hernández Alvarez [1967] 1976). In 1970, Puerto Ricans (844,303 people) made up approximately 11 percent of the New York City population; this figure has shown a steady but not precipitous decline, reaching 8.6 percent (728,947 people) by 2015.

The growth in the number of Puerto Ricans living in New York City between 1980 and 2015 has been low compared to previous decades. Despite the slight decline in the percentage of New York City residents who are Puerto Rican, an upsurge in Puerto Rican migration during the 2000–2015 period seems to have stabilized the long-term decline.

Migration from Puerto Rico exclusively drove the initial growth of the Puerto Rican population in New York City. From the 1970s, however, the natural increase in the population—that is, births minus deaths—determined population growth, at least until the upsurge in migration from 2000 to 2015. While Puerto Ricans remain a relatively younger group than the rest of the city's population, the gap in age structure is closing fast. In 1970 approximately 75 percent of Puerto Ricans residing in New York City and 53 percent of the whole city's population were younger than thirty-five, a twenty-two-point gap that shrank by half to an eleven-point gap in 1990.

Behind these changes in the age structure of the Puerto Rican population in New York City lie several demographic factors. First, they reflect the decline in Puerto Rican migration to the city until the 2000–2015 period. Second, they correspond to an upsurge in new, younger immigrants from the Dominican Republic, Central America, Mexico, and Asia. As younger immigrants arrive in the city, the demographic profile of Puerto Ricans more closely approximates that of the city at large. Third, the exodus of Puerto Ricans from New York City has been disproportionately of the younger population, particularly women of childbearing age. This has the effect of immediately shifting the age distribution upward and reducing birthrates. It is important to keep these demographic trends in mind when considering the changing socioeconomic and political conditions of the Puerto Rican population in New York City.

The Puerto Rican presence in the city of Hartford shares similar origins with that in New York City and in some respects can be viewed as an extension of the larger metropolis as well as being unique in and of itself (J. Cruz 1998). New York City certainly served as a feeder of Puerto Rican population to Hartford, but the latter also received direct migration from the island. Hartford began to see an influx of Puerto Ricans in the 1950s. They came to work on the agricultural farms in the surrounding region, particularly in the tobacco-growing areas. Many of these workers did not return to the island but remained in Hartford, where they found a growing community. Some light manufacturing took place in Hartford, the home of the Royal Typewriter Company, another source of employment for Puerto Ricans, but the city suffered a decline in its manufacturing base in the 1970s, as did much of the Northeast.

The Puerto Rican population in Hartford became particularly noticeable during the decade of the 1980s, when it grew by 55 percent. This growth was prompted by renewed migration from the island as well as an influx of Puerto Ricans from neighboring cities in the Northeast, including New York City. This period also saw considerable growth in the number of Puerto Ricans throughout Connecticut, as communities expanded in Bridgeport, Waterbury, New Haven, and New Britain. Whereas the 1950s was the decade of substantial growth in the numbers of Puerto Ricans in New York City, for Hartford the decade of most rapid growth was the 1980s (J. Cruz 1998).

The growth of the Puerto Rican population in Connecticut during the 1980s coincided with a period of relatively slow population growth in the state. As we have seen, this translated into a greater presence of Puerto Ricans within many cities in Connecticut, but none more so than Hartford. With Puerto Ricans representing 34 percent of Hartford's population, the city is one of a handful of US localities that has elected Puerto Ricans. The relationship between the Puerto Rican community and the wider Hartford citizenry has gone through tumultuous periods, as Puerto Ricans have sought greater representation and improvements in housing, education, health services, and the like.[9]

Chapter 6 explores the issue of socioeconomic progress among Puerto Ricans in Hartford. Hartford represents a good example of the community's political enfranchisement and use of identity politics for empowerment (J. Cruz 1998). The city with the third-largest concentration of Puerto Ricans in 2015, it has been the only major city in the United States that has elected two different Puerto Rican mayors. The question remains whether the aspirations of the Puerto Rican community for representation have been adequately met in light of their presence in this and other cities. It is also noteworthy that the Northeast corridor that includes Hartford, Connecticut, and Springfield and Holyoke, Massachusetts, has the most concentrated numbers of Puerto Ricans relative to the general population.

Orlando provides a strikingly different Puerto Rican experience from that of New York City or Hartford. The Puerto Rican population of Orlando grew substantially during a period of rapid and remarkable population growth throughout Florida. Orlando's Puerto Rican population is much smaller than Hartford's, but it has been growing at a much faster rate. The Puerto Rican percentage in Orlando (15 percent) is almost double that of New York City in 2015 (around 8.6 percent) but less than half of Hartford's (34 percent). As in Hartford, direct migration from Puerto Rico as well as movement from New York City and other parts of the Northeast has fueled the growth in Orlando's population. While 39 percent of all Puerto Ricans who left New York City between 1985 and 1990 returned to the island, 14 percent moved to Florida—many to Orlando (Rivera-Batiz and Santiago 1996, 148). However, migration from Puerto Rico is contributing to Orlando's Puerto Rican population growth to a much greater extent than it is in New York City or Hartford.[10]

The concentration of Puerto Ricans in the city of Orlando is noticeable but actually much smaller than that in the neighboring city of Kissimmee. In Kissimmee approximately 24 percent of the city population was Puerto Rican as of 2000 (compared to 9 percent for Orlando), and the figure has risen significantly since then. By 2015, Puerto Ricans constituted almost one-third of Kissimmee's population (Orlando's share was at 5 percent). Many of Florida's cities have a Hispanic flavor to them, as may be seen in restaurants, markets, and social clubs, but Kissimmee has a noticeable Puerto Rican taste.

Drawing Puerto Ricans to central Florida, particularly Orlando and Kissimmee, is the economic boom that the state experienced during the 1990s and the employment opportunities that became evident as tourism and other sectors flourished. Puerto Ricans seeking to retire and leave the colder Northeast and the bustle of life in Puerto Rico also have moved to central Florida. All in all, a heightened quality of life has induced many to resettle in Florida. An educated, professional, and middle-class Puerto Rican family is also likely to move to Florida in search of employment and educational opportunities. The higher income and positive labor market outcomes in Orlando and other parts of central Florida also attract this more affluent segment of the US Puerto Rican population (as will be discussed in Chapter 6).

New York City, Hartford, and Orlando present just three different demographic snapshots of the Puerto Rican experience in the United States. They are also communities with different trajectories and experiences. New York City remains the most significant destination for the majority of Puerto Ricans, and their experiences do not deviate significantly from the more traditional New York City immigrant one. Hartford, in contrast, better represents the experiences of Puerto Ricans who are struggling in cities whose economic heyday has long passed and coping with an economy in which skills and knowledge are most highly prized. Puerto Ricans in this setting have the advantage that they are a growing presence and have real opportunities to convert their numbers into greater political representation. Finally, Orlando encapsulates the more recent experience of migration into areas of growth. There a more highly educated Puerto Rican population, the core of an emerging middle class, is making inroads in such communities, although their impact is still nascent.

Other Migration Destinations

Despite the growth of the Puerto Rican population in cities like Hartford and Orlando, Philadelphia and Chicago still remained, after New York, the cities with the second- and third-largest percentages of the total US Puerto Rican population in 2015, respectively holding 2.6 and 2.0 percent. The arrival of Puerto Rican newcomers to these two cities took place during the postwar Great Migration period.

Elena Padilla (1958) was one of the first researchers to study Puerto Rican migration to Chicago and compare it with that of New York. She noted that the declining manufacturing base in both cities pushed a large number of Puerto Ricans into nonindustrial service and menial jobs. In later studies, Félix Padilla (1985, 1987) documented in more detail the evolution of the Chicago Puerto Rican community. According to Félix Padilla (1985), as the Puerto Rican population continued to grow during the late 1950s and early 1960s, "Puerto Ricans became evermore conspicuous, and the indifference with which they had been regarded in the early years changed to hostility. Ethnic tensions, police brutality, and the rise of a racist doctrine, which whites applied to Puerto Ricans, began to determine the status of the city's Puerto Rican population" and "accelerated the growth of a Puerto Rican ethnic consciousness" (60). He also noted that despite the initial dispersal of Puerto Ricans in several areas of the city, by 1960 there was a Puerto Rican enclave taking shape in the West Town/Humboldt Park area of Chicago. In the mid-1990s Division Street was renamed Paseo Boricua (Boricua Promenade), which today stands as one of the most vibrant Puerto Rican neighborhoods in the United States (see Chapter 7).

Part of the tumultuous history of the US civil rights movement manifested itself in the rioting that took place in many of the ethnic enclaves of the nation's largest cities. During 1966, Chicago's Puerto Rican riots were a response to segregation, racial conflicts, and the overall socioeconomic marginality experienced by the community. But some of the anger and frustration against the white-dominated power structures was channeled through social and political activism, as Puerto Ricans began to create new organizations to fight for their rights and foster social change (see Chapter 7). These organizations contributed to what Félix Padilla (1985) has described as "a we-feeling or consciousness of ethnic solidarity and community" (67).

The experience of Puerto Ricans in Philadelphia offers another example of postwar labor migration and the US economy's need for cheap labor. Earlier studies of Puerto Rican migration to this city (Siegel, Orlans, and Grier 1975; Koss 1965) showed a bidirectional pattern of migration of contract laborers, with individuals coming to work for a good part of the year on Pennsylvania farms and then often returning to Puerto Rico during the winter months. Carmen T. Whalen (2001) provided a more detailed and well-documented history, noting that Puerto Ricans were recruited in large numbers to engage in "farm and railroad work for men, domestic and garment work for women" (5). As in Chicago, Puerto Ricans faced the racial tensions and struggles of the civil rights era; they found themselves relegated to a subordinate status and labeled as belonging to "a culture of poverty" (G. Lewis 1963) or "an underclass" (Lemann 1991; Katz 1993). Whalen (2001) has argued that these paradigms "ignore labor recruitment, the impact of structural changes, and migrants' motivation in seeking work and a better life" (15).

Just as Puerto Rican migrants chose to settle in large US cities, they also came to smaller cities of the Northeast and Midwest. Agricultural work in Vineland, New Jersey, and factory work in Camden, New Jersey, are representative of the contract labor that started in the late 1920s and continued through the 1950s. Other cities, like Lorain, Ohio, recruited workers for the US Steel plant, providing the foundation for the larger Puerto Rican community that exists today in that city.

Notes

1. Luis Muñoz Marín assumed the governorship of the island in 1948 with a strong mandate and a slogan calling for "bread, land, and liberty" for the island population. This was a significant rebuke to the absentee and local agricultural elite that dominated the sugar industry. The hallmark of his administration was the deferral of discussions of political status until social and economic progress was well under way.

2. See Maldonado (1997) for an in-depth view of Moscoso's role in Puerto Rico's industrialization process.

3. The minimum wage boards were abolished in the mid-1970s, and parity with the US minimum wage level was achieved by 1980. For additional information on this issue, see C. Santiago (1989, 1991, 1993).

4. The average annual growth rate of the population of Puerto Rico was 1.6 percent from 1899 to 1950 and 1.1 percent from 1950 to 2000. In contrast, from 2000 to 2015 the average annual growth was −0.6 percent, indicating a pattern of population decline during this period.

5. In absolute terms, the largest population movements in recorded history include the forcible removal from the African continent of 18 million slaves during the African slave trade between 1500 and 1900; the emigration of 50 million Asians (many indentured servants) from India, China, Japan, and the Pacific Islands between 1820 and 1930; and the departure of upward of 60 million Europeans for the United States, Canada, Australia, New Zealand, and South Africa from 1820 to 1930. See "Labor Migrations, 1500–1930," August 26, 2003, http://www.sscnet.ucla .edu/classes/cluster 22/lectures/lecture3/ts1d002.htm.

6. One should keep in mind that population growth in Puerto Rico primarily, but not entirely, reflects changes in the population born on the island. However, the foreign-born population in Puerto Rico has increased considerably since 1960. Rivera-Batiz and Santiago (1996) wrote, "In 1990, the largest immigrant group in Puerto Rico was made up of those born in the Dominican Republic. The Dominican-born residing in Puerto Rico doubled during the 1980s, increasing from 20,558 in 1980, to 41,193 in 1990" (113). By 2010 the Dominican-born population in Puerto Rico was estimated to be close to 70,000 people.

7. Juan Carlos García-Ellín provides a comprehensive review of the interstate Puerto Rican migratory experience. He not only finds the US-based Puerto Rican population to be extremely mobile but also makes the case that a good many of the movers are US-born Puerto Ricans. See García-Ellín, "A Brief Look at the Internal Migration of Puerto Ricans in the United States: 2001–2011," in Meléndez and Vargas-Ramos (2014).

8. Chapter 6 takes up the issue of the changing socioeconomic status of Puerto Ricans in the United States and the geographic dimensions of this topic.

9. Much of the discontent among Puerto Ricans in Hartford erupted in 1969 when rioting broke out in the city, as Puerto Ricans decried discrimination, police brutality, and the lack of representation. See J. Cruz (1998).

10. For a more detailed review of Puerto Rican migration to Orlando, see Duany and Matos-Rodríguez (2005) and Duany and Silver (2010).

5

Economic Collapse, Hurricane Maria, and the New Millennium Migration

The previous chapter provided evidence of the dramatic increase in Puerto Rican migration that began during the first decade of the new millennium. Over the ten-year period from 2005 to 2015, Puerto Rican migration to the United States approximated levels not seen since the Great Migration of the 1950s and 1960s. In this chapter we examine some of the specific forces that brought about this dramatic upsurge in migration. We posit that the forces that gave rise to the dramatic increase in Puerto Rican migration began many years earlier. In addition, these forces interacted in complex ways, and many of the actions taken simply postponed the inevitable economic crisis.

In reviewing the causes and impact of the collapse of the Puerto Rican economy on migration to the United States, we focus primarily on policies and processes rather than personalities and politics, although we know that the latter are not unimportant in any comprehensive analysis.

In the midst of economic hardship, stagnation, and indebtedness, Puerto Rico was struck in September 2017 by the most devastating hurricane to hit the island in modern times. The island's power grid was virtually destroyed, and the cost of the devastation has been estimated at around $30 billion, although it is too early to fully understand the extent of the damage. This exacerbates an already difficult situation for island residents. Moreover, even months after the hurricane, predictions were that it would take six months or more to restore full power and even longer to repair or replace destroyed homes and businesses, and roads and bridges. The extent of the storm damages clearly demonstrated that the island's basic infrastructure was precarious at best. The Puerto Rican diaspora in the United States has already begun to step up efforts to help Puerto Ricans relocate

119

for temporary or permanent stays. Stateside Puerto Ricans have played a key role in assisting with donations and relief supplies.

Although it is too early to assess the full impact of Hurricane Maria on Puerto Rican migration, the prognosis is quite bleak. A recent newspaper article concluded, "Amid all the wreckage and upended lives in Puerto Rico, one thing is certain: Migration, already at historic levels before Hurricane Maria because of the island's bankruptcy and dire economic situation, is bound to sharply rise with untold consequences for the states that will take them in and the island they leave behind" (Fonseca and Aldridge 2017, 6). Speculation has already begun that we will see the largest migration of Puerto Ricans within a compressed period.

In the remainder of this chapter we focus on the impact of both economic collapse and Hurricane Maria on Puerto Rican migration. We also consider whether Puerto Rico has been experiencing a brain drain and the long-term ramifications of its current "demographic winter."

Economic Crisis and Long-Term Stagnation

The financial collapse that occurred in the United States in 2007, known as the Great Recession, was the culminating event of the economic debacle that struck Puerto Rico, although its fundamental origins began much earlier.[1] While a budget crisis was averted on the island in 2006 with an agreement to reform taxes and to increase the sales tax, by 2008 public indebtedness had risen to approximately $47 billion, growing at an even faster pace than the Puerto Rican economy.[2] The US Great Recession spelled the beginning of an economic depression in Puerto Rico. One might characterize it as the straw that broke the camel's back.

It is important to understand that movements of the Puerto Rican economy mirror those of the US economy, albeit in a nuanced manner. When the US economy is booming, the Puerto Rican economy will show some growth, albeit with a time lag and a moderated effect. The opposite case is often summed up in the popular expression "When the U.S. economy catches a cold, the Puerto Rican economy gets pneumonia." A recent report by the Federal Reserve Bank of New York (2014) indicated, "While Puerto Rico's economy has historically paralleled the U.S. mainland economy, the Island's latest downturn started earlier and was much steeper and more prolonged" (1). This observable fact is illustrated for 1981 to 2014 in Figure 5.1, taken from the Federal Reserve Bank of New York (2014, 3).

The events that come together to bring about an economic crisis include a weak or stagnant economy, falling tax revenues and growing government deficits, and ineffective policies to buttress declining standards of living through increasing borrowing and indebtedness. This downward spiral ultimately results in the imposition of austerity measures. But Puerto Rico's

Figure 5.1   Real GNP Growth in Puerto Rico and the United States, 1981–2014

Percent

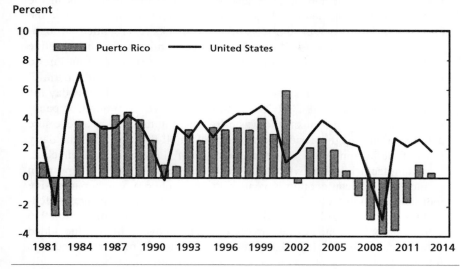

Source: Data from Puerto Rico Planning Board and US Bureau of Economy Analysis. Retrieved from Federal Reserve Bank of New York (2014).
Note: Puerto Rico's GNP is calculated on a fiscal year basis; US GNP is calculated on an annual calendar year basis.

economic depression is not simply the result of variations in the business cycle. The severity and length of the economic decline reflect deep-rooted structural imbalances that have, to this day, not been confronted.

While Puerto Rico's economic crisis follows the general pattern described above, its origins are more complex and predate, by decades, the collapse that coincides with the Great Recession of 2007. US private investment in Puerto Rico has shaped the local economy and, in many respects, plays a role in determining whether it expands or contracts over time. This pattern dates back to the early years of the US occupation, when coffee and sugar production dominated the island economy. It continued throughout the twentieth century until the present. Moreover, federal and local tax policies are particularly effective in shaping the changing industrial structure of the island economy, for better or worse.

Since the advent of Operation Bootstrap the economy has transformed itself from agriculturally based production, to basic manufacturing (paper products, apparel), to petrochemicals, pharmaceuticals, electronic products and scientific instruments, and financial services. In each transition, the nature and timing of federal tax exemptions often influenced the type of enterprises attracted to Puerto Rico and best suited to take advantage of the tax structure. Over time, the Puerto Rican economy was brought into the US economic orbit and became susceptible to further variations in the global economy. The demise of Puerto Rico's petrochemical industry in the early 1970s is just one example, as oil price shocks reverberated throughout the global economy and it was no longer economically feasible to refine petroleum in Puerto Rico. Unfortunately, the long-term impact on Puerto Rico was higher gasoline prices, environmental degradation, and a harmful impact on the health of residents living near the refineries. To this day the deteriorated remnants of CORCO (Commonwealth Oil Refining Company) smoke stacks, storage tanks, and waste-treatment units stand as an eye sore and a reminder of the acrid smoke and foul smell that pervaded the daily lives of the inhabitants of the southern towns of Guayanilla and Peñuelas.

Manufacturing employment has declined over time as the composition of the Puerto Rican economy went from low-technology, labor-intensive industries to high-technology, capital-intensive industries. Changes in federal tax-exemption policies, particularly with the elimination of Section 936 of the Internal Revenue Code, largely drove the move to high-value-added enterprises. Vélez Pizarro (2014) describes the impact of these changes as follows: "One of the effects the elimination of Section 936 had was a shift in the industrial composition of the island. Since it was repealed in 1996, a decrease in the number of intensive labor manufacturing plants (textiles, light manufacturing) while consolidation of capital-intensive companies (chemicals, medicine, electronics) took place" (27). This transformation signified that Puerto Rico could no longer compete in light manufacturing activities at the national and global level, leading to a concomitant increase in overall unemployment.

Government employment expanded to counteract rising unemployment as new public works projects emerged and the demand for health care, education, and other publicly provided services grew. Unemployment, however, remained relatively high on the island even in the best of economic times. As unemployment grew and labor force participation declined (as the long-term unemployed stopped looking for work), the local and federally funded safety net expanded. Borrowing on the part of public corporations, municipalities, local businesses, and individuals expanded rapidly as well. Cash-strapped local municipalities began to rely on the provision of electricity and water by government utilities on a largely subsidized basis.

To summarize: the standard analysis of Puerto Rico's economic collapse has many different elements. Economic stagnation gradually resulted in the government becoming the major employer on the island as revisions to, and ultimately the elimination of, federal tax exemptions reduced US investments. As stated earlier, this was particularly so with the elimination of the Section 936 tax incentives by the US Congress in 1996. Furthermore, the US social safety net for island residents was expanded; pension obligations, particularly for public-sector workers, remained underfunded; health-care costs increased substantially;[3] and private and public indebtedness grew. Once unleashed, subsidies were politically difficult to roll back. Many of these social programs began in the 1970s and were quickly integrated into the economic and social fabric of the island. In particular, the expansion of what was originally known as the federal food stamp program and the elimination of island-specific minimum wages to allow parity with the federal minimum wage have been cited as disrupting the island labor market.[4] The cost of labor in Puerto Rico quickly exceeded counterparts in the Caribbean and other areas of Latin America—Puerto Rico had lost the competitive advantage it once held to attract new US companies.

However, US investors were more than happy to financially underwrite this public-sector expansion as Puerto Rico represented a safe and lucrative destination for funds. Government and quasi-government utilities and public lending agencies such as the Government Development Bank were recipients, distributors, and users of these funds. Debt as a percentage of Puerto Rico's gross domestic product began to grow, ultimately to unsustainable levels. To say that Puerto Rico has been in an economic downturn for eleven years is an understatement. The government has experienced a budget deficit for the past seventeen years, which it has attempted to borrow its way out of. It has obviously been unsuccessful. The expiration of tax exemption under Section 936 in 1996 and the lack of a coherent long-term development strategy have clearly worsened the economic crisis.[5]

The Puerto Rican economic crisis exacerbated by the Great Recession became fully apparent when Puerto Rico's governor, Alejandro García Padilla, a member of the pro-Commonwealth party, announced in 2015 that the Commonwealth could not repay $72 billion of its debt.[6] This debt included general obligation bonds, pension obligations, and public utility debt, including that of the Puerto Rico Electric Power Authority (PREPA). The sheer magnitude of financial indebtedness brought a pall over Puerto Rico's economic future. Since bankruptcy is not a viable option for Puerto Rico, the island will likely be mired in an austerity plan to rival the most severe belt-tightening ever imposed by the International Monetary Fund (IMF) on a particular country.[7] Predictions are that the social safety net will weaken, retirees will see their pensions cut, weekly working hours of public employees might be reduced, little to no investments will be made in education at all levels, health and human services delivery systems will be jeopardized, health benefits will decline for an aging population, unemployment will remain high, and transportation and infrastructure projects will likely be delayed or abandoned altogether.

By 2013 Puerto Rico's outstanding public debt as a percentage of its annual gross national product surpassed 100 percent.[8] The government's annual general fund account was continually in deficit as the weak economy led to smaller tax revenues. The weaknesses in the local tax system had been acknowledged, and there was clear realization that the island had a thriving informal sector where official channels failed to capture literally millions of dollars.[9] The financial crisis manifested itself in the bond market as Puerto Rican bonds were judged to be of junk or near junk level. In other words, the value of the bonds was minimal, and this dissuaded lenders from buying them. At the same time, this further exacerbated economic conditions in Puerto Rico as government agencies and public corporations were running out of funding. Holders of these bonds, both in Puerto Rico and outside the island, also lost wealth as the assets depreciated in value.

The rush was on to determine who would be repaid first from whatever revenue might be coming to the Puerto Rican government. First in line for payments on Puerto Rico's obligations would be US bond holders, who would seek recourse in federal courts to recoup their losses. Retirees and pension recipients would also seek to ensure that payments continued. No doubt lawsuits would arise as debtor and creditor vied for positioning and leverage. Because Puerto Rico could not restructure its payments in bankruptcy court under Chapter 9 (as states and municipalities can do), the prospects for continued dysfunction were real. To forestall these disputes, the US Congress established the Puerto Rico Oversight, Management, and Economic Stability Act (PROMESA) to manage Puerto Rico's economic affairs. President Barack Obama signed the bill into law on June 30, 2016, and shortly thereafter named the members of the Junta de Supervisión Fiscal (Financial Oversight and Management Board), established to oversee the process of restructuring Puerto Rico's debt. Some argue that PROMESA is a needed measure to forestall short-run instability and the uncertainty of multiple legal actions. But the general consensus is that it will be ineffective in bringing about the conditions for long-term economic growth, which is what Puerto Rico most needs at this time (G. White 2016). Critics of PROMESA argue that it represents a brazen effort to undermine the democratic process as the unelected members largely have unfettered control over Puerto Rico's budget and finances. They equate it with the centralization of control brought about by the Foraker Act of 1900. With virtually unlimited powers, PROMESA will do more than just adjudicate debt claims: it will have a direct impact on the standard of living in Puerto Rico in both the short and the long term.[10]

So far, over a year after its appointment, the Junta has accomplished very little in the way of fiscal relief or debt restructuring for the island, except to endorse draconian austerity-based interventions that severely constrain the power and authority of Puerto Rico's government and municipalities and further enrich government consultants and corporate lawyers representing the Commonwealth and the numerous local and US investment banks and firms that for many years oversold Puerto Rico's municipal bonds to investors (Kolhatkar 2017; Pavlo 2017). Severe budgetary cuts in the island's operating budget already have produced the loss of hundreds of thousands of public employees, the closing of about 200 public schools (before Hurricane Maria), a proposed $450 million cut to the public University of Puerto Rico system,[11] a drastic reduction of government services, diminished government contributions to the pensions and health benefits of public employees, and proposed furloughs that would reduce the hours and salaries of regular workers.

Some see the economic crisis as the result of government ineptitude and mismanagement. Others see it as the result of investor greed by brokerage firms and banks and a system that encourages profligate spending on the part of local governments and individuals alike. Many of these critiques have questionable premises. As is typical, both perspectives contain an element of truth, but neither alone captures reality. No doubt the growth of government employment over the years has overtaken employment in manufacturing and other sectors and Puerto Rico's economy showed substantial weakness even before the United States entered the 2007–2009 Great Recession.

The confluence of forces that have generally resulted in an economic crisis in Puerto Rico include a natural downturn in the economy as it moves through the business cycle, industry-wide effects of changing federal and local tax policies, and negative trends in the global economy. These and other factors combined to transform a significant recession in the United States into an economic debacle for Puerto Rico.

As mentioned earlier, events in the continental United States have always had a disproportionate impact on the economic well-being of Puerto Ricans. The economic crises of the 1970s—which included skyrocketing oil and gas prices and the bankruptcy of the US city with the largest concentration of Puerto Ricans, New York City—resulted in dramatic effects in Puerto Rico. During that time, Puerto Ricans began returning to the island in increasing numbers, and public policies were enacted to keep them there. Social programs expanded, and local minimum wage provisions were dismantled, leading to the convergence of local and federal minimum wage levels. These policies particularly changed the structure of manufacturing as labor-intensive and petrochemicals industries began to give way to high-value-added sectors.

The severity of Puerto Rico's current economic decline is unprecedented and has led thousands of Puerto Ricans and their families to seek opportunities elsewhere. Puerto Ricans have long uprooted themselves and resettled in the United States in large numbers for a variety of reasons: to seek employment; to avoid social ills, such as drugs and violence; to escape political repression unleashed against nationalists and other pro-independence activists; or simply to improve their quality of life. The existence of long-established social networks in urban centers of the United States played an important role in the transmission of information. These networks served to confirm the validity of the information being transmitted and reinforced important decisions. Ultimately, the information provided by migrants moving back and forth between multiple locations reduces the uncertainty of the decision to move and the selection of a prospective destination.

Puerto Rican migration between the island and the United States ebbed and flowed over the years as circumstances changed in Puerto Rico as well as in stateside communities. Net out-migration predominated in the 1950s and 1960s, while substantial return migration characterized the 1970s. In the following two decades (1980s and 1990s), net out-migration averaged around 100,000 people, more than in the 1970s but significantly less than during the Great Migration. All of this changed during the ongoing New Millennium Migration, and significant net out-migration is likely be with us for years to come.

The next chapter highlights the extent to which the bankruptcy of New York City in the mid-1970s negatively impacted the Puerto Rican population residing there. During the decade of the 1960s net Puerto Rican migration to the United States surpassed 200,000 people, with most going to New York City and the Northeast. Yet during the decade of the 1970s, it fell to approximately 60,000 individuals. During the 1970s the standard of living of Puerto Ricans residing in New York City declined dramatically. This coincided with the bankruptcy and economic collapse of that city. It also resulted in increased numbers of Puerto Ricans returning to Puerto Rico.

Attempting to reconcile New York City's economic crisis of the 1970s with the simultaneous expansion of policies to increase incomes in Puerto Rico at that time will lead to the easy conclusion that the two are related. In fact, even without a clear connection, one could argue that policies to support incomes in Puerto Rico in the 1970s, such as minimum wage parity with US rates and increased food stamps and other social supports, were prompted to reduce migration to the United States (particularly to New York City) and to promote return migration from New York City. While there is scant conclusive evidence that policymakers in both Puerto Rico and Washington, DC, worked together to produce this outcome, one cannot deny the possibility.

As shown throughout this book, Puerto Rican migration flows have not simply been the result of market forces or the relative advantages of staying or leaving a particular location. Explicit government policies to promote migration have always influenced the timing and direction of migratory flows in and out of Puerto Rico (Edgardo Meléndez 2017). In its most recent past these policies have impacted the structure and growth of the Puerto Rican economy and standards of living on the island.

Hurricane Maria Compounds the Economic Crisis

No one will question that the economic downturn and Hurricane Maria, two disastrous and defining events that have abruptly altered the normal lives of both island and stateside Puerto Ricans, have shifted US and international attention to an island nation that represents one of the last vestiges of colonial domination around the globe. The current state of affairs is completely crippling the effectiveness and stability of the ostensibly self-governing Commonwealth to tackle its massive debt, which after the hurricane most experts now deem unpayable, and begin the process of rebuilding the country. The Junta declared to the media that the circumstances created by Hurricane Maria would force it to significantly modify its fiscal plans for dealing with the island's debt payments. Just a week after the hurricane federal judge Laura Taylor Swain, appointed under PROMESA to rule on all Puerto Rico debt proceedings, delayed forthcoming bankruptcy hearings and declared, "These Americans who were in the process of restructuring billions in debt through these PROMESA Title III proceedings in the hope of emerging from this economic crisis of unprecedented proportions, now face an even greater humanitarian crisis, one also that threatens their already challenging path back to economic stability" (Gleason 2017).

At a November 2017 appearance at a congressional hearing headed by Rob Bishop, chair of the Committee on Natural Resources, Junta executive director Natalie Jaresko requested "congressional affirmation" for the board "to be able operate quickly and decisively" in dealing with its now more complicated congressional mandate to stimulate "immediate recovery with long-term revitalization and building" for Puerto Rico (House Committee on Natural Resources 2017). Only time will tell if the message that goes out from this committee gets the attention of the legislative and executive branches to provide badly needed federal resources so that the process can move forward.

So far, the current Republican administration and US Congress have officially responded to Puerto Rico's plight by granting its government a $4.9 billion low-interest Treasury loan to support immediate liquidity problems and enable it to fully engage in hurricane emergency relief efforts, remove storm debris, and begin the monumental task of restoring electricity and water service to a completely blacked-out island. Almost six months after the approval of the loan, Puerto Rico has not received these funds. Moreover, in the context of an already fiscally strapped territory and with hurricane damage estimated at over $90 billion, the congressional loan gesture only underlines the unequal, second-class treatment of Puerto Ricans and the callous and almost tone-deaf reactions of US officials to the gravity of the island's present conditions. The appalling reality is that countries around the globe generally receive more generous foreign aid grants—rather than loans—from the United States or get more expeditious responses when facing multiple crises than the US citizens of Puerto Rico have (so far) received after

Hurricane Maria. Surprisingly, even US media coverage has been critical of the unequal hurricane aid response given to the island compared to the immediate disaster relief given to the states of Texas and Florida just a few weeks before due to the flooding and destruction caused by Category 4 hurricanes Harvey and Irma (August 26 and September 10, 2017, respectively) in these states. In February 2018, Congress briefly shifted its attention to the US disaster areas hit by major storms during the 2017 hurricane season (i.e., Florida, Texas, Puerto Rico, and the US Virgin Islands). It alloted $15 billion for Puerto Rico to be used for healthcare and reconstruction. Considering the magnitude of the destruction, it is not clear what impact the funds will have on the pace of recovery and rebuilding.

In the days after Hurricane Maria hit Puerto Rico, a compelling declaration by independent foreign debt and human rights experts affiliated with the United Nation's Human Rights Council in Geneva warned, "Puerto Rico remains without an effective emergency response more than a month after Hurricane Maria devastated the island" (UN Human Rights 2017) and further dramatized the island's devastating conditions and grueling path to recovery. One expert on foreign debt and human rights notes, "Even before Hurricane Maria struck, Puerto Rico's human rights were already being massively undermined by the economic and financial crisis and austerity policies, affecting the rights to health, food, education, housing, water and social security" (UN Human Rights 2017). A second team expert on housing rights points out, "We can't fail to note the dissimilar urgency and priority given to the emergency response in Puerto Rico, compared to the US states affected by hurricanes in recent months." Collectively, these experts are drawing global attention to Puerto Rico's present predicaments:

> We call on the United States and Puerto Rican authorities to remove regulatory and financial barriers to reconstruction and recovery. All reconstruction efforts should be guided by international human rights standards, ensuring that people can rebuild where they have lived and close to their communities. Reconstruction should aim to increase the resilience of Puerto Rico's infrastructure, housing and hospitals against future natural disasters. (UN Human Rights 2017)

Numerous Puerto Rican voices from the island and stateside communities fully recognize that in envisioning a path to recovery from fiscal insolvency and the widespread damage and destruction of most of the island's previous infrastructure, any reconstruction efforts must be sustainable, based on reducing reliance on fossil fuels and pursuing solar, wind, and other alternative energies, and conceived primarily by Puerto Ricans themselves. Such a plan also involves creating an economy that is based on expanding local agricultural production, supports small businesses and the tech-oriented startup companies of many island Puerto Rican Millennials, and makes eco-tourism a more efficient and attractive option for travelers. The challenges are how to pursue such goals, reduce reliance on the come-and-go US corporations seeking vulnerable low-wage labor around the world, and at least reduce the level of imported US goods. The repeal of the Jones Act cargo shipping laws would reduce the cost of US goods and allow Puerto Rico to engage in trade with other countries.

Island and stateside Puerto Ricans from all sectors of the population seem consistent in arguing that reconstruction endeavors should be based on meeting the immediate needs of those most affected by the storm, while also securing the long-term well-being of the citizens of Puerto Rico. Alternative solutions imposed by US officials, debt holders, or other external corporate and financial interests should be secondary in this time of crisis.

The less-than-competent response in the destructive aftermath of Hurricane Maria, the bureaucratic disarray, and slow pace of rescue efforts stood out in how US Federal Emergency Management Agency (FEMA) director William "Brock" Long brushed off the various urgent pleas of San Juan's outspoken mayor, Carmen Yulín Cruz. From day one after the hurricane, when met with the surrounding widespread destruction, unprecedented levels of flooding, and general collapse of the electrical and water grids and communications networks throughout the island, she cried out to the local and US media, "We are dying here." The image of a courageous mayor submerged in waist-high flood waters in a working-class neighborhood, bullhorn in hand, working like a first responder to save lives, rescue the elderly and those in need of immediate medical attention stranded in their flooded homes, comfort some of the rescued victims, and send a public message to the US administration—"Mayday! We are in trouble!"—made Cruz the national and international face and voice of the disaster swallowing up Puerto Rico. Shortly after Mayor Cruz's critical outcry about Puerto Rico's lopsided treatment in receiving a rapid response from FEMA and the US military during the bleak days that immediately followed the hurricane, President Donald Trump reprehensibly shifted blame for the disaster onto Puerto Ricans themselves for allowing the country's debt crisis to happen and letting its infrastructure deteriorate. He also criticized the mayor for her "poor leadership ability" and called her "nasty" for her criticism of FEMA and his administration.

Just a week after the hurricane, an intemperate Trump visited Puerto Rico. During the few hours he spent on the island holding a photo op press conference, he dismissed the criticisms of his administration's delayed and inadequate relief efforts, which the US media compared to those of President George W. Bush's administration in the aftermath of Hurricane Katrina (2005) in New Orleans. With a total absence of empathy and respect for hurricane victims, the current president joked about Puerto Rico's hurricane disaster putting the US budget "out of whack" and made baseless comparisons between Hurricanes Katrina and Maria aimed at diminishing the magnitude of the latter's destructive force on Puerto Rico because of the low number of recorded hurricane-related fatalities (at the time incorrectly reported to be sixteen; the "official" number has more than tripled since then and is expected to grow even more). Based on average monthly deaths in Puerto Rico over several years and the officially reported count since Hurricane Maria, some researchers have concluded that total hurricane-related deaths could amount to around 1,000. As if he had not said enough, Trump bragged about the "heck of a job" he was doing in providing assistance to Puerto Rico. Before leaving the island, he visited one of the shelters located in a middle-class neighborhood of Guaynabo, part of the metropolitan area, instead of going to one of the many destroyed and flooded poor neighborhoods in the region. The president proceeded to disrespectfully lob rolls of paper towels toward an audience of hurricane victims gathered at the shelter, a behavior covered by the local and international media and deemed disgraceful by Puerto Ricans, reporters and commentators, and a significant portion of the US general public. Then, upon his return to the United States, from his New Jersey golf club the US president dispatched a series of new tweets deriding Puerto Ricans for wanting "everything to be done for them when it should be a community effort" and declaring that Puerto Ricans should not expect for FEMA to be on the island "forever"; he totally disregarded the fact that the agency was just beginning its, to that point, ineffective relief efforts on the island (Rosenthal 2017).

The US president's callous behavior received wide rebuke from island and stateside reporters, commentators, some political and community leaders, and late-night comedians; it was covered by iconic television programs such as *60 Minutes* (see Kroft 2017). In its fall premiere episode, animated sitcom *The Simpsons* trolled the US president through the character of Moe, the bartender, showing empathy for the suffering hurricane victims in Puerto Rico, addressing the courageous mayor of San Juan, criticizing the president's humiliating paper towel tossing at the shelter, and collecting $25,000 to support hurricane relief efforts on the island. The episode's closing scene shows the cast of animated characters holding the Puerto Rican flag, with Marge also holding a sign bearing the word *Unido* (United)[12] and Lisa in the forefront shedding a tear, and makes a heartfelt appeal to all Americans to support the US citizens of Puerto Rico with their own donations. Mayor Cruz started the foundation Alguien Ayúdenos (Somebody Help Us) to seek public donations to assist hurricane survivors and has been making the rounds to keep alive Puerto Rico's struggle to get Congress and the US administration to support legislation that focuses on the immediate and long-term reconstruction of Puerto Rico. Other island and stateside Puerto Rican political leaders are also engaged in these congressional lobbying efforts for disaster aid.

The politicized responses of the US administration to obfuscate its prejudices and contemptuous treatment of Puerto Rico aside, outsiders expecting to profit from the island's current predicaments pose other impending dangers. US investment firms hold most of the island's debt, and the US Congress and federal government are succumbing to pressures exerted by Wall Street to apply "shock therapy" and "disaster capitalism" policies to an already fiscally bankrupt island (see Yeampierre and Klein 2017; Cintrón Arbasetti 2017; Kolhatkar 2017; Klein 2007; Sassen 2014). These drastic policies are similar to those applied globally to other countries and major cities experiencing similar economic crises in more recent times (e.g., Greece, Argentina, Detroit). The bulk of those policies generally promote large-scale privatization of government services (in this case PREPA is a favorite target), reduction in federal subsidies, stripping of crucial benefit protections from island unions and government employees, and the influx of US and other foreign predatory speculators wanting to acquire coveted damaged properties in areas of high real estate value and investment potential.

The halfhearted and patronizing responses from US officials in the executive and legislative branches have not deterred island and stateside Puerto Ricans from fully engaging in emergency relief efforts and using social media and calling for collective action to organize fund-raising campaigns for immediate help for hurricane victims. For weeks, almost everyone on the island had to deal with serious shortages of canned food, bottled water, batteries, emergency radios and generators, mosquito nets, insect repellant, and medical supplies. In smaller towns and isolated rural communities, neighbors and residents began helping each other in the desperate initial search for food, drinking water, and fuel to run their vehicles and electric generators, rescuing those in flooded areas or in need of immediate medical assistance, clearing debris from the streets and roads, and opening paths to those communities isolated by the collapse of paved roads or bridges and all forms of communication. New groups of volunteers emerged and rapidly mobilized to get basic survival aid to isolated areas FEMA took days and weeks to reach; existing nongovernmental and grassroots organizations sponsored collective kitchens and brought food and water to hurricane victims. Individuals and organizations used social media to solicit donations and supplies to meet the immediate survival needs of hurricane victims. Newly created and long-established groups, such as Mentes Puertorriqueñas en Acción, Foundation for Puerto Rico, Paz para la Mujer, Taller Salud, ComPRometidos's Maria: Puerto Rico's Real-Time Relief Fund, Fundación Comunitaria de Puerto Rico, Esfuerzo Ciudadano, Instituto Nueva Escuela, and Operación Agua, began to fill the initial vacuum created by a poorly prepared FEMA and island government responders by getting help to many of the most remote and damaged municipalities and poor and rural communities.

The challenge is immense, yet the support and outpouring of concern among stateside Puerto Ricans has been extraordinary. Many Americans have been calling for more effective support for Puerto Rico after the devastation caused by Hurricane Maria. Citizens throughout the United States of all persuasions have stepped up to offer support. In a time of human despair it is important to recognize the resilience of people who have gone far beyond their island's shores. They have created, and will again create, vibrant communities.

Mottos such as *Puerto Rico se levanta* (Puerto Rico rises up) and the widespread display of the Puerto Rican flag on vehicles and windows of buildings and houses, even those damaged by two feet of flash flooding, crashing mudslides, and fierce storm winds that often reached over 140 miles per hour, became symbols to inspire a resilient and spirited island nation to join together in dealing with the trauma, despair, and hardships left behind by Hurricane Maria.

Is Migration Draining the Island of Talent?

The question of whether out-migration has led to a brain drain on the island has been raised throughout Puerto Rico's history. *Brain drain* refers to the loss of the most educated and those with specialized training, which any economy can ill afford to lose. The common conception is that the migration stream from Puerto Rico has consisted disproportionately of the most educated. Doctors, engineers, scientists, and others with academic credentials and unique skills have often been cited as representing the brain drain.

There is little doubt that the educational attainment of more recent Puerto Rican migrants is greater than that of earlier migrants. But this observation per se does not constitute evidence of a brain drain. The educational attainment of migrants has increased with increasing overall educational attainment in Puerto Rico. In other words, the more educated migrant population, more than anything else, reflects the increased educational attainment of Puerto Ricans in general. Rivera-Batiz and Santiago (1996) made this point based on data from the late 1980s:

> The data presented suggest that persons who migrated from Puerto Rico to the mainland United States during the 1985–90 window had an age-standardized educational distribution almost identical to that of the Puerto Rican population. This means that, in terms of educational attainment, the recent emigrants represent a near cross-section of the Puerto Rican population. There is certainly not an overrepresentation of highly educated people. On the other hand, the migrants who left during the 1975–80 period included a greater proportion of less educated people. (52–53)

To determine whether the brain drain is truly characteristic of migration, one needs to compare the educational and occupational characteristics of those leaving with those of the population of origin at large. For instance, if the percentage of physicians among all migrants is greater than the percentage of physicians in the population at large, one can conclude that a brain drain is taking place, at least for this particular occupational group. Again, the perception of a brain drain does not correspond with reality. Of all employed out-migrants between 1985 and 1990, 44 percent had a white-collar occupation, compared to 51 percent of the employed on the island (Rivera-Batiz and Santiago 1996, 53).

Scant evidence confirms the common perception that Puerto Rican migration reflects a brain drain. A more recent analysis by Birson (2014) focusing on the 2006–2011 cohort of migrants comes to a similar conclusion:[13]

> Contrary to popular perception, the evidence from this study found no evidence of a brain drain [in] the aggregate educational or occupational categories relative to the Puerto Rican population of the island. Emigrants, in fact, were less educated, with the majority (59%) of those leaving having a high school education or less. Fifteen percent held a bachelor's degree and just 5 percent had attained a graduate degree, a slightly smaller representation than among those staying in Puerto Rico. (15)

Analysis focused on the occupational composition of the migration stream confirmed the conclusion of earlier studies: "These emigrants were also underrepresented in professional occupations and over-represented in lower-skill industries" (Birson 2014, 15).

Overall analytical studies of the Puerto Rican brain drain yield similar conclusions: the existence of a brain drain is more a perception than a reality.[14] Education levels and occupational mobility have increased among the island Puerto Rican population, and both are also reflected in migrants, but not disproportionately so.[15] One might certainly question whether this pattern will continue in the face of longer-term migration, such as that happening today. With continued economic decline and the devastation of Hurricane Maria, might the composition of the migrating population change from what it has been in the past? We might argue that in the immediate aftermath of Hurricane Maria the age composition will shift to the elderly as the island's health-care system has become seriously compromised.

The migration stream that results from the weather-related event in Puerto Rico is likely to provide new information regarding the likelihood of a brain drain. One might speculate that at the beginning migrants will fall on both the older and younger sides of the age distribution. With the disruption of schools, educational institutions, and medical facilities, we are likely to see a disproportionate number of the young and elderly among the migrants. One might also speculate about the income levels of those Puerto Ricans seeking to leave the island. On the one hand, low-income families are likely to be the most impacted by the storm as their homes are the least likely to have survived a hurricane the size of Maria. Moreover, mountainous and hard-to-reach communities, where relief efforts have been less effective, are more likely to be reflected in the migration stream. On the other hand, the wealthy have the means to more easily uproot themselves as the island's infrastructure is being rebuilt. Professionals and the more educated likely have more opportunities to continue their careers elsewhere if prospects for employment and advancement become truncated due to the hurricane's devastation. Time will tell whether a brain drain accompanies the next stage of Puerto Rican migration. In the meantime, unsupported claims and popular beliefs will likely continue to influence the debate.

Puerto Rico's Demographic Winter

The twenty-first century has brought a new and troubling reality to the Puerto Rican migratory experience. Whereas the need to promote industrialization following creation of the Estado Libre Asociado triggered the Great Migration of the 1950s, the migration patterns in the new millennium stem largely from economic collapse and unanticipated crises. The data cannot be clearer or starker. As Table 4.2 shows, in the ten-year period between 2005 and 2015, net migration grew to 443,443—reminiscent of the Great Migration of the 1950–1960 period. No one really imagined that such population movement was on the horizon, as approximately 13 percent of the island population migrated in that time span.[16]

While the magnitude of Puerto Rican migration over the first decade of the new millennium was, in absolute terms, almost at the levels of the 1950s, its impact on overall population growth on the island has been much more significant. Recall that during the 1940s the population of Puerto Rico was growing quite rapidly, whereas during the new millennium it has slowed down considerably. In the decade prior to the Great Migration, the population of Puerto Rico grew by 21 percent, whereas in the decade prior to the New Millennium Migration it grew by only 8 percent (Table 4.1).

The impact of migration on a growing population is fundamentally different from that on a stable population. Population growth slowed on the island during the Great Migration, but during the new millennium it has resulted in actual population decline. Both the magnitude of more recent migration and its impact on overall population decline on the island differ fundamentally from the past. As one author has suggested, the recent Puerto Rican migration experience has resulted in a "demographic winter."[17] A demographic winter is the result of an aging population, due to increased life expectancy on the one hand and declining fertility rates on the other. The outcome is a declining overall population as replacement rates fail to keep pace with mortality rates over time. Japan is often cited as a country in the midst of a "demographic winter." Other countries often cited as experiencing somewhat similar demographic effects include Spain, Germany, and Italy. Unlike for Puerto Rico, out-migration has not been perceived as contributing to the demographic winters of these more established economies.

Among the demographic characteristics we see playing out in Puerto Rico at present are (1) fertility rates that have stabilized below 2 births per woman, (2) an age-dependency ratio that began to increase around 2013,[18] (3) a birth rate that has fallen below 10 per 1,000, (4) an increasing death rate, and (5) life expectancy that has increased to seventy-nine years. The underlying forces that were the foundation of today's demographic changes were playing out thirty years earlier. Rivera-Batiz and Santiago (1996) noted, "The overall aging of the Puerto Rican population has been influenced by declining birth rates and by the net migration of Puerto Ricans to the mainland United States. Between 1980 and 1990, the proportion of children in the population fell by more than 5 percent. Migration has also left the island with an older population because out-migrants from Puerto Rico are generally younger than the average" (28).

The one element that differs from the experience of forty years ago is the sheer magnitude of net migration that we see in the new millennium. It has clearly exacerbated current demographic trends. One can only conclude that any migratory effects of Hurricane Maria will accelerate this process, leading to a more pronounced "demographic winter" than anticipated.

The long-term consequences of this demographic collapse are only now becoming evident. In effect, if a population is unable to replace itself, it faces a loss of human resource potential that limits its ability to grow economically and on other dimensions in the long term. Macarrón Larumbe (2014, 216–217) cites five potential effects of demographic decay, including substantial damage to the economy, a distortion of democracy, affective impoverishment, increasing marginalization of the elderly, and abandonment of the aging poor.

Recent migration is predominantly responsible for the island's "demographic winter" and represents a new and disturbing challenge to enhancing standards of living for residents. The impact of the recent hurricane can only reinforce this negative trend, although one can only speculate about what the age distribution will be for the outgoing population. Will the young continue to be overrepresented in the migration stream, or will the loss of basic services (including health services) lead to an outflow where the elderly are overrepresented? While we can certainly say that the impact of the storm will result in greater out-migration, the exact composition of the departing population is difficult to determine at this time.

Place-to-place migration is, in its most basic terms, determined by a combination of push-and-pull factors at the place of origin and the place of settlement. As argued in other work, however, this model of migration is quite simplistic in the Puerto Rican context, where people continuously flow back and forth between the island and the continental United States. Nonetheless, it does provide a good starting point in discussing the Puerto

Rican reality at the turn of the current century. The basic premise is that economic and social conditions on the island prompted individuals and families to seek opportunities elsewhere.

While the underlying origins of the massive Puerto Rican exodus during the first decade of this century contrast with those of the Great Migration of the 1950s, there are some similarities that go beyond the commonality of their sheer magnitude. The first is that Puerto Ricans do not leave the island for a random set of locations. As the previous chapter demonstrated, Puerto Ricans move to communities where other Puerto Ricans already reside. As the stateside Puerto Rican population has grown, more and more acceptable locations have been identified. Second, we will likely see some level of return migration once the current economic crisis in Puerto Rico abates, however long that takes.

Conceptualizing Puerto Rican Migration

In many respects, migration was at the heart of Puerto Rico's industrialization effort at the end of World War II (see Edgardo Meléndez 2017). It proved to be the catalyst that enabled the island to rapidly grow its per capita income, due to the impact it had on reducing island population growth. But today migration plays the role of safety valve in a different way.

In addition, one must underscore the fact that government policies also affect the magnitude and direction of migration. Examples abound of the impact of official government policies that inhibit migration and those that stimulate migration to one region or another. Puerto Rico's historical experience is a clear case in point. Both the federal government and the Puerto Rican government have introduced policies to promote or forestall migration. The Great Migration of the 1950s, the return migration of the 1970s, and the New Millenium Migration are perfect examples of the use of government policies that fundamentally impact an individual's likelihood to migrate.

Is there a way to adequately characterize the Puerto Rican migratory process and its variations over time? Are its salient features those of place-to-place migration, as experienced by the waves of European immigrants who came to the United States at the beginning of the twentieth century? Or is it more reminiscent of a return-migration process, as identified during the first decade after the Great Migration began? Perhaps it is neither and best described by the circular, or commuter, phenomenon that seems to prevail today, as Puerto Rican migrants continue to move with ease between the United States and the island.

Will researchers need to reconceptualize Puerto Rican migration in light of long-term economic decline on the island resulting from indebtedness and collapse of basic infrastructure? How will the composition of the migration stream change in response to short- and medium-term developments as the island rebuilds? How are the repercussions of long-term climate change going to impact the stability of the island population? These and other questions will likely occupy academics and researchers for years to come.

The one constant that has characterized the Puerto Rican migratory experience in the postwar period has been the continual ties to the island and the fact that stateside Puerto Rican communities are fed by waves of newer migrants, albeit until recently at rates lower than in the past. Moreover, new areas of settlement seem to be arising, populated initially by migrants already residing in the United States and shortly afterward by migrants from the island. Networks of family, friends, and acquaintances play a large role in the transmission of information across localities. Although these information networks have always been present in the Puerto Rican migratory experience, they have taken on an even larger role today than in the period of the Great Migration, when the Commonwealth government was more directly involved in promoting migration to the United States. With the increased frequency of movement that characterizes commuter migration, it seems reasonable to expect that information flows have become more accurate over time. In the earlier days of large-scale migration, many more people were involved in making the trek north, and the points of destination were fewer than today. At the same time, the primary sources of information were the Commonwealth government or the Migration Division offices in New York and other major cities, as well as family and acquaintances who first undertook the move. All of that has fundamentally changed.

Today, information flows are more complex, as more and more points of destination are identified throughout the United States, involving a wide variety of communities and labor markets. The increased frequency with which migrants are moving across these communities, from areas of "older" settlement to areas of newer settlement and from the island to these Puerto Rican enclaves, is further evidence of the importance of information flows in the process of migration. No doubt, technological improvements in transportation and communication continue to fuel these interactions, leading to enhanced mobility and migration. But, existing transnational connections, the high degree of mobility between island and stateside communities, and the increase in points of destination also create a variety of "patterns of attachment to place or emotional anchoring" (Aranda 2006) that will continue to influence the commuting experiences of Puerto Ricans.

What do these new and complicated patterns of mobility mean for the transmission of cultural, social, political, and economic institutions across space and time? While one may argue that processes of assimilation into Anglo-American society and Puerto Rican cultural autonomy may conflict in very complicated ways here, the links and ties between the island and the colonial metropolis remain strong, transforming individuals and communities in the areas of both origin and destination. The result is a hybridity and fluidity that calls us to assess and reassess just what it means to be a Puerto Rican living in the United States.

Notes

1. The National Bureau of Economic Research determines the timing and length of economic activities. The Great Recession spanned nineteen months, beginning in December 2007 and officially ending in June 2009.

2. See Vélez Pizarro (2015) for a useful perspective on the Puerto Rican debt crisis that highlights the role of federal and local tax exemption on the island's economic activity over time.

3. Freeland (2016) argues that health-care costs have been a major driver of Puerto Rico's indebtedness: "Puerto Rico's current debt is fueled in large part by healthcare costs. Over 60% of Puerto Ricans are enrolled in Medicare/Medicaid, and the health care industry makes up about 20% of the island's GDP. The sheer number of Medicare users is due to the poverty rate on the island" (17).

4. See Rivera-Batiz and Santiago (1996) for further discussion of this point. Also see C. Santiago (1989, 1993) for a discussion of minimum wage parity in the 1970s and its impact on Puerto Rican migration.

5. See Vélez Pizarro (2015) for a summary of this process. He highlights the long-term nature of Puerto Rico's economic decline, the annual public-sector deficits that resulted in the emission of bonds to cover the growing debt, and the role of changes to Section 936 of the Internal Revenue Code that led to declining investment and hence economic growth on the island.

6. See Cabranes (2015), 1.

7. Cabranes (2015) argues that the most effective way for Puerto Rico to deal with its current mountain of debt is to restructure all of its debt through the US Bankruptcy Code.

8. See Federal Reserve Bank of New York (2014).

9. An early article providing estimates of the size of Puerto Rico's informal sector can be found in Santiago and Thorbecke (1988).

10. See Trigo (2016) and Emmanuelli Jiménez and Colón Colón (2016) for a critique of the establishment of the control board.

11. During the past decade, numerous strikes and demonstrations against government budget cuts and tuition increases have been organized by students attending the various campuses of the University of Puerto Rico, the largest higher education public system on the island.

12. The correct word on the sign should be the plural *Unidos*.

13. See Birson (2014).

14. Still another publication that disputes the notion that Puerto Rico is experiencing a brain drain is Abel and Deitz (2014), although the authors qualify their conclusion by noting, "This finding does not mean that brain drain has not occurred or is not a concern, but rather that people with higher human capital are not particularly vulnerable to the forces leading to migration when compared with other education groups" (6).

15. Abel and Deitz (2014) reinforce the notion that, on average, educational levels in Puerto Rico have increased because "Puerto Rico's out-migrants tend to be from younger and, in recent years, less-educated segments of the population" (5).

16. While the migration streams in the Great Migration and the New Millennium Migration are relatively similar in size, their proportional impact is different. During the decade of the Great Migration Puerto Rico experienced a 21 percent migration rate compared to a 13 percent rate for the 2005–2015 period. The difference is obviously due to the different base population sizes for the two periods.

17. See Macarrón Larumbe (2014).

18. The total dependency ratio is the sum of the number of children under the age of fifteen and the number of elderly over sixty-five divided by the working-age population.

6

A Demographic and Socioeconomic Portrait

Multiple generations of Puerto Ricans have resided in the United States over the past century. These cohorts continue to reinforce each other through successive waves of migration from the island. Given the nature of the migratory processes described in Chapters 3, 4, and 5, a certain dynamic emerges wherein Puerto Ricans residing in the United States and those living on the island are continuously transmitting and exchanging their experiences and cultural endeavors from one location to another. There also have been significant transmissions of wealth—and poverty—across generations and across communities, both on the island and in the United States.

Among those included in the Hispanic/Latino umbrella designation, Puerto Ricans remain the second-largest group in the United States, after Mexicans/Chicanos/as. The increased dispersion of Puerto Ricans across the US continent, the multiple points of destination for migrants who come directly from Puerto Rico, and the urban character of both older and emerging settlements in different localities have brought a special dimension to Puerto Rican migrant experiences. Despite the relatively free mobility of people between the island and the continent facilitated by the unique citizenship status of Puerto Ricans, there are lessons to be learned and shared about their integration into US society and its cultural milieu.

In this chapter we review the socioeconomic status of Puerto Ricans residing in the United States and how they have fared relative to other ethnic and racial groups, focusing on issues of income and poverty. The labor market characteristics of the Puerto Rican population related to socioeconomic status also get some attention. Of particular interest is the changing income and poverty profile of the Puerto Rican population relative to that of other ethnic and racial groups in US society. Our question is, has the economic progress of the 1980s, 1990s, and 2000s suggested by increases in household income filtered down to the poorest Puerto Ricans? Or to what extent has a lack of uniform economic progress led to higher poverty rates among them? As we will see, the demographic and household characteristics associated with poverty shed some light on these issues. The age structure of a population, for instance, makes a significant difference in terms of poverty levels: except for the very old, as individuals age, they generally tend to have higher income than when they were younger. As a result, if the average age of a population declines, its average income may go down. Moreover, a key variable associated with poverty is the proportion of all households headed by women without a spouse present. Economists Sheldon Danziger and Peter Gottschalk (1993) observed, "Since these [female-headed] households have much lower income than married-couple families, this demographic shift places more families in the lower tail of the distribution and is clearly poverty-increasing" (14). In addition, differences in poverty levels related to gender, educational attainment, migrant status, and marital status are considered. Finally, the chapter explores the geographic distribution of poverty rates for metropolitan statistical areas (MSAs) as well as the levels of public assistance benefits. The chapter ends by showing the consequences of poverty for the standard of living of Puerto Ricans, focusing on the characteristics of households as well as the impact of poverty on children.

The most commonly used measure of economic status is income. The determinants of income and income generation are many and often interact in significant and complex ways. However, there are different ways to look at income and how it is distributed. In some cases, the size distribution of income is used to study income inequality. In this approach, individuals are ranked by income level and then grouped, often in quintiles. Thus, the top quintile would show the total share of income going to the 20 percent of the population with the highest income, and the bottom quintile would show the total share of income going to the 20 percent of the population with the lowest income. While this is a common approach in the study of income distributions, it is not useful for comparing relative income levels across time and among various ethnic and racial groups, as we want to do here.

Therefore, we take a different approach, using a measure of household income per capita to make the necessary comparisons. Because we rely on income levels as determined by the US Bureau of the Census, we use its definition of income, which is calculated in monetary units (dollars) and counts as income the amount of money earned before personal income taxes, Social Security contributions, union dues, and other deductions are made. At the same time, it excludes noncash benefits, which may be quite substantial for certain groups. Noncash benefits include such things as health benefits, food stamps, rent-free housing, employers' contributions to retirement and medical programs, among others.

The largest component of household income is earnings, although it certainly has many other important components.[1] Wages and salaries are by far the largest source of earnings. We review some of the many factors that determine the level of earnings and income in this chapter. As mentioned before, age is one of the most important determinants of income and income growth. Since earnings reflect the degree of labor market involvement by an individual, the extent to which an individual and other family members participate in the labor force over their lifetimes is another important determinant of earnings and hence income. Clearly, both the industry and the occupation in which someone is employed will have an important effect on his or her income, and one's level of education will influence the type of job skills that a labor force participant possesses.

To arrive at the appropriate income measure for our purposes—the mean, or average, household income per capita—we take average household income and divide it by the average household size.[2] When we examine the mean household income per capita for racial and ethnic groups in the United States from 1980 to 2015 (see Table 6.1), we can see the effect of household size, which varies considerably from group to group, on income. Hispanics have had significantly larger households than non-Hispanics, and their household income increased steadily from 1980 to 2015.

Among Puerto Ricans, average household size surpasses that of non-Hispanic whites and blacks, but the thirty-five-year trend for Puerto Ricans has been toward smaller households. All other things being equal, this decline in the number of people in Puerto Rican households has led to an increase in mean household income per capita.[3]

Puerto Rican household income per capita, though lower than similar figures for the entire United States, has been increasing at a relatively rapid rate. In fact, incomes among Puerto Ricans grew at a faster rate than the national average for the decades of the 1980s, 1990s, and 2000s. In 1980, income levels among Puerto Ricans were among the lowest for any ethnic and racial group in the country, and the prospects for a positive change were pessimistic. At that time, mean household income per capita among Puerto Ricans was only slightly over 50 percent of the US average. After reviewing the socioeconomic progress of Puerto Ricans in the United States in the 1970s, the US Commission on Civil Rights (1976) came to the following conclusion:

> The Commission's overall conclusion is that mainland Puerto Ricans generally continue mired in the poverty facing first generations of all immigrant or migrant groups. Expectations were that succeeding generations of mainland Puerto Ricans would have achieved upward mobility. One generation later, the essential fact of poverty remains little changed. Indeed, the economic situation of the mainland Puerto Ricans has worsened over the last decade. (145)

Table 6.1 Mean Household Income per Capita by Groups, 1980–2015 (nominal dollars)

	1980			1990			2000		
	Mean Household Income ($)	Number in Household	Mean Household Income per Capita ($)	Mean Household Income ($)	Number in Household	Mean Household Income per Capita ($)	Mean Household Income ($)	Number in Household	Mean Household Income per Capita ($)
United States	19,684	2.75	7,163	37,035	2.63	14,082	56,651	2.59	21,865
Non-Hispanic white	20,602	2.65	7,771	39,037	2.50	15,615	60,364	2.43	24,876
Non-Hispanic black	13,936	3.08	4,530	25,319	2.88	8,797	39,618	2.73	14,534
Hispanic	16,023	3.50	4,582	29,677	3.58	8,295	43,671	3.61	12,096
Mexican	16,016	3.76	4,260	28,681	3.86	7,423	42,831	3.92	10,939
Puerto Rican	12,631	3.31	3,813	26,633	3.19	8,343	40,151	3.00	13,399
Cuban	18,956	2.98	6,357	35,470	2.81	12,638	52,254	2.75	18,995
Other Hispanic	17,330	3.14	5,511	32,178	3.33	9,656	45,158	3.44	13,144
Asian	22,853	3.26	7,004	45,174	3.35	13,485	67,055	3.09	21,667

	2010			2015		
	Mean Household Income ($)	Number in Household	Mean Household Income per Capita ($)	Mean Household Income ($)	Number in Household	Mean Household Income per Capita ($)
United States	67,800.86	2.52	26,905.10	78,369.31	2.49	31,473.62
Non-Hispanic white	73,067.12	2.35	31,092.39	85,179.93	2.34	36,401.68
Non-Hispanic black	46,315.60	2.51	18,452.43	51,477.95	2.42	21,271.88
Hispanic	52,378.85	3.36	15,588.94	59,859.04	3.22	18,589.76
Mexican	49,920.82	3.61	13,828.48	57,693.61	3.45	16,722.79
Puerto Rican	50,732.18	2.79	18,183.58	57,737.20	2.71	21,305.24
Cuban	58,496.04	2.62	22,326.73	67,120.48	2.56	26,218.94
Other Hispanic	58,678.59	3.03	19,365.87	65,295.24	2.93	22,285.06
Asian	88,519.35	2.96	29,905.19	104,474.40	2.92	35,778.90

Sources: Integrated Public Use Microdata Series (IPUMS 5% sample files) 1980 and 1990; Census 2000, Public Use Microdata Sample (PUMS), 5% files; IPUMS USA 2010, 2015.

Note: IPUMS 1970 file does not have total household income information.

By 1990 the mean income of Puerto Ricans was 59 percent of the US average, and in 2000, it reached 61 percent of US mean per capita household income. By 2015 the ratio had increased to 68 percent. This upward trend in income among Puerto Ricans provides some evidence of a slowly emerging middle class. It also demonstrates that the dire appraisal of their socioeconomic progress in the mid-1970s was not entirely justified (Rivera-Batiz and Santiago 1994).

One important factor to keep in mind is that ethnic and racial groups in the US population vary considerably by age, which has an important effect on the household income of the group. For example, younger households generally have more children who do not earn an income, whereas older households are more likely to have multiple earners. The Puerto Rican population remains a relatively young one compared to the larger US population, although it has been aging. In part, this aging is due to the large number of people having grown up in the continental United States. Despite the resurgence of migration from Puerto Rico and the fact that migrants are generally younger than the nonmigrant population, there is little evidence that the aging of the stateside Puerto Rican population has slowed.

While 58 percent of the Puerto Rican population was under the age of thirty-four in 2015, only 46 percent of the total US population was under thirty-four (see Table 6.2). However, Puerto Ricans are, on average, slightly older than other Latino groups in the United States, with the exception of the Cuban population. Migrant populations are by and large younger than the nonmigrant native population. The stateside Puerto Rican population has continued to age, and other Hispanic groups represented in the more recent waves of immigration have been augmenting their numbers with younger members.

Age is reflected in other ways in household income per capita. We know that age is related to the timing of both entry into and exit from the labor market and that earnings change over the life cycle. Potential workers look for their first job at an early age or after they have completed some degree of schooling, and they retire at an age when their skills are generally on the decline. Figure 6.1 depicts this relationship between earnings and age. The curvilinear pattern of the age-earnings profile captures these life-cycle effects.

It is particularly noteworthy that the age-earnings profile reflects significant differences by gender. Over their lifetimes, Puerto Rican men residing in the United States earn substantially less than other men. This age-earnings gap is much larger than the one between Puerto Rican women and other US women. Nonetheless, for both the total US and Puerto Rican populations, men earn more than women over their lives. Note that the gender gap among Puerto Ricans is smaller than the gap within the total US population because Puerto Rican men earn so much less than other US men. A number of factors discussed below can also account for these differences. However, they do reflect some unknown level of discrimination in terms of gender, race, and ethnicity.[4]

Table 6.2 Age Structure of the US Population and by Groups, 1970–2015 (percentages of age group in the population group)

Age Group	Total US Pop.	Non-Hispanic White	Non-Hispanic Black	Hispanic	Mexican	Puerto Rican	Cuban	Other Hispanic Subgroups	Asian
1970									
0–34	58.2	56.4	66.0	70.6	72.5	68.8	55.3	67.9	52.2
35–64	31.9	32.8	26.9	24.8	23.3	21.4	38.6	26.4	32.1
Over 64	10.0	10.7	7.2	4.6	4.3	2.7	6.2	6.2	6.7
1980									
0–34	57.8	55.2	66.4	71.6	74.8	73.7	57.2	67.7	64.5
35–64	30.9	32.3	25.8	23.8	21.3	23.2	41.1	26.7	29.7
Over 64	11.3	12.5	7.8	4.6	3.9	3.0	11.7	5.6	6.0
1990									
0–34	53.4	49.9	61.6	68.7	72.2	67.8	44.6	64.8	60.0
35–64	34.0	35.7	29.7	26.4	23.2	27.8	39.5	29.8	33.8
Over 64	12.7	14.5	8.7	5.0	3.0	4.4	15.9	5.4	6.3
2000									
0–34	49.3	44.6	57.5	66.4	70.1	62.4	39.5	63.4	56.2
35–64	38.3	40.6	34.5	28.8	26.0	31.5	41.8	31.7	36.7
Over 64	12.4	14.9	8.0	4.8	3.8	5.6	18.8	4.9	7.1
2010									
0–34	47.16	41.1	52.78	62.67	65.72	60.84	42.09	57.06	48.82
35–64	39.76	42.49	38.25	31.79	29.79	32.55	41.21	36.06	41.6
Over 64	13.08	16.41	8.96	5.54	4.5	6.62	16.7	6.88	9.58
2015									
0–34	46.27	40.32	51.28	59.64	62.49	57.93	42.73	54.74	46.91
35–64	38.89	40.9	38.15	33.73	32.02	34.08	40.61	37.01	41.45
Over 64	14.85	18.78	10.57	6.63	5.49	8.0	16.67	8.24	11.64

Sources: Integrated Public Use Microdata Series (IPUMS 5% sample files) 1970, 1980, and 1990; Census 2000, Public Use Microdata Sample (PUMS) 5% files; IPUMS USA 2010, 2015.

Since earnings, the major component of income, are determined by whether an individual is employed or not, differences in labor force participation across ethnic and racial groups will clearly influence the relative level of income. The higher the level of labor force participation, the greater the likelihood that an individual will either have a job or secure employment over a particular period. The labor force participation rate captures the fraction of the total working-age population that is either currently employed or searching for work. If an individual decides not to continue looking for work and drops out of the labor force, the labor force participation rate will fall; this is known as the "discouraged-worker" effect.

The labor force participation rate among Puerto Ricans has, over a long period, remained below that of the total US population by approximately five to six percentage points, but it has also trended upward from 1970 to

Figure 6.1   Age-Earnings Profile for the US Population and the US Puerto Rican Population by Gender, 2015

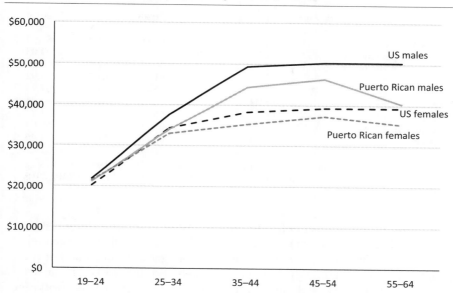

2015 (see Table 6.3). By 2015 the labor force participation rate among stateside Puerto Ricans had effectively reached the level of the non-Hispanic white population. Participation rates among Puerto Ricans have historically been among the lowest in the United States. But the aging of the Cuban population has led to significant declines in that group's labor force participation rate, so that since 2000, Cubans' labor force participation rate has been very similar to that of Puerto Ricans.

While the gap in labor force participation among Puerto Ricans and the total population has narrowed, unemployment among Puerto Ricans has tended historically to be high. Since 1980, unemployment among Puerto Ricans has stayed at nearly double-digit levels, peaking during the Great Recession of 2008 and closely paralleling unemployment rates among the African American population (see Table 6.4).[5] In 2010, as the effects of the Great Recession were still being felt in the labor force, the non-Hispanic black population experienced an 18 percent unemployment rate, while Puerto Ricans had a 16 percent unemployment rate. By 2015 the economic recovery was well underway, but the non-Hispanic white unemployment rate was still approximately half that of African Americans and Puerto Ricans.[6]

Table 6.3   **Labor Force Participation by Groups, 1970–2015 (percentages)**

	1970	1980	1990	2000	2010	2015
Total population	58.24	61.9	65.13	63.99	64.24	62.97
Non-Hispanic white	58.32	62.08	65.26	64.99	63.8	62.05
Non-Hispanic black	57.53	59.33	62.42	60.69	62.04	62.02
Hispanic	57.99	63.26	67.25	61.33	67.6	66.92
Mexican	56.36	64.45	68.08	62.17	67.61	67.19
Puerto Rican	53.5	54.58	60.27	58.62	61.82	61.91
Cuban	66.16	66	65.02	56.02	62	61.7
Other Hispanic	60.88	64.53	69.29	61.39	69.76	68.04
Asian	63.23	66.54	67.2	63.67	65.96	64.46

Sources: Integrated Public Use Microdata Series (IPUMS 5% sample files) 1970, 1980, and 1990; Census 2000, Public Use Microdata Sample (PUMS) 5% Files; IPUMS USA 2010, 2015.

High unemployment often reflects an inability to successfully match a worker's skills with a particular job or task, or a mismatch between jobs and skills. This may be due to the lack of more general (schooling) or specific (on-the-job training) know-how on the part of the worker. It can also mean that an inordinately long time passes before a person finds work. In some cases, a downturn in economic activity over the business cycle will result in layoffs of the more recently hired workers, known as the "last hired, first fired" phenomenon.

No matter what causes might exist for high unemployment, Puerto Rican workers in the United States experience unemployment at disproportionately high rates. As discussed below, the late arrival of the largest group of Puerto Ricans in the Northeast at a time when the manufacturing sector was in decline, together with their concentration in New York City when the city faced its most severe fiscal crisis, explains much of the hardship Puerto Ricans have faced in the US labor market.

During the 1950s Great Migration period, most migrants had relatively low skills for the US economy, and they often entered the low-paid service sector or the labor-intensive manufacturing sector, such as the apparel industry. Many of the migrants came from rural backgrounds, which made it difficult for them to find manufacturing employment upon their arrival.

In 1970, Puerto Ricans were disproportionately represented in the manufacturing sector, since 42 percent were employed in manufacturing compared to 25 percent for the population at large. They were underrepresented in the professional and related services sector, construction, and retail trade. By 1980, the manufacturing sector was in decline, particularly in the Northeast, affecting Puerto Ricans in particular: their employment in manufacturing declined approximately ten percentage points, while the national

Table 6.4   Unemployment Rate by Groups, 1970–2015 (percentages)

	1970	1980	1990	2000	2010	2015
Total population	4.31	6.39	6.2	5.73	10.82	6.31
Non-Hispanic white	3.93	5.6	4.91	4.36	9.11	5.05
Non-Hispanic black	6.84	11.44	12.51	11.32	17.93	11.35
Hispanic	6.22	8.75	10.31	9.27	12.89	7.29
Mexican	6.97	8.96	10.54	9.21	12.77	7.22
Puerto Rican	7.07	11.19	12.22	10.62	16.03	9.25
Cuban	5.74	5.74	6.92	7.14	14.06	6.53
Other Hispanic	4.87	7.94	9.7	9.27	11.93	7.06
Asian	3.5	4.68	5.3	5.4	8.57	5.22

Sources: Integrated Public Use Microdata Series (IPUMS 5% sample files) 1970, 1980, and 1990; Census 2000, Public Use Microdata Sample (PUMS) 5% Files; IPUMS USA 2010, 2015.

decline was only about 3 percent. This trend continued throughout the 1990s, when manufacturing employment among Puerto Ricans reached the national average of approximately 15 percent of the labor force. Thus, between 1970 and 2000, employment of Puerto Ricans in manufacturing declined by 27 percent, whereas the national decline over that same period was only nine points. Since 2000, the percentage of Puerto Ricans in the US manufacturing industry has fallen below that of the general population.

The Great Recession of 2007–2009 hit Puerto Ricans particularly hard and accelerated some underlying trends in industrial and occupational changes in the labor force. The trend toward the decline in Puerto Rican participation in US manufacturing continued unabated, and the increase in retail trade and services was also reinforced in the early part of the new millennium. We anticipate that these trends will likely continue with structural changes resulting from automation and advanced technological change.

There is no doubt that Puerto Ricans, more than any other group in the United States, suffered disproportionately from the deindustrialization of this country. Just as remarkably, Puerto Ricans increased their presence substantially in the personal, entertainment, and recreational services sector as well as the professional and related services sector. Although some Puerto Ricans left jobless in the manufacturing sector did eventually move to the lower-wage service sector, one can hardly make the case that they moved to professional services. These patterns do suggest a bifurcated labor market process where the loss of manufacturing employment among Puerto Ricans kept their unemployment rates high, at the same time that some degree of upward professional mobility was taking place among other, presumably younger Puerto Ricans.

To verify these patterns, it is useful to examine the occupational distribution of the US population from 1970 to 2015. Once again, a disproportionate number of Puerto Ricans (42.7 percent) served as operators, fabricators, and laborers in 1970. This percentage matches up with the 42 percent of the Puerto Rican labor force in manufacturing at the time. Puerto Ricans were disproportionately underrepresented in the managerial, professional, technical sales, and administrative support occupations in 1970. By 2015 the occupational distribution profile had dramatically changed, mirroring the changes in the industrial distribution of the Puerto Rican labor force.

Again, the decline in manufacturing occupations (operators, fabricators, and laborers) gave way to significant growth in the service occupations, where Puerto Ricans were overrepresented in 2015 compared to the larger US population. But one should note that the representation of Puerto Ricans in technical, sales, and administrative-support occupations surpassed that of the rest of the population. Moreover, although they continued to be underrepresented in managerial and professional occupations, 23 percent of Puerto Ricans were in these jobs, compared to just 5 percent forty-five years earlier. Thus, the Puerto Rican labor force has exhibited dramatic changes in occupational structure compared to other groups in US society.

Rising educational attainment among Puerto Ricans and their increased presence in managerial, professional, technical, sales, and administrative support positions are the main reasons for the improvements noted in terms of household income over the last thirty years. In 1970 over three-quarters of the Puerto Rican population did not have a high school education, and only 2 percent had a college degree. The rates of educational attainment were significantly higher for the total US population in 1970 (see Table 6.5). There is no doubt that twenty years after large-scale migration from Puerto Rico began in 1950, Puerto Ricans remained among the least educated of all groups in US society.

However, by 2000 the educational landscape for Puerto Ricans had improved dramatically: 63 percent had a high school diploma or higher, over 12 percent had completed a college degree, and almost a quarter had some college education. Although Puerto Ricans continue to have levels of educational attainment below those of the general US population, they no longer constitute the least-educated group, and the gains have been real. The improvements in educational attainment among stateside Puerto Ricans are consistent with the general improvement in educational attainment across the country since the 1970s.

One can argue that Puerto Ricans are now a greater part of the educational landscape and that the initial stages, in which a gloomy socioeconomic status largely dominated the profile of the migrant population, have ended. This is not to suggest that Puerto Rican educational attainment has no challenges: high school dropout rates remain relatively high; thus access to higher education is still limited. It has yet to be determined how rapidly the gap between Puerto Rican educational attainment and that of the broader US society will disappear. At present, approximately 50 percent of

**Table 6.5   Educational Attainment by Groups, 1970–2015
(percentage of group)**

	1970			
	Less Than High School	High School	Some College	College or More
United States	47.9	31.01	10.43	10.66
Non-Hispanic white	44.84	32.54	11.11	11.5
Non-Hispanic black	68.94	20.88	5.7	4.48
Hispanic	68.03	21.29	6.2	4.48
Mexican	76.23	16.69	4.78	2.31
Puerto Rican	76.28	18.21	3.35	2.16
Cuban	55.3	23.17	10.28	11.26
Other Hispanic	55.35	29.05	8.58	7.01
Asian	37.5	30.02	11.71	20.78
	1980			
United States	33.53	34.58	15.67	16.23
Non-Hispanic white	30.47	36.03	16.1	17.41
Non-Hispanic black	48.77	29.3	13.58	8.35
Hispanic	55.95	24.44	11.95	7.67
Mexican	62.34	22.35	10.41	4.9
Puerto Rican	59.82	24.49	10.12	5.57
Cuban	44.53	25.33	13.83	16.32
Other Hispanic	42.61	29.01	15.97	12.41
Asian	25.18	24.64	17.21	32.97
	1990			
United States	21.96	31.18	25.79	21.06
Non-Hispanic white	18.48	32.44	26.4	22.68
Non-Hispanic black	32.64	29.9	25.27	12.18
Hispanic	47.23	22.85	20.27	9.65
Mexican	53.37	21.69	18.36	6.57
Puerto Rican	43.69	25.52	20.74	10.04
Cuban	38.66	20.85	22.67	17.82
Other Hispanic	36.78	24.83	23.9	14.49
Asian	19.23	19.61	23.16	38
	2000			
United States	19.52	28.6	27.41	24.47
Non-Hispanic white	14.5	29.96	28.58	26.96
Non-Hispanic black	27.12	29.63	28.62	14.63
Hispanic	47.6	22.05	19.89	10.46
Mexican	54.19	20.8	17.53	7.48
Puerto Rican	36.81	25.97	24.69	12.53
Cuban	36.66	20.17	21.9	21.27
Other Hispanic	40.65	23.41	22.4	13.54
Asian	19.34	16.47	21.44	42.74

continues

Table 6.5   Continued

	2010			
	Less Than High School	High School	Some College	College or More
United States	14.4	28.49	28.89	28.22
Non-Hispanic white	9.28	29.28	30	31.44
Non-Hispanic black	17.84	31.79	32.42	17.95
Hispanic	37.7	26.4	22.78	13.13
Mexican	43.36	26.15	21.06	9.42
Puerto Rican	25.49	29.8	28.4	16.31
Cuban	23.62	28.7	24.04	23.63
Other Hispanic	26.76	25.49	26.41	21.34
Asian	14.33	16.06	19.44	50.16
	2015			
United States	12.83	27.52	28.99	30.65
Non-Hispanic white	7.73	27.92	29.61	32.72
Non-Hispanic black	15.14	31.5	33.16	20.2
Hispanic	33.94	27.49	23.59	14.98
Mexican	39.1	28.01	21.99	10.9
Puerto Rican	21.35	29.09	30.76	18.81
Cuban	20.65	28.78	23.95	26.63
Other Hispanic	25.51	25.46	25.85	23.18
Asian	13.39	15.47	18.58	52.56

Source: Integrated Public Use Microdata Series (IPUMS 5% sample files) 1970, 1980, and 1990; Census 2000, Public Use Microdata Sample (PUMS) 5% Files; IPUMS USA 2010, 2015.

the Puerto Rican population has some college and beyond. This is a remarkable achievement for a group that resided at the bottom of the education pyramid for decades. The upward mobility that education has provided stateside Puerto Ricans over the last generation is a testimony to those earlier migrants who sacrificed much for their children and grandchildren and put them on the path to an improved standard of living, as other immigrant groups have done in this country over time.

Overcoming Poverty

Although this chapter suggests real socioeconomic progress among Puerto Ricans in the United States since 1980, the gains have not been uniform across the population. In this section we take up the issue of Puerto Rican poverty and review the progress made at the lower end of the income spectrum.

Puerto Rican poverty has been an issue of some interest among social scientists but, for the most part, remains understudied (see Aponte 1990;

Massey 1993; Edwin Meléndez 1993a; Meléndez and Vargas-Ramos 2014). The research questions addressed have generally entailed just how much prevailing theories of poverty explain the Puerto Rican experience. Some analyses have focused on the geographic dimension by highlighting the fact that Puerto Ricans often reside disproportionately in cities that continue to lose their manufacturing base (called the "mismatch thesis"). The concentration of Puerto Ricans in the Northeast and in rustbelt urban centers contributes further to this notion. Others highlight Oscar Lewis's (1966) "culture of poverty," although scholars of Puerto Rico and stateside Puerto Ricans have severely criticized Lewis's deterministic view of Puerto Rican poverty. Still others focus on female single-headed households and welfare benefits, and proponents of the human capital approach tend to focus on individuals' educational attainment and skills in elevating productivity and hence incomes. And finally, Puerto Ricans have been identified as part of the urban poor in discussions of the "underclass" (Lemann 1991).

The real deficiency of many of these approaches in explaining Puerto Rican poverty is that they often lack a solid factual base, and the hypotheses that emanate from them are rarely subject to rigorous empirical testing. For the most part, they may explain a component or some aspect of stateside Puerto Rican experiences, but they simply do not comprehend the totality, or the majority, of them. Thus we are left with rather limited approaches that do not capture all of the changes that have been occurring in the stateside Puerto Rican community.

The one approach, although outdated, that seems to have received significant attention from academics and the media in the Puerto Rican context is that of the urban underclass. It is virtually impossible to reconcile the various notions that have become associated with this concept. Since the seminal work of Wilson (1987), numerous articles and books have attempted to bring coherence to the theoretical debates and consistency to the empirical evidence. In some, the urban underclass refers to the coexistence of concentrated and persistent poverty (Wilson 1987; F. Levy 1977). In this view, those in the underclass differ fundamentally from the working poor because the former have little labor force "attachment." Others use the term to describe the behavior of a particular group, often identified by race, age, and/or ethnicity, whose behavior lies outside that of common social mores (Auletta 1982). These include teenage unwed mothers, alcoholics, street criminals, urban gang youth, and those involved in illicit drug activities.

There appears to be consensus among researchers studying the Latino population in the United States that the notion of an underclass does not readily apply to Latinos/as (see Moore and Pinderhughes 1993; Edwin Meléndez 1993a). This is not because persistent poverty does not exist in some Latino communities but rather because the Latino/Hispanic umbrella encompasses so many different nationalities. The designation "Latino/a" is less a description of a reality than a term incorporating the varied political aspirations of those who have come to the United States from Spanish-speaking Latin America, the Caribbean, and Spain or who have always resided in what was once Mexico's northernmost provinces. An obvious omission from the US census's official definition for the Hispanic category is other Latin American nationalities, such as Haitians and Brazilians.

In the 1970s, the US Census Bureau arrived at the designation "Hispanic" to characterize the people who increasingly refer to themselves as Latinos/as. The panethnic Hispanic or Latino/a label includes groups that differ among themselves by nationality, race, age, geographic residence, educational attainment, family headship, occupation, industry, and, ultimately, income, labor force participation, poverty status, and migration history. This diversity is but one reason why the term "urban underclass" does not readily apply to Latinos/as. The current realities of Latino communities in the United States and the sociohistorical forces that forged these communities vary greatly.

However, an influential body of literature in the United States suggests that, in contrast to other Latino groups, Puerto Ricans have failed to achieve significant economic progress. Some have argued that Puerto Ricans were at risk of becoming an "underclass." Nathan Glazer and Daniel P. Moynihan (1963) first made this suggestion early in the 1960s in *Beyond the Melting Pot*. The idea was picked up in studies that suggested that the economic situation of Puerto Ricans was deteriorating over time instead of improving. Tienda (1989) noted, "Among Hispanics, between 1970 and 1985 Puerto Ricans experienced a sharp deterioration in economic well-being while Mexicans experienced modest, and Cubans substantial, improvement in economic status" (106).

As a result, it has been argued, "Puerto Ricans are the worst-off ethnic group in the United States" (Lemann 1991). One of the most vocal proponents of this viewpoint was Linda Chávez (1991) in *Out of the Barrio*, in which she suggested, "Puerto Ricans occupy the lowest rung of the social and economic ladder among Hispanics" (140). These widespread pronouncements bring us to the following questions: What about the Puerto Rican experience in the United States is so different from that of other Latino groups and has led to the characterization of Puerto Ricans as an urban underclass? Is this an accurate or adequate description?

One must first remember that Puerto Rican migration to the United States began essentially as a process of "expulsion." As we have seen, Puerto Rican and US leaders in the postwar period defined population pressure on the island as the biggest deterrent to economic growth and development.[7] Operation Bootstrap was never equipped to create the number of jobs necessary to gainfully employ the mass of Puerto Rican workers (largely coming from agriculture) without significant reductions in the population and the labor force. This does not mean that all Puerto Ricans who left Puerto Rico would have been better off if they had stayed, but certainly those who remained benefited economically from the migration of others. Emigration kept both population growth and unemployment rates on the island "artificially" low, as over 20 percent of the active labor force left the island between 1950 and 1960.[8] As a result, per capita income in Puerto Rico increased dramatically. Puerto Rican migration remains one of the largest in modern times as a percentage of the population of origin.

The sheer magnitude of Puerto Rican migration during the 1950s is a clear indication that emigration was actively promoted. The government of Puerto Rico encouraged migration by providing information about economic opportunities, allowing US companies to recruit workers for stateside agricultural and industrial work, and promoting an infrastructure to facilitate the ability of people to move (such as low-cost airfare). In the absence of these incentives, Puerto Rican migration would not likely have resulted in so large an outflow as actually occurred. While conventional human capital–based migration models posit that the likelihood of migration is highest among the more skilled, the Puerto Rican migration stream largely consisted of agricultural and low-skilled labor during the early decades of mass migration. In this sense, the state actively promoted migration of "surplus labor" as a method to increase the standard of living on the island, and emigration became the "safety valve" that it was envisioned to be.

Despite the importance of migration in the study of Puerto Rico and the stateside Puerto Rican population, we really have little knowledge of the links between the institutional and behavioral forces involved and the economic outcomes of the migrants themselves. In fact, much of the research on Puerto Rican migration has focused exclusively on its impact on the island economy. We do know that Puerto Ricans are a very mobile group, and the diaspora has been variously referred to as commuter migration, back-and-forth migration, and circular migration—the same individual moves frequently throughout his or her lifetime between the United States and Puerto Rico. Others refer to it as the *guagua aérea*, or airbus. In this context, some studies described how, to the extent that Puerto Rican migration has been circular in nature, migration disrupted work and schooling, leading to lower earnings over the individual's life. Tienda and Díaz (1987) supported this view: "Puerto Ricans have suffered disproportionately with the decline of inner-city manufacturing in the Northeast. But what separates them from other inner-city minority groups is their circular migration between the Island and the United States, which severely disrupts families and schooling, leading inevitably to a loss of income" (A31).

Another factor that must be considered in the assessment of Puerto Rican poverty in the United States is English-language proficiency. This affects the migration experience, since the ability to use the English language is important for economic mobility in the United States. The dominant language spoken in Puerto Rico is Spanish, and even after more than a century of US presence, the island's population is far from bilingual. According to the US census in 1980, 58 percent of the island's population (over five years of age) spoke no English, and another 28 percent indicated that they only spoke it with difficulty. In 2000 the fraction of the population that did not speak any English was down to approximately 45 percent, and 21 percent spoke English with difficulty. The percentages were virtually the same in 2015 as 44 percent of the population indicated they spoke no English, while 22 percent indicated they spoke English with difficulty. Perhaps this data can help us understand, at least partially, why English is popularly referred to in Puerto Rico as "El Difícil" (the difficult one) (L. R. Sánchez 1994).

Recent immigrants do not perform as well as natives in the US labor market. There is generally a period of adjustment in which the immigrant ultimately adapts to conditions in the local labor market. Eventually, however, immigrant earnings tend to rise rapidly and often outpace those of natives. The same phenomenon is present in the context of Puerto Rican migration. However, the gap in earnings, unemployment, and poverty is quite large between recent Puerto Rican migrants and nonmigrants residing in the United States. In fact, even with higher average levels of educational attainment on the part of migrants, their labor market performance (that is, earnings, unemployment, and poverty) tends to lag behind that of Puerto Rican nonmigrants. In this case, the fundamental difference between Puerto Rican migrants and nonmigrants residing in the United States is English-language proficiency. Recent Puerto Rican migrants indicate that they are considerably less proficient in the use of English compared to US-born Puerto Ricans.[9] Thus, the institutional features of Puerto Rican migration, the expulsive character of early migration, the circularity of recent migration, and the adherence to Spanish all produce an experience and economic outcome unique to stateside Puerto Ricans, one not readily captured by conventional explanations for the existence of an "urban underclass."

Poverty rates have come to represent important indicators of the lack of economic well-being in the US population. They are cited as evidence of economic disadvantage among ethnic and racial groups in society, serve to justify a host of social programs, and are also used to determine eligibility for as many as twenty-seven federal programs. Poverty rates are computed by designating an income threshold and indicating the fraction of the population with incomes below the threshold or poverty line. Poverty thresholds are computed by size of family and number of related children under eighteen years old. A family "below the poverty level" has an income below a minimum poverty threshold representing the lowest nutritionally sufficient (according to the government) standard of living for a family in the United States. The poverty threshold is revised annually to incorporate changes in the cost of living, as measured by the Consumer Price Index.

The average poverty threshold in the United States for a family of four persons (two adults and two related children) was $13,254 in 1990 and rose to $24,036 in 2015.[10] Use of the poverty threshold has come under criticism, but the extent to which it understates or overstates actual poverty is not really known.[11] The poverty rate generally understates the level of poverty by relying on outmoded, static, and unchanged determinants of a nutritionally sufficient living standard while simultaneously overstating poverty by relying on erroneous and underestimated levels of income.

For changes in the poverty rates of various ethnic and racial groups according to the decennial US census of population, see Table 6.6. In many respects poverty rates remained relatively unchanged between 1970 and 2015, fluctuating back and forth between 12 and 13 percent. In 1970, 13.8 percent of the population lived in households with income below the poverty level, and forty-five years later that figure stood at 13 percent. This slight downward trend was replicated for all major groups in the country, but important differences exist among Latino groups.

In 1980, after New York City's economic crisis, the Puerto Rican poverty rate was among the highest in the nation at nearly 37 percent—this contrasted with a lower poverty rate of not quite 30 percent just ten years earlier. By 2000 the Puerto Rican poverty rate had declined by ten percentage points, the largest absolute decline among the major ethnic and racial groups. The downward trend has continued over time, and in 2015 it reached 22 percent. This improvement ran contrary to notions of a lack of socioeconomic progress among stateside Puerto Ricans in the second half of the twentieth century. Nevertheless, poverty rates for Puerto Ricans were still among the highest in the nation. There have also been few efforts among the academic and public policy community to document the improvement empirically and to provide suitable explanations for it. More-

Table 6.6   Non-Hispanic and Hispanic Groups Below the Poverty Level, 1970–2015 (percentage)

Group	1970	1980	1990	2000	2010	2015
Total population	13.85	12.51	13.05	12.32	13.75	13.02
Non-Hispanic white	10.28	8.93	8.97	8.24	9.38	8.98
Non-Hispanic black	35.77	29.96	29.26	24.45	24.90	22.90
Hispanic	25.33	23.61	25.13	22.65	22.92	20.72
Mexican	29.30	23.34	26.07	23.50	24.80	21.76
Puerto Rican	29.87	36.70	31.52	26.05	24.68	22.21
Cuban	13.13	12.82	14.44	14.49	16.19	15.43
Other Hispanic	18.51	18.78	21.35	20.69	17.85	17.95
Asian	11.07	12.83	13.73	12.60	9.94	9.52

Sources: US Department of Commerce, 1970, 1980, 1990, and 2000 United States Census of Population and Housing, 5% Public Use Microdata Sample (PUMS); IPUMS USA 2010, 2015.

over, in the competitive politics of poverty relief and in the struggles for
ethnic representation in the United States, as well as in the promotion of
income maintenance programs, there is often little advantage to claiming
real economic progress.

Undoubtedly, the 1970s was a decade of real disappointment for the US
Puerto Rican population. Over 58 percent of the total migrant population
lived in New York City at the beginning of the decade, and the economic
downturn at the national and local levels hit Puerto Ricans very hard. Cruz
and Santiago (2000) describe the turn of events in the following way:

> By 1980, the Puerto Rican population in the United States was viewed as
> the group for which the "American dream" was just that—a dream. All of
> the relevant socioeconomic indicators pointed to this reality. In the nation-
> al context, Puerto Ricans had among the lowest income levels, highest
> poverty rates, low labor force participation and high welfare dependency,
> significant numbers of single female-headed households, and low educa-
> tional attainment. Yet, given their high concentration in New York City
> and the calamity that befell that city from 1974 on, could things have real-
> ly been any different? (15)

New York City's fiscal crisis and the accompanying economic downturn in the larger metropolitan area proved extremely detrimental to economic progress among Puerto Ricans between 1970 and 1980. As relatively
new immigrants to New York City, Puerto Ricans were subjected to "last
hired, first fired" policies in both the public and the private sectors. They
were also disproportionately represented in the manufacturing sector at a
time when manufacturing employment was in decline. Additionally, they
were overrepresented in the laborer and service occupations when technological innovation was changing the nature of these jobs and employer
demand for them. The fact that job skills and educational attainment among
Puerto Ricans were limited compared to other groups in society meant that
they were extremely vulnerable to economic downturns. If timing is everything, the concurrence of Puerto Rican migration with economic and industrial structural change in the United States in the postwar period resulted
in an environment that was not conducive to socioeconomic advancement
among this sector of the population.

Surprisingly in this context, between 1980 and 1990 Puerto Ricans made
real economic gains. According to Rivera-Batiz and Santiago (1994),

> Puerto Ricans exhibited substantial socioeconomic progress in the 1980s. . . .
> The median household income per capita of Puerto Ricans in the United
> States increased by close to 30 percent. The result was an upgrading in the
> relative economic status of Puerto Ricans vis-à-vis other Hispanic groups. . . .
> Poverty rates declined, welfare participation dropped, labor force participa-
> tion increased—especially among women—and so did earnings and occupa-
> tional advancement. (5)

The reversal of socioeconomic prospects for Puerto Ricans between 1980 and 1990 has been attributed to a number of factors, including increased educational attainment (particularly at the associate's degree level) and dispersion to other parts of the country where the economy was more robust. Rivera-Batiz and Santiago (1994) closed their study "by expressing awe at the resiliency and adaptability to change of the Puerto Rican population" (121). Although the economic progress among Puerto Ricans in the 1980s did manage to show itself in lower poverty rates,[12] its impact was comparatively small, considering the fact that Puerto Ricans continue to have one of the highest poverty rates among all ethnic and racial groups.

In 2015, the poverty rate among Puerto Ricans still remained the highest among US Latinos/as. This occurred despite the fact that mean household income per capita of Puerto Ricans surpassed that of most other Latinos/as. One implication is that there was greater income inequality among Puerto Ricans than among other Latino groups. The larger proportion of Puerto Ricans at the bottom of the income ladder explained the higher poverty rates. It also gave evidence of the continued emergence of a Puerto Rican middle class and persistent inequality, which Rivera-Batiz and Santiago (1994) had noted ten years earlier.

What variables are associated with higher poverty rates? The extensive literature on poverty in both the general and the Latino population points to several demographic factors.[13] More recent migrants have had higher poverty rates than both older migrants and the general population partly because of the adjustment period required to find gainful employment once in the continental United States. Indeed, as immigrants increase their English-language proficiency, find more information about the local labor market, and cope with their new environment, their income rises substantially, which can be expected to reduce poverty rates (see Chiswick 1978; Borjas 1985; Rivera-Batiz 1991, 1992). This pattern is representative of the Puerto Rican experience in the United States.

In 2015 the highest poverty rates among Puerto Ricans occurred for the most recent migrants, those who migrated to the United States between 2001 and 2010 (see Table 6.7). The poverty rate of these migrants was equal to 23.3 percent, compared to a 20.9 percent poverty rate among Puerto Ricans who moved to the United States during the 1991–2000 period and an 18.1 percent poverty rate among those migrating between 1981 and 1990. The poverty rate among US-born Puerto Ricans (16.4 percent) remained lower than that of migrants. This pattern held true substantially for earlier decades as well.

Higher educational attainment is associated with lower unemployment, higher labor force participation, and, ultimately, higher earned income. Therefore, higher educational attainment should lead to a lower poverty rate. Thus, educational attainment and poverty rates are expected to be

Table 6.7   Puerto Ricans Below the Poverty Level, 1980 to 2015, by
Migrant Status, Education, Gender, Marital Status, and Age
(percentage)

	1980	1990	2000	2010	2015
Migrant status					
Born in the United States	22.44	20.4	19.45	18.84	16.44
Migrated between 2001–2010				27.01	23.27
Migrated between 1991–2000			31.3	23.81	20.89
Migrated between 1981–1990		35.39	25.88	20.53	18.1
Migrated between 1970–1980	33.46	30.98	23.83	20.46	18.51
Migrated before 1970	27.61	22.42	19.97	18.01	17.38
Educational attainment					
Less than high school	37.74	38.5	40.22	40.32	39.04
High school	19.89	20.33	21	21.64	20.4
Some college	17.06	14.12	12.95	15.23	14.65
Finished college	8.31	7.44	6.42	5.29	6.25
More than college	11.13	5.52	4.93	3.5	2.71
Gender					
Male	20.38	18.33	17.75	15.67	14.54
Female	35.52	30.44	26.26	24.11	21.71
Marital and headship status					
Never married	37.08	34.22	31.83	27.62	24.42
Married	18.1	13.11	12.1	10.27	9.43
Divorced	38.45	31.12	25.84	22.38	19.28
Separated	58.22	48.08	40.9	32.22	25.61
Widowed	45.6	40.51	39.54	27.7	32.96
Female-headed household	28.35	24.73	22.22	35.45	29.86
Age					
20–29	30.86	28.08	25.6	24.26	21.06
30–39	29.59	24.38	21.67	20.02	18.51
40–49	24.6	21.2	19.5	16.2	14.82
50–55	23.56	21	20.5	18.25	16.66
Over 55	27.24	26.48	24.94	20.8	19.87

Sources: US Department of Commerce, 1980, 1990, and 2000 United States Census of Population and Housing, 5% Public Use Microdata Sample (PUMS); IPUMS USA 2010, 2015.

inversely related. Indeed, this seemed to have been the case for stateside Puerto Ricans, as indicated in Table 6.7. But more importantly, the disparity in poverty levels was particularly acute between those who had completed a high school education and those who had not.

Individuals who had not completed high school had almost twice the poverty level of those who had, irrespective of the time period selected. The poverty rate of persons in 2015 with less than a high school diploma was 39 percent, compared to a poverty rate of 20 percent for those with a high school education, 15 percent for those with some college, 6 percent for those completing college, and 3 percent among persons with educational attainment greater than a college degree. A significant change in the Puerto Rican population during the 1980s was a notable increase in the number of people with some college education but not a completed degree. For those individuals with some college education, poverty rates declined substantially compared to those with only a high school education.

Poverty rates vary considerably by marital status. Married persons tend to have lower poverty rates, owing to the pooling of resources associated with marriage. Conversely, marital dissolution is associated with higher poverty rates. But there is some difference in poverty rates by marital status: poverty rates for those divorced are lower than for the widowed or separated. Previous research has also shown that two major trends have affected the demography of the Puerto Rican island population. Rivera-Batiz and Santiago (1996) pointed out, "The trend toward delayed marriage in Puerto Rico has been accompanied by another significant social trend: marriages on average are lasting shorter periods of time. This is reflected in a rapidly rising divorce rate" (37–38). Puerto Rico's divorce rate is the highest in Latin America and the Caribbean, rapidly approaching US levels (which are among the highest in the world). These trends have had an obvious impact on the Puerto Rican population residing in the United States.

Among stateside Puerto Ricans, those who were married in 2015 had sharply lower poverty rates than unmarried people. Among married persons in the twenty-to-fifty-five age range, the poverty rate was 9.4 percent, which contrasts with a 24.4 percent poverty rate among persons who had never married, 19.3 percent among divorced persons, 33.0 percent for widows, and 25.6 percent for the separated. The high incidence of marital dissolution among Puerto Ricans has resulted in significant numbers of female-headed households experiencing very high poverty rates. Although the 30 percent poverty rate for female-headed households (in 2015) shown in Table 6.7 is for women ages twenty to fifty-five, the rate is substantially higher when younger cohorts are included.

The declining proportion of married-couple families among Puerto Ricans represents an important factor in explaining their resilient poverty rates. In New York City, for example, the proportion of all households consisting of married-couple families declined from 58.2 percent in 1970 to 33.5 percent in 1990. By 2015, the percentage of married-couple families had stabilized around 30 percent. During this same period, the proportion of all Puerto Rican households in New York City consisting of a female householder with no husband present rose from 25.4 percent in 1970 to 34.5 percent in 1990. It reached 37 percent in 2000 (City of New York 1993). As poverty rates among stateside Puerto Ricans have declined overall more recently, we also see a stabilization of the proportion of female-headed Puerto Rican households, so that by 2015 approximately 30 percent of households in New York City were headed by women—a number unchanged from 2010.

Except for the elderly (those over sixty-five years of age), older work-ers tend to have higher incomes and lower poverty rates—this is the typical life-cycle age-earnings pattern. The highest poverty rates occur among the younger populations (Table 6.7). For those in their twenties, the poverty rate in 2015 was 21 percent, down from 31 percent for a similar age cohort in 1980. Among persons in their thirties, the poverty rate was 18.5 percent; for those in their forties, it was 14.8 percent; for persons aged fifty to fifty-five, the proportion was close to 17 percent. For those over fifty-five years of age, the poverty rate increased to approximately 20 percent, noticeably higher than for the previous cohort.

Because of structural inequities in the US labor market, women gener-ally earn less income than men and tend to have higher poverty rates. Poverty among women is especially high among households headed by one adult with no spouse present. This is particularly important because of the rising proportion of female-headed households in the United States. As sociologists William Julius Wilson and Kathryn Neckerman (1986) have noted, "The rise of female headed families has had dire social and eco-nomic consequences because these families are far more vulnerable to poverty than other types of families. Indeed, sex and marital status of the head [of household] are the most important determinants of poverty status for families, especially in urban areas" (240).

Poverty rates among Puerto Rican women in 2015 were substantially higher than among men, although the gap has been declining (see Table 6.7). Over 21 percent of Puerto Rican women aged twenty to fifty-five were below the poverty level in 2015, compared to 14.5 percent among men. This situation has been linked to the growing proportion of female-headed households among the Puerto Rican population. An interesting anomaly is that despite the growing number of female-headed households among Puerto Ricans, the percentage of female-headed households below the poverty level has not changed significantly. Whereas 28.3 percent of all Puerto Rican female-headed households found themselves in poverty in 1980, that figure was similar in 2015 at 29.9 percent. A caveat, however, is that in the midst of the Great Recession, poverty rates among Puerto Rican female-headed households spiked at 35.4 percent.

Increases in the percentage of female-headed households in the US population are evident by race and ethnicity. The proportion of female-headed households rose for all groups by about ten percentage points (from 24.3 to 34.9) between 1970 and 2000 but declined somewhat by 2010. Among Puerto Ricans the rate rose dramatically from 31.7 percent in 1970 to 47.3 percent in 2000—almost 16 percentage points and the largest increase for any group (see Table 6.8). Since then, however, the rate has declined to 40.7 percent for Puerto Ricans, mirroring the trend among the broader population.

Table 6.8   Female-Headed Households Among Non-Hispanic and
Hispanic Groups, 1970–2015 (percentage)

	1970	1980	1990	2000	2010	2015
Total population	24.3	27.74	32.5	34.87	31.16	31.11
Non-Hispanic white	21.55	25.83	30.26	32.54	28.45	28.34
Non-Hispanic black	39.69	44.35	51.98	54.17	49.96	49.59
Hispanic	29.2	26.48	30.75	32.84	30.55	30.8
Mexican	16.67	21.96	26.16	27.55	27.18	27.75
Puerto Rican	31.7	40.57	45.42	47.31	42.54	40.67
Cuban	19.93	23.05	28.56	32.54	31.39	30.92
Other Hispanic	26.52	29.3	33.96	37.07	33	32.83
Asian	14.29	21.01	23.52	27.65	22.38	22.21

Sources: US Department of Commerce, 1970, 1980, 1990, and 2000 United States Census of Population and Housing, 5% Public Use Microdata Sample (PUMS); IPUMS USA 2010, 2015.

In conjunction, the five variables discussed here encompass most of the dimensions of the poverty present within the Puerto Rican population. How is poverty distributed across Puerto Rican communities? Do benefit levels vary significantly across MSAs, generally considered extended cities? What consequences does the high rate of poverty among Puerto Ricans have for the present and future standard of living of the population? The remainder of the chapter discusses these questions.

Differences Among Communities

A crucial finding of this chapter is that geography matters. Where you reside influences your earnings and job prospects, housing, and the provision of educational services. We know that the Puerto Rican population is very mobile, both within the continental United States and between the island of Puerto Rico and the United States. Thus, unsurprisingly, poverty is also spread across communities in a nonuniform manner.

A look at poverty rates in cities with the largest concentrations of Puerto Ricans yields some conclusions (see Table 6.9). First, Puerto Rican poverty was quite high in specific urban areas of the Northeast. Of the top twenty-five metropolitan areas where Puerto Ricans reside, nine exhibited poverty rates of 30 percent or higher in 2015 and most were located in the Northeast. For example, poverty rates in Providence, Rhode Island, and Springfield, Massachusetts, were 45.6 percent and 42.1 percent, respectively, among Puerto Ricans. Second, Puerto Rican poverty was very low in other areas, such as the extended Washington, DC, area or Long Island, New York. From a public policy perspective, the varying concentration of poverty in these communities means that interventions might be more effective when applied within specific geographic areas. In

Table 6.9   **Puerto Rican Poverty Rates in Cities with Largest
Concentrations of Puerto Ricans**

	1980	1990	2000	2010
New York, NY PMSA	41.81	37.26	35.71	33.7
Philadelphia, PA–NJ PMSA	44.96	44.62	39.39	33
Chicago, IL PMSA	33.05	31.16	21.83	18.6
Orlando, FL MSA	18.82	15.43	15.25	20.3
Newark, NJ PMSA	38.84	31.93	26.69	23.7
Miami, FL PMSA	25.97	23.48	21.13	20.9
Nassau–Suffolk, NY PMSA	15.66	10.24	11.55	11.8
Tampa–St. Petersburg–Clearwater, FL MSA	20.37	20.37	18.77	26.3
Hartford, CT MSA	56.79	47.09	33.98	33
Springfield, MA MSA	60.28	56.11	45.41	42.1
Bergen–Passaic, NJ PMSA	—	22.18	17.91	18.3
Boston, MA–NH PMSA	53.33	40.19	32.3	33.3
Jersey City, NJ PMSA	39.16	29.84	26.39	25.4
Fort Lauderdale, FL PMSA	10.07	12.07	13.29	11.9
Cleveland–Lorain–Elyria, OH PMSA	31.45	40.63	29	44.9
Middlesex–Somerset–Hunterdon, NJ PMSA	—	13.87	12.23	13.3
Los Angeles–Long Beach, CA PMSA	19.58	18.77	20.47	14.8
Bridgeport, CT PMSA	38.15	34.79	23.09	25.4
Allentown–Bethlehem–Easton, PA MSA	48.5	40.66	35.61	41.3
Rochester, NY MSA	35.05	42.46	39.64	32.1
Washington, DC–MD–VA–WV PMSA	10.19	6.08	7.53	10.1
New Haven–Meriden, CT PMSA	49.9	38.92	36.87	32.3
Providence–Fall River–Warwick, RI–MA MSA	50.65	49.22	51.24	45.6
Monmouth–Ocean, NJ PMSA	—	16.72	14.44	18.6
West Palm Beach–Boca Raton, FL MSA	22.9	25.57	17.09	17.9

Sources: US Department of Commerce, 1980, 1990, and 2000 United States Census of Population and Housing, 5% Public Use Microdata Sample (PUMS); IPUMS USA 2010.

addition, one-third of these areas—such as Hartford, Connecticut; Springfield, Massachusetts; and Chicago, Illinois—saw very large drops in poverty. Many cities that had large concentrations of Puerto Ricans and high rates of poverty in 1980 saw significant declines in their poverty rates just twenty years later, and these trends continue to the present.

The public assistance beneficiary rate is the proportion of the population receiving some public assistance income. For Puerto Ricans there has been considerable correspondence between poverty rates and beneficiary rates in primary metropolitan statistical areas (PMSAs) and MSAs. Metropolitan areas with high poverty rates (Table 6.9) also had high beneficiary rates (see Table 6.10). The correlation coefficient between poverty and beneficiary rates in metropolitan areas has remained quite high over the past thirty years.[14] Nevertheless, on average, beneficiary rates were significantly less than poverty rates. In other words, a substantial portion of the Puerto Rican population with incomes below the poverty line did not receive income from public assistance. Given beneficiary levels significantly lower than poverty rates, relative mean public assistance income was not likely a major determinant of Puerto Rican mobility.

Poverty relates directly to a family's inability to sustain minimum nutritional standards. However, it is also associated with a failure to sustain other basic needs, such as housing, health, and children's welfare. This failure, in turn, negatively affects the ability of current and future generations to lead productive lives, perpetuating a vicious cycle of poverty.

The comparatively high poverty rates among the Puerto Rican population also potentially affect the economic welfare of children. In 2015, over 40 percent of all school-age Puerto Rican children resided in households living below the poverty level (see Table 6.11), a 9 percent drop from 1990. Although progress has been slow, it is important to note that in 1980 almost 55 percent of Puerto Rican school-age children resided in households below the poverty threshold.

The decline in the poverty rate of school-age children for the Puerto Rican population replicated the trend among the general population. For the United States overall, the proportion of school-age children living in poor households fell from 39 percent in 1980 to 34 percent in 2015. Still, of all population groups considered in Table 6.11, Puerto Ricans ranked second in percentage of children living in poor households, with only Mexicans having higher rates.

The issue of adequate housing and home ownership is very important in discussions of poverty. As of 2015, Puerto Ricans had the lowest rate of home ownership in the United States compared to other groups (see Table 6.12). Only slightly more than 40 percent of US Puerto Ricans own the house they live in, far less than the 64 percent home ownership in the total population. The more recent housing and financial crisis in the new millennium erected further barriers to Puerto Rican home ownership.

A major element driving the lower home-ownership rates among Puerto Ricans is the dearth of single-family housing in New York City, where the largest percentage of Puerto Ricans reside. Home ownership is 18 percent among Puerto Ricans residing in the New York City MSA and 37 percent among the total population. But home ownership among all Hispanics in New York City is extremely low. In addition, there is some evidence that the number of persons who reside in a Puerto Rican household is

Table 6.10   Distribution of Public Assistance Benefits Among Puerto Ricans in Cities with Largest Puerto Rican Populations

	1980		1990		2000		2010	
	Total PR Population Receiving Benefits (%)	Mean Public Assistance Income Among PR ($)	Total PR Population Receiving Benefits (%)	Mean Public Assistance Income Among PR ($)	Total PR Population Receiving Benefits (%)	Mean Public Assistance Income Among PR ($)	Total PR Population Receiving Benefits (%)	Mean Public Assistance Income Among PR ($)
New York, NY PMSA	14.7	3,051.39	14.06	3,961.75	7.13	3,527.87	8.33	3,250.65
Philadelphia, PA–NJ PMSA	13.15	3,234.67	12.87	3,750.98	6.16	3,120.12	10.48	3,303.92
Chicago, IL PMSA	8.83	2,961.87	9.86	3,423.39	3.08	2,450.68	3.39	3,353.4
Orlando, FL MSA	1.14	2251	2.95	3,341.93	1.91	1,720.83	1.82	7,186.33
Newark, NJ PMSA	10.28	3,307.98	8.54	4,212.05	4.08	3,271.77	5.07	2,290.97
Miami, FL PMSA	4.82	2,415.49	4.34	3,331.1	3.61	2,511.47	1.34	2,209.45
Nassau–Suffolk, NY PMSA	4.34	3,605.71	3.39	5,474.95	1.15	3,789.49	6.79	5,656.25
Tampa–St. Petersburg–Clearwater, FL MSA	1.98	1,791.36	3.35	3,066.6	2.61	1,894.62	2.47	2,320.16
Hartford, CT MSA	13.68	3,461.06	14.62	4,664.09	7.96	3,463.58	12.41	5,007.89
Springfield, MA MSA	15.87	3,401.6	18.59	5,777.3	7.9	4,236.27	10.11	4,386.77
Bergen–Passaic, NJ PMSA	—	—	4.72	3,919.99	3.11	3,088.83	4.63	4,215.4
Boston, MA–NH PMSA	14.08	3,569.11	13.61	4,787.45	3.87	3,611.14	12.36	2,984.26
Jersey City, NJ PMSA	9.62	2,858.73	9.42	3,927.55	3.74	3,067.9	8.94	5,067.1
Fort Lauderdale, FL PMSA	2.55	2,520	2.35	,3242.14	1.37	2,234.04	0.94	5,166.14
Cleveland–Lorain–Elyria, OH PMSA	10.12	2,373.46	13.08	3,350.66	4.6	2,077.81	5.06	3,379.48
Middlesex–Somerset–Hunterdon, NJ PMSA	—	—	3.72	3,056.95	1.89	2,161.29	5.74	3,356.99

Continues

Table 6.10 Continued

	1980		1990		2000		2010	
	Total PR Population Receiving Benefits (%)	Mean Public Assistance Income Among PR ($)	Total PR Population Receiving Benefits (%)	Mean Public Assistance Income Among PR ($)	Total PR Population Receiving Benefits (%)	Mean Public Assistance Income Among PR ($)	Total PR Population Receiving Benefits (%)	Mean Public Assistance Income Among PR ($)
Los Angeles–Long Beach, CA PMSA	8.05	2,897.67	8	5,493.57	3.28	3,628.33	10.59	4,423.08
Bridgeport, CT PMSA	11.8	3,464.14	10.1	4,604.95	4.62	4,215.95	6.36	4,240.97
Allentown–Bethlehem–Easton, PA MSA	12.92	2,846.38	10.46	4,116.08	4.83	4,033.74	9.8	2,853.86
Rochester, NY MSA	8.23	3,086.74	13.02	4,393.01	8.4	3,515.76	11.19	3,062.8
Washington, DC–MD–VA–WV PMSA	1.09	2,440	1.39	3,840.47	0.66	2,807.09	1.03	2,485.82
New Haven–Meriden, CT PMSA	11.75	3,897.28	12.26	5,457.21	6.48	3,273.06	7.5	5,413.83
Providence–Fall River–Warwick, RI–MA MSA	12.66	2,819.5	11.23	5,604.63	9.37	4,285.67	11.49	2,539.89
Monmouth–Ocean, NJ PMSA	—	—	5.77	2,970.55	2.22	4,294.96	0.6	1,900
West Palm Beach–Boca Raton, FL MSA	1.31	605	3.37	3,113.39	1.38	3,077.4	2.39	4,192.39

Sources: US Department of Commerce, 1980, 1990, and 2000 United States Census of Population and Housing, 5% Public Use Microdata Sample (PUMS); IPUMS USA 2010.

Table 6.11   **Children Living in Poor Households Among Non-Hispanic and Hispanic Groups, 1980–2015 (percentage)**

	1980	1990	2000	2010	2015
Total population	39.17	37.62	36.45	36.2	33.94
Non-Hispanic white	32.17	30.36	28.61	26.98	24.53
Non-Hispanic black	47.53	45.26	44.64	41.92	38.44
Hispanic	50.94	46.95	44.94	46.74	44.6
Mexican	52.59	49.15	46.88	49.86	47.95
Puerto Rican	54.84	49.05	44.48	45.54	41.4
Cuban	25.4	23.63	20.99	24.16	25.24
Other Hispanic	44.63	40.84	42.47	38.48	36.98
Asian	38.99	36	31.1	25.34	22.83

Sources: US Department of Commerce, 1980, 1990, and 2000 United States Census of Population and Housing, 5% Public Use Microdata Sample (PUMS); IPUMS USA 2010, 2015.

quite high compared to the population at large (Rivera-Batiz and Santiago 1994, 52). Although home ownership has been rising among Puerto Ricans, it remains quite low.

In evaluating the socioeconomic progress of the stateside Puerto Rican population over the second half of the twentieth century, one would probably reach a mixed conclusion. On the one hand, the Puerto Rican population has without a doubt faced, and continues to face, significant economic hardship, obstacles, and challenges. The fact that Puerto Ricans came to the United States in ever-increasing numbers just as the US economy was in the early stages of transforming from an industrial one based on manufacturing to one dominated by high-skill and high-paying jobs in the technology sector certainly impeded their full economic integration into US society. The extent of Puerto Rican poverty and its many dimensions—female-headed households, job insecurity, geographic and urban concentration, circular migration, youth in their formative years, and inadequate housing—have all posed serious obstacles to those with the task of alleviating poverty in these communities.

On the other hand, real progress has been made. Household income has increased, poverty rates continue to decline, educational attainment has risen, and a middle class has slowly emerged. Academics and policymakers need to come to grips with these realities. To some it may seem new, but they have been emerging since the 1980s. As long as opportunities are available to augment education and labor market skills, relocation to regions and parts of the country where jobs are available is possible, and these skills and training are appropriately compensated, the stateside Puerto Rican population will continue to make noticeable economic gains. The economic hardship of the 1970s should never be repeated, since Puerto Ricans took the brunt of New York City's fiscal crisis.[15] The Great Reces-

Table 6.12   Rate of Ownership of Living Quarters Among Non-Hispanic
and Hispanic Groups, 1980–2015 (for US and NYC)

	1980	1990	2000	2010	2015
United States					
Total population	65	64.22	66.09	73.1	63.14
Non-Hispanic white	69	69.05	72.07	75.82	74
Non-Hispanic black	45.37	43.77	45.95	47.13	43.56
Hispanic	44.16	42.25	45.68	50.31	48.12
Mexican	49.82	46.92	48.44	51.64	49.79
Puerto Rican	21.1	25.85	34.36	43.19	40.71
Cuban	44.32	50.93	57.63	61.79	57.15
Other Hispanic	45.4	37.99	42.86	47.6	45.22
Asian	52.01	52.63	52.59	64.67	63.6
New York City					
Total population	31.55	32.89	34.73	36.65	
Non-Hispanic white	39.54	43.6	46.59	49.51	
Non-Hispanic black	19.64	21.87	26.34	28.56	
Hispanic	11.89	12.41	14.93	17.04	
Mexican	16.55	9.05	8.41	10.25	
Puerto Rican	9.19	11.32	15.26	18.33	
Cuban	19.93	21.58	25.84	34.32	
Other Hispanic	15.05	12.87	14.78	16.77	
Asian	25.81	32.62	35.65	42.27	

Sources: US Department of Commerce, 1980, 1990, and 2000 United States Census of Population and Housing, 5% Public Use Microdata Sample (PUMS); IPUMS USA 2010, 2015. Note: No data available for 2015 New York City.

sion of 2007 to 2009 likewise impacted Puerto Ricans disproportionately. Recovery has been slow but sustained.

The consequences of continually high poverty rates, for both current and future generations of Puerto Ricans, are serious. Low standards of living, reflected in such essential ways as inadequate housing conditions and high rates of children living in poor households, permeate the daily lives of a large portion of the stateside Puerto Rican population. That so many Puerto Rican children find themselves in circumstances of significant poverty should be a major concern to politicians, policymakers, and others, as we may be leaving a generation behind if steps are not taken to address these conditions. There is a need to focus on crucial support structures, such as local schools, in ensuring a secure future for this sector of the population.

The reasons for the increase in Puerto Rican income per capita during the 1980s and beyond provide some guide as to how Puerto Ricans are attempting to overcome poverty in the medium to long term. One answer is mobility, and the second is educational attainment. Those Puerto Ricans who did leave areas of economic distress and relocated to more favorable labor markets benefited from their move. The loss of manufacturing employment in the

Northeast during the 1970s and 1980s represented a particularly difficult challenge to Puerto Ricans. Approximately 40 percent of the Puerto Rican population in the United States was engaged in manufacturing then. In 2015 less than 11 percent of the population was in that line of work. Given this severe sectoral dislocation, those able to find jobs in expanding labor markets, often far from their original residence, managed to improve their economic lot.

The second key, not unrelated to the first, is educational attainment. The increase in educational attainment among Puerto Ricans during the 1980s and 1990s, as well as during the new millennium, was most pronounced among those completing two-year and associate's degrees. Individuals acquiring these skills managed to find employment in the expanding service and technical fields (for example, nursing). Nevertheless, it is easy to identify the individuals most at risk among the population. Clearly, those with less than a high school education experienced a dramatic decline in income from 1980 to 2015, as manufacturing employment dried up and the lack of skills made it impossible for them to compete effectively in the areas of emerging employment growth. To many, the alternative continues to be precarious low-wage service-sector employment.

A major concern is the extent to which the changes since the 1980s have resulted in greater inequality within the Puerto Rican community. The concentration of Puerto Ricans in midsize cities of the Northeast—cities with declining employment and tax bases—is leading to pockets of extreme poverty surrounded by an infrastructure in decline. It is ironic that despite difficult economic times in these cities, Puerto Ricans continue to gravitate to them.[16] The economic challenges facing Puerto Rican communities in the Northeast present a serious threat to the ability of these communities to maintain themselves as viable agents of social and economic progress.

Notes

1. Among the components of income designated by the US Census Bureau as outside earnings are "unemployment compensation, worker's compensation, social security, supplemental security income, public assistance or welfare payments, veteran's payments, survivor benefits, disability benefits, pension or retirement income, interest income, dividends, rents, royalties, estates and trusts, educational assistance, alimony, child support, financial assistance from outside of the household, other income, and government transfers." See the US Bureau of the Census (http://www.census.gov) for complete definitions of these items.

2. According to the Census Bureau, "A household consists of all the people who occupy a housing unit. A house, an apartment or other group of rooms, or a single room, is regarded as a housing unit when it is occupied or intended for occupancy as separate living quarters; that is, when the occupants do not live and eat with any other persons in the structure and there is direct access from the outside or through a common hall. A household includes the related family members and all the unrelated people, if any, such as lodgers, foster children, wards, or employees who share the housing unit. A person living alone in a housing unit, or a group of

unrelated people sharing a housing unit such as partners or roomers, is also counted as a household. The count of households excludes group quarters." See "Current Population Survey," United States Census, http://www.census.gov/population /www/cps/cpsdef.html.

3. The decline in household size can reflect a decline in family size (fewer children) or fewer adult members of the household. Although in purely mathematical terms, the decline in average household size would reduce mean household income per capita, the underlying nature of household size will impact average (mean) household income.

4. Puerto Ricans identify themselves according to various racial classifications, including white and black. See C. Rodríguez (2000a) for an informative discussion of race and the census in the Puerto Rican context.

5. The period from December 2007 to June 2009 has been labeled the Great Recession as it turned out to be the most pronounced economic downturn in the United States since the Great Depression of the 1930s. What began as a housing crisis quickly spread to the labor market as incomes fell and unemployment increased. It is estimated that the US labor market lost 8.4 million jobs, or approximately 6 percent of all payroll employment. For corroborating information, see "The Great Recession," The State of Working America, http://stateofworkingamerica.org/great -recession.

6. For a more detailed and nuanced analysis of the impact of the Great Recession on unemployment, earnings, and poverty among Puerto Ricans in the United States, see Kurt Birsin and Edwin Meléndez, "Puerto Rican Economic Resiliency After the Great Recession," in Meléndez and Vargas-Ramos (2014).

7. See Maldonado (1997) for a detailed description of the protagonists, their policies, and the debates during Operation Bootstrap.

8. In comparing post–World War II population growth among export-oriented open economies, Carlos Santiago (1992) found that Puerto Rican population growth was extremely low, due entirely to migration rather than natural increase in the population. For example, Puerto Rico exhibited a population growth rate of 0.6 percent in 1950–1960, compared to Hong Kong (4.4 percent), Israel (5.2 percent), Singapore (4.7 percent), and Taiwan (3.4 percent).

9. Santiago-Rivera and Santiago (1999) found a complex relationship between migrant status, English-language proficiency, and educational attainment among stateside Puerto Ricans; they concluded, "Both English-language proficiency and educational attainment influence decisions regarding the frequency of migration and a migrant's length of stay in complex ways. It appears that educational attainment alone is not sufficient to assure a Puerto Rican migrant's success in the US labor market if the person's English-language skills are inadequate. While English-language proficiency may compensate for low educational attainment among Puerto Rican migrants, one cannot say that the reverse is true" (241).

10. For more details on the determination of poverty thresholds as used by the US Census Bureau, see "How the Census Bureau Measures Poverty," August 11, 2017, https://www.census.gov/topics/income-poverty/poverty/guidance/poverty -measures.html.

11. A 1995 report by the National Academy of Sciences recommended that modifications be made to the definition of poverty in the United States. The proposal suggested making additions to an individual's income by including transfer payments such as food stamps, school lunches, and public housing, while simultaneously subtracting taxes, child-support payments, medical costs, health insurance premiums, and a number of other work-related expenses. See Galvin (1995).

12. A legitimate question is whether the decline in poverty rates for Puerto Ricans from 1980 to 1990 might have been reversed during the early 1990s, coinciding with the economic slowdown in the United States. Information from the Current Population Survey (1990) indicates that the poverty rate among Puerto Ricans did rise somewhat after 1990 but did not reach its 1980 level. This demonstrates the cyclical sensitivity of poverty rates to the business cycle and also reinforces the notion that Puerto Ricans did make real economic gains during the 1980s.

13. For surveys on the determinants of poverty, see Tienda and Jensen (1988), Lynn and McGeary (1990), and Edwin Meléndez (1993a).

14. The coefficient of correlation between beneficiary and poverty rates was 0.68, 0.53, 0.48, and 0.62 for 1980, 1990, 2000, and 2010, respectively.

15. To this date, New York City continues to carry a debt burden from the 1970s. In 2004 the city's debt was around $50 billion, the highest in the country.

16. One reason for the continued migration of Puerto Ricans to these midsize cities is that housing rental rates are relatively low, and for a renter population such as Puerto Ricans, this provides a real alternative to the high housing costs of a metropolis like New York City.

7

Social, Civil Rights, and Empowerment Struggles

In the mid-1970s, a report about Puerto Ricans in the United States sponsored by the US Commission on Civil Rights (1976) made reference in its subtitle to their "uncertain future." This assessment of their overall status was based on an analysis of all the available census data, which showed that Puerto Ricans remained at the bottom of the socioeconomic ladder, part of that unprivileged "other America" (Harrington 1962), the significant segment of the US population still living in poverty and afflicted by socioeconomic and racial inequalities and segregation. According to all official indicators, in the 1970s Puerto Ricans were far from reaping the benefits of many of the reforms that came out of the mid-1960s Great Society programs promulgated by President Lyndon B. Johnson's administration. The report's data called into question the traditional "melting pot" model of immigrant assimilation leading to social mobility and integration into mainstream society, since it did not seem to apply to minority populations of color, such as Puerto Ricans, African Americans, and Native Americans (Glazer and Moynihan 1963; A. Torres 1995).

Overall, the civil rights achievements and reforms of the 1960s and 1970s did not significantly improve the underprivileged status of stateside Puerto Ricans, leading to some simplistic generalizations by researchers and policymakers that gave continuity to a view of migration from the island as "the Puerto Rican problem." Subsequent socioeconomic studies about the stateside communities introduced notions of a "Puerto Rican underclass" (Tienda 1989; Lemann 1991) or referred to "the Puerto Rican exception" (L. Chávez 1991) to overstate the persistence of poverty among Puerto Ricans. The combined effect of these characterizations was a portrait of a population lagging behind other nationalities lumped together by the US census within the broader Hispanic/Latino category. The unfavorable socioeconomic status of Puerto Ricans also served to reinforce the argument that whether they had been born in Puerto Rico or the continental United States, the advantage of holding US citizenship did not necessarily make them better off than other Latinos/as or, for that matter, other US populations of color. It also allowed some policymakers and scholars to continue putting forward debasing or limited explanations regarding the underprivileged status of Puerto Ricans by blaming the victim or arguing that their condition was largely "self-inflicted" (L. Chávez 1991, 161). These appraisals frequently disregarded the structural socioeconomic conditions and racist barriers that perpetuate inequalities and in general diminish equal access for populations of color to opportunities for educational and socioeconomic advancement, which in the United States tend to accrue to the white population. Moreover, most of these disparaging assessments of the stateside Puerto Rican population lacked a more discerning sociohistorical analysis of how the particular colonial relationship between Puerto Rico and the United States and the control of the island's economy by US industries limit the autonomy of the local government regarding economic development and trade policies. For instance, the major post–World War II shift in Puerto Rico from an agricultural to an industrial economy, one primarily dependent on US capital investments in exchange for generous tax exemptions and lower labor wages for US industries located on the island, created the conditions that propelled the largely working-class Great Migration (1950s–1960s) that continued for several decades (see Chapter 4).

For generations of stateside Puerto Ricans, living in a racially segregated and socially stratified environment along with the structural conditions that deter social mobility have contributed to their slow progress in overcoming their underprivileged status.

When scholars and policymakers refer to the status of Puerto Ricans and other ethnoracial minorities, they generally focus on the discouraging picture that comes out of official socioeconomic data without giving enough credit to the idea that those groups that remain marginalized because of their lower socioeconomic indicators are far from resigning themselves to lives of deprivation and hardship and, for the most part, do not inevitably or passively accept their poverty status. Closer to reality are the multiple ways in which working-class Puerto Rican migrants have fought for civil rights and social justice, combatted unequal treatment, and shared aspirations for social mobility for their families and communities, much like other prior immigrant groups. Their limited representation in the ruling structures of the cities and states where they have settled and their limited political power at the state and national levels still remain major obstacles in achieving faster and more dramatic improvements in their socioeconomic status.

Against unfavorable odds, Puerto Ricans and other US populations of color have a long history of challenging the power structures and a wide range of institutions on specific issues in their pursuit of social and political change. This history includes their survival struggles to overcome pervading inequalities and injustices, based on intersections of class, gender, ethnicity, and race, that often impair their social progress (Rodríguez, Sánchez Korrol, and Alers 1996). Regardless of these barriers and evidence that since the 1990s more encouraging patterns of socioeconomic progress and increased political participation are developing in certain geographic areas where Puerto Ricans reside, pervasive disadvantages and a polarized widening gap between the wealthy and the poor in US society will continue to hinder the possibilities for significant change for lower-income Puerto Rican workers, other populations of color, and even the white working class.

In general, the struggles of Latinos/as for social justice are a neglected component of the civil rights movement and of the mainstream of US history of social and political movements. The bulk of the literature on these movements shows a propensity to describe the civil rights movement as largely an arena for African American battles against racism, segregation, and voting rights. At the time, blacks were the largest minority group still dealing with a long-standing history of social injustice, systemic racism, disfranchisement, and violence that persisted after the American Civil War and their emancipation from enslavement. Hence, historical narratives focused on the civil rights movement have a tendency to omit or offer a cursory examination of the activism of Puerto Ricans, Chicanos/as, and other Latinos/as of various national origins. Native Americans and Asians also have had parallel experiences of racial oppression and unequal treatment and have actively engaged in their own forms of struggle and resistance (see Takaki [1993] 2008).

The few early studies about civil rights activism among Latinos/as focused on recognizing the wide range organizations and engagement of Chicanos/as (Acuña 1972) or offering a more panoramic view of the struggles for social justice and empowerment of diverse groups of Latinos/as (Cockcroft 1995). A wave of subsequent studies aimed to document the crusades of specific organizations or provide testimonial accounts of prominent men and women activists involved in different areas of collective action that were part of a broader Chicano/a movement (Gutiérrez 1999; Gonzales 2001; López Tijerina 2000; J. Levy 2007; M. García 2008; Sánchez and López 2017). Those studies about the Puerto Rican movement emphasized different areas of engagement and the organizations that emerged to mobilize their respective communities (Torres and Velázquez 1998; J. Cruz 1998, 2017; M. Meléndez 2003; Acosta-Belén 2011–2012; Song-Ha Lee 2014; Wanzer-Serrano 2015; I. Morales 2016).

For Puerto Ricans in particular, these studies illustrate that the written accounts of both researchers and activists, as well as of some of the participants in the main organizations demanding freedom from different forms of oppression and equal rights to transform and empower their communities, continue to unveil and record the history of the diaspora and its multiple spheres of activism. As a whole, these studies draw a different portrait of stateside Puerto Ricans, one that is far from the widely held stereotypes of docility or political apathy and transcends catchy but often demeaning portrayals or sweeping generalizations made in a substantial portion of the previous scholarship and commonly recycled by the mainstream media. As noted in previous chapters, for Puerto Ricans these depictions included being branded as part of "the culture of poverty" (Lewis 1966) or "the culture of public welfare" (Horwitz 1960), or as suffering from "self-inflicted wounds" (L. Chávez 1991) or a "lack of community organization" (Glazer and Moynihan 1963). Subsequent scholarship has contested most of these old notions and generalizations. However, for mainstream society, Puerto Ricans, like other Latinos/as and African Americans, still fit the portrait of an impoverished and disenfranchised community, beleaguered by unemployment and dependent on social assistance programs, beset with gang violence, drug abuse, and incomplete education, and blamed for most of the social ills generally associated with poverty. These problem-oriented or "blaming the victim" sweeping characterizations, which for decades dominated the social science literature on Puerto Ricans, share a common thread: denying agency to the efforts and battles of working-class migrants arriving in the United States with the same dreams of socioeconomic prosperity and a better future as held by most immigrants. Less attention is given to the sources and conditions that account for the enduring systemic and institutionalized ethnic and racial bigotry and structural marginality experienced by populations of color. Much too frequently, these populations are scapegoated in order to conceal the real sources of socioeconomic disparity, labor exploitation, and the debasing nature of racialization and prejudice.

Chapters 4 and 5 have already analyzed in detail some of the reasons for the unprivileged status of many stateside Puerto Ricans, especially before the 1990s. A good portion of the traditional scholarship tended to overemphasize the most pressing problems faced by Puerto Ricans and other minorities without considering their collective struggles and economic and cultural contributions both to the development of their own communities and to mainstream society. By examining concrete examples of Puerto Rican collective action, in this chapter we provide a more balanced portrait by focusing on the different social, political, and educational battles that burgeoned in the various stateside Puerto Rican communities, first during the civil rights era and then in later decades. These different forms of engagement solidified a foundation that provides continuity and inspires subsequent struggles and forms of collective action.

It is important to reiterate that multiple generations of Puerto Ricans, Chicanos/as, and other Latinos/as waged many battles during earlier historical periods in defense of their rights or around an array of pressing issues related to the general conditions and needs of their respective communities. Thus their record of activism in the civil rights movement represents a more visible continuation of fighting back against unequal treatment and violation of their rights as US citizens and human beings. Trespasses included the outright neglect, injustice, and abuse perpetrated by the governing power structures, law enforcement authorities, and the legal and prison systems, as well as severe inequalities and deficiencies in public schools, health and social services, and private and public housing prior to some of the protections granted by the Civil Rights Act of 1964. Earlier struggles to improve these conditions, therefore, took place in a society torn by segregation and racial violence unleashed by white supremacists with impunity and that afforded fewer legal protections and assigned a lesser value to people of color. For many decades most of these populations remained on the margins of the dominant Anglo-American mainstream, and the FBI even subjected some of their most radical or active organizations working for change to surveillance and persecution. Moreover, rarely did the local or national media pay attention to Puerto Ricans outside reference to issues or incidents that, more often than not, portrayed them in a negative light.

Prior to the 1960s, it was rare for federal or state government agencies or established mainstream organizations to fully address minority concerns or develop agendas for change. To deal with their specific concerns and most urgent needs, these populations therefore had to create their own professional and grassroots organizations and media outlets, which had more limited success in denouncing pervasive inequalities and racism or getting government officials and legislators to act on improving conditions. Early-twentieth-century organizations focusing on Puerto Rican or pan-Latino/a affairs ranged from mutual-aid societies to social and cultural clubs, churches, businesses, professional associations, legal services, advocacy groups, community agencies, organized labor, and even political organizations.

The Legacies of the Puerto Rican Movement

Back in 1998, when Torres and Velázquez released *The Puerto Rican Movement: Voices of the Diaspora*, they were acknowledging the meaning of giving recognition to the wide range of political and collective strategies of stateside Puerto Ricans and the organizations they created to seek social justice, empower their communities, and engage in the anticolonial struggle. These groups, along with others that emerged during the same and subsequent decades, have forged legacies of cultural, social, political, and educational activism that allow new generations of Puerto Ricans to draw meaningful lessons from their experiences, accomplishments, and shortcomings. These social movements and endeavors also show a community organizing and mobilizing in multiple ways to combat the social and racial injustices and socioeconomic marginality its members experience. In the area of community activism, stateside Puerto Rican political organizations were among the most radical during the 1960s and 1970s. Racism and related issues of inequality and social justice, and the lack of political representation, were central to the Puerto Rican agenda, as they were for other populations of color. Along with some of the radical groups, a number of progressive social and political organizations were more willing to engage in negotiations with the power structures and use the growth of their communities and their ethnic identity to state their claims for equal treatment and for increased representation and participation, which would enable them to alleviate critical socioeconomic and educational conditions (J. Cruz 1998, 2000, 2017). However, the most militant Puerto Rican political organizations established during the civil rights era also reflected political concerns of some stateside and island Puerto Ricans, particularlyPuerto Rico's colonial relationship with the United States and the release of Puerto Rican political prisoners. Prominent Nationalists involved in the 1950 and 1954 shootings at Blair House and the US Congress, respectively, already had been confined to federal prisons for over two decades.

Within the Puerto Rican communities, organizations and community organizers sponsored voter registration campaigns aimed at increasing electoral participation in general elections and Puerto Rican representation in city and state governments and the US Congress. Some of the organizations encouraged Puerto Ricans to join the mainstream political parties by establishing clubs affiliated with them in order to address some of the most critical problems and issues affecting the predominantly working-class populations of their communities.

The issue of Puerto Rico's colonial status often linked some of the most militant stateside political organizations to those on the island. This generated an expectation that a shared concern about the liberation of Puerto Rico would bring the communities of the island and the diaspora closer to one another in the pursuit of common political goals. But, understandably, most stateside Puerto Rican political leaders affiliated with the Democratic and Republican parties were more concerned with expanding their political presence and influence at all levels and addressing the immediate socioeconomic needs and inequalities engulfing their own communities. Therefore, they were less concerned with broader political debates about Puerto Rico's political future.

Since the late 1960s the large majority of the island's electorate has been almost evenly divided between support for the Commonwealth status quo and for future statehood for the island, with less than 4 percent of general voters supporting independence.[1] Notwithstanding, this electoral reality did not deter the most militant stateside Puerto Rican political organizations, especially during the 1970s and 1980s, from supporting the island's independence, even when the specific concerns of their local communities were also central to their agendas. The socialist orientation and defense of Puerto Rico's liberation from US colonial control central to some of the organizations, however, had a more limited appeal to a majority of stateside Puerto Ricans.[2]

One of the few issues that resonated with Puerto Ricans from both shores was the release of political prisoners. The hanging of the Puerto Rican flag on the forehead of the Statue of Liberty in 1977 by a group of Puerto Rican activists supporting the prisoners' freedom dramatized and drew US media attention to their cause. Two years later, President Jimmy Carter commuted the sentences of four Nationalists: Oscar Collazo, involved in the 1950 attack on Blair House, the temporary residence of President Harry S. Truman; and Rafael Cancel Miranda, Irving Flores, and Lolita Lebrón, involved in the 1954 attack on the US Congress (see Chapter 3). All of these political prisoners had served twenty-five years or more in federal prisons, far longer than most others sentenced for similar or worse offenses.

Added to the list of political prisoners in later years were leaders and members of two clandestine pro-independence radical organizations operating in Puerto Rico and the United States in the 1970s and 1980s: Fuerzas Armadas de Liberación Nacional (FALN, Armed Forces for National Liberation) and its successor, Ejército Popular Boricua (Boricua Popular Army), better known as Los Macheteros (The Machete Wielders). In some cases, relatives and friends of members were also persecuted or imprisoned. These groups were deemed responsible for multiple acts of sabotage on the island that included the bombing of an electric power plant and of aircraft at a military installation in Puerto Rico. Stateside, there were numerous bombings of government buildings, department stores, and a New York City tavern, which resulted in an explosion that killed four people and injured more than fifty customers. Los Macheteros were also known for carrying out a multimillion dollar robbery of a Wells Fargo armored truck depot in Hartford, Connecticut (see R. Fernández 1987). The mastermind behind the heist was Filiberto Ojeda Ríos, leader of FALN and Los Macheteros, and a fugitive hiding for many years in a rural area near the town of Hormigueros, where, in 2005, the FBI surrounded him in his house. He was shot by an FBI sharpshooter and denied medical attention until he bled to death. The island government and civil rights organizations condemned the act as an "illegal killing." Another prominent political prisoner, Oscar López Rivera, a FALN member who considered himself an anticolonialist combatant, was convicted of "seditious conspiracy" for his involvement with FALN's sabotage bombings and robberies, although he was never accused of injuring any individuals. After he had spent thirty-five years in a federal prison, the island and stateside communities mobilized to demand his release. Political leaders, members of Congress, community activists, students, and those who believed

that López Rivera's original sentence had been too harsh and his imprisonment too long, considering the nature of his legal offenses, supported sustained campaigns for his release. President Barack Obama commuted his sentence in 2017. President Clinton had done the same in 1999 with sixteen
FALN members convicted for their participation in robberies or of firearms
and explosives violations, but not charged with harming people. By the 1990s
most of the underground Puerto Rican liberation groups had faded away.

Due to the unrelenting poverty and racial segregation that engulfed the
stateside Puerto Rican community during the 1970s, a significant number of
the political organizations that emerged during the civil rights period in major
US cities with large concentrations of Puerto Ricans fighting for social and
political change had a liberal orientation or deployed more radical strategies to stake their demands. The latter approach was common among many
minority organizations, as well as organizations associated with the Vietnam
anti-war movement and the antiestablishment counterculture revolution that
overwhelmed the United States and most other Western nations. Socialism
proved a useful tool for activists in denouncing workers' exploitation and
socioeconomic disparities and racial divisions perpetuated by a corrupt capitalist system and US military interventions in Third World countries. For
many Puerto Ricans critical of US colonialism, the rejection of compulsory
military service during the Vietnam War was an important rallying issue.
However, the demands for new civil rights protections for equal treatment
and increased economic and educational opportunities, as well as for more
effective responses to the overall plight of the poor in the richest country in
the world, provided a broader context for waging these particular struggles.
Massive anti-war demonstrations by students, labor and hunger strikes,
economic boycotts, and other forms of mobilization mirrored some of US
society's wider political and racial unrest during those years when a multitude of voices clamored for significant change.

Torres (1998, 5) identified eight core groups that represented the radical
political spectrum within the Puerto Rican diaspora during this period: the
Young Lords Party (later the Puerto Rican Workers' Party), El Comité–MINP
Movimiento de Izquierda Nacional Puertorriqueña (Puerto Rican National
Leftist Movement), the Puerto Rican Student Union, the Movimiento de Lib-
eración Nacional (MLN, Movement for National Liberation), the Fuerzas
Armadas de Liberación Nacional (FALN, Armed Forces for National Liber-
ation), the Partido Socialista Puertorriqueño (PSP, Puerto Rican Socialist
Party), the Partido Nacionalista Puertorriqueño (PN, Puerto Rican National-
ist Party), and the Partido Independentista Puertorriqueño (PIP, Puerto Rican
Independence Party). Several of these organizations originated in the United
States, but a few others, such as the PSP, PN, and PIP, were branches of
political parties originally founded in Puerto Rico, all of them calling for the
island's independence.

Of the different range of organizations listed above, the Young Lords Party best represents the concerns of stateside Puerto Rican urban youth and their commitment to making a difference in dealing with the everyday problems of the inner-city barrios. The group originated in Chicago in 1969; its founders had been part of a Latino youth gang encouraged by members of the city's Black Panthers to channel their activities into the more constructive path of social and political activism aimed at improving conditions in their poor neighborhoods. Several Puerto Rican college students from New York had come together to form the Sociedad Albizu Campos (Albizu Campos Society), an organization that defended Puerto Rico's right to self-determination. They heard about the activism of Chicago's Young Lords and went to that city to meet José "Cha Cha" Jiménez, the group's leader. Inspired during the visit by the grassroots-centered agenda of Chicago's Young Lords, they secured the group's consent to start their own chapter in New York (Guzmán 1998). Eventually, the New York chapter of the Young Lords became the most visible and active, although branches also were established in Philadelphia, Newark-Hoboken, Bridgeport, and Puerto Rico. In their organizing efforts, the Young Lords tried to reach out not only to those living in the urban barrios but also to students on college campuses, community professionals, and other activists who could help them advance the organization's social and political goals.

New York's Young Lords were most effective in mobilizing youth and other grassroots communities for their campaigns to create breakfast programs for needy children and people's health clinics for the detection of lead poisoning, tuberculosis, diabetes, and other illnesses. Additionally, they fought for the improvement of hospital services and prison conditions and pressured local officials to make inner-city schools more responsive to the educational needs of migrant children with limited English proficiency. They supported bilingual education and curricular reforms that incorporated a student's cultural heritage. The Young Lords even engaged in more mundane undertakings, such as mobilizing the community to help pick up the garbage on the streets of the barrios and force the city's municipal government to improve its garbage-collection practices.

Feminist women members of the organization were also fully engaged in these community-focused initiatives. They played a key role in exposing *machista* (male chauvinist) and sexist treatment within an organization whose leadership was largely controlled by men. Even with these critical challenges, they claimed their place in the leadership of the organization and fought from within to bring to the forefront women's issues and concerns in such areas as violence against women, reproductive rights, health, LGBTQ issues, education, leadership training, political representation, and women's liberation. Women members were particularly instrumental in defining an agenda focused on the empowering of grassroots Puerto Rican women and other women of color.

Iris Morales (2016), the first woman to join the New York branch of the Young Lords, collected some of the individual and collective experiences of these "rebel women" in the organization. During her post–Young Lords life, Morales became a lawyer and worked tirelessly on media projects aimed at contesting stereotypical representations of Puerto Ricans and other Latinos/as and on documenting and preserving the history of the organization. The impact of her work is best represented by the documentary film *¡Palante, Siempre Palante! The Young Lords* (1996), which introduced younger generations of stateside Puerto Ricans to the organization and to an important chapter in the Puerto Rican movement. The film has become a classroom staple for learning about the Young Lords' activism and their impact on the community. Through her scholarship and public speaking, Morales is also contributing to the wider process of building a historical memory of different forms of activism within a wider range of Puerto Rican civil rights struggles during the late 1960s and 1970s. Morales's personal account of her Puerto Rican journey to becoming a Young Lord, along with those of other members of the leadership, form part of *Palante: The Young Lords Party* (Young Lords Party and Abramson 1971),[3] which introduced to the general public the stories and hopes for a more just society that inspired the emergence of the organization. The book includes writings by party leaders and photographs of their activism taken by Michael Abramson. Morales was behind the publication of a second edition of the book, *Palante: Voices and Photographs of the Young Lords, 1969–1971* (Young Lords Party and Abramson 2011), which also allows new generations of Puerto Ricans to learn about grassroots mobilization in pursuit of social change and a more just society. Ensuring preservation and full acknowledgment of the tireless work and resilience of the women members of the Young Lords, Morales's (2016) *Through the Eyes of Rebel Women: The Young Lords, 1969–1976*, is a powerful testimony to the wisdom, vitality, and determination that feminist women bring to the struggle for equality and liberation from patriarchal oppression. Additionally, the volume is an honest and balanced assessment of the Young Lords Party's accomplishments and shortcomings. Morales continues to be a strong advocate for women's reproductive rights and health.

Former male members of the Young Lords also have recorded their experiences in the movement. In *Harvest of Empire: A History of Latinos in America*, Juan González ([2000] 2011), now a journalist and investigative reporter and formerly minister of education of the Young Lords, charts a full history of the multiple territorial, economic, and political US imperialist interventions in the past and present that account for the growing presence and activism of Latinos/as in the United States. Joining his former comrades in the efforts to document the social and political activism of the Young Lords, Miguel "Mickey" Meléndez (2003), also a member of the Young Lord's Central Committee, wrote *We Took the Streets: Fighting for Latino Rights with the Young Lords*. His account delivers an insider's view of the organization's bold platform and its defiance of the established order in its determination to "take over the streets." Propelled by a mixture of idealism, outrage, and sense of purpose, the Young Lords managed to mobilize community members for collective action in battling for their rights around basic issues that impaired the quality of their daily lives and their neighborhoods. Several other male and female members of the Young Lords have chosen careers in journalism and broadcast media, have founded community organizations, or remain engaged in different forms of community organizing and activism. Others are teaching and writing or involved in social and legal work, as well as other creative or socially and politically meaningful endeavors.

The Young Lords' newspaper, *Palante* (1970–1973), was an important vehicle for denouncing injustices and violence against the Puerto Rican and other Latino communities, as well as a consciousness-raising tool.[4] The group's popular slogan, *Tengo Puerto Rico en mi corazón [sic]* (I carry Puerto Rico in my heart)[5] was more than a reflection of its members' pride in their cultural roots and heritage. It conveyed a political agenda that transcended the borders of the Puerto Rican communities of the diaspora—a platform that recognized the presence of Puerto Ricans in the United States as a colonial migration impelled by decades of US socioeconomic policies and control over the island. Thus, central to this platform was a militant nationalistic stance regarding the liberation of Puerto Rico. The Young Lords proclaimed clear positions against US imperialism and colonial domination of Puerto Rico and in support of the island's independence. But their platform also reflected a broader social and political consciousness and denunciation of capitalist exploitation of the working class and a call for socialist revolution to eradicate the impoverished status of Puerto Rican workers.

The militant outlook of many of the organizations mentioned above stemmed from a view of capitalism, colonialism, and racism as the main sources of workers' oppression. The United Nations invigorated their commitment to Puerto Rico's self-determination in 1972, when it called for an end to the colonial relationship between the island and the United States (see Gautier Mayoral and Argüelles 1978). In addition, these organizations were consistent in their demand for the freedom of Puerto Rican political prisoners, most of them former members of the Nationalist Party or of the clandestine FALN and Los Macheteros.

As indicated in Chapter 3, the repressive measures against Puerto Rican Nationalists were part of a sustained effort, begun in the mid-1930s and lasting for most of the twentieth century, aimed at incarcerating their leaders, intimidating their followers, and discouraging support for Puerto Rico's independence among the island's population. These coordinated measures involved the FBI, the CIA, and the island's police and government agencies. Most notorious for its domestic covert operations during the 1960s and 1970s was the FBI's counterintelligence program, known as COINTELPRO, which carried out a broader war against political dissent in the United States (see Churchill and Wall 1990). For more than half a century, US and Puerto Rican public officials systematically used imprisonment, blacklisting, surveillance, and other forms of political persecution to suppress or neutralize militant pro-independence groups or any groups labeled "subversive" merely for their opposition to US colonial rule in Puerto Rico (see Acosta 1987; Bosque Pérez and Colón Morera 1997). The local police and the FBI created *carpetas* (files) for all suspected subversives. The Intelligence Division of the Puerto Rican police kept files on over 150,000 Puerto Ricans (Bosque Pérez and Colón Morera 1997, 303). Along with these repressive measures, island institutions, the school system in particular, were used from the early years of US rule to "Americanize" Puerto Ricans and create a consensus to justify US control over the island (see Negrón de Montilla 1971; Méndez 1980; Silva Gotay 1997; del Moral 2013). These sometimes overt, other times covert practices deflected the perception that Puerto Rico was under the yoke of US imperialism and substituted the more agreeable notion that, at best, the relationship between the two countries was the result of "a compact" or "mutual agreement" and, at worst, a reflection of "colonialism by consent."

In the continental United States, the 1950s were characterized by Cold War anti-communist hysteria and witch hunt tactics instigated by Senator Joseph McCarthy and the House Un-American Activities Committee (HUAC). During the now infamous era of McCarthyism, numerous liberal and radical groups and individuals throughout the United States became the targets of a concerted congressional campaign of questionable investigations, baseless accusations of subversive activity, and intimidation, all in the name of protecting the country from the threat of communism. These HUAC hearings created an environment of communist paranoia that violated basic civil liberties and destroyed the lives of many US citizens and government employees.

While US society focused on the communist threat, racial violence and segregation continued to affect the lives of African Americans and other populations of color. This was more vivid in the southern states, where segregation and voter suppression were still legal, although it also was a problem in northeastern and midwestern inner cities with large concentrations of ethnoracial minorities. For Puerto Rican migrants and other populations of color living in this environment, US citizenship did not prove advantageous, since they were considered nonwhite and, based on this racialization, denied the same rights and opportunities shared by the more privileged white majority.

Several Puerto Rican political organizations of the civil rights era consistently denounced the abuses of capitalism and the virtues of socialism, even though they frequently ventured away from this ideological agenda. Their solidarity with grassroots efforts to deal with specific community issues is well known, and they were most effective when they collaborated with local groups or organizations. Puerto Ricans came together to denounce abuses by the police and slumlords, mass incarcerations, inadequate and segregated schools, poor health services, discrimination and mistreatment in factories and farms, street violence, and overall failure by local city officials to address most of the conditions that afflicted poor neighborhoods.

It is noteworthy that the more radical positions espoused by some of the political organizations, mainly on issues related to the island's independence and socialist revolution, appealed less to the majority of a migrant population striving to make a living in an environment where socioeconomic prosperity was largely elusive. Since the mid-twentieth century, independence has not been the preferred status choice of Puerto Rico's electorate, especially after the coming into power of the Partido Popular Democrático (PPD, Popular Democratic Party) in 1948 and the subsequent inauguration of the current Commonwealth in 1952. The downturn in support for Puerto Rico's independence during the second half of the twentieth century was due in part to the success of Luis Muñoz Marín's populist movement, since his party discarded this political alternative in favor of a permanent, albeit subordinate, relationship with the United States (see Chapter 3). Other important factors in the decline of political support for independence were apprehension and fear, instilled by government officials and the media, regarding violent incidents involving Nationalists and other radical groups. The systematic persecution of these particular groups by the island government in collaboration with US authorities often failed to distinguish between the most militant and more moderate sectors of the independence movement and several times ended with police beatings, mass arrests of demonstrators, and the killing of university students (see Nieves-Falcón 2009; Nelson 1996; Nieves-Falcón, García Rodríguez, and Ojeda Reyes 1971).

Stateside, the murders of Young Lord members in Chicago and New York and multiple incidents at political rallies and mass demonstrations also led to mass arrests, police beatings, and deaths.[6]

In more recent decades, island and stateside Puerto Ricans have come together in support of political causes linked to Puerto Rico's colonial status. Their combined activism was clearly demonstrated during the Vieques movement that drove the US Navy off the small island (Acosta 2002; Barreto 2002; McCaffrey 2002), in the campaigns to free Puerto Rican political prisoners, and in their support for Puerto Ricans' struggle to put islanders' well-being over debt holders' profits during the current fiscal crisis. More recently, many stateside Puerto Rican organizations and communities, along with prominent figures from the entertainment and movie industries and political and community leaders, have mobilized to aid the island in dealing with the destruction and humanitarian crisis created by Hurricane Maria, covered in Chapters 1 and 5.

Working to subvert or tear down the establishment's social and political power structures was by no means the preferred course of action of existing Puerto Rican organizations or institutions. However, most of them would not have emerged or maintained their vitality without the activism and engagement of both island and stateside Puerto Ricans. For the latter, legal challenges to segregation, discrimination, and voting rights violations yielded some landmark results in the battle for civil rights reforms. Following the model of the National Association for the Advancement of Colored People in its advocacy for African Americans, Chicanos/as and Puerto Ricans established their own legal institutions to seek social justice and challenge the constitutionality of segregation and unequal treatment. With seed grants from the Ford Foundation, the Mexican American Legal Defense and Education Fund (MALDEF) was founded in 1968, and the Puerto Rican Legal Defense and Education Fund (PRLDEF; now LatinoJustice, www.latinojustice.org) got its start in 1972. Based in New York City with a focus on litigation, public policy, and education, PRLDEF's legal team initiated landmark class action lawsuits, the most notable being the successful ASPIRA consent decree (discussed below). In more recent decades, PRLDEF was behind Proyecto Ayuda (Project Aide), aimed at securing benefits for the families of the victims of the September 11 terrorist attacks. PRLDEF also offered legal support to the people of Vieques in their efforts to force the US Navy to discontinue its military target practices, which were having negative effects on residents' health and the environment. Stateside it was involved in challenges to gerrymandering in the redistricting of Latino/a communities. In 2008, the organization changed its name to LatinoJustice due to increases in New York City's population of Latinos/as of other national origins.

These particular groups had an increased demand for legal expertise in areas related to immigration policy, the rights of the undocumented, including those protected by the Deferred Action for Childhood Arrivals (DACA) program, challenging anti-immigrant ordinances, and protecting voting rights of Latinos/as who are US citizens. LatinoJustice also aims to train a new generation of Latino/a lawyers and leaders committed to the advancement of their communities. Shortly after the destruction of Hurricane Maria became evident to stateside Puerto Ricans, many community organizations, activists, people with relatives and friends on the island, and other volunteers, along with the US general public, began to show solidarity with Puerto Rico by making donations or actively participating in relief efforts. LatinoJustice's immediate "Rebuilding Puerto Rico" initiative is providing Puerto Rico residents with much-needed bilingual legal assistance in dealing with insurance coverage claims and applying for FEMA aid and unemployment benefits for those who lost their jobs. It is also one of many stateside organizations that tried to secure, without success, an extension of the Jones Act beyond the initial ten-day period granted by the US administration right after the hurricane in order to allow the free flow of cargo ships with critical deliveries of food and medical supplies.

The National Congress for Puerto Rican Rights (NCPRR), founded in the South Bronx in 1981, with chapters later established in Boston, Philadelphia, and San Francisco, is another advocate for Puerto Ricans' human and civil rights. Through rallies and mass demonstrations NCPRR tries to influence policy (J. Cruz 2000). It prides itself as an independent entity that does not rely on government funding for its local or national campaigns "against environmental racism, police abuse, racially-motivated violence, and other forms of discrimination" (NCPRR 1996).

Puerto Rican political representation in state and national electoral politics has been limited. Only five stateside Puerto Ricans are currently serving in the US Congress, all elected to the House of Representatives. This in part reflects the continuous growth of the stateside Puerto Rican population but relatively low rate of Puerto Rican participation in US electoral politics. Increasing electoral participation within the stateside communities still represents a major challenge, considering that over 80 percent of voters in Puerto Rico generally cast their vote in island elections. It also reflects how slow the Democratic and Republican parties have been in fully engaging Puerto Ricans and other Latinos/as in the electoral process. Two of the stateside Puerto Ricans serving in Congress in 2017, José E. Serrano and Nydia M. Velázquez, are Democrats representing New York City districts; a third representative, Luis V. Gutiérrez, is a Democrat representing a Chicago district. A new Puerto Rican representative, Darren Soto, also a Democrat, was elected in 2016 by an Orlando-Kissimmee district. The only Republican Puerto Rican representative is Raúl Labrador from Idaho, elected in 2010. All the Puerto Rican Democratic representatives have districts with large Puerto Rican communities; they are known for supporting the institutions and organizations that serve the needs of Latinos/as and national initiatives such as the Patient Protection and Affordable Care Act (aka Obamacare). Congressman Gutiérrez's (2013) *Still Dreaming: My Journey from the Barrio to Capitol Hill* recounts his formative years in a Chicago Puerto Rican neighborhood and in a rural town in Puerto Rico and his path to the US Congress. He has established a visible national profile in advocating for immigration reform and policies and has underscored the contributions of millions of undocumented workers to the US economy. He has forcefully defended the granting of work permits to and a path to citizenship for DACA Dreamers, the offspring of undocumented immigrants brought to and raised in the country by their families and for whom the United States is the only home they have ever known. He and Congresswoman Nydia Velázquez have been strong advocates for Puerto Rico in matters related to the debt crisis and, more recently, persuading Congress to cancel the debt and abolish the Jones Act shipping laws as part of a reconstruction and renewal plan for the island. Congressman Labrador is a member of the Congressional Freedom Caucus, an ultraconservative group known for wanting to end programs such as Social Security, Medicare, Medicaid, and other social services that are part of the safety net for low-income US citizens, the elderly, and the large majority of the US population. He does not show a record of supporting legislation that reflects the concerns of island or stateside Puerto Ricans or Latinos/as in general.

The late Herman Badillo was the first Puerto Rican representative in the US Congress and the only one for most of the 1970s. Robert García, a former assemblyman and senator in the New York State legislature, replaced Badillo when he gave up his congressional seat in the 1980s to join the New York City mayoral administration of Ed Koch and eventually pursue his unrealized aspirations to become the city's first Puerto Rican mayor. After García resigned his congressional seat, he was replaced in 1990 by Serrano, a former member of the New York State legislature. Two years later, Serrano was no longer the only voting representative of Puerto Ricans in Congress when Velázquez and Gutiérrez joined him in the House.

Many stateside Puerto Rican community organizations have been making voter registration a priority issue and sponsoring voter registration campaigns during major election years. As a result Puerto Ricans have been doing better than ever before at getting elected to state and municipal legislative posts. According to the National Puerto Rican Coalition (1999), there were ninety-five Puerto Rican elected officials in legislative positions around the country, but this data has not been updated.

Only a few Puerto Ricans have been elected mayor of a large city. Maurice Ferré, nephew of the late Luis A. Ferré, former governor of Puerto Rico in the late 1960s and founder of the pro-statehood Partido Nuevo Progresista (PNP, New Progressive Party), served in the early 1970s in Miami. Puerto Rican mayors have been elected in Hartford, Connecticut, a city where Puerto Ricans represent almost a third of the total population, and in East Chicago, Indiana. More recently, Michelle de la Isla was elected in 2017 to become the first Puerto Rican woman mayor of Topeka, Kansas, the state capital. Neither of the latter two cities has a large Puerto Rican population.

Most prominent of all presidential appointments was that of Sonia M. Sotomayor to the US Supreme Court by President Barack Obama in 2009. A graduate of Princeton University and Yale Law School, she was a strong advocate during her student years for these Ivy League institutions to recruit more Latino/a students and faculty. A few years after her appointment to the Supreme Court, Justice Sotomayor (2013) published *My Beloved World* (simultaneously published in Spanish as *Mi mundo adorado*). This memoir is a gripping and inspirational account of her experiences growing up Puerto Rican in the Bronx and the achievements of this US-born daughter of migrants, won through intelligence, hard work, self-confidence, resiliency, and a drive to learn and excel in any undertaking she pursued.

José Cruz (2017) documents the political history of New York's Puerto Rican community from the 1960s to the 1990s. In his study, he validates Puerto Ricans' reliance on ethnic identity and the liberal democratic process as a positive and effective strategy in seeking to expand their participation and representation in the US political system at municipal, state, and national levels. Cruz also argues that in pursuing this approach New York City's Puerto Rican political elites have placed themselves "out of the margins and right in the mainstream of city politics as significant contributors to urban democracy" (xxiii). In a prior assessment of the political accomplishments and challenges of stateside Puerto Ricans, Cruz (2000) noted that elected officials tended to focus on "amelioration and the short term" (56), without a good balance with longer-term objectives; he argued that for the diaspora "the political system has failed most of its members" (56) and pointed to the lack of "a two-pronged policy agenda, seeking both economic growth and equality" (57). Cruz provided a few examples of what he describes as "convergence," where radical agendas gave way to political compromise and electoral mobilization in order to get more representation in municipal administrations, city councils, and state legislatures, as happened in cities like Hartford and Philadelphia (50). He also made the discouraging but realistic statement that the US Congress had a long history of treating island Puerto Ricans with "selective inattention" and stateside Puerto Ricans with "oblivious disregard" (57). Even when the whole world was watching with empathy and compassion, the official response from the Donald Trump administration and Congress in sending relief to the distraught US citizens who had survived Hurricane Maria in Puerto Rico was another sobering example of this treatment.

In 2017, of thirty-eight Latinos/as serving in the US Congress, only the aforementioned five representatives and the island's nonvoting resident commissioner were Puerto Rican. Occasionally, Latino/a elected officials have come around in support of some common issues that transcend the different needs of the wide range of nationalities placed by the US census under the Hispanic/Latino rubric. Nonetheless, although the majority of them are Democrats, as a whole, they do not represent a unified political force in Congress. The rapid population growth among Latinos/as, which has made them the largest minority group in US society since 2003, is increasingly forcing the major political parties to seek their vote; therefore it is reasonable to assume that eventually this considerable population growth will translate into more political power for Puerto Ricans and other Latinos/as in future years.

The most obvious accomplishments of the Puerto Rican civil rights movement were in the educational arena (see Chapter 6). Many persistent problems and challenges faced by students in New York City's public schools and those of other large US cities where the majority of Puerto Ricans resided made it relatively easy to define an agenda for change. Among the most pressing educational policy issues were high dropout rates at the secondary school and college levels, the practice of pushing high school students to pursue vocational training rather than a college career, the lack of bilingual education and instruction in English as a second language for new migrants and their children, the underrepresentation of Puerto Ricans and Latinos/as among teachers, administrators, and members of city educational boards and town councils, and the inadequate physical conditions and services of many public schools in segregated communities of color. Community involvement in condemning these conditions and demanding better school facilities, more inclusive multicultural curricula, and more effective and equitable educational experiences was central to the pursuit of much-needed reforms.

No agency has influenced and continues to advance Puerto Rican and other Latino/a youth educational goals more than ASPIRA (*aspira* means "aspire" in Spanish; see www.aspira.org). Established in New York City in 1961 under the visionary leadership of the late community leader Antonia Pantoja, this organization reached out to high school students to increase their motivation and preparation to complete secondary school, develop leadership skills, and pursue a college education.

In the 1950s, Pantoja had been a founder and president of the Hispanic Young Adult Association (HYAA), an organization that strove to make the New York City government more responsive to the needs of the expanding Puerto Rican migrant population. During its early years HYAA held voter registration drives and worked toward improving conditions in shelters for the homeless and fostering educational and leadership development among youth. Puerto Rican professionals Alice Cardona, Louis Núñez, Josephine Nieves, and several others joined Pantoja in these efforts. As the organization expanded, HYAA decided to focus on the specific needs of the Puerto Rican migrant community and, in 1954, changed its name to the Puerto Rican Association for Community Affairs (PRACA). Three years later, Pantoja and other leaders founded the Puerto Rican Forum (PRF, later the now defunct National Puerto Rican Forum). The PRF was originally conceived as "a launching-pad" for new community organizations and service programs (Pantoja 2002, 92). The organization originally aimed to assess the community's main problems and priorities and to facilitate the creation of new institutions to deal more appropriately with specific areas of need. It strove "to conceive ways of ensuring self-sufficiency and effective citizenship for the new wave of Puerto Ricans emigrating to the United States." Under the directorship of Frank Bonilla, during its early years the PRF concentrated on developing leadership and increasing educational opportunities for Puerto Rican youth and planted the seeds for the subsequent creation of ASPIRA. The PRF also provided services in adult literacy, English as a second language, and job placement. Another important accomplishment of the PRF was the creation of Boricua College in 1972, the first private Latino/a bilingual higher education institution in New York City. With offices in New York, Chicago, and Río Piedras, Puerto Rico, for many years the PRF served the educational and employment needs of low-income Latinos/as.

The War on Poverty, launched by the Johnson administration in the mid-1960s, provided the resources for a new wave of antipoverty programs. These new opportunities led to perhaps the best-funded endeavor aimed at alleviating the poverty of most Puerto Rican New Yorkers: the Puerto Rican Community Development Project (PRCDP). With the involvement of Pantoja and other PRF members, the PRCDP brought together the various professional agencies and grassroots organizations serving the community to develop "a model for comprehensive community development and advocacy" (Pantoja 2002, 114), aimed at reducing Puerto Rican poverty. But the project fell short of fulfilling its major goal. Stiff competition for federal funding and other power struggles between members of the PRF and the Commonwealth's Migration Division provoked the resignation of Pantoja and many others from the PRCDP board.

The lack of federal government oversight of antipoverty programs led a few of the barrio leaders administering them to use some of the jobs funded by these programs for political favors in their own city boroughs, intensifying power struggles and divisions within the community and sometimes undermining their respective efforts. As with many of the antipoverty programs of this period, their positive effects were short-term; they gradually disappeared when the US Congress reduced and eventually eliminated federal funding for these programs, curtailing their potential for any long-term impact.

On the other hand, organizations such as ASPIRA, Boricua College, and Hostos Community College are among the most successful and dynamic educational institutions founded by Puerto Ricans in New York City. In later years, they inspired Puerto Ricans to seek more advanced higher education degrees and appointment to academic research and administrative positions. In recent decades, some have become presidents, chancellors, deans, department chairs, and productive scholars at a wide range of colleges and universities throughout the United States.

Antonia Pantoja's multiple pioneering contributions to the US Puerto Rican community were recognized nationally when President Bill Clinton awarded her the Medal of Freedom in 1996. The former factory worker, schoolteacher, social worker, and activist dedicated over half a century to the various community-building activities described above, playing a leadership role in the creation of several of the most prominent organizations that continue to serve Puerto Ricans, Dominicans, and other Latinos/as in New York City and other parts of the country.

As the leading advocacy agency for New York Puerto Ricans and other Latinos/as, ASPIRA joined forces in 1972 with the newly created PRLDEF and filed a legal case against New York City's Board of Education demanding the implementation of bilingual education programs for students with limited English proficiency. The outcome of *ASPIRA v. Board of Education* was a consent decree that mandated bilingual instruction in certain New York City schools. The most visible advocates of bilingual education throughout the state included educators such as Hernán La Fontaine, Luis Fuentes, Carmen Pérez, María Ramírez, Luis O. Reyes, and Awilda Orta. La Fontaine and Pérez were among the founders and former presidents of the National Association for Bilingual Education, also established in 1972. Pérez and Ramírez played a leadership role in promoting bilingual and international education in New York State's Department of Education. For more than three decades, Pérez headed the Bilingual Education Bureau, which monitored the implementation and effectiveness of these programs. Reyes is a member of New York's Board of Regents, a research associate at the Center for Puerto Rican Studies, and a former member of New York City's Board of Education.

Grassroots organizations in working-class communities, in particular, stood out in the struggle for better schools and against segregation. Worthy of mention is United Bronx Parents, Inc., founded in 1964 under the leadership of Evelina López Antonetty. A dedicated grassroots activist, López Antonetty rallied Puerto Rican parents to form an alliance with African American parents in order to advocate more effectively for school desegregation, the physical and curricular improvement of schools, and increasing efforts to motivate students to seek college degrees. For many decades, the New York City Board of Education and the powerful United Federation of Teachers and American Federation of Teachers, which were controlled by the white majority, curtailed the licensing of Puerto Rican and Latino/a teachers in general. It was common practice for a Puerto Rican teacher with a Spanish accent to be denied a license by the board and relegated to the corps of auxiliary teachers with limited possibilities for career advancement. This practice affected other teachers with foreign accents as well. Parents demanded the hiring of more Puerto Rican and Latino/a teachers and administrators and the establishment of bilingual education and a multicultural curriculum as a way of improving student retention rates, academic achievement, and motivation to pursue higher education. Additionally, they denounced the common practice of "tracking" students of color into vocational areas rather than encouraging them to go to college, as well as the overall disregard for their cultural heritage and the Spanish language, which had detrimental effects on their self-esteem and how they valued education. Other demands included administrative decentralization and more community control over schools.

Several other founders of HYAA have occupied leadership positions in organizations that promote the well-being and advancement of their communities. A notable figure was Alice Cardona, the program coordinator of United Bronx Parents and cofounder of the Hispanic Women's Center, known as HACER (*hacer* means "to do, make, or build"). This latter organization focused on the particular educational needs of women. Another HYAA founding member, Louis Núñez, was among the founders and directors of the National Puerto Rican Coalition (NPRC) in Washington, DC. Since 1977 the NPRC has concentrated on advocacy and public policy issues, drawing attention to the concerns of the stateside Puerto Rican community.

Influencing legislation and formulating public policy at the municipal and state levels constituted two of the original goals of the nonpartisan Institute for Puerto Rican Policy (IPRP), the predecessor of today's National Institute for Latino Policy (NILP; www.nilpnetwork.org). Established in New York in 1982 by Angelo Falcón, the institute has for many years concentrated on analyzing the patterns of Puerto Rican and Latino/a participation in New York's electoral politics and on redistricting issues. It also tracks demographic changes in the state population. In 2000, the PRLDEF and the IPRP combined their legal and public policy expertise and merged into one organization. This alliance was dissolved in 2005, when they became separate organizations again. For several years, the IPRP served as the policy and advocacy division of the PRLDEF, coordinating projects on a variety of issues, such as Latino/a municipal priorities, voting rights and electoral reform, bilingual education, and advocacy training. The NILP shifted focus to national issues in order to be more inclusive of the wider range of intersecting policy issues impacting the lives of most US Latinos/as, but it continues to play an important advocacy role in identifying the state and national needs of Puerto Rican communities.

Other Community Organizations

For almost four decades the Migration Division (1951–1989) of the Department of Labor (i.e., the Commonwealth Office), established during the administration of Luis Muñoz Marín (see Chapter 3), tried to facilitate Puerto Rican migrants' introduction to the New York environment and that of other major US cities. Additional branches were established subsequently in other urban centers with large concentrations of Puerto Ricans. The office provided orientation and employment services, housing information, and English-language classes and also promoted cultural activities. According to Cabán (2005), the Migration Division was an important component of the island's industrialization program, making it easier for migrants to find employment and housing. But the office also played a role in diverting the stream of migrants from the larger cities of settlement to multiple smaller locations where industrial, agricultural, or service labor was most needed. Migration was a way of reducing the number of unemployed workers in Puerto Rico; thus Puerto Rico's government influenced many of the division's policies and activities. But through the years, with changes in its leadership and the emergence of new grassroots organizations that understood better the day-to-day problems and struggles of the migrant population and the racism and deplorable working conditions they sometimes faced, the Migration Division became an important presence within the largest communities of the diaspora. With time, it was subject to political changes in Puerto Rico. The office tended to receive more attention when the PPD was in power and less when the PNP took control of the island's government. In 1991, the division became the Department of Community Affairs, which was abolished in 1994 when PNP candidate Pedro Roselló was elected governor. It was replaced by the Puerto Rican Federal Affairs Administration (PRFAA; prfaa.pr.gov). For some years, one of the agency's most notable efforts was its voter registration campaigns aimed at increasing political representation and engaging more Puerto Ricans and Latinos/as in the US political process. However, the PRFAA's current mission is to engage in "the task of ably representing and advancing the needs of the Government of Puerto Rico before federal, state, and local governments." With regional offices in New York, Orlando, and Washington, DC, the agency does not offer employment and housing services; nor does it focus on migrants' needs. After shifting the focus of its mission, the office mostly engages in lobbying efforts and a broad legislative agenda on bills and programs that maintain the flow of federal funds to Puerto Rico also received by the states. PRFAA also promotes the economic and public policy initiatives of the island government. Under the PNP leadership, however, PRFAA is often perceived as serving to promote the party's pro-statehood agenda.

On another front, the Puerto Rican Family Institute, Inc. (PRFI; www .prfi.org), is a health and human service agency founded in 1960 by a group of Puerto Rican social workers in New York City. PRFI focuses on services to Puerto Rican and other Latino/a families. Among its multiple services are home-based crisis intervention, mental health clinics, home-care services, HIV/AIDS education and prevention, outreach services to the homeless, a lifeline program for seniors, a Head Start program for children, and other educational services. PRFI strives to avoid the disintegration of poor families because of socioeconomic or health-related hardships, as well as other problems migrants and immigrants experience in their adjustment to a culturally and linguistically different environment.

Grassroots activism has led, through the years, to the emergence of numerous Puerto Rican–focused community organizations in New York and other cities that service the stateside communities in multiple areas. As the stateside Puerto Rican population continues to increase, many of these organizations enjoy the opportunity to carry on and expand the scope of their endeavors. A good example is provided by La Casa de Don Pedro (www.lacasanwk.org) in Newark, named for Pedro Albizu Campos and started in 1972 by ten migrant families striving "to achieve self-sufficiency and empowerment." The organization now serves Puerto Ricans and other Latinos/as, as well as African Americans residing in Newark's North End area. Among La Casa's early initiatives were the opening of New Jersey's first bilingual day-care center and services for at-risk youth. It now runs multiple programs focused on community-based social services and comprehensive community development, with initiatives for affordable housing, workforce development and job placement, health services, and a vast array of other grassroots outreach activities.

Professional Puerto Rican women in the United States came together to form the National Conference of Puerto Rican Women (NACOPRW) in 1972 in Washington, DC, to deal with the "dual discrimination" they experienced because of their ethnicity and gender. The notion of women "organizing for change" was at the core of the organization's goals (NACOPRW 1977). Additional chapters were established in New York City, Chicago, and Hartford. The NACOPRW was an early advocate of the Equal Rights Amendment to the US Constitution. Additionally, it promoted women's leadership training, fought for equal representation of women in government agencies, and tackled neglected issues related to women's poverty, family planning, and health. The organization's visibility reached its peak during the United Nation's International Women's Year in 1975 and subsequent Decade for Women (1975–1985), since it was the only women's group with a national reach voicing the concerns and needs of Latinas. Some of the Puerto Rican leaders involved in the early years of the NACOPRW were Aída Berio, Lourdes Miranda King, Paquita Vivó, Carmen Delgado Votaw, and Alice Cardona. Although not as visible as during its early years, the NACOPRW continues to hold annual conferences, and the regional chapters now concentrate on issues specific to their particular local communities.

Bringing together the combined strength and expertise of several established US-based Puerto Rican organizations to promote cultural enrichment, El Comité Noviembre (the November Committee) was established in New York City in 1987. November has been designated as Puerto Rican Heritage Month, since it marks the arrival of the Spanish to the island on November 19, 1493. Organizations such as ASPIRA, the Center for Puerto Rican Studies, the Museo del Barrio, PRLDEF, NCPRR, and the PRFAA all support a wide range of cultural events under the umbrella of El Comité Noviembre. Additionally, the organization sponsors a scholarship program and was instrumental in mobilizing the community around issues such as a solidarity campaign on behalf of the people of Vieques and the release of political prisoners. Its annual programs highlight Puerto Rican contributions to the state and nation.

This sampling of the many community institutions and organizations created by stateside Puerto Ricans mostly highlights some of the longest standing and most successful in making an impact within their local communities and those achieving some state and national recognition for their work. With the wider geographic dispersion of the stateside Puerto Rican population, it is not possible to do justice to the many other worthy manifestations and concrete outcomes of their collective spirit and activism.

Community Resistance and Empowerment Struggles

During the 1960s and 1970s, urban renewal projects targeted some of the older low-income minority neighborhoods of inner cities and made the land available to private developers to build new and more profitable housing and commercial buildings that would in turn increase property tax revenues at the expense of displacing and replacing entire communities and historic areas. Some of these neighborhoods were located in strategic areas where it was certain that real estate values would significantly increase with more luxurious new apartment buildings, restaurants, and businesses. The community dislocations prompted by the wave of urban renewal projects in major US cities also produced an upsurge of grassroots activism and protests among minority communities against city authorities and developers. Under these adverse conditions of inner-city decay and housing displacement, the Puerto Rican community of Chicago's Lincoln Park, the first neighborhood where Puerto Ricans settled during the years of the Great Migration and where a Puerto Rican youth turf gang named the Young Lords emerged in the early 1960s, was eventually torn down.

After a few years of gang life on the streets and in and out of jail for drug-related offenses, one of the Young Lords members, José "Cha Cha" Jiménez, decided to turn his life around and become a community activist. Inspired by the militancy and impact of the Black Panthers' efforts to empower African American communities, in 1968 Jiménez became the leader of the Young Lords, and the group was transformed into an organization determined to mobilize the community into collective action to denounce police brutality, segregation, urban renewal housing displacement projects, and the city government's failure to provide basic services to the citizens of poor neighborhoods. The Young Lords' militant style in defying Chicago's political machinery and government bureaucracy and in empowering the community encouraged other activist groups and organizations to join in denouncing decades of neglect and abuse by the power structures and in stating their demands for change and social justice. Before long other branches of the Young Lords appeared in New York, Philadelphia, and a few other cities (see Young Lords Party and Abramson ([1971] 2011); Whalen 2001; I. Morales 2016). While some members of these communities saw the Young Lords as a radical fringe organization, and its revolutionary ideology and paramilitary structure did not generate extensive support throughout the country or in Puerto Rico, younger generations of community organizers and civil rights activists see it as a symbol of successful community mobilization and empowerment in the struggles for social justice. In later years, the early activism of the Young Lords and other community organizations of the 1960s and early 1970s help lay a foundation for subsequent struggles for increased community control of ethnic neighborhoods in several US cities facing urban renewal and gentrification projects.

Two of the most outstanding models of Puerto Rican grassroots organizing and mobilization against federal and local governmental urban renewal drives to displace communities are Chicago's Paseo Boricua (Boricua Promenade) and Boston's Villa Victoria (Victory Village). The symbolic importance of Puerto Rican communities like these in carving out what Ramos-Zayas (2003) characterizes as "spaces of resistance and autonomy," whereby these communities "Puerto Ricanized" and imprinted their respective neighborhoods with a distinctive cultural and political character, is undeniable. In both localities, the communities have managed to assert relative control in shaping their development and future. Moreover, the vitality and engagement of Puerto Ricans and other Latinos/as in projects and activities sponsored by these communities is obvious to anyone who visits them.

Defining itself as the "flagship" of Puerto Rican neighborhoods in the United States, Paseo Boricua in Chicago emerged from the upheaval and resentments caused by the aforementioned years of urban renewal projects that eventually displaced Puerto Ricans from the Lincoln Park to the Humboldt Park area of the city. Long-lasting patterns of racial profiling and abuse by Chicago's police, combined with poor housing and schooling conditions and the city's disregard for the well-being of its less privileged citizens, provoked, in the summer of 1966, three days of violent confrontations and a neighborhood uprising known today as the Division Street Riots. The shooting of a young Puerto Rican man by the police during a Puerto Rican parade was a major catalyst of the riots. But the violent events also motivated the emergence of community organizations that would give visibility to the many pressing concerns of a neglected Chicago Puerto Rican community. Over a decade later, in the summer of 1977 during the annual parade festivities, confrontations and the killing of two Puerto Rican young men by the police fueled several days of rioting in the Humboldt Park area that left more than a hundred people injured and also led to multiple arrests. Both the Division Street and Humbold Park riots were the culmination of many years of fermenting anger over "systematic oppression" deployed by law enforcement and city authorities against the poverty-stricken, displaced, and abandoned community that created the "psychological climate" for the violence (Padilla 1987, 150–153).

Since 1995, Paseo Boricua in Chicago, a six-block area of Division Street, has proudly boasted of being the only officially recognized Puerto Rican neighborhood in the United States. Today it stands as a symbol of the resilience of Puerto Rican grassroots mobilization and agency that empowered this particular community to transform its surrounding environment into a distinctively Puerto Rican space. Two towering cross-street Puerto Rican flags made out of steel are the gateways to Paseo Boricua. The award-winning flag sculptures have architectural flair and are a nod to the many Puerto Rican migrants who labored in Chicago's steel mills during the decades of the Great Migration. The neighborhood is also home to the Juan Antonio Corretjer Puerto Rican Cultural Center (PRCC), the administrative propeller of most of Paseo Boricua's major community-centered initiatives. Under the visionary and charismatic leadership of José Elias López and through the commitment and hard work of its staff and many other community members, PRCC defines itself as "a community-based grassroots educational, health, and cultural services organization founded on the principles of self-determination, self-actualization, and self-sufficiency that is activist-oriented" (see PRCC n.d.a). Through *La voz* (The voice), the community's bilingual newspaper, PRCC keeps residents informed of events and issues of interest or concern to the neighborhood and is an important outlet for recognizing the contributions and achievements of Puerto Ricans.

Paseo Boricua's unequivocal historical, cultural, and political Puerto Rican flavor is found in the numerous colorful murals that embellish the PRCC area and in many of the neighborhood buildings, schools, and parks. The murals, sculptures, and other paintings that adorn these community spaces celebrate moments in Puerto Rican history, prominent island and stateside Puerto Ricans of the past and present, and the collective struggles and self-determination of this remarkable community and the Puerto Rican people. Puerto Rican nationalism and the liberation of Puerto Ricans are very much present in these public artistic expressions and the names of various buildings and schools.

Among the community's educational accomplishments is the Dr. Pedro Albizu Campos High School on Division Street, a charter school founded in 1972 as part of the Alternative Schools Network. One of the PRCC's most recent undertakings is the "Community as a Campus" comprehensive education initiative introduced in 2015. This community-based plan centers on educational enhancement that will revitalize the Roberto Clemente Community Academy, a Chicago public high school, and the several public elementary schools that feed students into it.

Health services are also central to the community. The Integrated PASEO (Promoting Actions That Support Recovery Through Services and Outreach) project sponsors a series of initiatives in health education, prevention, and screening through inclusive programs that strive to serve "Chicago's most vulnerable populations" (see PRCC n.d.b).

Since 2014, the National Museum of Puerto Rican Arts and Culture (NMPRAC) has widened the scope of and built on the work initiated by the Institute for Puerto Rican Art and Culture in the 1990s. Located in a renovated historic building in the Humboldt Park vicinity, it is currently the only museum in the United States that focuses entirely on Puerto Rican arts and culture. Under the leadership of Billy Ocasio, its chief executive officer, a former Chicago City Council ward alderman and a current advisor to the Illinois governor, NMPRAC's vast program of exhibits and visiting Puerto Rican artists and other cultural events enriches the lives of Paseo Boricua's residents and visitors. Moreover, based on its belief in "the power of art to change lives," the NMPRAC dedicates an entire wing of its building to art education programs for students in Chicago's public schools that include hands-on arts and crafts workshops in a wide range of art forms.

Another important center of cultural and social activity is La Casita de Don Pedro (The Little House of Don Pedro), constructed in 1997. The house was designed to resemble a typical Puerto Rican wooden house still found in the island's rural areas and most towns.

The Casita has a community-based garden-gallery designed with the participation of Pedro Albizu Campos High School students and other neighborhood residents. The red mosaic garden has a white-stone star-shaped design built to resemble the Puerto Rican flag when viewed from above. The gallery holds a collection of Puerto Rican photographs and artisan crafts. A statue of Nationalist leader Pedro Albizu Campos in the middle of the stone star, a painting of the Casita's front iron gate made to resemble a Puerto Rican flag, and another of former Nationalist political prisoner Lolita Lebrón welcome visitors to the site.

Inquilinos Boricuas en Acción (IBA, Boricua Tenants in Action) was founded in 1968 in the South End of Boston, where the residents of this Puerto Rican neighborhood fought tirelessly and successfully against displacement from their homes and community and for the right to control its development. Out of one of the most successful grassroots battles against urban renewal abuses emerged IBA's Villa Victoria (Victory Village), an affordable-housing complex constructed for residents on the land that occupied their former homes (see Small 2004; Matos Rodríguez 2005). At the entrance to the village is Plaza Betances, with its impressive mosaic mural that displays a collage of Puerto Rican history and culture, and an attractive sign that bears the name Villa Victoria above the dictum *Lucha puertorriqueña, "Orgullo Borincano"* (Puerto Rican Struggle, "Source of Pride for

Boricuas"); words that hail the success, pride, solidarity, and resilience of this community. Today, in an increasingly Latinoized city environment, IBA sponsors preschool, after-school, and summer programs, youth development, a Community and Technology Center, a Center for the Arts, and an educational and financial development project with Bunker Hill Community College, all aimed at enhancing opportunities for individuals and families of several Latino/a national origins to build a more prosperous future.

The shift in focus of the study of Puerto Rican migration from New York City to other cities was initially slow but is growing at a steady pace in recent decades. So far, it has yielded well-documented and engaging historical narratives and portrayals of the different waves of Puerto Rican workers and families and the conditions they faced as newcomers and residents in other places.

The expanding body of scholarship on the history and presence of Puerto Ricans in a variety of US cities and states broadens the scope to analyze the particular factors and circumstances that brought Puerto Rican migrants to other major locations at different points. These studies represent fertile ground for pursuing comparative studies of a wider range of communities and the more specific factors that account for major differences in socioeconomic and educational indicators, as well as the conditions that may or may not contribute to Puerto Ricans' social mobility and their incorporation into the political process. Considering the ongoing geographic dispersion of stateside Puerto Ricans to different cities, states, and regions, comparative approaches would also provide valuable insights into how communities were established and evolved through time, the scope and impact of the organizations and institutions they created, and what they have contributed with their labor, small businesses, and cultural creativity to the development of multiple US cities. Furthermore, it would allow scholars to assess the extent to which a long history of segregation, disparaging and racialized characterizations of the community, and unequal treatment is replicated in older and newer geographic settings. The end result would be a more nuanced profile of those areas where Puerto Ricans have made substantive progress in climbing the socioeconomic ladder or expanding their political power and an enhanced understanding of their range of interactions with other communities of color and the white population, depending on the particular racial, ethnic, and class composition of their places of residence. But equally important are the legacies and traditions bestowed by pioneer generations of Puerto Ricans across the country that give continuity and a sense of community and belonging to US-born generations, as well as to the uninterrupted influx of new migrants.

Comprehensive foundational studies of migration to Philadelphia, now the city with the second-largest concentration of Puerto Ricans, during the post–World War II Great Migration years and those of the interwar period have allowed a more discerning understanding of the historical evolution of this community. Whalen's (2001) study of migration in the postwar period broke ground in revealing stories of the range of Puerto Rican men and women workers struggling to make a livelihood in a less than welcoming setting. By relying on a mix of oral interviews and archival sources, Whalen put a human face to their labors and survival struggles: men arriving as contract laborers brought to the area for jobs in agriculture, women laboring in garment factories, others employed in other blue-collar occupations. Her analysis also shows how changes in the global economy, most notably the decline in manufacturing and other sectors of the city's economy, affected their lives. By describing their productive lives, organizations, and traditions that brought some cohesion to the community, she challenges prevailing negative views of underprivileged Puerto Rican migrants. Whalen also gives visual recognition to the Puerto Rican historical presence in the city in *El Viaje: Puerto Ricans of Philadelphia* (2006) by unveiling photographs from archival sources to show early Puerto Rican settlers and the generations that succeeded them in a variety of environments, ending the invisibility of migrants coming to Philadelphia since the early decades of the twentieth century.

A more recent additional contribution to the study of Philadelphia's interwar years (1917–1945) is Vázquez-Hernández's (2017) *Before the Wave: Puerto Ricans in Philadelphia, 1910–1945*. This particular study focuses on the formative stages of the community, the interactions of Puerto Ricans with other immigrant groups in the city, and how they established what is now a long-standing Puerto Rican presence in Philadelphia. Whalen points out that this study will allow other scholars "to think more comparatively" when examining Puerto Rican migration experiences in this and other areas of settlement and their particular interactions with other ethnic and racial groups.

For a long time Chicago housed the second-largest concentration of stateside Puerto Ricans; Philadelphia now occupies that position. But Chicago is still second, after New York City, in terms of generating scholarship about the history and presence of its Puerto Rican community. The pioneering contributions of anthropologist Elena Padilla, an outcome of rigorous ethnographic work in Chicago while she was a master's student at the University of Chicago and, later on, for her book *Up from Puerto Rico* (1958), which was the first major study of Puerto Rican migrants in New York City carried out by a Puerto Rican researcher, introduced new approaches for studying less privileged communities.

Further comprehensive research on Puerto Ricans in Chicago did not occur until Félix Padilla's (1985) *Latino Ethnic Consciousness: The Case of Mexican Americans and Puerto Ricans in Chicago*. His study pointed to their shared similar experiences during the 1960s and 1970s and how their strong ethnic and racial consciousness and collective panethnicity strengthened them in their battles to influence social and political change on behalf of their respective communities. The politics of race, citizenship, and space are at the center of Ramos-Zayas's (2003) groundbreaking ethnographic study about the "national performances" of Puerto Ricans in Chicago, which show a confluence of political and cultural nationalism but also address important differences within the community and in the interactions of Puerto Ricans with other groups. The prospects and hurdles to a shared panethnic consciousness of *latinidad* among Puerto Ricans and Mexicans in Chicago, what De Genova and Ramos-Zayas (2003) refer to as "Latino crossings," are further explored in their ethnographic analysis of the politics of race and citizenship within these two communities. Both the Paseo Boricua and La Dieciocho (Pilsen–Eighteenth Street) are community spaces for Puerto Ricans and Mexicans, respectively, where the performance of nationalism is illustrative of the individual cultural, social, and political engagements and distinctive identities of these two groups. Lilia Fernández (2012) examines connections between Mexicans and Puerto Ricans in postwar Chicago during an earlier period (1940–1960) in an in-depth study of their "distinct racial position" and the racial tensions and conflicts that emerged from their interactions with African Americans and Italian Americans. Neighborhood encroachments and later the urban renewal projects instigated by the white power structures and developers triggered this situation and caused the displacement of Latinos/as and African Americans from their previous neighborhoods. Another noteworthy Chicago-focused publication is Mérida Rúa's (2012) ethnographic study of "the grounded identity of Puerto Ricans" in the city. Rúa refers to the foundational stages of the community, such as the enrollment of University of Puerto Rico students in the University of Chicago in 1945 (many later became part of the crop of new technocrats who guided Operation Bootstrap, which transformed the island into a modern industrial society) and the recruitment of Puerto Rican women for domestic work and other laborers for foundry industries in the area. Puerto Rican connections with other Chicago communities and the circular nature of transnational connections with communities in Puerto Rico are the focus of Gina Pérez's (2004) ethnographic research into Puerto Rican families in different locations, such as Chicago, Florida, and San Sebastián, Puerto Rico.

Adding to the more in-depth scholarly studies briefly described are visually appealing vintage photographic histories of a wide range of iconic US communities, part of the Images of America series. So far, the series includes only Puerto Rican communities in New York City (Matos-Rodríguez and Hernández 2001; Sánchez Korrol and Hernández 2010), Chicago (W. Cruz 2004), and Philadelphia (Whalen 2006).

Sharing the histories of neglected Puerto Rican communities is at the heart of *The Puerto Rican Diaspora: Historical Perspectives* (Whalen and Vázquez-Hernández 2005). The editors have taken another step in also promoting the work of other scholars that will foster comparative work on

Puerto Rican migration in a wide range of geographic locations. Some of these scholars continue to expand their research on their chosen communities of focus. Such is the case of Iris López, whose chapter in that volume recounts the history of Puerto Rican migrations to Hawaii in the early 1900s but also brings readers into the present as a result of her ethnographic work and interviews with descendants of the contract workers brought to the islands. She had begun to examine *Borinki* identity issues of this population in a prior publication (with Forbes 2001). A chapter by Rivera gives readers a taste of the experiences and struggles of Puerto Rican workers recruited to work, side by side with Mexicans, at a steel mill in Lorain, Ohio—part of a larger project to document and unveil the history of Lorain's Puerto Rican community. Both Lorain and Cleveland, Ohio, are key cities in documenting the understudied recruitment and settlement of Puerto Rican workers to different US industrial areas during the years of the Great Migration. Focusing on gender and class issues, Maura Toro-Morn highlights the neglected contributions of Puerto Rican working-class women recruited for domestic work in Chicago and of professional women and the struggles to balance paid work and family life. Bringing us back to the East Coast, Félix Matos Rodríguez's essay acknowledges the symbolic importance of the urban renewal battles that gave rise to Boston's Villa Victoria but also addresses some of the most pressing concerns stemming from the increasing Latinization of Boston.

The fastest-growing stateside Puerto Rican population is now in Florida, concentrated mostly in Central Florida but also found in Tampa, Miami, and other areas of South Florida; it will soon surpass the New York Puerto Rican population. The pace and pattern of Puerto Rican population growth in Florida became more evident in the 1980s when the Puerto Rican population reached 88,361, almost three times what it had been in 1970 (28,766). The pattern of growth continued at a faster pace and reached a figure of 194,443 by the dawn of the new millennium. By then, the "Puerto Ricanization" of Florida (Duany and Silver 2010) had become a palpable reality and was drawing increased attention from migration researchers. Most recent data show that 21 percent of the stateside Puerto Rican population is still in New York, but Florida has closed the gap, with 19 percent of the total (Meléndez and Vargas-Ramos 2017). The 109 percent rate of Puerto Rican population growth in Florida during the 2000–2015 period indicates the degree of demographic change in Florida.

With a current population estimate of slightly over a million in 2015, the Puerto Rican presence in Florida, however, is long-standing. For instance, during the early 1900s some working-class Puerto Ricans were drawn to the tobacco factories of Tampa, most notably labor organizers and writers such as Luisa Capetillo, a pioneer of Puerto Rico's first-wave feminist movement, and Angel Dieppa, also a socialist anarchist labor activist who wrote for the labor press and published a book about the future of humanity. It has been documented that a few Puerto Ricans had their own cigar-making workshops (Duany and Silver 2010). Larger numbers of Puerto Ricans came to Tampa in the 1950s to work in agriculture and the garment industry, especially after the latter began to decline in New York City. They also came to Central Florida to work in agriculture and other jobs, at a time when land speculators were coming to Puerto Rico to entice people to purchase inexpensive parcels of land in Central Florida, when that area was still less populated and undeveloped—a striking contrast to the fantasy land and tourist entertainment mecca that it is today for families from all over the world.

Substantive studies, stimulated by the seminal work of Duany and Matos-Rodríguez (2006) on Puerto Ricans in Orlando and Central Florida, offered a detailed historical and socioeconomic profile of the growing population. This body of research expanded so much that four years later a special issue of *Centro Journal* focused on Central Florida. Duany and Silver (2010) introduce the volume by providing the historical framework of the community's evolution and its current status. The research essays selected for the volume represent a vast array of in-depth topics, including home-ownership, housing segregation, health, issues of adaptation, identity discourses, political participation, and schooling experiences. They all contribute to a more nuanced understanding of the realities and experiences of Puerto Ricans in a geographic setting that has experienced significant transformations since the 1950s and where they were interacting with Latinos/as of different national origins.

Puerto Rico's economic woes and the specific factors that have propelled the New Millennium Migration to Florida and other states were analyzed in previous chapters. No one anticipated that the ravaging effects of Hurricane Maria on the island would change dramatically both Puerto Rico and Florida within just a few weeks. While Puerto Rico was experiencing a state of emergency that continued for several months, a tsunami of Puerto Ricans (over 130,000 left the island) came primarily to Central Florida and a few other US destinations. Chapter 5 discussed the implications of this major exodus for both Puerto Rico and Florida. Considering Puerto Rico's current financial insolvency and the resources required for the posthurricane process of reconstruction and recovery, it is realistic to expect that migration will continue and that a significant portion of those who left the island will remain in that area or other US localities.

All of these communities have over time developed their own cultural legacies and traditions shared with other Puerto Ricans and non–Puerto Ricans in the areas where they live. The most prominent stateside Puerto Rican celebration is the Puerto Rican Day Parade in New York City. Similar parades or festivals are currently held in Philadelphia, Chicago, Hartford, Orlando, Philadelphia, Newark, Jersey City, Boston, and Cleveland, to name only a few, but none has yet attracted the large crowds and media coverage of the New York City event. Originally known in Spanish as *el Desfile Puertorriqueño*, this vital tradition started in New York in 1959 as a symbol of the unity and strength of a growing community. The parade's content and attendance have expanded significantly since the earlier days (see Alicea and Velásquez 2007). Gilberto Gerena Valentín, a community activist and labor organizer in New York City for more than half a century, was involved in the early years of the parade. He was a founder of the Congreso de Pueblos (Council of Hometown Clubs), which for many years was central to the organizing of this annual event (see Gerena Valentín and Rodríguez-Fraticelli 2013).

The importance of hometown clubs in fostering solidarity and coalescing a sense of community within the early Puerto Rican *colonias* was underscored by Sánchez Korrol ([1983] 1994) in her pioneering book on this period. Each club was created by Puerto Rican migrants coming from the same town in Puerto Rico. Sánchez Korrol ([1983] 1994) also noted that these clubs "provided a home away from home predominantly oriented toward sociocultural and political affairs" (12).

Estades (1980) also had noted that the parade was inspired by the proliferation of Puerto Rican hometown clubs throughout the city. Town mayors of many of Puerto Rico's municipalities annually bring delegations to New York City to participate in the parade, and many government officials and other celebrities join the cultural and social gatherings related to what is now an institutionalized annual summer event and one of the largest parades in the country, generally attracting about a million spectators.

Another memorable tradition that emerged within the diaspora was the building of *casitas* (small wooden houses), which started in the 1970s. Only a few of them still remain in New York, but when they appeared in the South Bronx, they served important functions for some struggling communities. These wooden houses were built to bring aspects of the Puerto Rican countryside and popular folklore to the inner city. Often sited on empty or abandoned lots in decaying urban areas, the *casitas* were erected on stilts and painted in bright colors by members of the community, resembling country houses back in Puerto Rico, and landscaped with vegetable and flower gardens or other types of foliage. Used for community celebrations, meetings, social gatherings, and political rallies, the *casitas* in many ways attempted to recreate visual images and cultural practices of the homeland and provide remembrances of Puerto Rican life relocated in urban environments. Most of the *casitas'* names reflected the nostalgia of displaced migrants for their homelands: Villa Puerto Rico (Puerto Rican Village), Rincón Criollo (Downhome Corner), or Añoranzas de Mi Patria (Yearning for My Homeland). During the period when they emerged, the *casitas* were regarded as "a true architecture of resistance subverting the traditional city" (Aponte-Parés 1995, 14).

One of the remaining New York *casitas* is Rincón Criollo, originally built in 1978 in the South Bronx by the late José "Chema" Soto, a neighborhood resident. Thus the structure is unsurprisingly also known as La Casita de Chema (The Little House of Chema). After the city reclaimed the lot where this particular *casita* had been built, the community persuaded city officials to allow them to rebuild it on a nearby lot. The city government eventually tore down most of the New York *casitas* in the South Bronx.

In Chicago, the previously mentioned Casita de Don Pedro (The Little House of Don Pedro) at Paseo Boricua, built in 1997, remains a lively cultural and social site for Puerto Ricans. Less known is Puerto Rican House, located at Hawaii's Plantation Village, an outdoor museum and botanical gardens located in Waipahu, a town not far from Honolulu. This museum was built on the old plantation where contract laborers were brought in the early twentieth century to work in the sugarcane fields, usually under wretched working conditions. Amid some restored buildings and artifacts from the old plantation, these particular small houses were constructed by the government to recognize the labor and multiple contributions of immigrants of several national origins—Filipinos, Puerto Ricans, Portuguese, Koreans, Chinese, and Japanese—to the historical and cultural legacies of the Hawaiian Islands. Some of the groups represented in these replicas of typical homes from the immigrants' respective homelands are still an integral part of the state's population, and they frequently use them for cultural and social events and festivities.

Decolonizing Knowledge

In the early 1970s, the late Frank Bonilla (1974), founder of the Centro de Estudios Puertorriqueños in New York City, in his essay "Beyond Survival: *Por qué seguiremos siendo puertorriqueños* [Why we will continue being Puerto Rican]," deplores the negative portrayals of Puerto Ricans perpetuated in most of the social science literature. He argued then for the need to break away from the barrage of recurrent and confining negative images and from the internalized inferiority complex that for a long time dominated the discourses about the Puerto Rican people and were, on the whole, by-products of their subordinate colonial experiences. Bonilla (1974) also stresses the urgency of "an unprecedented job of psychological and cultural reconstitution and construction" in order for Puerto Ricans "to grow affirmatively as a culturally integrated and distinctive collectivity" (363–364). This process would make it possible for them to move beyond the mere notion of survival as a community and engage in developing "a collective vision that reaches out to Puerto Ricans everywhere" (370).

Foreseeing the pressing need to decolonize knowledge about the Puerto Rican people, which is crucial to the process of unveiling and preserving a historical memory and constructing new decolonial imaginaries within the diaspora, Bonilla's discerning comments pointed to basic biases and short-comings in the available scholarship up to that point—a body of knowledge that often reiterated shortsighted, misinformed, and problem-oriented per-spectives and unflattering representations of Puerto Ricans. Before the 1970s, little had been done to document the multifaceted full history of a predominantly working-class Puerto Rican migration to the United States (Centro History Task Force 1979, 1982). With few exceptions, studies about stateside Puerto Ricans were written by US and other foreign schol-ars and thus markedly skewed in their recycling of similar myths and stereotypes—a blueprint that dominated most studies about racially and ethnically diverse impoverished communities. But, above all, there was also a recognition of an existing wedge between island and stateside communi-ties. Intermittently, Puerto Rico's media and the general public subscribed to similar negative stereotypes or were either indifferent to or uninformed about the lives and survival struggles and poverty conditions faced by their migrant fellow citizens living in the United States. These statements stand out even more, if one considers that for island Puerto Ricans migration con-tinues to be a common choice. For many decades, the separation between the two communities was more palpable than it is in the present, and many islanders tended to perceive stateside Puerto Ricans as mostly poverty stricken, welfare dependent, and culturally deficient, the same negative stereotypes shared by a large segment of the general US population. Notwithstanding, it is appropriate to add that, since the 1970s, the separa-tion between both communities is being bridged by a large number of writ-ers, artists, musicians, scholars, activists, educators, political and civic lead-ers, and industrious Puerto Rican individuals and families, continuously navigating these two different cultural and linguistic worlds, yet driven to hang on to a distinctive and resilient sense of Puerto Ricanness.

Significant changes have occurred since the 1970s, mainly a result of the initiative, vision, and commitment of many US-based Puerto Rican studies scholars, educators, students, and activists, who, like the late Frank Bonilla, contested old assumptions, rectified omissions, and produced new knowledge and critical approaches that depict more accurately the wide range of experiences and contributions of stateside Puerto Ricans. These concerted efforts aimed to end their invisibility in the annals of both US and Puerto Rican history. But on the whole, a generalized lack of knowl-edge prevails within the white US mainstream society about what in a few more decades will be a majority population of color.

Now a legitimate and fairly institutionalized academic endeavor, the field of Puerto Rican studies emerged in the late 1960s and early 1970s and was first conceptualized and shaped by the experiences and struggles of Puerto Ricans as a disenfranchised ethnoracial minority. Part of a broader

206 Puerto Ricans in the United States

ethnic studies movement that engulfed many US universities and schools during those years, scholars, teachers, and community activists pushed for new perspectives and paradigms to address more effectively the experiences of those ethnic and racial groups remaining on the margins or left out of the mainstream of academic disciplines. The emergence of these new fields of inquiry, which also included feminist, gender, women's, and what is now LGBTQ studies, was made possible by the advocacy and vision of those wanting to challenge the exclusions and limitations of Western intellectual traditions and their Eurocentric, patriarchal, racializing, and heteronormative discourses and theoretical paradigms that perpetuated others' historical marginality or invisibility. It is indisputable that in the United States, Puerto Rican studies and other nontraditional interdisciplinary fields made important strides in transforming knowledge by generating new scholarship and teaching endeavors that focused on analyzing the intersectionalities of socially constructed categories of class, gender, race, and sexuality. In addition, they gave due recognition to the multiracial and multiethnic character and experiences of many groups excluded or misrepresented in conventional historical narratives. This groundbreaking research also exposed some of the traditional biases and normative assumptions of the traditional disciplines and their canons regarding depictions of groups relegated to the periphery of the homogenized "American experience" as defined up to then.

Under Bonilla's vision and leadership, the Centro de Estudios Puertorriqueños (Center for Puerto Rican Studies) was established in 1973 at the City University of New York (CUNY). Currently based at Hunter College's School of Social Work in Spanish Harlem, Centro's Library and Archives are regarded as the main and largest repository of archival materials on Puerto Rican migration and the stateside diaspora. Centro researchers and archivists continue to be part of a vanguard of scholars, activists, and practitioners offering new interpretations of Puerto Rican migration to the United States and drawing attention to the less known histories of a growing number of communities within the diaspora.[7] A few years earlier, the Centro de Estudios de la Realidad Puertorriqueña (CEREP; Center for the Study of Puerto Rican Reality), established in Puerto Rico in 1971, sponsored similar efforts in the ambitious and intricate intellectual project to decolonize scholarship about island Puerto Ricans.[8] CEREP researchers' early work inspired a boom of groundbreaking scholarship on the island in what was later referred to as "the new Puerto Rican historiography."[9] Consequently, since the early 1970s new generations of US-based and island researchers have been developing a more nuanced understanding of the historical roots, structural conditions, and unequal power relations between the colonizer and the colonized that explain Puerto Rican migration, including an analysis of the uninterrupted transnational circuit between island and stateside Puerto Rican communities.

The emergence of Puerto Rican studies programs at various US universities, in particular those affiliated with the CUNY, State University of New York (SUNY), and Rutgers University systems, paved the way for dispelling many of the myths about Puerto Ricans perpetuated in the scholarly literature. New research and teaching endeavors exposed some of the shortcomings of the traditional scholarship and inspired new approaches to the study of Puerto Ricans. Foremost among the efforts of this generation of Puerto Rican scholars was documenting the multifaceted experiences of a working-class diaspora, both in relation to the island's colonial condition and as a marginalized ethnoracial minority within the United States. Researchers then began to establish the link between Puerto Rico's colonial experience and the "internal colonialism" (Blauner 1972) being experienced by Puerto Ricans and other disenfranchised groups. Unquestionably, Puerto Rican studies scholars and activists continue to play a central role in the efforts to "decolonize" traditional interpretations of Puerto Rican migrant experiences, which often replicated the negative views and prejudices of the wider society. Puerto Rican studies scholars concentrated their efforts on documenting and recovering a collective presence and heritage that had been largely distorted or excluded from conventional histories of the United States. They also encouraged the analysis of power relations and of the structural conditions that contribute to perpetuating social and racial disparities.

Puerto Rican and other ethnic studies programs were the result of the collective activism of students, community members, and professionals directed toward making higher education more responsive to the needs of Puerto Ricans and other students of color. These programs were geared toward providing students with new knowledge about their historical and cultural roots; in addition they promoted important paradigm shifts within the academic disciplines in their study of ethnic, racial, and gender differences and raised awareness about the conditions afflicting communities of color and the multicultural diversity and character of US society. Moreover, they were instrumental in incorporating constructions and intersections of ethnicity, race, gender, class, and sexuality into the analysis of socioeconomic inequalities and the cumulative effects of these forms of oppression (A. Torres 2011–2012). Researchers also concentrated their efforts on documenting the multiple ways in which Puerto Ricans have contributed to the development of this nation. Their critical view of the shortcomings, biases, and exclusions of the traditional disciplines with respect to populations of color generally made it difficult for these programs to become institutionalized or gain acceptance as a legitimate part of the academic enterprise. Many white scholars and administrators tended to view them as "identity politics" and sources of "political correctness." These critics failed to acknowledge their own Eurocentric and patriarchal perspectives and biases, which for centuries had privileged the production of knowledge and marginalized or erased the experiences of women and populations of color, generally viewing them as subordinate or peripheral to established intellectual traditions.

Among the pioneering and subsequent wave of scholars involved in the administrative leadership of Puerto Rican studies departments and programs during their early years were Josephine Nieves, María Sánchez, Virginia Sánchez Korrol, and María Pérez at Brooklyn College; María Canino and Pedro Cabán at Rutgers University; Rafael Rodríguez and Jesse Vázquez at Queens College; Federico Aquino and Gabriel Haslip-Viera at City College; Eduardo Seda-Bonilla at Hunter College; María Teresa Babín and Clara E. Rodríguez at Lehman College; Antonio Pérez, Edna Acosta-Belén, and Elia H. Christensen at the University at Albany, SUNY; and Alfredo Matilla and Francisco Pagán at the University at Buffalo, SUNY. Fordham University and John Jay College, CUNY also established programs during the early 1970s.

By and large, Puerto Rican studies scholars tend to be representative of the "organic intellectual," combining a commitment to the advancement of knowledge and scholarship about Puerto Ricans with meaningful pedagogical and mentoring experiences for students, advocating for the needs of their local communities, and striving to change the biases and exclusionary practices of the traditional disciplines and their respective institutions and professions. Community service is also an important component of these programs, since it often includes internships and field experiences for students, along with opportunities for applied or basic research and activism that promotes social change.

The emergence of Puerto Rican studies as a legitimate academic field of inquiry brought about a debunking of the old myths and stereotypes about Puerto Ricans and new opportunities for scholarly research. The impact of these programs is far reaching, as they opened up new venues for the training of future generations of professionals with an increased knowledge and a more positive view of their cultural heritage and better preparation to work for the socioeconomic and political empowerment of their communities. They also brought new perspectives into mainstream scholarship and ended the exclusion of populations of color as producers of knowledge and enriched the teaching and learning process.

Since the 1970s, the vitality of Puerto Rican studies research and scholarship has been reflected in the many new scholarly books and doctoral dissertations in the social sciences, humanities, and professional fields focusing on multiple aspects of the realities and conditions of stateside Puerto Ricans, the histories of their communities, their institutions and organizations, and their cultural expressions, which have been published and influenced subsequent research and activism.

Puerto Rican and other ethnic studies programs introduced white students to important and uncomfortable issues of racial and gender power relations and multicultural diversity. In a broader sense, and despite the current backlashes and setbacks, focusing on these issues generates a more accurate understanding of the United States as a nation built with the labor and survival spirit of multiple immigrant and migrant groups of many different nationalities and races.

A lack of institutional support and adequate resources through the years caused the demise of some of the early Puerto Rican studies programs, but a respectable number survived and became more established. Some of the remaining programs later joined forces with more institutionalized Latin American and Caribbean area studies programs or expanded their scope to include the growing and broader panethnic field of Latino/a studies.[10] The emergence of Latino/a studies was propelled by an unprecedented population growth among Latinos/as in many different cities and states, which became more diversified because of the influx of new migrants from other Latin American and Caribbean nationalities in the 1980s and subsequent decades that eventually made them the largest US population of color in 2003. As of 2015, Mexicans, Puerto Ricans, and Cubans still represent the three largest national groups. Some of these expanded programs promoted postcolonial and transnational hemispheric approaches to studying the interactions and dynamics between the realities and conditions faced by US Latinos/as and those of their national counterparts in their respective countries of origin or ancestry (see Cabán 2009, 2011–2012).

The creation of the Centro de Estudios Puertorriqueños in 1973 was an important outcome of the overall Puerto Rican ethnic revitalization movement. With the initial support of the Ford Foundation and under the visionary leadership of Frank Bonilla, Centro sponsored new research and publications in neglected areas and began the long process of documenting the history of the Puerto Rican diaspora by engaging the community in this challenging endeavor. A vital aspect of these initial efforts was the development of its Library and Archives, presently located at Hunter College Silberman School of Social Work, part of CUNY. Through the years Centro's Library and Archives have become the leading repository of documents and materials about the Puerto Rican presence in the United States (Hernández 2011–2012). The indefatigable efforts of librarians and archivists Nélida Pérez, Pedro Juan Hernández, and Amílcar Tirado during its earlier years, and subsequently of Alberto Hernández-Banuchi and other dedicated staff members, have made the library's special archival collections an indispensable site for Puerto Rican studies researchers and students from all over the world. In most recent years, under the leadership of Centro director Edwin Meléndez, some of the most used archival collections are being digitized in order to make them more accessible to researchers and the general public. Centro Press was established to publish scholarship based on some of the donated collections by prominent Puerto Rican public figures, community leaders, writers, and artists. Two Diaspora Summits were held in 2016 and 2017 respectively, to engage island and stateside Puerto Ricans in increasing understanding of the effects of Puerto Rico's debt and hurricane crises on island and stateside Puerto Ricans, seeking ideas for influencing policies, and recommending potential solutions to seemingly long-term predicaments.

The Puerto Rican Studies Association (PRSA) was created in 1992 as a professional organization that brings together scholars, community activists, and students to discuss their research and other endeavors. PRSA also promotes linkages between island and stateside scholars and organizations and holds a major biennial conference (see Sánchez Korrol 2011–2012).

Back in the 1970s, Puerto Ricans and other groups of color were at the forefront of the battles for open admissions to the CUNY system. Organizations like the Puerto Rican Students Union were instrumental in the push for open admissions as a way of providing access to a higher education to those groups underrepresented in public and private colleges throughout the United States. Educational activism brought about the establishment of minority student recruitment programs, such as SEEK (Search for Education, Elevation, and Knowledge) and EOP (Educational Opportunity Programs), and affirmative action programs to recruit more faculty and professional support staff in fields or units where they were not generally represented.

Cultural Citizenship

The concept of cultural citizenship, developed by Chicano anthropologist Renato Rosaldo (1987), refers to the process by which Latinos/as "claim and establish a distinct social space" within US society (Flores and Benmayor 1997, 1). Defining this "distinct social space" involves Latinos/as asserting their rights, defining their different cultural domains, and contesting and renegotiating power relations with the wider society. These activities are all part of an empowering process taking place within their various stateside communities. This process allows Puerto Ricans and other groups marginalized by mainstream society to reclaim their own historical, cultural, and racial spaces and to dispel some of the negative images ascribed to their communities. Moreover, it fosters awareness of their presence and their many contributions to the building of the United States.

Many island Puerto Ricans recognize that they hold "a second class" US citizenship because they are not fully represented in Congress or able to vote in presidential or congressional elections and because of the unequal treatment they generally receive from Congress and other US officials. However, they seem oblivious of the contradiction that, at least in theory,

Puerto Ricans are entitled to full citizenship rights if they reside in any of the fifty states. That this is the case does not change in any significant way the fact that stateside Puerto Ricans are also collectively subjected to unequal treatment and not only face serious socioeconomic and educational disparities when compared to the US white population but also experience political disenfranchisement, racism, and segregation. Because of these disparities, they are continuously struggling to overcome these conditions and uphold their civil rights. In many ways, island politicians and voters, most notably statehood and commonwealth supporters, repeatedly fail to grasp the historical weight of their colonial experience and of structural inequalities and institutionalized racism on the lives of stateside Puerto Ricans and other populations of color.

Almost every locality in the United States with a large concentration of Puerto Ricans or Latinos/as has cultural centers or social clubs aimed at fostering their cultural heritage and sense of community. These organizations promote cultural enrichment that allows members of their communities to connect with their heritages and identities and share experiences with other immigrants/migrants in the process of adaptation and integration into a more hostile cultural setting. Additionally, they provide spaces for social interaction, cultural pride, and entertainment in the form of musical and theater performances, art exhibits, dancing, parades, festivals, and the consumption of typical foods.

Several firmly established institutions play a leading role in promoting Puerto Rican arts and the overall cultural enrichment of the various stateside Puerto Rican communities. These are discussed in more detail in Chapter 8.

In a newspaper article published in 1948, community activist and journalist Jesús Colón ([1960] 1982) posed the following questions: "Why have the reactionary newspapers unleashed a concerted campaign against the Puerto Ricans coming to New York? Why do they describe the Puerto Ricans in the worst light they can imagine?" Colón's questions, articulated during the years of the Great Migration of Puerto Ricans to New York City, came as a reaction to the frequently biased reporting and sensationalist media that depicted the growing presence of Puerto Rican migrants in the city as a social problem, depriving them of their human dignity and denying their capacity to improve their individual and collective lives. A man with a strong social consciousness, Colón understood the racial and social conditions that surrounded him and the historical invisibility endured by the working class, ethnic immigrants and migrants in particular. He foresaw the need to document the lives and struggles for survival and social justice of Puerto Rican migrants and to give due recognition to their efforts in building their own communities. As a committed progressive activist and writer, he considered these struggles essential components of the process of forging a legacy for younger generations of Puerto Ricans. Jesús Colón, his brother Joaquín Colón, Bernardo Vega, and many other progressive migrant pioneers were early contributors to these endeavors (see Chapter 8). These forerunners offer an alternative view of migrant life, with all its problems and challenges, but centered on people working hard to make a living, engaging individually and collectively to defend their rights and foster social change during the decades that preceded the Civil Rights Act of 1964, and reclaiming and defining their own historical and cultural legacies within US society. New generations are giving continuity to similar and newfound struggles for survival, recognition, and empowerment.

Notes

1. For detailed data on Puerto Rico's election results for each political party from the 1920s to the present, see the Elecciones en Puerto Rico/Elections in Puerto Rico website (http://eleccionespuertorico.org).
2. Although many stateside Puerto Rican political organizations in the United States of the past and present have advocated for Puerto Rico's independence, there is no evidence of any significant support for this political status alternative for the island among the stateside Puerto Rican community. The Institute for Puerto Rican Policy conducted the National Puerto Rican Opinion Survey in 1989, asking 615 Puerto Rican respondents their preference among the various status options: statehood, independence, and the current Commonwealth. The majority of the respondents chose the Commonwealth status quo.
3. The motto *Palante, siempre, palante*, used by the Young Lords, means "Forging ahead, always forging ahead." The Puerto Rican popular colloquial expression *siempre pa'lante, nunca pa' atrás* (always forge ahead, never go backward) inspired the slogan. See Iris Morales, "Palante, Siempre, Palante: The Young Lords," in Torres and Velázquez (1998); and Young Lords Party and Abramson ([1971] 2011).
4. The Chicago Young Lords Newspaper Collection is part of the Digital Collections of DePaul University's Special Collections and Archives. It was donated by Omar López, the organization's minister of information in 2004.
5. The Spanish slogan coined by the Young Lords was not grammatically correct. The correct expression in Spanish would be *Tengo a Puerto Rico en mi corazón*. The missing preposition was in itself indicative of the differences between island and diaspora Puerto Ricans in their command of the Spanish language.
6. In 1970, Young Lord Julio Roldán was arrested and in the custody of the New York Police Department. The police alleged that he committed suicide by hanging himself in his cell at the Manhattan Detention Center. In 1969, Manuel Ramos, an unarmed Chicago Young Lord, was killed by a police officer. Another Chicago Young Lord, José (Pancho) Lind, a dark-skinned Puerto Rican, was beaten to death by a white gang.
7. An impressive founding conference on Puerto Rican historiography was sponsored by Centro at CUNY's Graduate Center Conference in New York City in 1974. The conference brought together prominent island and stateside scholars to engage in substantive and wide-ranging discussions on topics related to Puerto Rico's colonial condition in shaping Puerto Rican historiography. However, the conference's major focus on migration stressed the need for producing new and transformative scholarship, critical approaches, and interpretative paradigms to study the

presence, histories, and legacies of stateside Puerto Ricans. The proceedings were initially published in *Taller de Migración, Conferencia de Historiografía, Abril 1974*.

8. This new generation of island intellectuals included Angel Quintero Rivera, Marcia Rivera, Rafael Ramírez, Gervasio García, Fernando Picó, Isabel Picó, and Arcadio Díaz Quiñones, among others.

9. For a critical discussion of the "new Puerto Rican historiography," see García (1989); Castro Arroyo (1988); and Manuel Negrón Portillo and Raúl Mayo Santana, "Trabajo, producción y conflictos en el siglo XIX: una revisión crítica de las nuevas investigaciones históricas en Puerto Rico," *Revista de Ciencias Sociales* 24, nos. 3–4 (1985): 470–497.

10. Illustrative of this evolution is the University at Albany's Puerto Rican Studies Program, initiated in 1970. The program became a full-fledged academic department offering a major in 1974. In the early 1980s, the department evolved into the current Department of Latin American, Caribbean, and US Latino Studies (LACS), offering a master's and PhD in LACS cultural studies, the latter a joint initiative of LACS and the Spanish section of the Department of Languages, Literatures, and Cultures.

8

Cultural and Artistic Legacies

I was not born in Puerto Rico
Puerto Rico was born in me.
—Mariposa Fernández,
"Ode to the Diasporican"

In Chapter 4, we examined the Puerto Rican presence in US society dating back to the second half of the nineteenth century. Numerous examples support the assertion that for many Puerto Rican migrants coming to the United States since then—whether for a brief stay or for a longer and more permanent residence—the experiences of migration and displacement have influenced and continue to be central to their cultural expressions and artistic creativity. For most of these migrants, the journey from the island to the continent meant dealing with a different cultural and linguistic milieu, nostalgia for their homeland, a more inclement climate, and, above all, a society beset with racial and social inequalities. As a racially mixed population, most Puerto Ricans share these disparities with other US populations of color.

The Anglocentric "melting pot" image, which has served for over a century as the metaphor for immigrant assimilation and social mobility within US society, has proved elusive for Puerto Ricans and other ethnoracial minorities. Grouped under the label "populations of color," Puerto Ricans and other Latinos/as confront deeply rooted prejudices and exclusion, factors that impair their social progress and contribute to their unprivileged status. Like previous groups of immigrants and migrants, Puerto Ricans and other Latinos/as also share the "American dream," hoping to forge a more prosperous life for themselves and their families in their new setting. However, racial and cultural differences, along with prevailing structural inequalities and unequal treatment, have been barriers not easily overcome, more conspicuously before the civil rights reforms and legislation of the 1960s. The social and political changes that came out of the civil rights era banned discrimination and segregation and aimed at creating a more equitable society. New legislation facilitated access to more socioeconomic and educational equal opportunities and fostered inclusiveness for these groups. But even the new US-born generations of Puerto Ricans, who now constitute 68 percent of their total population, have not yet been able to overcome the realities and consequences of decades of poverty, racial injustice, and socioeconomic disadvantage. More recent back-lashes and rollbacks to many of the civil rights legislative accomplishments of the past include voter-suppression practices by conservative white nation-alists and other political extremists, who are constantly pressing for legisla-tion to weaken the rights of women, LGBTQ individuals, and populations of color in the workplace and other spheres of civil life. These rollbacks clearly demonstrate that the struggles against these inequalities are far from over and continue to threaten the democratic fabric of this nation. Attempts to rollback civil rights gains for these groups will likely persist until doing so stops being a useful divisive political strategy, as it is at present.

The working-class origins and lower socioeconomic indicators shared by a significant portion of stateside Puerto Ricans when compared to the non-Hispanic white population, particularly before the 1990s, explain the general tendency to undervalue their cultural expressions and contributions to US society. Easily labeled as part of "an underclass" (Tienda 1989) or "a culture of poverty" (Lewis 1966), Puerto Ricans had to deal with the stigma of their racialized unprivileged status. The generalized assumption that liv-ing in poverty also means experiencing a "poverty of culture" and the elitist notion that the working classes have little to offer as producers of worthy cultural expressions explain the neglect by scholars or critics of this aspect of their lives. However, despite these preconceptions, since the 1970s schol-ars and critics have been contesting these assumptions and paying increased attention to documenting and analyzing the historical and cultural legacies of the Puerto Rican diaspora. This chapter outlines the sociohistorical and political context shaping the various forms of cultural production that con-tinue to engage stateside Puerto Ricans.

The Spanish-Language Press

Since the second half of the nineteenth century, Puerto Rican migrant and sojourner writers, artists, and other intellectuals have been coming to the United States and actively participating in the cultural life of New York and other stateside communities with large concentrations of Puerto Ricans and/or other Latinos/as (see Chapter 3). Thus, their work represents a valu-able source for a deeper understanding of the different stages in the evolution of these communities. Puerto Rico's literary canon, for instance, recognizes the writings of some Puerto Ricans who migrated to the United States but eventually returned to the island, especially those who write in Spanish, and the views many island Puerto Ricans share of their stateside counterparts were in part initially shaped by their portrayals in this creative literature.

Among the most valuable sources of information on the development of Puerto Rican and other communities of Latinos/as in the United States is the still understudied Spanish-language press. Since colonial times, newspapers and other periodicals have been important outlets for journalistic and creative endeavors and discussions of multiple issues with a bearing on the collective and individual lives of Latinos/as from diverse national origins and their respective communities, their survival struggles and injustices faced, their interactions with Anglo-American society, and their connections with the countries of origin. Initially, Spanish-language newspapers in the pioneer communities were part of an immigrant press that kept the population informed of local and national events as well as what was happening back in their native countries. These newspapers also represented the voice of a marginalized population facing some of the same civil rights and socioeconomic problems and challenges that other racially mixed groups have endured at different historical periods. The earliest Spanish-language newspaper identified to date is *El Misisipí* (The Mississippian), published in New Orleans and dating back to 1808 (Kanellos and Martell 2000, 4).

By the late 1820s most of the former Spanish New World colonies had achieved their independence, with the exception of the Hispanic Caribbean islands of Cuba, Puerto Rico, and the Dominican Republic. Most of the Spanish territory in today's Southwest was ceded by Mexico to the United States at the end of the Mexican-American War (1846–1848). In Chapter 3 we presented a detailed analysis of how the repressive measures of Spanish authorities on both islands forced many independence supporters into exile, turning US cities such as New York, Philadelphia, New Orleans, Tampa, and Key West into important sites of activity for an expatriate Antillean separatist movement. The presence in the United States of leading separatist intellectuals and political leaders, many of them journalists and literary figures, catalyzed the emergence of Spanish-language newspapers aimed at promoting the liberation of Cuba and Puerto Rico from Spanish rule and envisioning their future as independent republics. These publications were also important outlets for creative writing. The most fundamental ideas about the future of the islands after they had secured their sovereignty, including their future relationship with the United States, were first discussed in many of these newspapers.

Several Puerto Rican émigrés who were among the most respected and fervent voices of the separatist cause—Ramón Emeterio Betances, Eugenio María de Hostos, Francisco "Pachín" Marín, Lola Rodríguez de Tió, Sotero Figueroa, and Arturo Alfonso Schomburg, among others—spent some time in New York during this early period. Besides their political and cultural activities, discussed in depth in Chapter 3, they were among the most prominent frequent contributors to the Spanish-language newspapers in New York and other cities where Latinos/as were concentrated. In newspapers such as *La revolución* (Revolution) and *Patria* (Motherland) Betances, Hostos,

Rodríguez de Tió, Marín, and Figueroa promoted solidarity and unity among Puerto Ricans and Cubans in the common struggle for freedom and expressed their patriotic sentiments for Puerto Rico's independence from Spain (Ojeda Reyes 1992; Edgardo Meléndez 1996).

The idea of US annexation of both islands ran contrary to the post-independence political vision of the most prominent Puerto Rican separatists. Hostos's vision of a federation of sovereign Antillean republics, to include Cuba, Puerto Rico, and other non-Hispanic Caribbean islands, was the subject of many of his writings. A number of his essays on these issues first appeared in the pages of New York's *La revolución*. Betances, the leading voice of Puerto Rico's separatist movement in exile, was even more adamant about the possibility of a US intervention to put an end to the Spanish-Cuban War. His pronouncement "The Antilles for the Antilleans," promoting a sense of a unified Antillean struggle, was important not only for achieving the sovereignty of both islands but also for keeping them out of the hands of the United States.

There were many social, racial, and political divisions within the Antillean separatist movement, but several of its most ardent supporters worked ceaselessly to promote unity and solidarity. Cuban leader José Martí proclaimed, "With all, and for the good of all" to signify this goal (Poyo 1989). Similarly, Puerto Rican poet Lola Rodríguez de Tió (1968a) called for a unified Antillean struggle in the immortalized verses of her poem "A Cuba" (To Cuba):

> Cuba y Puerto Rico son
> de un pájaro las dos alas
> reciben flores o balas
> sobre el mismo corazón.
> [Cuba and Puerto Rico are
> the two wings of a bird.
> They receive flowers and bullets
> on the very same heart.]
> (Stavans 2011, 259)

The newspapers created by Antillean separatists and labor activists in the city also document the presence and political activities of Puerto Rico's "pilgrims of freedom," such as Rodríguez de Tió and others in the formation of New York City's Spanish-language community, constituted mostly by Cubans, Puerto Ricans, Dominicans, and other less represented Latin American countries. For Puerto Ricans, the writings of these patriots that appeared in the Spanish-language press during this period are particularly important from a nation-building perspective. Living in exile allowed these freedom fighters to freely articulate their vision of a sovereign Puerto Rico and reaffirm a sense of national identity unbound from Spain. In the poem "Autógrafo" (Autograph), Rodríguez de Tió fervently repeats the verse "Porque la Patria llevo conmigo" (Because I carry the Motherland within me), emblematic of her nostalgia and longing for the homeland she was forced to leave and a life of exile in the struggle for freedom.[1]

Artisans Sotero Figueroa and Arturo Alfonso Schomburg arrived in New York in the early 1880s and were among the most active and dependable supporters of the Antillean separatist movement. Under the leadership of José Martí, the Partido Revolucionario Cubano (PRC) had welcomed Puerto Rican separatists, who also created their own PRC-affiliated clubs. An experienced typographer, Figueroa ran his own printing press and undertook the role of administrative editor of *Patria*, founded by Martí in 1892. In this capacity, Figueroa wrote many of the newspaper's editorials and other articles, especially when Martí went on his fund-raising campaign trips to the émigré communities in Florida and other parts of the United States. Worthy of mention is a series of six articles Figueroa published under the title "La verdad de la historia" (The truth about history). The various installments of the essay traced the long struggle of Puerto Ricans to liberate their country from the tyrannical Spanish colonial regime. He was the first to underscore the historical importance of Puerto Rico's Grito de Lares revolt of 1868 and the heroic activities of the revolutionaries who risked or gave their lives fighting for freedom. Figueroa (1892) also tried to dispel the island autonomists' claim that there were no separatists in Puerto Rico:

> The conquered people never accept passively the yoke imposed by their conquerors, and battle to break away from the chains of slavery until finally they do so.
>
> Puerto Rico like Cuba has not been able to extract itself from that violation of its dignity, and even if it is just a childish tactical strategy or to divert suspicion from being considered accomplices or sympathizers, the coryphaeus of the liberal organizations in Puerto Rico have said repeatedly that there are not and never have been separatists there, which is, according to a vulgar expression, wanting to cover the sun with one hand. This categorical denial tends to refute what is historical truth and makes those Puerto Ricans who are aware of their future destiny and who have and are fighting for freedom degraded slaves without faith or regional aspirations who tolerate insults and do not have the pride to ask for satisfaction and who accept the punishment and submissively kiss the hand of those who mistreat them. (1, author's translation)

Martí's death in 1895 brought out old ideological and social divisions within the Antillean separatist movement, giving an upper hand to the separatists favoring US intervention in the Spanish-Cuban War and its annexation of the islands. Figueroa kept the newspaper *Patria* going for several more years and remained active in the Sección de Puerto Rico of the PRC, which founded the short-lived newspaper *Borinquen* in 1898. The year after the US invasion of the islands, he left New York for Havana, where he held administrative posts in the Cuban government and continued writing for the newspapers of the new republic.

When Schomburg lived in Puerto Rico, like Figueroa, he had worked in an Old San Juan printing shop and developed close friendships with other artisans, particularly *tabaqueros* (cigar rollers) and typographers. Schomburg did some typographic work at a San Juan stationery shop before departing for New York. Upon his arrival in the city, he immediately connected with other artisans residing there. Through the club Las Dos Antillas (The Two Antilles), Schomburg collaborated with Puerto Rican labor activist and cigar roller Flor Baerga and Cuban Rafael Serra, also a cigar roller, as well as other artisans in seeking financial assistance to secure weapons and medical supplies for the fighting rebels in Cuba. After the War of 1898 and US takeover of Cuba and Puerto Rico, Schomburg remained in the United States and shifted his intellectual and political energies to collecting and documenting the experiences of African peoples around the world. An avid bibliophile, Schomburg amassed an invaluable collection of books, maps, and other materials, which he sold to the New York Public Library in 1926. Schomburg was not a prolific writer, but in the handful of articles he published during his lifetime, he emphasized the importance of blacks' learning about their past and advocated the establishment of a chair for Negro studies, foreshadowing the African American studies programs that emerged in US universities during the late 1960s and 1970s. He also wrote a few biographical profiles highlighting the contributions of previously ignored black personalities from different parts of the world. The Schomburg Collection for Black Culture is now internationally known among researchers of the African experience.

The journalistic activities of separatist poet and typographer Francisco Gonzalo "Pachín" Marín were mostly devoted to his own revolutionary newspaper, *El postillón* (The courier), which had been the main cause for his exile from Puerto Rico, but his poems and articles also appeared occasionally in *Patria*. His 1892 article "La bofetada" (A slap in the face) was quick to condemn Puerto Rican liberal autonomists back on the island for making compromises in pursuit of reforms from the Spanish government rather than choosing the path of revolution to secure independence. He also wrote a series of *crónicas* (personal vignettes) for *La gaceta del pueblo* (The people's gazette) that reflected his views of different cultural and linguistic aspects of being an exile in the large New York metropolis. The 1892 *crónica* "Nueva York por dentro: un aspecto de su vida bohemia" ("New York from Within: A Phase of Its Bohemian Life" 2002) offered the ironic perspective of a newcomer overwhelmed by an environment in which wealth and poverty existed side by side:

> To attain an intimate knowledge of this elephant of modern civilization, you will need to set foot on the ground without a quarter to your name, though you may bring a world of hope in your heart.
> Indeed! To arrive in New York, check into a comfortable hotel, go out in an elegant carriage pulled by monumental horses every time an occa-

sion presents itself, visit the theaters, museums, *cafés*, chantants, cruise the fast-flowing East River, . . . visit Brooklyn Bridge—that frenzy of North American initiative—and the Statue of Liberty—that tour de force of French pride—, . . . frequent, in short, the places where elegant people of good taste gather, people who can afford to spend three or four hundred dollars in one evening for the pleasure of looking at a dancer's legs, oh!, all that is very agreeable, very delicious, and very . . . singular; but it doesn't give you the exact measure of this city which is, at one and the same time, an emporium of sweeping riches and rendezvous-point for all the penniless souls of America. (Kanellos 2002, 342).

The US takeover of Cuba and Puerto Rico put an end to the political activities of Antillean separatist émigrés but opened the gates to increased migration. With the new colonial regime in Puerto Rico, the flow of businessmen and well-known political and intellectual figures to the United States intensified. More privileged island Puerto Ricans came to the United States to advance their educations, for professional and leisure activities, or to distance themselves from the unfavorable political environment in Puerto Rico. Working-class island Puerto Ricans were recruited by stateside industries, and contract labor was heavily promoted by the colonial government in order to deal with the high levels of poverty and unemployment in Puerto Rico and to provide these US industries with a steady source of low-wage labor.

In 1901, autonomist political leader and journalist Luis Muñoz Rivera left the island and settled in New York during a period when the supporters of US annexation for Puerto Rico had the upper hand in influencing the policies implemented on the island by the new US colonial regime. Muñoz Rivera's concern about how little US citizens knew about Puerto Rico and his opposition to the misguided policies of colonial officials inspired him to start the bilingual *Puerto Rico Herald* (1901–1904). He remained in New York only a few years before returning to his former political life in Puerto Rico. There he joined the Partido Unión Puertorriqueña (Unionistas, or Unionist Party), a political organization fighting to increase Puerto Rican representation in the US colonial government and seeking new measures for self-government. With the Unionists' support, Muñoz Rivera was elected to the post of resident commissioner, a nonvoting representative of the island to the US Congress, a position he occupied from 1908 until his death in 1916.

A number of Puerto Ricans from the most privileged social sectors saw in the island's relationship with the United States opportunities for expanding their educational and professional careers and those of their offspring. Muñoz Rivera's tenure in Washington, DC, for instance, allowed his son, Luis Muñoz Marín, to attend Georgetown University, and in the United States the young Muñoz Marín developed his journalistic and creative writing vocation. His formative years in the United States were crucial in setting the course of his future political life. Muñoz Marín shuttled back and forth between Puerto Rico, Washington, and New York from his childhood until the early 1930s, when he finally settled in Puerto Rico to become more involved in island politics. A good number of the articles and poems reflecting his early social and political views were written in English and published in well-established journals, such as the *American Mercury*, *New Republic*, *Nation*, and *Poetry*, or in widely read newspapers such as the *New York Tribune* and *Baltimore Sun*. During the years he lived in New York City's Greenwich Village in the 1920s, with his North American wife, suffragist poet Muna Lee, Muñoz Marín befriended a wide circle of liberal and socialist thinkers and artists who helped shape the ideology that was to guide his political career and actions in Puerto Rico in subsequent decades (Acosta-Belén et al. 2000). Lee was close to Ruby Black, a prominent feminist journalist in Washington, DC, who had access to Eleanor Roosevelt, first lady of the United States from 1933 to 1945. Fewer than two decades after Muñoz Marín returned to Puerto Rico, he was set to become the first elected Puerto Rican governor of the island and the mastermind of its political, social, and economic transformation from the 1940s to the 1960s.

During the formative years of largely working-class Puerto Rican communities in Brooklyn and Spanish Harlem (late 1910s–1920s), a number of community journalists and civic and political leaders articulated their perspectives and social and political concerns through the articles, columns, and editorials of newspapers such as *Gráfico* (1927–1931), initiated by Afro-Cuban dramatist and actor Alberto O'Farrill and later purchased by Bernardo Vega, and *Nuevo mundo* (1928–1930), aimed at a wider Spanish-language readership. These and other small publications kept community readers abreast of news and issues back on the island, entertained them with creative writings and cartoons, and provided information about community events, businesses, and services. The larger and more commercialized newspapers *La prensa* (a weekly established in 1913; a daily paper since 1918) and *El diario de Nueva York* (established in 1947), which merged in 1963 into *El diario–La prensa*, held the greatest circulation in reaching the Spanish-speaking communities in New York's metropolitan area.

Another important Spanish-language publication during the 1930s was the *Revista de artes y letras* (Review of arts and letters, 1933–1939), founded by Puerto Rican feminist activist Josefina "Pepiña" Silva de Cintrón. This monthly magazine circulated widely in the professional sector of New York's Spanish-speaking community and in Puerto Rico and a few other Latin American countries. *Artes y letras* fostered a panethnic sense of *hispanismo* or *latinismo* (affirmation of Hispanic or Latino/a roots) within the United States by calling for the preservation of the Spanish language and Hispanic heritage (Sánchez Korrol [1983] 1994). During this early period, most of the Spanish-origin population in New York City, composed primarily of Spaniards, Cubans, and Puerto Ricans, was referred to as "Spanish" or "Hispanos," while terms such as "Hispanic" or "Latino/a" were not commonly used throughout the United States until the 1970s and beyond. Thus the panethnic intellectual and literary focus of *Artes y letras* and the reputation and editorial leadership of Silva de Cintrón attracted the collaboration of many well-known writers from the Spanish-speaking world and the New York community. Some frequent contributors to the journal were Puerto Rican writers Pedro Juan Labarthe, Clotilde Betances Jaeger, and Pedro Caballero, whose publications were mostly in Spanish. Caballero is also author of the Spanish-language novel *Paca antillana* (Paca, the Antillean woman; 1931). But Labarthe was one of the exceptions. He wrote the novel *Son of Two Nations: The Private Life of a Columbia Student* (1931), the first published autobiographical narrative written in English by a Puerto Rican migrant.

Artes y letras paid special attention to women's issues and community concerns, and Clotilde Betances Jaeger, grandniece of the patriot Ramón Emeterio Betances, was a frequent contributor. She wrote about women's rights and the historical significance of the Grito de Lares insurrection and the expatriate Antillean separatist movement. She was also a regular contributor to the Spanish anarchist newspaper *Cultura proletaria* (Proletarian culture) and Vega's *Gráfico*, and her understudied legacy as a woman of letters and defender of progressive ideas still awaits further attention (Acosta-Belén 1993; Vera-Rojas 2010, 2010–2011). Most of her journalistic articles are dispersed throughout these publications and a few others in Puerto Rico, Cuba, and Spain.

Promoting Puerto Rican–focused issues, as well as a panethnic sense of *hispanismo* (Hispanism), was at the core of *Alma Boricua* (Boricua soul, 1934–1935), which called itself an "órgano defensor de la integridad boricua" (a publication protecting Boricua integrity). One of its founders was Joaquín Colón, Jesús Colón's brother. The magazine started publication in 1934 during the years of increased political activity by Puerto Rican Nationalists and their persecution by colonial authorities.

In the 1940s, Spanish-language newspapers were an important vehicle for Spanish Civil War exiles in New York City fighting Spain's fascist Francisco Franco regime and for the increasing number of Puerto Ricans coming to the city during the early years of the Great Migration. Two of the best-known newspapers were *Pueblos hispanos* (Hispanic peoples, 1943–1944), founded by Puerto Rican Nationalist poet Juan Antonio Corretjer, and *Liberación* (Liberation, 1946–1949), started by Spanish exiles but a frequent publisher of articles and creative literature by Puerto Rican writers and journalists. These publications fostered a panethnic sense of *hispanismo* and solidarity based on common political causes: denouncing fascism in Spain and other parts of Europe, US colonial domination in Puerto Rico, and racism against Hispanics and the exploitation of their labor in US society. Both newspapers also promoted the writings of Latinos/as from many different nationalities. Bernardo Vega, for instance, wrote a few pioneering articles about Puerto

Rican migration to the United States for *Liberación*.[2] Puerto Rican migration was already showing an increasing pattern of growth by the mid-1940s.

As extensively documented by Kanellos (2011), there is no doubt that the Spanish-language press in the United States represents one of the most valuable sources for understanding the evolution of the Puerto Rican and other national communities of US Latinos/as, the multiple issues of concern and interest to the populations of particular localities, and how their citizens saw themselves at different times, in relation first to the Spanish colonial power and, after Latin American independence, to their specific countries of origin and the United States. Newspapers kept Puerto Ricans and other Latinos/as living in the United States abreast of what was happening back in their native countries and issues impacting their developing communities, as much as they contributed to their adaptation and interactions with the surrounding white Anglo-American society. Moreover, the Spanish-language press played a vital role in the publication of creative literature that has facilitated the unveiling of a valuable literary heritage to younger generations. Newspapers also were important outlets for community businesses and organizations to advertise their respective services and activities, and they played a key role in highlighting the creative pursuits of community members (Kanellos and Martell 2000; Kanellos 2002, 2011). Although some Spanish-language newspapers are still being published in the stateside communities, by the mid-twentieth century they had stopped being an important outlet for the publication of literature. Authors wanting to publish their writings had to rely on publishing houses, and for the most part mainstream publishers had no interest in the US Latino/a experience or Latino/a writers and generally questioned their marketability. Self-publishing was another option used by some authors to get their writings out to the reading public, but few writers achieved national recognition outside the boundaries of their own communities until the 1960s.

Since New York was an important refuge for Puerto Rican Nationalists between the 1930s and the 1950s, by coming to the city many nationalists distanced themselves from the relentless blacklisting and persecution they had faced in Puerto Rico. Initially, the large metropolis provided a much-needed sanctuary and opened opportunities for Nationalists to establish bonds of solidarity with fellow migrants or with political exiles from Spain and Latin America living in the city. However, during the early days of the Cold War and fears of the spread of communism and Communist Party infiltration of the US government, the political environment in the country became more difficult for socialists and progressive individuals and organizations due to the congressional committees and hearings of what came to be known as the McCarthy era.[3]

Among the most prominent Puerto Rican Nationalists living in New York during this period were Corretjer and his wife, Consuelo Lee Tapia, who helped administer and occasionally wrote for *Pueblos hispanos*; feminist poet Julia de Burgos, a regular columnist for the newspaper; and poet Clemente Soto Vélez, a regular contributor to this and many other New York Spanish-language newspapers. These authors were known in Puerto Rico, and a good portion of their work was tied to the island, but often their writings also reflected aspects of their lives in the New York metropolis. Julia de Burgos, for instance, left a rich legacy of poems about loneliness and abandonment, unrequited love, and connection with her homeland's lush rural landscape during her growing up years; she also wrote poems addressing the social, racial, and gender inequalities and political issues that affected the lives of working-class Puerto Ricans (Acosta-Belén 2017; Pérez-Rosario 2014). In addition, she penned a cultural column for *Pueblos hispanos*. Nonetheless, Burgos (1997) is best remembered for her emblematic feminist and revolutionary poems, such as "A Julia de Burgos" (To Julia de Burgos), "Desde el Puente Martín Peña" (A view from the Martín Peña Bridge), and "Yo misma fui mi ruta" (I was my own route):

> Yo quise ser como los hombres quisieron que yo fuese:
> un intento de vida,
> un juego al escondite con mi ser.
> Pero yo estaba hecha de presentes
> Y mis pies planos bajo la tierra promisora
> No resistían caminar hacia atrás,
> Y seguían adelante, adelante...
> Burlando las cenizas para alcanzar el beso
> De los senderos nuevos.

[I wanted to be like men wanted me to be: / an attempt at life / a game of hide and seek with my being. / But I was made of nows; / and my feet leveled upon the promised land / would not accept walking backward, / and went forward, forward, / mocking the ashes to reach the kiss / of the new paths.] (56–57, editor's translation)

The poet suffered from severe alcoholism, an ailment that contributed to deteriorating health and an early death. Burgos collapsed in the streets of New York's Spanish Harlem at the age of forty-four. Although the large majority of her poems were in Spanish, she wrote her last poems, "Farewell in Welfare Island" and "The Sun in Welfare Island," in English while she was convalescing at the city's Goldwater Memorial Hospital. These particular poems capture the loneliness and despair that overwhelmed the final days of Burgos's life and foreshadowed her death:

> Where is the voice of freedom,
> freedom to laugh,
> to move
> without the heavy phantom of despair?
> My cry that is no more mine,

but her and his forever,
the comrades of my silence,
the phantoms of my grave
It has to be from here,
forgotten but unshaken
among comrades of silence
deep into Welfare Island
my farewell to the world.
("Farewell in Welfare Island"; Burgos 1997, 357)

The iconic stature of poet Julia de Burgos within the stateside Puerto Rican diaspora was established by Vanessa Pérez-Rosario's (2014) valuable study *Becoming Julia de Burgos: The Making of a Puerto Rican Icon*. Pérez-Rosario sees Burgos as a cultural, social, and political "border icon." In a commentary about Pérez-Rosario's book, Acosta-Belén (2017) supports this characterization of Burgos's posthumous iconic stature among stateside Puerto Ricans, which is illustrated by "the ample evocation of Burgos's name, image, and verses in the streets, cultural centers, schools, parks, women's shelters, and murals that today adorn the walls of many New York City buildings and public spaces" and the widespread impact and influence of her poetry (190). Over six decades after her death, Burgos's iconic stature also transcends the confines of New York and spills out into other stateside communities and to the island, where scholars, educators, activists, writers, visual artists, poets, and musicians from all sectors are devotedly inspired by her poetic legacy and rebellious spirit. With nationalistic fervor, in the 1930s she was a fighter for Puerto Rico's freedom, defiantly challenged colonial authorities, and celebrated the fallen martyrs of the cause in her poetry and political speeches. With the courage of a feminist warrior, she derided hypocritical social conventions and double standards imposed on women's behavior and affirmed the agency of women to chart and follow their own paths. In this regard the second wave of the feminist movement that flourished in the 1970s on the island and stateside and numerous Puerto Rican and Latina writers, poets, scholars, visual artists, and activists continuously evoked her name. True to her humble upbringing in a rural barrio of Puerto Rico, through her poetry Burgos was a voice that spoke to the proletarian masses of exploited workers, inciting them to revolution. In condemning racial oppression and the insidiousness of slavery, she became "the people's rebel soul poet" and the national poet of Puerto Rico and its diaspora (Acosta-Belén 2017).

Another Nationalist poet, Clemente Soto Vélez, had been incarcerated in a federal prison for several years along with Juan Antonio Corretjer and party leader Pedro Albizu Campos. Not allowed to return to Puerto Rico after his release, Soto Vélez put down roots in New York during the early 1940s and remained there until the 1980s; he died in Puerto Rico a few years later.

Soto Vélez was a regular contributor to Spanish-language newspapers such as *Pueblos hispanos* and *Liberación* and was involved in the community's political life, including the campaigns of East Harlem Italian-American representative Vito Marcantonio, a strong advocate of Puerto Rican causes from 1935 to 1951. He was also involved in the political campaigns of the American Labor and Communist parties in the city. As a small business owner, in 1945 he founded the Puerto Rican Merchants' Association as a unified front to protect the interests of community businesses. He was particularly involved in organizations that promoted the creative work of Spanish-language poets and writers and was a generous mentor to many stateside Puerto Rican and Latino/a writers. He founded the Club Cultural del Bronx (Bronx Cultural Club) and presided over the Círculo de Poetas y Escritores Iberoamericanos (Circle of Ibero-American Poets and Writers), in addition to founding the short-lived newspaper *La voz de Puerto Rico en Estados Unidos* (The voice of Puerto Rico in the United States). His collection of poems *La tierra prometida* (The promised land, 1979) denounces US imperialist domination over Puerto Rico and gives voice to his vision of independence for his beloved homeland.

The negative experiences endured by working-class migrants in US society, who at the time constituted the larger sector of the community, were central to the literary and artistic production of stateside Puerto Ricans. One of the best known and most powerful early depictions of the effects of migration on a Puerto Rican family is the classic drama *La carreta* (The oxcart, 1951–1952) by René Marqués, a well-recognized playwright, prose fiction writer, and essayist in Puerto Rico and throughout the Spanish-speaking world. Marqués, also a supporter of Puerto Rico's independence, lived in New York in 1949 while he was studying theater at Columbia University. There he began to write *La carreta*, a play that island Puerto Ricans used for many years as a point of reference for portraying the migrant experience.

La carreta focuses on the migratory journey of a peasant family forced by poverty and the lack of work opportunities to move from the Puerto Rican countryside to an urban slum in San Juan and later to New York's Spanish Harlem. The play illustrates how the uprooted peasant family members deal with the individual and collective effects of their difficult and alienating life, first in the island's capital and then in the New York metropolis. The family's experiences are filled with tragedy. They lose the oldest son in a factory accident, an event that forces the remaining family members to return to the abandoned Puerto Rican homeland. Marqués's tragic view of migrant life tends to downplay the social and political dynamics of migration by focusing on the poor personal choices of individual family members, even when they are forced into them by prevailing social and political conditions. In the end, the surviving characters of *La carreta* realize that they have "betrayed" the Puerto Rican homeland by abandoning it and that their only "redemption" is to return to the island. In reality, that was not the choice made by the large majority of migrants for whom the United States became their permanent home, regardless of the many hardships or survival struggles they had to confront. *La carreta* was first performed in New York in 1953 and in Puerto Rico's major theater festival a few years later. The play was well received by critics, and its popularity as a representation of the migrant experience lasted for several decades.

Other island writers of Marqués's Generation of 1950, such as José Luis González, also spent brief periods in New York. González's stay in the city inspired his short novel *Paisa* (Fellow countryman, 1950) and subsequent collection of short stories, *En Nueva York y otras desgracias* (In New York and other tragedies, 1973). In these early narratives, he denounces the labor exploitation of Puerto Ricans and their desperation to make a living but also shares Marqués's tragic view of migrant life. Both Marqués and González were perceptive in their portrayal of the distressing socioeconomic circumstances, racial injustices, and labor exploitation faced by Puerto Ricans in New York City. However, both focused on the tragic effects of migration rather than on migrants' struggles to lead productive lives in the United States since many of them chose not to return to Puerto Rico. González's provocative 1980 essay "El país de cuatro pisos" ("The four-storeyed country," 1993) made some powerful arguments about the need to acknowledge the importance of Afro-descendants in the formation of the Puerto Rican nation and the neglected and suppressed blackness in the island's historiography, but overlooked the presence of an evolving and growing Puerto Rican diaspora. Subsequently, stateside Puerto Rican scholars referred repeatedly to the missing "fifth floor" in the architectural metaphor González constructed to define the various historical stages and cultural formations that hindered the development of a strong national consciousness among Puerto Ricans, a process ultimately thwarted by the US invasion and the beginning of yet another colonial relationship.

The writings of other island authors of the same generation also replicated this despairing or tragic view of migrant life. The poignant short stories of Pedro Juan Soto's acclaimed 1956 collection *Spiks*, a common ethnic slur used to deride Puerto Ricans and Spanish-speaking people, along with his novel *Ardiente suelo, fría estación* (Hot land, cold season, 1962), and Emilio Díaz Valcárcel's novel *Harlem todos los días* (Daily life in Harlem, 1978), both available in English translations, are among the most recognized Puerto Rican migration narratives of that period. All these narratives share a pessimistic undertone but manage to capture some of the cultural and social conflicts, sense of displacement, and marginality experienced by so many Puerto Rican migrants during the mid-twentieth-century Great Migration years.

The creativity of Puerto Ricans in the United States spans a broad range of genres and themes, reflecting long-standing notable accomplishments in literature, the visual arts, music, film, and television. The bulk of these cultural expressions are influenced by the dislocations, cultural conflicts, and adjustments that are part of overarching migrant experiences. The cultural legacies of the diaspora started with the contributions of sojourner writers, artists, and performers and those who lived in the United States for longer periods and eventually returned to the island, as well as other working-class migrant pioneers whose writings, for the most part, are still scattered in Spanish-language newspapers and other periodical publications.

Two significant works bear testimony to the working-class experiences of early Puerto Rican migrants to the United States. These are *Memorias de Bernardo Vega* (Memoirs of Bernardo Vega), written in the 1940s and published in 1977, and *A Puerto Rican in New York and Other Sketches* by Jesús Colón ([1961] 1982). Both Bernardo Vega (1885–1965) and Jesús Colón (1901–1974) were of working-class origin and came to New York from the mountain town of Cayey, Puerto Rico. They emigrated to the United States as young men, Vega in 1916 and Colón in 1918. Back in Cayey, then a tobacco-growing area, both men were exposed during their formative years to the culture of the socialist *tabaqueros* (cigar rollers and other tobacco industry workers), who represented an enlightened sector of the Puerto Rican working class, since they commonly hired *lectores* (lectors, or readers) to read to them from raised platforms at the tobacco factories and workshops and also engaged in study groups and avid discussions outside the workplace. Having *lectores* allowed these workers to become familiar with many of the classics of world literature and social and political writings, as well as with the news of the day. Thus, most members of this artisan class were socialists or anarchists well versed in local issues and events. Additionally, they shared a vast knowledge of international labor movements and workers' struggles. The *lectores* tradition was replicated in the late nineteenth and early twentieth centuries by cigar industry workers in the United States, most of them of Cuban, Puerto Rican, Spanish, and Italian origin (see Mormino and Pozzetta 1987; Ingalls and Pérez 2003).

Vega's and Colón's writings are largely autobiographical. In these texts they give testimony to the hardships and struggles that they and other early migrants faced trying to make a living in a society that devalued their presence. Although these two highly committed community activists occasionally returned to Puerto Rico to visit relatives and friends, each resided in the United States for about half a century. Hence their personal accounts of the migration experience shed light on an important period in the evolution of New York's Puerto Rican community, times not well documented in previous studies of the diaspora. Vega's and Colón's narratives go back in time to the second half of the nineteenth century, the years when Cuban and Puerto Rican political émigrés started coming to the United States and established *colonias* (neighborhoods) in New York, Philadelphia, and a few other US cities. They provide detailed information about many of the expatriates forced into exile because of their involvement in the struggle to liberate Cuba and Puerto Rico, Spain's last two colonies in the Americas. They also intended to recognize the working-class laborers employed in factories, in the tobacco industry and workshops, and in the sweatshops of the garment industry, as well as others toiling in grueling service and menial jobs or in agricultural fields for meager wages. The tobacco sector of the US economy was booming, especially after the 1880s, and relied to a large degree on immigrant labor (see Mormino and Pozzetta 1987; Ingalls and Pérez 2003).

In their respective writings, Bernardo Vega and Jesús Colón offer an engaging composite of the struggles, challenges, and contributions of working-class migrants during the formative stages of New York's Puerto Rican community in different areas of the city. These two migrant pioneers emphasize the interethnic and class solidarity among workers. They describe the importance of informal networks and a community where social and political activism combined with intellectual and other cultural pursuits. In this community, workers frequently stood side by side with members of the intellectual and political elites, whether to defend the cause of Antillean independence and their civil rights, condemn US colonialism in Puerto Rico and fascism in Spain, or denounce exploitative workplace and housing conditions and discrimination and violence against members of the community. Although there were racial and social class differences within the community, most groups and organizations aimed at improving the quality of life and defending residents from the abuses of landlords, employers, and the police. Vega and Colón also drew attention to the numerous grassroots organizations, newspapers, and individuals contributing to these endeavors. Their own socialist formation and active involvement in the cultural, social, and political life of Puerto Ricans provides valuable insights missing from mainstream accounts of Puerto Rican migrant experiences.

Vega's *Memorias* is abundant with details about important events, the emergence of all kinds of community organizations and groups, and the names of the people involved in these endeavors. But the recorded information does not hide his critical views of the socioeconomic and racial ills of US society. Aware of the importance of creating a historical record of the community's early years, Vega clearly understood the significance of documenting his experiences and those of other working-class migrants.

Vega's interest in journalistic endeavors expanded in the late 1920s. He bought the Spanish-language newspaper *Gráfico* (Illustrated, 1927–1931), originally founded by Afro-Cuban actor and writer Alberto O'Farrill, and turned it into an important forum for informing New York's Latinos/as about events and issues that had a bearing on their daily lives. Furthermore, the newspaper was an effective tool for consciousness-raising around social and political issues impacting the community and for fostering activism, as well as a source of entertainment. The December 2, 1928, issue compared Harlem's Lenox Avenue to the Latin Quarter of Paris, with Harlem's bohemian nights likened to nightlife in other cosmopolitan cities such as Madrid, Rio de

Janeiro, and Buenos Aires. This was in part an overflow of the cultural vitality that characterized the pan-African and Harlem Renaissance movements during the 1920s and 1930s, but the contributions of the Puerto Ricans and other Latinos/as also enriched this environment.

Jesús Colón was a regular columnist for *Gráfico*, as were several other labor activists, journalists, and creative writers from New York and Puerto Rico. Besides his writings in *Gráfico*, Colón left a rich legacy of articles published in various other New York newspapers, including *Pueblos hispanos*, *Liberación*, the *Daily Worker*, *Mainstream*, the *Worker*, and the *Daily World* (see Acosta-Belén and Sánchez Korrol 1993; Colón 2001). Colón's weekly columns "Lo que el pueblo me dice" (What I am hearing from the people) and "As I See It from Here" for the *Daily Worker* (later to become the *Worker*, 1955–1968) are excellent examples of his critical views of capitalism and imperialism and of the working-class socialist and communist perspectives that dominated his writings. After his death in 1974, some of his unpublished writings were donated to the Center for Puerto Rican Studies Library and Archives and collected in the volume *The Way It Was and Other Writings* (Acosta-Belén and Sánchez Korrol 1993).

In some of his newspaper columns, chronicles, and short stories, which he called "sketches," Colón deplored the lack of bibliographic sources on labor organizations and trade unions, even though at the time the majority of New York City's Puerto Rican population was working-class. Thus, like his countryman Bernardo Vega, Jesús Colón was aware of the need to forge a historical record for posterity about the building of a Puerto Rican community from the labor and survival struggles of working-class migrants. Both writers offered a male working-class perspective on migrant life, but they also tried to acknowledge women's contributions to the community. At the time, the great majority of women identified themselves as homemakers, but they often did home-based piecework for the needle industry, worked outside the home as self-employed seamstresses, sold homemade pastries and typical foods, took in boarders, and engaged in other activities such as child care (Sánchez Korrol [1983] 1994). Around one-fourth of all the migrant women worked outside the home in the garment and tobacco industries; others did clerical work, and a smaller group were teachers, librarians, social workers, creative writers, and journalists.

Two Puerto Rican feminist activists and tobacco workers' union organizers, Luisa Capetillo and Franca de Armiño, migrated in the early decades of the twentieth century. These two women were involved at different times in the activities of Puerto Rico's Federación Libre de los Trabajadores (Free Federation of Workers). Capetillo arrived in the United States in 1912 and spent a couple of years working in the tobacco factories of Ybor City, Florida, and New York City, where she was a reader, one of the few women to hold that post during those years. She then lived in Cuba and Puerto Rico and returned to New York again in 1919. As she did when living in Puerto Rico, Capetillo frequently contributed essays and plays to the Spanish-language labor press. Her experiences working in the United States shaped some of the writings in her 1916 book *Influencia de las ideas modernas* (Influence of modern ideas). These writings illustrate Capetillo's anarchofeminist ideology and a revolutionary utopian vision that challenged social conventions that oppressed women, defended free love, and denounced prevailing inequalities among the various social sectors and between men and women (Capetillo [1911] 2004; Valle Ferrer 2008; Capetillo [1916] 2009).[4]

While still living in Puerto Rico during the early 1920s, Franca de Armiño had been the leader of a tobacco stripper's union and president of the Asociación Feminista Popular (Popular Feminist Association), a suffragist workers' organization. There is some evidence that she lived in New York in the late 1920s and 1930s, since she published a couple of articles about the need for workers to organize in Bernardo Vega's *Gráfico*. Her little-known revolutionary play *Los hipócritas* (The hypocrites) was published in New York in 1937. This play, which takes place in Spain, decries the abuses of capitalist employers and class prejudices during the years of the Great Depression and reaffirms the author's revolutionary ideals about the power of workers to change society; it also reveals her concerns about the looming Spanish Civil War.[5] The play was staged in 1933 at the Park Palace.

Sharing the activist spirit of his brother Jesús Colón, Joaquín Colón López also felt the need to recognize those Puerto Ricans migrating to the United States in the early decades of the twentieth century. His *Pioneros puertorriqueños en Nueva York 1917–1947* (2002) (Puerto Rican pioneers in New York 1917–1947) was not published until almost four decades after his death, but its importance is indisputable, since it documents in detail the activities of a wide range of grassroots organizations and different areas of activism within the early Puerto Rican community. The book's introduction, written by literary scholar Edwin Karli Padilla Aponte, addresses the difficulties faced by early migrants and how they struggled to improve their conditions. There is a clear sense in Joaquín Colón López's (2002) writings that the trials and tribulations that migrants had to endure only increased their social consciousness and activism, a view far from the stereotypical portrayal of the apathetic or despairing poor migrant:

> From that harsh, strange, anticivic environment some action had to flourish.
> . . . That life sharpened the senses of our fellow compatriots and defiant men
> and women ready to engage in civic struggles were molded there. Parades,
> demonstrations, picketing, leaflets, and political rallies garnered the warmest
> support from a multitude of people and a great deal of the progressive legis-
> lation that we enjoy today came from there. Many of our compatriots
> became experts in housing and health regulations, and the importance of
> civil rights. (43, author's translation)

In *Pioneros puertorriqueños* (2002), Padilla Aponte's introduction summarizes the main themes that guided Joaquín Colón's autobiographical narratives in the volume: bringing recognition to migrant pioneers who opened the way to subsequent generations of Puerto Rican migrants to learn from their prior experiences; emphasizing Puerto Rican values and traditions preserved by the New York communities; revealing the neglect and discrimination experienced by Afro–Puerto Ricans within their own culture and in US society; and criticizing the lackluster accomplishments of a stateside Puerto Rican leadership that, up to that point, had not been able to represent Puerto Ricans of all social sectors and races.

Bringing Puerto Rican folklore and oral traditions to the New York Puerto Rican community was the life endeavor of librarian Purá Belpré, the first Puerto Rican librarian in the New York Public Library system. Her early experiences in the 1920s working at the branch that later became the Schomburg Center solidified her lifelong commitment to introducing the children of a working-class diaspora to their Spanish, Taino, and African cultural roots through storytelling. Belpré's folklorist interests, civil rights concerns, and pride in her Puerto Rican cultural heritage are best represented in her books for children, *Pérez and Martina* (1932), *The Tiger and the Rabbit, and Other Tales* (1946), and *Once in Puerto Rico* (1973). This devoted advocate of children worked as a librarian for more than half a century. As an Afro–Puerto Rican, Belpré had to deal with the blatant racial and ethnic prejudice and segregation endured by her community during the pre–civil rights years. These concerns often surfaced in her allegorical tales (Sánchez González 2001, 2013).

Cultural Discourses of the Diaspora

As the vicissitudes and experiences of Puerto Rican migrants living in the United States were not central issues to, and for many decades were basically ignored by, their compatriots in Puerto Rico, the separation between island and stateside communities was more than a matter of geography. Many island Puerto Ricans could not conceive of engaging in a discussion about stateside Puerto Ricans without making emphatic points about the obvious cultural, linguistic, or class differences of those generations born or raised in the United States. A view prevailed that stateside Puerto Ricans were not only beleaguered by poverty and discrimination but also culturally and linguistically "deficient" compared to Puerto Ricans on the island. In some ways islanders often regarded the diaspora as a distorted mirror of what it meant to be Puerto Rican. They frequently perceived their counterparts in the United States as too assimilated into Anglo-American values and unable to speak Spanish well or at all, both considered indicators of their disregard for or rejection of their own cultural heritage. In some ways, stateside Puerto Ricans embodied some of the lingering apprehensions about the Americanization process that island Puerto

Ricans had resisted in their own country since the US takeover; for this reason, they were quickly dismissed for not being "true" or "authentic" Puerto Ricans or were even regarded as "pseudo–Puerto Ricans" (see Seda Bonilla 1972). The words "Nuyorican," "Neorican," and just "Rican" were coined to differentiate stateside Puerto Ricans from the ostensibly "real" or "genuine" Puerto Ricans on the island.[6] The term "Nuyorican," which was the most commonly used of all the newly coined labels, was adapted from New York Puerto Rican and thus had its obvious geographic limitations for identifying the whole stateside population. However, it was adopted by a group of Puerto Rican poets born or raised in New York to differentiate themselves from island Puerto Ricans. They stripped the neologism of its original negative connotations and adopted it to define distinctive New York–based constructions of Puerto Rican identity. The decision to subvert the original meaning was in part the result of a visit to the island by poets Miguel Algarín and Miguel Piñero. Someone overheard them speaking "Spanglish" and used the term to describe them. As the stateside Puerto Rican population continued to grow and disperse geographically to other cities and states in later decades, the more encompassing term "Diasporican" was adopted, along with other geographically influenced labels, such as "Chicagorican" or "Orlandorican." With the current patterns of geographic dispersion and settlement of Puerto Ricans, the possibilities for location-based, newly coined identities to emerge are firmly planted.

As objectionable as the separation was to many Puerto Ricans, the widespread tendency to distinguish between the populations of the island and of the diaspora was deeply rooted in history. After the US invasion of Puerto Rico, the ill-advised Americanization policies implemented by the colonial government during the first four decades of occupation had left island Puerto Ricans with a bitter taste. These policies included the imposition of English as the official language of Puerto Rico and its public school system and the concomitant undermining of Spanish, the native language of island Puerto Ricans. Public education aimed at indoctrinating Puerto Ricans into white Anglo-American values and ways of life with an overall disregard for local history and cultural traditions. Protestant religious proselytizing was another tool used to convert a primarily Catholic island population.

All these cultural policies and actions contributed to making island Puerto Ricans extremely sensitive and defensive about cultural and language issues vis-à-vis US influence and colonial domination. Clearly, these issues have generated frequent and heated debates. Over the years there have been numerous writings and discussions regarding the preservation and erosion of Puerto Rican national identity and cultural traditions, the strong US "cultural aggression" (Méndez 1980) in Puerto Rico, and the inexorable connection with the island's political status. These discussions, however, often fail to transcend the political context of the colonial status dilemma or tend to lead to a fervent protectionism of an immutable set of Hispanicized Puerto Rican cultural traditions and the Spanish vernacular. Decades ago they generated intellectual and political denunciations of a professed transculturation in which all cultural and linguistic changes taking place in Puerto Rico were erroneously attributed to an unrestrained Americanization process (de Granda Gutiérrez 1968). This defensive and protectionist stance is part of a deeply rooted tradition of Puerto Rican cultural nationalism that historically has overpowered any forms of political nationalism aimed at extricating the island from the US colonial grip (Maldonado-Denis 1972).

One aspect of this national debate is the question of the cultural identity of those Puerto Ricans living in the United States or, as described more accurately, "the identity in question" (Sandoval-Sánchez 1992). An obvious shortcoming of these identity discussions is that essentialist and monolithic conceptions of identity tend to dominate them. For island Puerto Ricans, the identity of those in the diaspora represents another layer of complexity in an already sensitive and controversial national debate.

Unquestionably, discussions of Puerto Rican national identities now transcend island borders, drawing more attention to a diaspora that keeps growing in leaps and bounds and that surpassed Puerto Rico's population in 2003. The demographic reality and the transnational commuting nature of Puerto Rican migration have attenuated the sense of separation between island and stateside Puerto Ricans, despite the generalized propensity to focus more on their differences than on the issues that have brought both communities together in the past and present.

Among the first to point to the separation between these communities were Nuyorican writers. Island intellectuals were often predisposed to ignore or view critically stateside Puerto Rican authors who identified themselves as Puerto Rican but did not necessarily speak or write Spanish fluently, perceived as a clear indication of their assimilation into Anglo-American culture. More than in the past, the work of these authors—who write primarily (although not exclusively) in English or bilingually—is no longer regarded as a mere extension of US literature, and there is more acceptance of the significance and interrelationships of the diaspora's literary and cultural expressions with those of the island (see Flores 2009). Other times, appreciation of the diaspora's cultural expressions did not transcend the simplistic notion that they were evidence of a "Nuyorican identity crisis," suggesting that this particular identity issue was totally disconnected from the island and its colonial relationship with the United States (see Acosta-Belén 1992a, 2009).

Since the early 1970s, Puerto Rican scholars at US universities and colleges have concentrated their efforts on recovering and documenting the historical roots and evolution of the stateside Puerto Rican presence in the United States, examining the different ways in which Puerto Ricans construct and reaffirm a collective sense of identity within the various communities of the diaspora. Stuart Hall (1990) aptly captured the significance of the overall process of historical recovery and affirmation of cultural identity for diasporic populations when he stated, "Cultural identity . . . is a matter of 'becoming' as well as of 'being.' But, like everything which is historical, [identities] undergo constant transformation. . . . [I]dentities are the names we give to the *different ways* we are positioned by, and position ourselves within the narratives of the past" (22, emphasis added).

Hall stressed the importance for migrant populations of constructing a historical memory of their experiences in the host society as a way of validating who they are and where they come from. This process involves an interplay between the cultural traditions of the country of origin and those of the host society. In the case of Puerto Ricans and other Latinos/as, they share a heritage that has been slighted in mainstream historical narratives. Thus, recovering these legacies and telling these stories provide present and future generations with an empowering knowledge about their place in and contributions to US society. Doing so has been as important to Puerto Rican migrants as to US populations of color and other immigrant groups.

Adding another layer of complexity to the heated Puerto Rican national identity debate has been difficult at best, but now more than ever before the communities of the island and the diaspora are interested in discovering the issues and conditions that both separate and bring them together. This is due in part to generations of stateside Puerto Ricans trying to document the histories of their respective communities and determined to understand themselves and their identities not solely in reference to Puerto Rico but as part of the larger configuration that is the United States. Within the US context, Puerto Ricans are also part of a wider diversity of Latinos/as and share many of the urban barrios and suburban neighborhoods with other Latin American and Caribbean nationalities, African Americans, and other immigrant and nonimmigrant populations. It is quite ironic that because of its association with the United States, Puerto Rico has long struggled for acceptance as a "legitimate" Latin American or Caribbean nation; yet in the United States, Puerto Ricans not only receive a reconstituted Latino/a identity but, whether white, black, or multiracial, are racialized and placed in the ambiguous "people of color," or nonwhite, category. This racialization and labeling of Puerto Ricans and other Latinos/tends to homogenize them and obscure their multiracial backgrounds and long history of *mestizaje*, or racial mixture (e.g., Indian, African, Asian). The notion that because of this multiracial reality Latinos/as tend not to experience racial prejudice within their own cultures is more myth than reality. Historically, indigenous and African populations in Latin America and the Caribbean have endured the ravages of slavery, violence, and discrimination, which disputed theories of racial harmony should not obscure or silence.

The cultural expressions of Puerto Ricans and other ethnoracial minorities demonstrate the creative ways in which writers and artists deal with the inequalities and conflicts that arise from their collective interactions with the white Anglo-American mainstream society. They are also illustrative of how individuals and particular racialized ethnic groups address and negotiate these conditions from their subaltern position. Serving a variety of functions, these cultural expressions create a link with the past and the countries of ancestry, while at the same time, in Eric Hobsbawm's terms, "a tradition is invented" (Hobsbawm and Ranger 1983). Many of these traditions are brought from their home countries; others are shaped from their interactions with the new setting. Within the Puerto Rican diasporic communities, new cultural configurations emerge that play a fundamental social, political, and psychological role in the process of constructing more positive identities. These also play a role in building a historical record and memory of their presence and in the multiple ways they plant roots, build their communities, and become part of this nation. Stateside Puerto Rican writers and artists view countercultural responses to their position in US society and their straddling the two cultural locations as a sign of resistance to their marginality and mistreatment. Their creativity empowers them to expose racial and social conditions shaped by their own personal experiences and those of their communities and to connect with their own cultural origins and legacies.

For Puerto Ricans and other Latinos/as, defining their place in US society and connecting with their respective legacies represents both a challenge and an endeavor that does not necessarily conform to outmoded assimilation theories. Instead, these groups are introducing new forms of cultural affiliation and citizenship that do not rely entirely on "giving up" one's ethnic and racial heritage in order to be embraced as part of the American polity. As historian David W. Noble (2002) pointed out, "By the 1970s . . . Anglo-Protestants had lost their claim to represent the universal national and to monopolize agency within the history of the English colonies and the United States" (260). This statement implies that the historical authority of Anglo-American exceptionalism has been subjected to the same intellectual challenges that questioned the ethnocentric assumption that mostly white privileged elites in Western societies were the primary historical agents and producers of worthy historical and cultural achievements. These major paradigm shifts have validated the many different cultures and immigrant and migrant groups coming from "different shores" (Takaki 1993) and becoming part of the US cultural mosaic (A. Torres 1995).

A factor that contributes to a strong sense of Puerto Rican identity within the diaspora is the geographic proximity between Puerto Rico and the United States and the commuter and transnational nature of Puerto Rican migration. The sustained migratory flow and influx of first-generation migrants reinforces meaningful transnational interconnections between the island and stateside communities that foster cultural straddling and hybridity. Other Latino/a groups also experience different levels of these interactions with respect to their own countries of origin.

Only 32 percent of stateside Puerto Ricans are first-generation migrants, meaning that about 68 percent of the total population was US born in 2015. The ongoing New Millennium Migration might alter those figures, since large numbers of first-generation migrants are now leaving the island for the United States, but it would be hard to predict at this time the possibility of any significant decrease in the percentage of US-born Puerto Ricans. As a result, we can expect that cultural continuity from one generation to another will be accompanied by substantial changes and transformations in the multiple ways that writers and artists translate their experiences and relationships with US society and their Puerto Rican descent. These generational differences create a fluid Puerto Rican cultural context in which there is a constant influx of new arrivals from the island joining and interacting with those generations born and/or raised in the United States.

These differences are quite evident in the area of literary expression. For instance, there are Puerto Rican writers currently living in, or who once lived in, the United States and whose works are generally studied as an extension of the island's literature because they write primarily in Spanish and were born or raised in Puerto Rico. But the island's literary establishment often overlooks those born or raised stateside, whose primary language is usually English, and only a small number have published Spanish translations of their writings. This snobbish disregard has provoked critical reactions in the past from some stateside writers. In the words of renowned New York Puerto Rican prose fiction writer Nicholasa Mohr (1989),

> The separation between myself and the majority of Puerto Rican writers in Puerto Rico goes far beyond a question of language. The jet age and the accessibility of Puerto Rico brought an end to a time of innocence for the children of the former migrants. There is no pretense that going back will solve problems, bring equality and happiness. This is home. This is where we were born, raised, and where most of us will stay. Notwithstanding, it is my affection and concern for the people and the land of my parents and grandparents which is my right and my legacy.
>
> Who we are and how our culture will continue to blossom and develop is being recorded right here, by our writers, painters, and composers; here, where our voices respond and resound loud and clear (116).

Mohr echoed the voices of the generations of Puerto Ricans who felt "at home in the USA" (Turner 1991) but were replacing the myth of assimilation with a Puerto Rican sense of identity that straddles two different cultures and languages (Flores [1988] 1993; Acosta-Belén 1992a). These writers have carved out new hybrid cultural spaces to navigate and interpret their experiences and legacies and define their identities.

The literature of stateside Puerto Ricans has tended to be critical of the white Anglo-American mainstream, its history of racism against people of color and pervasive social and racial inequalities, and US colonial domination of the island. Writers have not necessarily been more benevolent in their views of their ancestral island and culture. Tato Laviera's (1950–2013) poetry is a case in point. The title of his 1979 book *La Carreta Made a U-Turn* demythified the inevitability of René Marqués's tragic view of migration in the play *La carreta*. Instead, Laviera affirmed the resilience of the Puerto Rican spirit and the capacity of New York's migrant community to find creative responses to the obstacles and challenges Puerto Ricans face in their daily lives. In the poem "nuyorican," Laviera's (1985) poetic voice decries the rejection he felt from his island compatriots because of his "American ways" but also denounces a cultural double standard imposed on Nuyoricans since the island also has "Americanized" in some ways:

> I fight for you, Puerto Rico, you know?
> I defend your name, you know?
> I come to your island, I feel a stranger, you know?
> but you with your slanderous accusations, deny me a smile . . .
> you despise me, your look is demeaning, you attack my speech,
> while you eat McDonald's in American discoteques.
> (53, author's translation)

The perceived rejection described in Laviera's verses impelled the foundational writers of the Nuyorican movement to define a distinctive identity that validates the cultural and linguistic back-and-forth and the hybrid nature of their working-class migration experiences and, in tandem, rejects the widespread ethnocentric and elitist views of white Anglo-Americans and island Puerto Ricans. In general, the more blatant nativism and white nationalism represent a backlash against how the country's changing demographics are replacing Anglocentric characterizations. It is also a response to an increased validation of cultural and linguistic diversity that reveals the oppressive experiences of most of these writers as they were growing up in the United States. Their reconstituted sense of identity, which in Laviera's poetry is both American and Puerto Rican—or to use his own coined term, "AmeRícan"—reaffirms a proletarian sense of individual and collective liberation rather than embracing a mythical "melting pot" that strives to erase all cultural differences that fall outside the Anglo-conformity model (see Flores [1988] 1993; Acosta-Belén 1992a). Also included in Laviera's (1985) collection *AmeRícan* is the poem "asimilao," with a redefined meaning of what it means to be a Nuyorican:

> assimilated? qué assimilated,
> brother, yo soy asimilao,
> asi mi la o sí es verdad
> tengo un lado asimilao.
> (Laviera 1985, 54)[7]

Nuyorican poet Miguel Piñero (1946–1988) called Puerto Rico "the slave-blessed land / where nuyoricans come in search of spiritual identity / and are greeted with profanity" ("This Is Not the Place Where I Was Born," Piñero 1980, 14). Piñero's verses offer another illustration of how the generations of Puerto Ricans born or raised in New York and wishing to drink from the ancestral fountain of "spiritual identity" repeatedly felt some degree of cultural rejection and prejudice from island Puerto Ricans. The bigotry and marginality Puerto Rican migrants also experience in US society further exacerbated this particular feeling of uprootedness.

Another prominent Nuyorican poet, the late Pedro Pietri (1944–2004), in his "Love Poem for My People," included in his acclaimed collection *Puerto Rican Obituary* (1973), which was published in Spanish by the Institute of Puerto Rican Culture in 1977—an unusual occurrence for a Nuyorican writer back then—called upon his people to trade the trappings of a materialistic US society for Puerto Rican pride and self-reliance:

> turn off the stereo
> this country gave you
> it is out of order
> your breath
> is your promised land
> if you want
> to feel very rich
> look at your hands
> that is where the definition of magic is located at. (78)

Only a handful of women poets were part of the early years of the Nuyorican poetic movement. Sandra María Esteves is the most recognized from this period. The publication of her first collection, *Yerba Buena* (1980), established that in the early days of this literary movement women writers explored similar cultural, racial, and class experiences and added new gender and sexuality perspectives to the mix. They were carving their own spaces to give voice to the subordination of women within Puerto Rican culture and introducing a feminist outlook that is now ingrained in most of the literature produced by stateside Puerto Rican women writers, as examined later in this chapter.

Some of Esteves's poems also capture the identity fragmentation and straddling so intrinsic to the Puerto Rican and Latina cultural experience in the United States. This is best represented in some of her early poems, such as "Not Neither" from *Tropical Rains: A Bilingual Downpour* (Esteves 1984):

> Being Puertorriqueña Dominicana,
> Borinqueña Quisqueyana,
> Taína-Africana
> Born in the Bronx. Not really jíbara

Not really hablando bien
But yet, not gringa either
Pero ni portorra[8]
Pero sí, portorra too
Pero ni qué, what am I? Y qué soy? (26)

Early studies of the diaspora's cultural expressions (Acosta-Belén 1978; Barradas and Rodríguez 1980; Flores [1988] 1993; Aparicio 1988) viewed this artistic production as a source for validating and affirming a distinctive collective sense of Puerto Rican identity. These new expressions were counterresponses to the detrimental effects of the socioeconomic and racial exclusion experienced by stateside Puerto Ricans and the pressures to assimilate into a society that rendered them almost invisible or minimized their presence. The cultural effervescence found in New York, Chicago, and other cities where Puerto Ricans resided was also part of a wider burgeoning consciousness among ethnoracial minorities in the United States during the late 1960s that expanded significantly in later decades. Some of the foundational poets and writers of the Nuyorican movement continue to write, publish, and perform.

As indicated previously, use of the terms "Nuyorican" and "Neorican" became common in the early 1970s to identify those Puerto Ricans born or raised in the United States and to differentiate them from those on the island. Besides the initial negative connotations, the Nuyorican label also had some obvious geographic limitations, since not all stateside Puerto Ricans lived in New York and, therefore, not all identified with the term. Its origin is unclear, but as early as 1964, island artist and writer Jaime Carrero used the word "Neorican" in the title of his poetry collection *Neorican Jetliner/Jet neorriqueño*. The Nuyorican variation first appeared in the literature in an essay by anthropologist Eduardo Seda Bonilla (1972) in *Requiem por una cultura*, but he claimed that the term was already "in the air."

In the early 1970s a group of New York Puerto Rican writers came together to share their work. Frequent gatherings of many of these writers at Miguel Algarín's home evolved into the Nuyorican Poets Cafe, which opened in 1974 (Turner 1991). Most of the Nuyorican poets got their first public exposure and support from their readings at this venue. Located in Manhattan's Lower East Side (renamed Loisaida by these poets), the cafe was closed in 1982 and reopened in 1989 at a new East Side location with a broader artistic vision. The cafe is now recognized as a New York City cultural institution that provides a stage for performers from many nationalities who dare to participate in its animated and provocative poetry slams (see Algarín and Holman 1994; Noel 2014).

Less than a year after the opening of the café, in 1975, Miguel Algarín and Miguel Piñero published the anthology *Nuyorican Poetry: An Anthology of Puerto Rican Words and Feelings*, introducing a more meaningful and positive ideological context for using the term "Nuyorican." For these authors, adopting this label was an affirmation of their culturally and linguistically hybrid experience; it reflected their new sense of Puerto Rican identity grounded in shared working-class realities and experiences of poverty and racism growing up in the various urban barrios of New York City (Spanish Harlem, the Lower East Side, Washington Heights, Los Sures, the South Bronx). "Nuyorican" was meant to differentiate those Puerto Ricans born or raised in the United States from those living in Puerto Rico. The Nuyorican experience was said to include a new language based on the mixing of English and Spanish linguistic codes (technically known as code switching) and the morphological adaptation of words from both languages, commonly described as "Spanglish" (Acosta-Belén 1977; Aparicio 1988; Stavans 2003). The experiences of most Nuyorican writers were deeply rooted in the streets of the urban barrios, where Puerto Ricans faced the consequences and challenges of the social and racial ills of life in the city and the wider US society. Nuyorican artistic expression frequently underscored African and indigenous cultural influences, as well as those of other Latinos/as of other national origins with whom Puerto Ricans shared the urban barrios.

The *Nuyorican Poetry* anthology featured the writings of Pedro Pietri, Sandra María Esteves, José Angel Figueroa, Jesús Papoleto Meléndez, Louis Reyes Rivera, and a few others, in addition to Algarín and Piñero. Since then Algarín has published several books of poetry, with *Mongo Affair* (1978) being among the best known. His work as a cultural activist was key to the establishment and institutionalizing of the Nuyorican Poets Cafe. Algarín also directed the Nuyorican Playwrights/Actors Workshop and the Nuyorican Theater Festival (Algarín and Griffith 1997). Piñero became an award-winning playwright when his play *Short Eyes* (written in 1974), a depiction of the harshness of the prison life he had experienced at a young age, received a New York Critics' Circle Award and the Obie for best off-Broadway play and was later made into a film. In 1980, Piñero published the poetry collection *La Bodega Sold Dreams* as well as a few short plays. He became a TV actor and played a recurring role in the *Miami Vice* (1984–1989) action series. A few years after his death, his life and writings were featured in the motion picture *Piñero* (2001).

After the publication of *Nuyorican Poetry*, some of these poets began to produce their own single-author collections and emerged among the most recognized performing poetry voices of the diaspora. Pedro Pietri received critical acclaim for his volume *Puerto Rican Obituary* (1973), and his recordings and dramatic readings of his own poems showed that oral communication, performance, and interaction with an audience were an essential part of the Nuyorican creative experience.

José Angel Figueroa's *Noo Jork* (1981) was the first Spanish-language poetry collection by a Nuyorican poet published in Puerto Rico. After the early poems of his first published collection, *East 110th Street* (1973), Figueroa proved to be one of the most innovative pioneers of the vibrant Nuyorican poetic movement of the 1970s and 1980s. According to Acosta-Belén (2013), four decades later, the poems collected in Figueroa's latest comprehensive collection, *A Mirror in My Own Backstage* (2013), show

> the author's social and political warrior soul of earlier times, but similarly reveal the creative imagination of a poet with a deliberate "consciousness of Art." For as much as Figueroa's poetry speaks to issues of equality and social justice, it is also an effective aesthetic tool for articulating allegorical visions and ontological musings about our place in a dysfunctional world and the overall human condition.
>
> What makes Figueroa's poetry so refreshingly unique, is how he branches out from the prescribed social and political messages of the Nuyorican movement and ends up with a more aesthetically and conceptually rich and complex poetry, often tinged with surrealistic tropes or the surprising juxtaposition of images that are simultaneously subversive, healing, and deeply rooted in notions of human freedom and dignity. (1–2)

While many of Figueroa's poems give voice to a sense of identity and heritage for a colonized Puerto Rican people, other poems in this volume reveal a more introspective, philosophical, and Shakespearean dimension of his writing—the world is a stage where the poet stands as "a mirror in [his] own backstage," striving to visualize and reflect the unseen, make sense of a wounded universe, and bring to it some healing and poetic harmony. Clearly, *A Mirror in My Own Backstage* also illustrates Figueroa's poetic evolution. The collection includes some of his most classic poems, along with a new crop of innovative work by this accomplished and gifted artist who has mastered his craft.

There were other poets not affiliated with the Nuyorican Poets Cafe movement who often performed their poetic compositions at that venue and published their work before or during those years. One of the first to publish a single-author collection was Víctor Hernández Cruz, author of *Papo Got His Gun* (1966) and *Snaps* (1969), the first full poetry volumes by a New York Puerto Rican. Many of Hernández Cruz's poems emphasize Afro-Caribbean cultural imagery, musical rhythms, and the magical realism so characteristic of the contemporary Latin American literary tradition. Subsequent poetry collections, such as *Mainland* (1973), *Tropicalization* (1976), *Rhythm, Content, and Flavor* (1989), and *The Mountain in the Sea* (2006), among several others, have made Hernández Cruz one of the most prolific and widely anthologized stateside Puerto Rican poets. In 1981, *Life* magazine included him on a list of best American poets. His most recent collection, *Beneath the Spanish* (2017), brings him back to Puerto Rico, the place where he was born and returned to live for a period of years, and allows him to play with the intersecting structures and rhythms of the languages and cultures that make him both a Puerto Rican and an American poet. Literary critic Nicolás Kanellos described Hernández Cruz as a "traveling troubadour," since he often incorporates into his poetry his trips around the world and exposure to other cultures and languages. His poem "Borinkins in Hawaii" captures the journey and historical circumstances that account for the long-standing Puerto Rican presence there—an outcome of the exploitative contract labor of immigrants from several countries in the early twentieth century—and the cultural hybridity, "Of islands / Which emerged / Out of the tears" (Hernández Cruz 1989, 100–101).

New Generations

Literary and artistic production among stateside Puerto Ricans continues to flourish, and the spirited creative drive has expanded considerably since the emergence of the foundational writers of the Nuyorican movement that dominated the 1970s and 1980s. Many of the poets, prose fiction writers, and visual artists included in the early anthologies of US Puerto Rican and Latino/a literature and those focused on the visual arts continue to add to their bodies of work; others are no longer publishing or painting, while a smaller number have passed away. The significance of the literary and artistic contributions of those who broke ground in making the Puerto Rican presence and experience visible to their communities and the general public is an undeniable testament to the creative imagination of less privileged sectors of US society. A substantive number of original and gifted writers and artists who came on the scene in the 1970s and 1980s drew recognition from critics and scholars and, by doing so, began to forge a space in an American literary and artistic tradition that, for the most part and up to that point, had excluded the work of writers and artists of color. They stand today as valued precursors to and inspirers of the contemporary muses and voices that are seizing the pages, stages, canvases, walls, and public spaces of creativity that touch our minds and souls and enrich our senses.

The emergence of new voices and images of a more geographically dispersed Puerto Rican diaspora is compelling cultural critics to shift their focus to the abundant cultural production of the 1990s and the early decades of the new millennium. Substantive scholarship about this period is far from abundant, and with few exceptions New York still appears to be drawing the larger portion of critical attention.

Even major literary undertakings, such as *Herencia: The Anthology of Hispanic Literature of the United States* (Kanellos 2002) and the *Norton Anthology of Latino Literature* (Stavans 2011), are currently missing numerous talented Latino/a writers from younger generations from a wide range of nationalities, but are also illustrative of the prolific creative spirit of stateside Puerto Ricans and other Latinos/as. Moreover, the process of selecting and including representative writers, as well as consideration of periodization and canonizing issues that generally guide the labor of anthologizing, is never all-encompassing. Occasional omissions of talented writers are unavoidable, the result of editorial or publisher decisions and other limitations, such as reprinting fees charged by copyright holders.

A significant portion of the creative endeavors from the first and subsequent waves of writers and artists of the Nuyorican cultural movement and of those based in other parts of the country remains understudied. One of the most outstanding and recent critical contributions that sheds light on a subsequent wave of performance poets is Urayoán Noel's 2017 *In Visible Movement: Nuyorican Poetry from the Sixties to Slam*. This indispensable scholarly study yields new insights into the significance of the foundational Nuyorican poets, but it then moves on to a typically more neglected part of the diaspora's cultural and literary heritage: the generations of Nuyorican performing poets of the slam era and beyond (1990s–2010s) in New York City and other parts of the country. Noel clearly establishes that the original creative spirit and literary heritage of the foundational Nuyorican poets is still very much alive and being transformed in multiple provocative and innovative ways by younger generations of the late-1980s and 1990s slam and spoken word def poetry jam scenes of the early 2000s. These new generations are also expanding vital literary and artistic traditions in the cultural life of the diaspora and ongoing social and political battles for equality and justice of its various stateside Puerto Rican and Latino/a communities, now being marketed and reaching broader audiences. Despite what was then regarded as the avant-garde experimental nature of poetry that seized the countercultural and revisionist stances of the first generation of Nuyorican poets, the slam-era performing poets continue to adopt the "counterculture" and "revisionist" stances of their precursors while also acknowledging multiple influences from other American, African American, Caribbean, and Latino/a writers (Noel 2014). These other generations are part of another wave of innovators with access to new and changing technologies and social media that open endless and always provocative poetic paths.

Younger poets, prose fiction writers, and playwrights started to enrich US Puerto Rican literary and artistic production in the late 1990s. The second opening of the Nuyorican Poets Cafe in 1989, a joint venture between Algarín and Bob Holman, also a performing poet with vast experience in producing and directing theater, film, and television, marked a renewal phase for a venue that had propelled a foundational generation of Puerto Rican performing poets. Some of these poets had been celebrated and anthologized by both stateside and island communities, and by the US cultural and literary mainstream. In its new reincarnation, however, the cafe became known for its performing poetry slams and broader multiculturalist vision. It transformed itself into an open setting for an emerging crop of Puerto Ricans and

Latinos/as of various national origins, as well as performers from other eth-
nicities and racial backgrounds who were motivated and brave enough to
share a coveted competitive stage for introducing and performing their
work. According to Noel (2014), "This new Cafe opened its doors to new
generations of poets attuned to hip-hop and (post) punk cultures" (124). He
also notes, "The term Nuyorican was beginning to circulate globally as a
metonymy of the physical space of the Cafe, decontextualized from community histories and identifications" (124). Whether the latter was a good thing
or not, the revitalized cafe turned into a well-recognized presence in New
York and an indispensable stage for performing poets. What better indication
of the Nuyorican Poets Cafe's widespread reputation than its coverage in a
2012 segment of *60 Minutes* and the numerous *New York Times* articles
about its wide range of poetry, theater, and musical performances.

The list of younger and talented poets includes the names of María
Teresa (Mariposa) Fernández and Willie Perdomo. Fernández's "Ode to the
Diasporican" (1998) was originally titled "Ode to the Nuyorican," when it
first appeared in 1993. The title was changed by the poet to be more inclusive of a growing stateside Puerto Rican diaspora. Considered her most
emblematic poem, it is a powerful affirmation of a redefined Puerto Rican
identity shared by those Boricuas born or raised, in her case in the Bronx, but
also throughout the United States. Mariposa's album *Ode to the Diasporican
Boogaloo* (2016) adds rhythms from the boogaloo musical genre, popularized in the 1960s in New York by Puerto Rican and other Latino/a musicians,
to this and other of her signature poems:

> Some people say that I am not the real thing
> Boricua, that is
> Cause I wasn't born on the enchanted island
> Cause I was born on the mainland
> North of Spanish Harlem
> Cause I was born in the Bronx. . . .
> What does it mean to live in between
> What does it take to realize
> That being Boricua
> Is a state of mind
> A state of heart
> A state of the soul
> No nací en Puerto Rico
> Puerto Rico nació en mi.[9] (78)

Raised in East Harlem, Willie Perdomo was lauded by African American
writer Claude Brown as an incarnation of the revered Harlem Renaissance
poet Langston Hughes, and the title of his first poetry collection, *Where a
Nickel Costs a Dime* (1996), comes from a line in a Hughes poem. The volume includes a CD, on which Perdomo performs his work to the beat of

Latino musical rhythms. His poetry blends the language of the streets with the creative imagination of a skilled performing poet. Emblematic poems such as "Nigger-Rican Blues" mix the conversational street language of Nuyoricans and African Americans as the author's poetic persona has a back-and-forth street conversation with friends that mocks never-ending identity dilemmas: "—Hey Willie, What are yu, man? Boricua? Moreno,[10] Que? Are you Black? Puerto Rican?" After denying his blackness and being deemed to have "the nigger-rican blues," he reveals his self-awareness by repeatedly shouting, "I'm a spic! I am a nigger! . . . / Spic, spic, spic. I ain't noooooo different than a nigger!" Subsequent works by Perdomo include *Postcards of El Barrio* (2002), *Smoking Lovely* (2004), and *The Essentail Hits of Shorty Bon Bon: Poems* (2014).

Other older and newer women's voices have added to what was for many years, with few exceptions, a more visible Nuyorican Poets Cafe performance poetry tradition dominated by Puerto Rican male poets and their "street poetry." The wide range of creative output by the indefatigable, multitalented poet, playwright, performing artist, teacher, national speaker, and feminist social activist Magdalena Gómez represents decades of building an impressive and critically recognized body of work and artistic endeavors celebrated by numerous audiences. Thus the reach of Gómez's exceptional creative mind and spirit goes beyond her modest number of published books. Noel (2014) sees her work as "a bridge between the founding Nuyorican poets and a new generation informed by slam and def poetry" (118), but he also notes that "the significance of her work . . . cannot be gauged primarily to her print output" (119). This assertion can be easily supported by Gómez's full range of artistic work.

Her several performance poetry recordings, including the CD *AmaXonica: Howls from the Left Side of My Body* (2004), not only convey the innovative performing character that runs through her creative work, blending poetry, music, and acting, but also reveal a contemporary Amazon warrior in pursuit of social justice, a "shameless woman"—the title of her 2014 poetic memoir—who dares to provoke, entertain, and inspire audiences and readers. Gómez is also a dismantler of stereotypes about Puerto Rican women's femininity and submissive roles imposed by patriarchal cultural values and religion, as noted by Golder (2011–2012, 156–157). A subsequent CD release, *Bemba y Chichón* (2008), relies on satiric humor to disrupt an array of stereotypes generally expected by marketers and consumers of Puerto Rican and Latino/a creative expression (Noel 2014). At her home base in Springfield, Massachusetts, Gómez cofounded Teatro V!da (www.teatrovida.com) in 2007; for over a decade, it has served as an important community venue to get youth involved in the arts and develop their creative, critical, and leadership skills and strengthen their connections with their communities and their surrounding realities. Her volume *Bullying: Replies, Rebuttals, Confessions, and Catharsis* (2012), coedited with María Luisa Arroyo, draws much-needed attention to one of the most serious and challenging problems experienced by our children and youth in schools and individuals in other settings. A wide multicultural selection of compelling real and fictional stories, essays, and poems aims at consciousness-raising about the pervasive pattern of abusive behavior and envisions strategies for dealing with its damaging effects and stimulating social change.

Since the release of *Teeth* (2007), her first published collection, Aracelis Girmay has been part of a younger generation of talented stateside Puerto Rican poets receiving wider recognition in US poetic circles, and not enough in Puerto Rican ones, even though her writings "explore the transnational and cross-cultural resonances of the diaspora" (Noel 2014, 174). Not getting their due recognition has happened, at least initially, to more than a few stateside poets whose work is shaped by a broader spectrum of artistic and cultural influences and more experimental poetic twists and turns than found in most of the foundational Nuyorican poets and their more explicit cultural, social, and political discourses. Girmay was born and grew up in Southern California but acknowledges the importance of having "roots in Puerto Rico, Eritrea, and African America." Thus she is among a growing number of stateside writers, artists, and women's voices formed or working in a wider range of geographic locations throughout the United States, some coming from a blend of diverse cultural and racial backgrounds that account for a more complex and nuanced understanding of the cultural production of the stateside diaspora. This new wave of poets transcends the borders of a New York City–centered perspective about Puerto Rican experiences that dominated the poetry and prose fiction writings of the 1970s and 1980s. Girmay's subsequent poetry books include *Kingdom Animalia* (2011) and *The Black Maria* (2016), recipient of the 2015 Whiting Award for Poetry. The latter volume illustrates the poet's interest in giving poetic rendering to African diasporic historical experiences and US racialized identities.

Poet Edwin Torres is also among the most original of the recent generation of experimental performers.[11] He is a self-proclaimed "lingualisualist," since sight and sound are intrinsic to his performing endeavors, book publications, and recordings. He noted in an interview, "The fascinating aspect of a poem's creation to me, is that its life on the stage gets to have a rebirth when experienced on stage" (see Walker 2010). Published by independent presses that work with numerous talented poets but do not necessarily reach a wide national market, a few of Torres's books include *Fractured Humorous* (1999), *The All-Union Day of the Shock Worker* (2001), *In the Function of External Circumstances* (2010), and *Ameriscopia* (2014), some of which Noel (2014) discusses in more detail.

Noel's aforementioned scholarly study is the most comprehensive analysis of the evolution of Nuyorican poetry available to date that gives continuity to earlier and more recent generations of Nuyorican performing poets and to the diaspora's creative role in producing decolonial imaginaries. However, perhaps its most obvious omission is that as Noel is a scholar and author of an invaluable piece of literary criticism and history, who is also one of the most innovative and recognized contemporary performing poets, he chose not to include himself among the Nuyorican poetic voices discussed in his book. Since he has demonstrated a level of creativity and talent that should not be ignored, we would be remiss not to highlight his body of work to date.

Noel describes himself as "a stateless poet" because of his "flux between island and mainland, and between textual forms (print, body, and web)"; he also calls himself a "postpunk parodist" (see www.urayoannoel.com). His first bilingual collection of poems, *Kool Logic/La lógica kool* (2005), immediately caught the attention of island and stateside critics and readers. He leads a very active career as performing poet, creative writer, university professor, and scholar. In a style that Noel would appreciate, poet Mónica de la Torre inventively praises and captures the essence of his 2010 collection *Hi-Density Politics*: "Urayoán Noel's plurilingual, polyphonic, & polymorphous text works are images are performance scores are records of poetry actions are homophonic translations are poems are homages to some of Latin America and the Caribbean's greatest innovators."

A few years later, Charlie "Isa" Guzmán, in a review of Noel's 2015 volume *Buzzing Hemisphere/Rumor hemisférico*, notes how "the poems bombard the reader with several languages, stylized formats, mistranslations, images, and playing." As a performing poet and artist of the most recent reiterations of millennial avant-garde poetics and performing poetry, Noel, in his texts and performances, reveals an artistic consciousness that explores the almost endless creative possibilities of how a text can metamorphose when it is being written, performed, accompanied by music or other sound effects, imbued with different cultural and linguistic wordplay and meanings, inscribed by spoken tones and body movements, or transformed by experimentation and the disruption of conventional poetic forms, styles, and traditions. Noel's (2010) "HI THEN [salutation]," included in *Hi-Density Politics*, is a good example of his "disrupting" poetic approach: "You can keep the poem that anoints— / That represents—that narrates or 'gives' voice— / Find the voice that *poems*—that disjoints!" (37–39).

However, New York is not the exclusive location for Puerto Rican creativity. In his *Defending Our Own in the Cold: The Cultural Turns of Puerto Ricans*, Marc Zimmerman (2011) unveils the rich tradition of a vital but neglected cultural production that developed beyond the geographic confines of New York City and includes other cities with large concentrations of Puerto Ricans, in this case, Chicago. Earlier efforts to introduce emerging writers and artists from that city, which at the time had the second-largest concentration, included *Nosotros* (1977) (a special issue of the

Revista Chicano-Riqueña), edited by performance poet David Hernández (1946–2013). Hernández, also a band leader, was regarded as a performing poet of Chicago's streets who made "rhythms with words," a generous mentor to younger artists, and an inspiring educator. In 1971 he founded Street Sounds, a celebrated music and spoken word group. Chicago poets and graphic artists, with samples of their poetry, photography, and art, appeared in several issues of the short-lived Chicago-based journal *The Rican* (1971–1974). Founded in 2005, Café Teatro Batey Urbano, a theater café located in Chicago's Paseo Boricua and linked to the Puerto Rican Cultural Center, has been an important venue for the city's performing poets for over a decade (Zimmerman 2011; Noel 2014).

Award-winning performing artist, poet, and playwright Rane Arroyo (1943–2010), a talented Chicago Puerto Rican gay writer, did not get due critical attention from Puerto Rican literature scholars, partly because the critical focus was, for a long time, on the Nuyorican cultural movement. Arroyo's openly gay and often erotic writings were more distanced from Nuyorican poetic trends and reflected the generalized neglect of LGBTQ writings (see La Fountain-Stokes 2009). Arroyo authored eleven books of poetry, three published plays, and a short fiction collection. Zimmerman (2011) examines the significance of Arroyo's body of work, which includes the poetry collections *Pale Ramón* (1998), *The Portable Famine* (2005), and *Same-Sex Séances* (2008), among others, and plays collected in the volume *Dancing at Funerals: Selected Plays* (2010).

Included among several well-recognized authors writing from different US localities was Boston-based poet Rosario Morales (1930–2011) and her California-based daughter Aurora Levins Morales, who continues her literary and historical writings and other creative endeavors. Back in 1986, the mother and daughter's groundbreaking joint collection of poetry and personal narratives, *Getting Home Alive*, introduced a radical feminist perspective into stateside Puerto Rican literary expression. Moreover, this particular volume captured the experiences of two Puerto Rican women from different generations as they acknowledged their multiple oppressions and defined and brought together the different components of their identities into a new cultural and racial synthesis, illustrated by their jointly authored "Ending Poem":

> I am what I am.
> *A child of the Americas.*
> A light-skinned mestiza of the Caribbean.
> *A child of many diaspora, born into this continent at a crossroads,*
> I am Puerto Rican. I am US American. . . .
> We are new . . .
> *History made us . . .*
> *And we are whole.*
> (Levins Morales and Morales 1986, 213)

Over a decade later, in 1998, Levins Morales published *Remedios* (Remedies) and *Medicine Stories: History, Culture, and the Politics of Integrity*, books that include a mix of testimony, historical account, and storytelling and reveal the author's uncompromising feminist outlook and keen sense of the history of the Americas viewed through the oppressive experiences of women and colonized indigenous and African cultures.

Another critically acclaimed Puerto Rican poet is Martín Espada. During his prolific career, Espada has combined his literary writing with a law practice and the teaching of creative writing at the University of Massachusetts, Amherst. His first collection of poems, *The Immigrant Iceboy's Bolero* (1982), includes photographs of barrio life taken by his father, Frank Espada, which provide visual images of the social milieu that inspired the poems. The poet is also author of *Rebellion Is the Circle of a Lover's Hand* (1990), a bilingual collection that focuses on the exploitative lives of immigrants and workers. Subsequent volumes include *Imagine the Angels of Bread* (1996), winner of an American Book Award, and *A Mayan Astronomer in Hell's Kitchen* (2000). As a whole, his body of work combines an intense political and social consciousness with his commitment to fighting oppression. Espada (1998) sees poetry as a form of revolutionary practice:

> Poetry of the political imagination is a matter of both vision and language. Any progressive social change must be imagined first, and that vision must find its most eloquent possible expression to move from vision to reality. . . . Political imagination goes beyond protest to articulate an *artistry* of dissent. The question is not whether poetry and politics can mix. The question is a luxury for those who can afford it. The question is how *best* to combine poetry and politics, craft and commitment, how to find the artistic imagination equal to the intensity of the experience and the quality of the ideas (100).

Several US Latina writers, inspired by the groundbreaking efforts of Chicana writers Cherríe Moraga and Gloria Anzaldúa (1981), editors of *This Bridge Called My Back: Writings by Radical Women of Color*, and Asunción Horno-Delgado, Eliana Ortega, Nancy M. Scott, and Nancy Saporta Sternbach (1989), editors of *Breaking Boundaries: Latina Writings and Critical Readings*, were instrumental in bringing attention to the intersectionalities of gender, race, ethnicity, and sexuality.

Poet Luz María Umpierre-Herrera (1987), author of *The Margarita Poems*, was one of them. Born and raised in Puerto Rico but living in the United States for several decades, she is also a well-known literary critic and has taught Latin American literature at various US universities. *The Margarita Poems* is a courageous bilingual collection of poems about love among women that defies social and patriarchal conventions and adds an important contribution to expanding the conventional scope of Puerto Rican and US Latino/a literature. As the poet describes on her website, this book represents "the coming out" period of her writing at a time when there were few LGBTQ voices included in US Latino/a and Latin American literatures. Critics now regard Umpierre-Herrera as a leading author of the Latina lesbian feminist poetic tradition. An early effort to introduce a wide range of LGBTQ experiences and topics was Juanita Ramos's (1987) edited collection *Compañeras: Latina Lesbians*, which includes the writings and testimonials of feminist women of color marginalized by their sexuality, exposing a myriad of social and cultural forces and patriarchal power structures that perpetuate their oppression. Subsequently, Lawrence La Fountain-Stokes's (2009) comprehensive groundbreaking study *Queer Ricans: Cultures and Sexualities in the Diaspora* underscored the importance of considering how different sexualities influence and shape the migration experiences and lives of stateside Puerto Ricans, including their cultural production. Critical of the nationalist or colonial perspectives of Puerto Rican cultural politics, the collection of essays *Puerto Rican Jam: Rethinking Colonialism and Nationalism*, edited by Frances Negrón-Muntaner and Ramón Grosfoguel (2008), added invaluable insights and approaches and expanded the scope of these discussions.

Growing-Up Narratives

An important tradition in Puerto Rican literature in the United States is the *bildungsroman*, or the coming of age narrative, which relates the events and experiences that shape the protagonist's personality from childhood through adulthood. Many writings by Puerto Rican authors portray the adventures, challenges, and risks of growing up Puerto Rican in the segregated barrios of urban cities and the harmful effects of racism and unequal treatment as part of a marginalized minority. As a whole, writers of color were not able to penetrate the US publishing market until the tumultuous civil rights battles of the 1960s, when US publishers began to show interest in autobiographical accounts of what it meant to grow up as a person of color in a society founded on the principle that all citizens are "created equal" but where racism, segregation, and violence against nonwhite groups by white supremacists still prevailed. Inspired by the civil rights and Black Power movements, African American writers such as Claude Brown, Malcolm X, and Eldridge Cleaver were among the first to publish their autobiographical novels. The pioneering autobiographical novel *Down These Mean Streets* (1967) and its sequel, *Savior, Savior, Hold My Hand* (1972), by Piri Thomas (1928–2011) were written along the lines of Brown's *Manchild in the Promised Land* (1965). Thomas's poignant autobiographical accounts of surviving racism, drugs, and imprisonment, among the first by a Puerto Rican of mixed race born in Spanish Harlem during the years of the Great

Depression, exposed the harsh realities of life on the streets of the inner city. For Thomas, the vicissitudes of growing up in the racially charged environment of the 1930s to 1950s made his story even more compelling. He openly related the nature and consequences of his self-destructive behavior and actions, including seven years' imprisonment for drug-related felonies, but his narratives were also a testament to his ability to overcome these conditions, turn his life around, and launch a successful career as a freelance writer and public speaker. His imprisonment and path to redemption and a productive life were at the center of *Seven Long Times* (1974), which allowed him to expose the dehumanizing environment of New York's prison system. The book was published only a few years after the tragic riot at New York's Attica Correctional Facility in 1971 that caused the deaths of thirty-three convicts and ten correctional officers and employees. Inspired by Piri Thomas's novels, other Puerto Rican male writers, such as Lefty Barreto, author of *Nobody's Hero* (1977), published their own narratives, albeit without achieving similar literary success.

The great majority of Thomas's narratives introduce readers to the lives and trials of working-class migrant families. New York–based author Edward Rivera (1944–2001) offered a different account of his own formative years in the stories of *Family Installments: Memories of Growing Up Hispanic* (1982). Although Rivera was a white, middle-class Puerto Rican, his more privileged background did not deter him from skillfully showing an awareness of the conflictive and sometimes degrading multiethnic environment of New York City. However, he did not dwell on the crude and bleak realism of many earlier testimonial accounts but rather relied on satiric humor to relate some of his thorny experiences in school, at home, and in his community and their relationship with the wider US society. In a 1996 interview with Ilan Stavans, Rivera mentioned the difficulty of getting his book published because he did not fit preconceived notions of "underclass lit." For many years, Rivera combined his writing with an academic career teaching English at City College and mentoring young Latino/a writers.

Author Ed Vega (who in later years used his full name, Edgardo Vega Yunqué; 1936–2008) also tried to break away from prescribed ethnic narratives. Vega relied on satire to combat ethnic stereotypes and challenge the conventions of "ghetto literature." He published the novel *The Comeback* (1985) and the short story collections *Mendoza's Dreams* (1987) and *Casualty Report* (1991). His last novel, *The Lamentable Journey of Omaha Bigelow into the Impenetrable Loisaida Jungle* (2004), continued to show his disdain for formulaic narratives and displayed his talent as one of the most powerful, complex, and original stateside Puerto Rican prose fiction writers.

Male-authored novels of inner-city life also include those of Edwin Torres. A writer and a justice of the New York State Supreme Court, Torres published a series of novels focused on city crime and clashes between members of minority groups and the police. These novels, which appealed to popular audiences, also tend to reinforce some common stereotypes. Torres's novels *Carlito's Way* (1975) and *Q&A* (1977) have been made into major action films.

Writer Abraham Rodríguez, from a younger generation, expressed the outrage and frustration of those caught up in the destructive effects of poverty and racism in his collection of short stories, *The Boy Without a Flag: Tales of the South Bronx* (1992), and the novels *Spidertown* (1993), *The Buddha Book* (2001), and *South by South Bronx* (2008). If Piri Thomas is regarded as the main raconteur of the lives and hardships of Puerto Ricans in Spanish Harlem, clearly Rodríguez adopts a similar role for those growing up in the South Bronx, a community that endured urban unrest and destruction during the late 1960s and 1970s.

It became common for Puerto Rican male narratives to highlight the violence and despairing realities of street life in the urban barrios, which often led to a self-destructive path or a search for the inner strength and determination to beat the odds. Underlying many of Rodríguez's writings is his outrage and frustration with Puerto Rican youth getting caught in the turbulent world of the streets and unable to overcome the detrimental effects of an underprivileged status.

In contrast to male authors, Puerto Rican women writers have preferred to explore the unequal power relations between the sexes and oppressive roles and traditions. Their stories frequently highlight the whole gamut of interpersonal relationships and interactions among women family members of different generations. A distinguished pioneer in this genre is Nicholasa Mohr. In her early career, she had to struggle with mainstream publishers to make them realize that growing up in the urban barrios was not always the self-destructive experience described up to that time by most of the published male accounts (see Acosta-Belén 1978, 2009). The hardships and discrimination faced by her Spanish Harlem community are very central to Mohr's work, but her narratives weave an impressive tapestry of working-class characters who reveal the compassion and human solidarity that is also part of daily life in the urban barrios. Mohr is author of the novel *Nilda* (1973) and the short-story collections *El Bronx Remembered* (1975), *In Nueva York* (1977), *Rituals of Survival: A Woman's Portfolio* (1985), and *A Matter of Pride and Other Stories* (1997). As she is a feminist writer, the focus of the latter two collections are resilient Puerto Rican women characters dealing with the *machista* conventions that constrain them along with the hardships faced by most working-class migrants but always forging ahead. Mohr's short stories are frequently anthologized and praised by critics, and her novels are often required reading in schools and universities. Mohr is also a graphic artist and has illustrated some of her books with drawings and silk screens, especially her children novels, such as *Felita*

(1979) and its sequel, *Going Home* (1986), and the illustrated story *The Song of El Coquí/La canción del coquí* (1995), done in collaboration with the most prominent island visual artist, Antonio Martorell. Mohr's coming-of-age memoir, *In My Own Words: Growing Up Inside the Sanctuary of My Imagination* (1994), encourages young readers to fulfill their dreams by exploring their creative imaginations, advice given to her by her loving mother before she passed away when Mohr was only fourteen years old.

Poet and novelist Judith Ortiz Cofer (1952–2016), raised in Paterson, New Jersey, and holding the distinguished title of Emeritus Regents' and Franklin Professor at the University of Georgia in Athens, where she taught creative writing for over twenty-five years, joined other feminist women in their attempts to capture the subordinate roles and experiences of different generations of Puerto Rican women and the tensions between the island/ stateside cultural worlds they share. After her early collection of poems, *Terms of Survival* (1987), Ortiz Cofer, a skillful storyteller and prolific writer, combined poetry and short fiction in the volumes *Silent Dancing: Remembrances of a Puerto Rican Childhood* (1990) and *The Latin Deli* (1993). For the most part, her writings also have depicted her coming-of-age experiences straddling Paterson, New Jersey, where many Puerto Rican families settled in the 1950s, and Puerto Rico. Her hometown of Hormigueros is also the setting of many captivating life stories about family members and town residents in Puerto Rico that were passed along to her by her grandmother, mother, and uncle. Ortiz Cofer's autobiographical novel *The Line of the Sun* (1989) was well received by critics and has been translated into Spanish as *La línea del sol* (1996). The back-and-forth movement between her two cultural locations was a vital part of most of Ortiz Cofer's writing. Her multigenre memoir *Woman in Front of the Sun: On Becoming a Writer* (2000) is driven by her reflections on her creative process and the role of ethnic literature in the United States. Ortiz Cofer's last autobiographical publication, *The Cruel Country* (2015), is her most moving and painful story about the weeks that preceded and followed the terrible loss of her mother from lung cancer. Her mother was an important presence in many of her writings. This was also Ortiz Cofer's last homecoming in a lifetime of straddling her two cultural locations. Over a year after the publication of *The Cruel Country*, Ortiz Cofer passed away in 2016, when she lost her own battle with cancer. She had been inducted into the Georgia Writers' Hall of Fame in 2006.

Another critically acclaimed writer in the prolific women's *bildungsroman* genre is Esmeralda Santiago, author of the autobiographical novel *When I Was Puerto Rican* (1993) and its sequel, *Almost a Woman* (1998). The sequel was made into a PBS television film. Santiago's writing depicts a wide range of experiences and motivations in Puerto Rican women's lives. The title of her first novel suggests another major theme in her work: the recovery of memory and the construction of identity against a backdrop of cultural straddling and flux. In alternating scenes of life back in Puerto Rico and in their respective stateside communities, both Ortiz Cofer and Santiago use humor to point out conflicts and contradictions that derive from the clash between cultures and among different generations. Due to growing interest in the stateside experiences of Puerto Ricans and other Latinos/as in their countries of origin, several of these leading authors' best-known works, including those of Ortiz Cofer and Santiago, have been translated in recent years from the original English into Spanish.[12]

The Role of Latino Publishers

It is well known that for a long time mainstream US publishing houses did not see a market for the writings of Puerto Rican or other Latino/a authors. These publishers, assuming that most Latinos/as did not have the levels of education to sustain a reading audience and market, easily bought into generalized stereotypes and prejudices about an alleged "poverty of culture" within these communities. Additionally, there was a generalized assumption that Latino/a lives and experiences would not interest non-Latino/a readers and that, overall, their creative writings were not marketable.

These widespread assumptions explain why the publication of works by Puerto Rican, Chicano/a, and other Latino/a writers was made possible, at least initially, not by mainstream publishers but by small ethnic presses and a few literary and cultural studies journals, generally individual or collective initiatives by Puerto Rican and Chicano/a scholars. These small presses and journals were located at the home institutions of the university professors who founded them. That was the case with the founding of *Revista Chicano-Riqueña* (subsequently the *Americas Review*) in 1973 by Puerto Rican literature scholar Nicolás Kanellos while he was a faculty member at Indiana University. A few years later, Kanellos moved to the University of Houston with the journal and founded Arte Público Press, first home to a large number of literary works by Puerto Ricans, Chicanos/as, Cubans, and Dominicans. Making available another key publishing outlet to Latino/a writers and readers, a year after the release of *Revista Chicano-Riqueña* Chicano scholar Gary H. Keller initiated the journal *Bilingual Review/La revista bilingüe* (1974) while he was a faculty member at York College, City University of New York. Keller also founded the Bilingual Press, and both are now based at Arizona State University.

In subsequent years, an unprecedented number of Puerto Rican and other Latino/a authors' first works were published either by Arte Público or Bilingual Press and became known to their communities. Some drew critical attention from literary scholars, rousing the interest of mainstream publishers in Latino/a literature. Some writers continued publishing with these small presses that had helped them launch their writing careers out of loyal-ty or as a way of supporting them in continuing their publication endeavors. Frequently, mainstream publishers tried to impose sensationalized or formulaic accounts of a particular author's ethnic, racial, or gender experiences growing up in the segregated barrios of different US cities, versions that repeatedly bordered on the perpetuation of some of the most common stereotypes. Moreover, it took until the 1990s for many of the major publishing houses to look at US Latino/a literature and the whole gamut of individual writers from different Latino/a national origins in a serious manner and to fully recognize their diversity of experiences, the abundance of talent, and the market potential for this literature for both English- and Spanish-speaking readerships. Another factor that made this possible was the significant growth of the US Latino/a population, a pattern that started in the 1970s and by the early years of the new millennium had turned Latinos/as into the largest population of color in the United States.

A few worthy attempts have been made in Puerto Rico to disseminate the wealth of literary creativity coming out of the diaspora, but most available anthologies published on the island have focused primarily on poetry. Writings by the best-known authors are translated and made available in Spanish more frequently than in the past. The 1980 poetry collection *Herejes y mitificadores: Muestra de poesía puertorriqueña en los Estados Unidos* (Heretics and mythmakers: a sample of Puerto Rican poetry in the United States) was the first to introduce Nuyorican poetry to an island audience. One of the editors, Efraín Barradas, noted that for Nuyorican authors, Puerto Rico represented a mythical fountain of images and symbols in their quest for self-definition. These island images and symbols that the *poetas neorriqueños* (Neorican poets) invoked in their poetry were accepted, rejected, or modified by the cultural and linguistic contact that Puerto Ricans have shared with other ethnic groups and the wider Anglo-American society. Barradas, a leading critic of US and island and stateside Puerto Rican literature (and Caribbean and Latin American literature and art as well), was among the first to bring the work of Nuyorican poets to the attention of Puerto Ricans and other Spanish-speaking literary critics and readers. Barradas is also the author of *Partes de un todo: Ensayos y notas sobre literatura puertorriqueña en los Estados Unidos* (The sum of the parts: Essays and notes on Puerto Rican literature in the United States, 1998), a volume that collects his most outstanding essays about foundational authors of what is now an established and flourishing literary tradition.

The poetry anthologies *Los paraguas amarillos: Los poetas latinos en Nueva York* (I. Silén 1983) and *Papiros de babel* (López-Adorno 1991) illustrate the presence and coexistence in the United States of Puerto Rican and other Latino/a authors from different generations writing in English or Spanish or bilingually. Most of these poets' writings are a powerful repository of images conveying a strong sense of *puertorriqueñidad* (Puerto Ricanness) that transcends island borders but also redefines what it means to be Puerto Rican in the US colonial metropolis (Acosta-Belén 1992a; Flores [1988] 1993). Thus a sense of Puerto Rican identity is rooted in the notion of being part of a stateside marginalized ethnic and racial minority. In fact, many of the authors included in these collections are read and known on the island, but the writers born or raised in the United States tend to write mainly in English and are mostly absent from the island's literary canon. Note, however, that some publishing houses in the United States, Mexico, Puerto Rico, Cuba, the Dominican Republic, and Spain are publishing Spanish translations of works originally written in English by Latino/a writers, proof that there is a viable readership and market, and some of the works of the more successful Puerto Rican and other Latino/a authors also are being translated into other languages. Interviews have been a preferred way for critics and readers to enter the creative imagination of stateside Puerto Rican authors and understand what drives their writing. In *Puerto Rican Voices in English*, journalist Carmen Dolores Hernández (1997) skillfully accomplishes the stated goal in her comprehensive and engaging volume of interviews. For many years, through her weekly cultural column in the island newspaper *El nuevo día*, Hernández played a leading role in introducing island readers to and reviewing the work of stateside Puerto Rican writers.

The bilingual 2012 volume *Breaking Ground: Anthology of Puerto Rican Women Writers in New York, 1980–2012*, edited by poet and fiction writer Myrna Nieves, represents trailblazing efforts to collect and draw attention to an abundant body of literature produced by Puerto Rican women in the city. The anthology shows that, whether originally written in English, Spanish, or a mix of both languages, the selected texts are, as Nieves (2012) argues, "Part of a Puerto Rican, North American, and universal discourse as evidenced by their themes, references, and inter-textuality" (21). Nieves also underscores the oral tradition and performative aspects that characterize spoken word or urban poetry, the perceptible literary influences of African American and Afro-Caribbean writers, and the poets' innovative use of elements from mixed media and postmodern technologies. This anthology is also the primary result of Nieves's leadership in cofounding the Boricua College Winter Poetry Series of readings and performances, which she directed for two decades. But considering the general neglect of Puerto Rican women's writing in New York and other US locations—in part because for a long period the foundational Nuyorican poets of the 1970s and 1980s (the majority of them male writers, with few exceptions) received most of the critical attention (Golder 2011–2012)—Nieves (2012) strove to make women the focus of her work and to "document their struggles, pains, joys, disappointments, successes, and challenges" (20).

Literary scholarship of Puerto Rican literature in the United States has produced new critical perspectives and approaches. In *Writing Off the*

Hyphen: New Critical Perspectives on the Literature of the Puerto Rican Diaspora, Carmen Haydée Rivera and José L. Torres-Padilla (2008) were among the first to compile a series of critical essays that cover the writings of leading stateside Puerto Rican authors and show the importance of this literature to both island and American literary traditions. Carmen S. Rivera's critical 2002 study *Kissing the Mango Tree* shows how several Puerto Rican women writers are rewriting American literature. Another critical study, *Dancing Between Two Cultures* by William Luis (1997), relies on the writings of leading Cuban, Puerto Rican, and Dominican authors to illustrate how their cultural straddling (or metaphorical dance) between Anglo-America and their cultures of origin evolves into new cultural forms of resistance and mediation.

Theater and Film

The history of Puerto Rican theater in the United States is linked to a long professional and working-class tradition in this genre that dates back to the second half of the nineteenth century and continued to flourish especially in New York City from the 1920s through the 1940s. In his well-documented, comprehensive *A History of Hispanic Theatre in the United States*, Nicolás Kanellos (1990) notes that New York was an important "model in solidifying diverse Hispanic nationalities on the stage" (xv). As the largest group of Latinos/as in the city, Puerto Ricans made their presence felt on the stage as writers and performers. Kanellos uncovered several published and unpublished plays by Puerto Rican and other Latino/a writers from the early decades of the twentieth century. These plays reveal many topics and themes of interest to a wide range of playwrights from diverse Latin American and Caribbean national origins living in the city and attest to the level of cultural activity taking place in these communities. Some of these plays aimed to provide entertainment and cultural enrichment or dealt with issues of interest to specific Latino/a nationalities.

Several plays stand out in reflecting the social and political concerns of the Puerto Rican community during those years. These include Gonzalo O'Neill's *Pabellón de Borinquen o bajo una sola bandera* (Borinquen pavillion or under one flag, 1934) and *La indiana borinqueña* (The indigenous Borinquen, 1922). Both plays upheld the pro-independence and anti-imperialist ideals of the Puerto Rican Nationalist movement during its burgeoning years. O'Neill's comedy *Moncho Reyes* (1923) took a satirical view of the controversial Americanization policies promoted by E. Montgomery Reily, the US-appointed governor of Puerto Rico at the time. The name chosen by O'Neill as the title for his comedy is a Spanish adaptation of the governor's name, coined by Puerto Ricans to ridicule his misguided policies. Over a decade later, another playwright, Frank Martínez, wrote *De Puerto Rico a*

Nueva York (From Puerto Rico to New York, 1939), which was performed but never published. According to Kanellos (1990), this play was an important antecedent to René Marqués's *La carreta* (1952).

A popular entertainment form among Puerto Rican and Cuban performers during the 1920s and 1930s was the humorous *teatro bufo-cubano*, which combined elements of vaudeville and African American minstrel theater shows. Puerto Rican actor, producer, and playwright Erasmo Vando was known for his contributions to this popular genre and for writing and producing the play *De Puerto Rico al Metropolitan o el caruso criollo* (From Puerto Rico to the Metropolitan or the creole Caruso, 1928).

Many theater productions during the Great Depression years aimed to raise consciousness among working-class audiences. The *teatro obrero* (workers' theater), a genre linked to the labor movement of numerous countries, was very popular in Puerto Rico in the latter decades of the nineteenth and early decades of the twentieth century (Dávila Santiago 1995). Community organizations such as the Mutualista Obrera Puertorriqueña (Puerto Rican Mutual Aid Society) and Ateneo Obrero (Workers' Athenaeum) regularly sponsored performances by professional companies and also provided space for amateur productions (Kanellos 1990). The previously mentioned *Los hipócritas*, by Puerto Rican feminist and labor activist Franca de Armiño (1937, 2013), focused on the exploitation of workers by the capitalist system, the aftereffects of the Great Depression, and workers' struggles in a Spain threated by a looming Civil War. The play was performed in 1933 at East Harlem's Park Palace Theatre, for many years an important venue for many of these community productions.

The Nuevo Círculo Dramático (New Dramatic Circle, 1953–1960) was established in New York by playwright Roberto Rodríguez Suárez, director of the premiere performance of Marqués's *La carreta*. In subsequent decades, the productions of the Puerto Rican Traveling Theater, founded in 1967 by theater and film performer Miriam Colón (1936–2017), brought theater to the people of the barrios of New York and offered new opportunities to actors and playwrights. The Traveling Theater was initially a vehicle to introduce the work of island writers to community audiences, but in later years it showcased the work of stateside Puerto Rican and Latino/a playwrights. Colón is considered the *gran dama* (great lady) of Puerto Rican theater in the United States for her efforts in promoting this genre and her numerous acting contributions to island and US film and television. Before her death, Colón was instrumental in merging the Puerto Rican Traveling Theater with the Bronx-based Teatro Pregones (www.pregonesprtt.org).

Under the artistic direction of Puerto Rican actor, director, and playwright Rosalba Rolón, Teatro Pregones was founded in 1980, according to its website, to promote a "cultural legacy of broad impact" through the creation and production of original musical theater and Latino plays rooted in

Puerto Rican/Latino cultures. Pregones is regarded as a vital stage for young actors, playwrights, producers, directors, and musicians to flourish and be mentored by more experienced professionals.

Nuyorican performing poets Miguel Piñero, Pedro Pietri, and Tato Laviera have also published several plays, and other writers have been achieving recognition on the Broadway and off-Broadway theater circuits. The remarkable success of Lin-Manuel Miranda, a playwright, actor, and composer, stands out. He has won two Tony Awards for his musical *In the Heights* in 2008 and one for his musical *Hamilton*, which also won a Pulitzer Prize for best musical and drama in 2016. Two Grammy awards, an Emmy Award, and the MacArthur Fellowship (aka "Genius Grant") have made Miranda one of the most acclaimed and successful playwrights and theater performers in the United States.

Puerto Rican playwright José Rivera, author of *Marisol* (1994), a futuristic and apocalyptic dark comedy about urban violence and breaking down male and female stereotypes, received an Obie Award. Rivera's autobiographical play *The House of Ramón Iglesia* (1983), based on his own Puerto Rican experiences, was first produced for television by PBS's *American Playhouse* series in 1986. Rivera won a second Obie Award for the play *References to Salvador Dalí Make Me Hot* (2003) and was nominated for an Oscar for the screenplay of the film *The Motorcycle Diaries* (2004), based on the memoirs of Ernesto "Che" Guevara during the years that preceded his revolutionary activities in Cuba and other parts of Latin America. Also doing laudable theater work is Puerto Rican playwright Carmen Rivera, author of *Julia: Child of Water* (2014), first produced in New York in 1999 by the Puerto Rican Traveling Theater, a feminist play that challenges traditional women's roles and evokes the poetic rebelliousness of Julia de Burgos. Rivera won an Obie award in 1996 for *La gringa*, a play about the painful quest for identity and belonging of the protagonist, perceived as an Americanized *gringa* when visiting Puerto Rico but defined as a Puerto Rican in the United States.

Theater and film roles for Latino/a actors have never been abundant. Actors constantly struggle for recognition, and most are conscious of the pitfalls of the ethnic typecasting that dominates the US film and television industries. Clara Rodríguez (2000b, 2004) has documented and analyzed many of the stereotypical images and representations of Latinos/as propagated in the US media and their demeaning effects at the individual and collective levels. Rodríguez (2004, 243) notes that Latinos/as in general continue to be "the most underrepresented ethnic group in films and primetime television" despite the unprecedented growth in this population since the latter decades of the twentieth century.

Several Puerto Rican performers have achieved recognition and praise in theater, film, and television. Only a handful launched successful careers during times when opportunities for Latino/a performers were scarcer and limited by typecasting or stereotyping. José Ferrer was the first Puerto Rican to receive an Academy Award in 1950 for his leading performance in the film *Cyrano de Bergerac*. Rita Moreno received an Oscar for a supporting role in the 1961 musical *West Side Story*. Her versatility in theater and television make her one of the few performers to have also received Tony and Emmy awards in later years. Raúl Juliá had a prominent career in film and theater, receiving numerous critical accolades for some of his roles and an Academy Award nomination for his leading performance in the film *Kiss of the Spider Woman*. But he is widely known for his portrayal of Gomez, husband of Morticia, in the *Addams Family* films of the 1990s. In 2002, actor Benicio del Toro received an Oscar for his supporting performance in the film *Traffic*.

The Visual Arts

Puerto Rican visual artists from the island have been among the most frequent sojourners and migrants to the United States since the 1950s. Because of the nature of their trade, many of these artists have studied, resided, exhibited, or received recognition off the island. Even many of the artists based in Puerto Rico maintain a continuous exchange with other stateside Puerto Rican artists, involving many technical, stylistic, and thematic aspects or their respective art circles, including issues of cultural identity and survival similar to those found in literary expressions.

The challenges and accomplishments of Puerto Rican visual artists during the past seven decades in developing their craft involve some of the uncertainties and creative angsts faced by most artists, even those that eventually achieve fame. Part of their journey often involves leaving their home countries to travel to other parts of the world seeking training, mentorship by established foreign artists, or opportunities to polish their own styles or enhance their artistic visions and presence, and thereby their chances for a more successful and productive career. Nostalgia for and evocation of the Puerto Rican landscape and traditions and the difficult adaptation to a culturally different and more alienating US environment shape the work of most visual artists of the diaspora.

According to Torruella Leval (1998), the activities of stateside Puerto Rican artists occurred in three different cycles. The first, beginning in the 1950s, opened the dialogue between artists from both shores around cultural issues of self-definition. The second cycle took place during the ethnic revitalization movement of the 1960s and 1970s and focused on social protest and community empowerment. The third one began in the 1980s and linked Puerto Ricans to the cultural debates and struggles of a wider panethnic Latino/a experience within US society.

Efforts to promote Puerto Rican culture within the United States were part of the mission of the Migration Division (see Chapter 4). The decades prior to the 1950s had witnessed the arrival of a few Puerto Rican artists, but they worked mostly without the benefit of a supportive artistic environment, often in isolation from one another, and their work was therefore less known to the community.

A few names stand out among notable artists of the pre–World War II Great Migration period. Juan De'Prey, an underrecognized painter of Puerto Rican and Haitian ancestry, who came to New York from Puerto Rico in 1929, became known for landscapes that conjure a nostalgia for his native land and his mulatto racial background. De'Prey's work has often been compared to that of Paul Gauguin, particularly his portraits of children (Bloch 1978).

Before becoming one of the most acclaimed visual artists in Puerto Rico and internationally, Lorenzo Homar lived in New York in the 1930s and worked as a designer for the famous Cartier house of jewelers. Another island painter, Rafael D. Palacios, arrived in New York in 1938 and developed a prominent career as a book illustrator and cartographer for US publishing houses. Olga Albizu was another painter to achieve some prominence in New York before the 1960s. She exhibited her work at the Organization of American States Gallery and did many designs for RCA record album jackets (Benítez 1988).

The cultural and intellectual environment promoted in Puerto Rico during the 1950s influenced cultural activities within the diaspora. Reacting to the rapid changes occurring on the island during the Operation Bootstrap years, the administration of Governor Luis Muñoz Marín sponsored Operación Serenidad (Operation Serenity). This ambitious cultural endeavor strove to maintain a balance between the overwhelming US economic and cultural influences on the island and preservation of Puerto Rico's cultural uniqueness and traditions. Some of the government-sponsored initiatives under Operación Serenidad included incentives in the form of scholarships, travel grants, performances, exhibits, films, and publications that often brought Puerto Ricans from the island to the United States to work on joint creative projects with other artists. Many of these activities were coordinated by the Migration Division in New York, then headed by Joseph Monserrat. This office sponsored the Oller-Campeche Gallery, which allowed many Puerto Rican artists to introduce their work to the New York community. Organizations such as the Puerto Rican Institute, directed at the time by Luis Quero Chiesa, also fostered Puerto Rican fine arts in New York. The presence in New York of prominent Puerto Rican visual artists Rafael Tufiño and Carlos Osorio during this period also enriched the diaspora's artistic circles (Torruella Leval 1998).

Graphic arts were a central component of the work of the Division of Community Education (DIVEDCO) in making the silkscreen poster a primary medium for communicating and highlighting the commemoration of important historical and cultural traditions and introducing a vast array of Puerto Rican artists to the public. DIVEDCO's popular education goals aimed at engaging the population of a developing nation with issues related to ongoing transformations, health and living conditions, and even migration (see Anderson and Moreno 2012). The art poster craft made its way to New York and other stateside Puerto Rican communities and was used in similar ways to announce commemorative events or activities of the stateside Puerto Rican communities' cultural life during the years of the Great Migration. Graphic art *talleres* (workshops), such as Taller Boricua in New York and Taller Puertorriqueño in Philadelphia, originated in the late 1960s and continue to welcome and mentor new artists. They work to preserve the artistic vitality of their locations and to support many other similar collective endeavors in their respective communities.

Prior to the ethnic revitalization movement of the civil rights era, it was not easy for Puerto Rican or other Latino/a visual artists to make significant incursions into US mainstream artistic circles. This situation began to change when members of the community started to design opportunities for artists to train, create, and exhibit. The founding of Los Amigos de Puerto Rico (Friends of Puerto Rico) in 1953 by Amalia Guerrero served those purposes. For more than two decades some of the best-known island artists came to New York to teach or learn at Guerrero's workshop (Torruella Leval 1998).

Notwithstanding, not until the 1960s and 1970s did Puerto Rican artists born or raised in the United States begin to make their mark with works that combined the images, colors, symbols, and traditions of the homeland with some of the harsh realities of New York's urban life. Through murals, sculptures, paintings, silk screens, art posters, and photographs, the artistic world of the diaspora began to flourish and to capture what it meant to be Puerto Rican in a bicultural and racialized environment. These artists also depicted the struggles of marginalized working-class Puerto Rican stateside communities and gave increased visibility to their productive cultural lives.

In the 1970s in most US cities, graffiti murals and designs covered the walls and buildings of public spaces and subway cars with a barrage of colors, unconventional designs, and sometimes just unintelligible scribbles of rebelliousness. Many Puerto Rican artists found creative outlets to channel their feelings of disaffection and anger at prevailing social injustices or to celebrate and affirm their heritage through artistic expression. Public art began to bring a mythical Puerto Rico—its landscape, history, and cultural traditions—to the many stateside communities where Puerto Ricans had settled. The reproduction of African and Taino indigenous motifs and folkloric traditions was very popular among these artists. According to Miramar Benítez (1988), "The walls of Puerto Rican business places, particularly those of La Marketa[13] . . . began to blossom with murals painted by folk artists. . . . Artists such as Johnny Vázquez and Millito López painted the rural scenes they had left behind" (78).

Some additional notable examples of public art include Rafael Ferrer's sculpture *Puerto Rican Sun* (1979), located in the South Bronx. The sculpture brought a tropical flavor to a sterile environment in the form of palm trees holding up a shining sun. Manuel (Manny) Vega's mural *Playa de amor* (Seaside of Love, 1988) displays Afro–Puerto Rican dancers celebrating their musical traditions. His subsequent impressive and colorful mosaic murals commissioned in 2015 by the New York City Housing Authority, depicting the vibrant presence of Puerto Ricans in Spanish Harlem (El Barrio), are now displayed on the walls of several East Side subway stations. Back in 1989, New York's Metropolitan Transportation Authority hired Nitza Tufiño to create a monumental ceramic mural also located in one of El Barrio's subway stations. The imposing mural *Neo-Borikén* reproduced Taino Indian petroglyphs in bright colors. Marina Gutiérrez, a high school art teacher, tried to capture elements of Puerto Rican social and political oppression on the island and in the United States (Torruella Leval 1998). Among her most impressive contributions to public art was her 1996 installation of colorful suspended mobile structures that visually captured images of Julia de Burgos's poetry. This installation is displayed in the atrium of the Julia de Burgos Latino Cultural Center on Manhattan's East Side.

Other artists, such as Pedro Villarini, created paintings that transported Puerto Rico's rural landscape and traditions to the cold and colorless environment of the city. His *El artesano en Nueva York* (The artisan in New York) is a tribute to the religious woodcarving tradition. Capturing different aspects of life in the urban barrios is another important theme, as demonstrated by the works of Ralph Ortiz, exposing the violence often experienced by members of these communities (Benítez 1988). Curricular materials, illustrated anthologies, posters, and covers of El Comité Noviembre's annual magazine displayed the work of Ernesto Ramos-Nieves, a talented artist who passed away at a young age. El Comité Noviembre, established in New York in 1987 to institutionalize the celebration of the month of November as Puerto Rican Heritage Month, was founded through the joint efforts of several community organizations; its annual publication highlighted the work of Puerto Rican artists and the overall cultural life of the community.

The works of Juan Sánchez, one of the most critically acclaimed and prolific visual artists of the diaspora, display the images, traditions, dilemmas, and "Rican-constructions"[14] of Nuyorican barrio life. Sánchez's powerful paintings and collages incorporating photos, newspaper clippings, written words, verses from poems, and quotes from patriots are displayed in many museums and buildings and on the covers of numerous books and journals. Jiménez-Muñoz and Santiago (1995) summarized the essence of Sánchez's body of work:

> Isn't this part of what being Puerto Rican is all about, particularly in the US: being caught between Spanish and English, being the Caribbean/tropical hybrid in Niuyol City's cold wasteland, trying to negotiate between American-ness and Latin American-ness, between "el welfare" and "las 936," crossing "el charco" in "la guagua aérea," etc.? It is no accident that practically all of these are themes which Sánchez has included (explicitly or implicitly) in recent paintings. (22)

One of Sánchez's most compelling works, *Conditions That Exist*, reiterates some of the crucial identity issues that since the 1930s have been central to many island Puerto Rican writers and artists. The words Sánchez included in this collage reveal the identity quest and feeling of estrangement so integral to many stateside Puerto Rican cultural expressions: "¿Dónde está mi casa? / ¿dónde está mi país? / ¿para dónde vamos?" (Where is my home? / Where is my country? / Where are we going?). Another piece, *A Puerto Rican Prisoner of War and Much More*, highlights the active role of the diaspora in the campaigns to free political prisoners.

The few institutions founded to promote artistic endeavors within the Puerto Rican community have been quite successful in achieving their goals. Two of the leading ones are the already mentioned Museo del Barrio and the Taller Alma Boricua (better known as the Taller Boricua), both established in New York in 1969. Founded in East Harlem by a group of Puerto Rican artists and educators, the Museo is now a key cultural and educational resource for a growing and more diverse population of Latinos/as of other

Conditions That Exist (1990), a triptych by artist Juan Sánchez that underscores some fundamental Puerto Rican identity questions: *¿Dónde está mi casa? ¿Dónde está mi país? ¿Para dónde vamos?* (Where is my home? Where is my country? Where are we going?). Reprinted by permission of the artist.

national origins. In addition to its many rotating exhibits, education programs, and publications, the museum has a permanent collection. Artists Martha Vega, Rafael Montañez Ortiz (also known as Ralph Ortiz), and Hiram Maristany were among the founders of this prominent institution. One of its major early exhibits, *The Art Heritage of Puerto Rico* (1973), a joint initiative with the Metropolitan Museum of Art, displayed a vast array of Puerto Rican artistic expressions: Taino *cemíes* (indigenous stone carvings) and other stone and ceramic crafts, *santos* (wooden carvings of religious figures), classical and modern paintings, art posters, silk screens, and sculptures. Since then, the museum has sponsored numerous art exhibits by Puerto Rican and other Latinos/as, in addition to many other cultural activities. Worth mentioning is the 1978–1979 exhibit at the Museo del Barrio, *Bridge Between Islands*, aimed at fostering connections between Puerto Rican artists from the island and the diaspora. After the Museo del Barrio widened its scope and vision to become a major center for Latino/a art and culture, the exhibition *New York 1613–1945* (2007), a collaboration with New York's Historic Society, documented a largely neglected and unrecognized part of New York City's history (see Sullivan 2010).

Puerto Rican artists Marcos Dimas, Carlos Osorio (1927–1984), Manuel "Neco" Otero, Armando Soto, Jorge Soto (1947–1987), Adrián García, Martín Rubio, and Fernando Salicrup (1946–2015) cofounded the Taller Boricua as a center for community art education in East Harlem. A large number of the most talented Puerto Rican artists, from both the island and the United States, have spent time working there. The Taller provides a setting for artists to work and exchange ideas. During its early years the artwork produced at this workshop often explored the roots of what it means to be Puerto Rican, especially by emphasizing Taino and African symbols and traditions (Torruella Leval 1998).

Described as a "Nuyorican visionary" who integrated Taller Boricua's "Afro-Taino aesthetics" (Ramírez 2005, 23), Jorge Soto is remembered for deconstructing and subverting two Puerto Rican iconic art pieces: Francisco Oller's classic 1893 painting *El velorio* (The wake) and Lorenzo Homar's 1957 design of the emblem of the Institute of Puerto Rican Culture (ICP). Soto's *El velorio de Oller en Nueva York* (1975) changes the geographic context of the original masterpiece by the mere fact that Soto is a Nuyorican artist sharing different social and cultural experiences as a racialized Puerto Rican in the United States. But the painting's almost radiographic, surreal images of gaunt characters accentuate their poverty, affliction, and racially mixed existence. Similarly, the ICP's circular emblem designed by Homar, one of the most recognized island graphic artists of the 1950s, defines the essence of the Puerto Rican nation by reference to its main cultural and racial roots, represented on the emblem by three male figures: on the left-hand side is an indigenous Taino, placed in the center is a Spanish conquistador, and an enslaved African is on the right-hand side. This representation reaffirms the traditional view of Hispanic centrality in Puerto Rico's racially mixed culture. In his "Rican-struction" (Ramírez 2005, 33) of the ICP emblem, Soto replaces the image of the indigenous male with that of a Taino woman, in this way subverting the patriarchal character of the original design. He also replaces the central image of the Spanish conquistador holding Nebrija's 1492 first grammar of the Castilian language with a male figure with a skeleton-like face, holding in his hands a skull surrounded by Uncle Sam caricatures, respective symbols of the genocide behind the Spanish colonizing enterprise and the subsequent aggression of US colonialism toward Puerto Ricans. The third original figure of the African holding a drum is substituted by an image of an African-featured man holding a skull and rapier to indicate his "Kongo ancestry" and the spirits that empower him (Ramírez 2005, 36). Soto's rein-terpretation of the ICP emblem is a way of validating subjugated African and Taino cultures. Although Soto's life was cut short—he was thirty years old when he died in 1987 from an undisclosed illness—he was one of the most original visual artists of the diaspora.

In Philadelphia, the Taller Puertorriqueño, founded in 1974, initially played a role similar to New York's Taller Boricua. With a new building for its cultural center, it has expanded the scope of its activities and now regards itself as the cultural heart of Latino Philadelphia. This community-based cultural education organization now houses a cultural awareness pro-gram, a gallery, a bookstore, and a museum collection and archives.

Chicago also has been an important center in promoting Puerto Rican arts and culture. The Juan Antonio Corretjer Puerto Rican Cultural Center (PRCC) plays a key role in maintaining the overall vitality of the Paseo Boricua, considered "the cultural and economic heartbeat" of the city's Puerto Rican community. The Paseo is the site of an impressive architectural display of two steel Puerto Rican flags that run across Division Street, part of this vibrant Puerto Rican neighborhood. The PRCC supported the development of the Institute of Puerto Rican Art and Culture, which evolved into today's National Museum of Puerto Rican Arts and Culture. Numerous murals by Puerto Rican artists are found on the walls of the PRCC and other buildings in Paseo Boricua's surrounding areas. A mural that illustrates the vitality of Puerto Rican nationalism within the diaspora is *Sea of Flags* by Gamaliel Ramírez and Star Padilla, who engaged community youth in the process of painting the mural, commissioned by the PRCC for the Jornada Albizu Campos (Albizu Campos Day) in 2004. A portion of the mural was displayed on the front cover of the first paperback edition of this book and is now among the art photos included in this chapter. The mural shows a multitude holding Puerto Rican flags and surrounding Nationalist leader Lolita Lebrón (in the center) holding the revolutionary flag used at the Lares Revolt of 1868, in which protestors clamored for the island's independence from Spain.

Against the backdrop is one of the two Puerto Rican steel flags that embellish Chicago's Paseo Boricua.

The cover of the second paperback edition is a partial view of the *Unidos para triunfar* (Together we overcome, 1971), also known as the *Justicia* mural, painted by renowned Chicago muralist John Pitman Weber (www .jpweberartist.com) with the collaboration of late Latino artist José Guerrero (1938–2015) and located in an area of Division Street. Within a year a city gang from outside the neighborhood had defaced the mural; Weber repainted it in 1974 with some major alterations. The artist restored it once again in 2003 with the collaboration of Chicago Puerto Rican artist Josué Pellot (www.josuepellot.com), and Lolita Lebrón was present at its rededication. The coffin added to the original mural memorializes Orlando Quintana, a young community organizer killed by a Chicago off-duty police officer in 1973. This mural captures community battles for social justice and against city-sponsored urban renewal projects that displaced Puerto Ricans from some of their old Chicago neighborhoods to promote gentrification through construction of businesses and expensive apartment buildings. Despite the lesser success of some community struggles to protect a few old neighborhoods from the steam-rolling government and private capital behind urban renewal projects, Paseo Boricua stands today as a triumph.

The arrival of the Internet created room in cyberspace for the dissemination of the works of stateside Puerto Rican visual artists. This new generation of experimental artists is best represented by photographer and visual

Sea of Flags (2004), mural by Gamaliel Ramírez and Star Padilla located at Paseo Boricua in Chicago. The mural was commissioned by the Juan Antonio Corretjer Puerto Rican Cultural Center (PRCC). Reprinted by permission of PRCC.

artist Adal Maldonado. He cofounded with Nuyorican writer Pedro Pietri the website El Puerto Rican Embassy in 1994, although artist Eddie Figueroa (1991) is responsible for the original Embassy concept, which he developed on another website called El Spirit Republic de Puerto Rico back in 1991. Prior to this project, Figueroa had opened the New Rican Village in 1976, also located on the Lower East Side not far from the Nuyorican Poets Cafe. In an interview, Figueroa described this performance venue as "the home of Afro-Caribbean music's avant-guarde" (Morales 1990).

Maldonado and Pietri expanded on Figueroa's original concept by creating a Puerto Rican "passport," appointing ambassadors of the arts, and writing a manifesto and a "Spanglish" Puerto Rican national anthem. El Puerto Rican Embassy's founders describe it as a "sovereign state of mind," an ironic take on Puerto Rico's "unsovereign" political status, but also a statement about decolonizing minds and using art as a tool of subversion and resistance. Maldonado's collection of photographs *Out of Focus Nuyoricans*, which is displayed on the website, "expresses the political and psychological conditions of the Puerto Rican and Nuyorican identity" (Bercht, n.d.). This site demonstrates that political and cultural issues related to the colonial subordination of Puerto Ricans continue to be important to both island and stateside Puerto Rican artists.

Increasingly, artists are using the Internet to display and promote their work. Soraida Martínez (n.d.a), creator of what she calls "Verdadism," or a philosophy of truth, describes her style as "a form of hard-edge abstraction in which paintings are juxtaposed with social commentaries." Martínez (n.d.b) has made the following comments about her 1992 painting *Puerto Rican Stereotype: The Way You See Me Without Looking at Me*:

> Throughout my life I have met lots of people that have never experienced meeting or getting to know a Puerto Rican woman. I have had some people admit to me their feelings on what they thought a Puerto Rican woman looked and acted like. "Puerto Rican Stereotype: The Way You See Me Without Looking at Me" is a satirical painting based on the false information given to me by the media and other life experiences.

Yasmín Hernández is creating some outstanding and powerful visual art. Her work, as she herself has acknowledged, is inspired by the theme of Puerto Rican liberation. Hernández's art captures the wide range of social, racial, and gender intersectional realities that account for Puerto Rico's colonial history and contemporary political conditions, in addition to the experiences and legacies of the Puerto Rican diaspora. Her impressive body of work to date includes multiple paintings that expose the persecution and brutality endured by female and male Puerto Rican patriots throughout the island's history. Her *Soul Rebels* series of individual-panel murals, exhibited in 2005 at the Museo del Barrio, celebrates the rebellious work of stateside

Puerto Rican writers and musicians who have inspired the community and "risked their careers and/or lives creating art as protest to bring about justice" (Y. Hernández 2018b). Not only is Hernández's work grounded in historical, social, and political realities, but it also conveys a sense of spirituality and determination that is part of Hernández's artistic vision. Her art "explores personal, political, and spiritual liberation" (Y. Hernández 2018a).

One of Hernández's most recent works, *De-Debt/Decolonize* (2017), also displayed in this chapter, establishes the link between Puerto Rico's debt crisis and the island's colonial condition and affirms the resiliency of a nation carving its path toward decolonization.[15] This comes at a time when Puerto Rico is experiencing some of greatest challenges in its long colonial history and is therefore at a critical crossroads. The face of political prisoner Oscar López Rivera, finally released from many years in federal prison in 2017 by President Barack Obama, floats in a nebula over the island as a symbol of struggle and resistance and a reminder of the persecution and sacrifices endured by numerous patriots fighting for the liberation of their homeland. Another of Hernández's most creative and gripping installations focuses on the struggles for peace and justice of the people of Vieques, still fighting and waiting for the US government and the Pentagon to clean up the environmental contamination and destruction caused by decades of bombing training exercises, which have had detrimental effects on the health of the small island's population.

A few years ago, Hernández moved with her husband and children to Moca, Puerto Rico. In an October 12, 2017, letter to the organizer of a Debt Fair panel at the Museo del Barrio, which she was unable to attend due to the destruction caused by Hurricane Maria, Hernández points out that since her move to Puerto Rico, her work has explored "nebulae to transcend the abyss of colonialism and oppression, to claim ancestral connection and to affirm our spiritual space in the cosmos. Moreover, painting our ancestors in transparent layers of nebulae is how I combat the invisibility imposed by colonialism."

Also among the most inventive Nuyorican artists of the younger generation is Miguel Luciano. Many of his earlier works disrupted the labels of commercial products or fast-food chains with humorous and cartoonish images that convey powerful social, racial, and political messages about the colonized experiences of Puerto Ricans. This includes the almost insatiable consumption of fast foods and other US products on the island. Among the best known is the series based on labels of canned "Porto Rican yams" sold in Louisiana during the early twentieth century. The original labels racialized "Porto Ricans" by using stereotyped images of an African American kitchen worker dressed in a white uniform wearing a chef hat.

Innovation and opening new paths to reach wider audiences through graphic art are also at the heart of Edgardo Miranda-Rodríguez's work. His experience working for Marvel Comics inspired him to create a Puerto

De-Debt/Decolonize (2017), acrylic collage on canvas by Yasmín Hernández. The Spanish words above the island mean "Your free soil. Your lone star." Reprinted by permission of the artist.

Rican superwoman for his comic book, *La Borinqueña* (2016). The title is both the name of the protagonist and Puerto Rico's national anthem and frequently used to refer to a native from the island. What better way to introduce such a character to New York's Puerto Rican community than to have her ride on a float in New York's 2016 Puerto Rican Day Parade—an annual event attended by hundreds of thousands of Puerto Ricans and other New Yorkers and city visitors—wearing a superhero costume that recreates the colors and lone star of Lares's revolutionary flag.

Miranda-Rodríguez's independent, enterprising, and successful endeavor adds to the still limited presence of Latino/a characters in American comic books and comes at a time when Puerto Ricans are facing overwhelming

La Borinqueña, the protagonist of the comic book of the same name written and created by Edgardo Miranda-Rodríguez and published in December 2016 by Somos Arte in Brooklyn, New York. Reprinted by permission of the artist.

challenges prompted by the debt and hurricane humanitarian crises. La Borinqueña is Marisol Ríos de la Luz (her first name alludes to the sea and sun; her last name alludes to rivers and light), a millennial Afro–Puerto Rican geological sciences student at Columbia University. She comes from the Puerto Rican barrio of Williamsburg, Brooklyn, known as Los Sures (the southern section), and travels to Puerto Rico to live with her grandparents while she does research for her senior thesis. After exploring most of the island's underground caves, she visits the only remaining one before an impending tropical storm makes it impossible to do so. She is drawn to a legendary, magical sparkling star-shaped wayfinder crystal, *la estrella del camino* (the star that lights the path), whose existence is only recorded in the oral tradition of indigenous tales. Finding the star-shaped crystal allows her to channel the powers of the ancient Taino deities of the earth, sea, and wind—Atabex, Yocahú, and Juracán—which will guide her quest to champion Puerto Rican causes on the island and stateside. In his insightful review of the comic book, Acosta-Ponce (2017) argues that the Borinqueña character "embodies the virtues of an idealized 'Boricuahood' without resorting to a *jíbaro* archetype or some nostalgia-rooted image" (5) and commends the artist for "moving away from a Euro-elitist vision that many 'white' Puerto Ricans have and embracing her Afro-Caribbean heritage" (5–6). He also concludes, "For Puerto Ricans, the *La Borinqueña* comic book functions as a fictionalized account of the struggle of an entire nation, whereas for non–Puerto Ricans, it functions as an educational tool that challenges preconceptions and beliefs about Puerto Rico and its people." The symbolic impact of *La Borinqueña* and its enthusiastic reception by Puerto Ricans and other audiences indicate its popularity. Miranda-Rodríguez is producing a 2018 Somos Arte anthology of stories about Puerto Rico, *Ricanstruction: Reminiscing and Rebuilding Puerto Rico,* with the collaboration of several artists and illustrators. The front cover will showcase La Borinqueña with Wonder Woman holding a Puerto Rican flag. The book proceeds will go to Hurricane Maria relief efforts (see Gustines 2018; www.somosarte.com).

Of course, New York is not the only art scene for Puerto Ricans. In Chicago, acclaimed painter Arnaldo Roche Rabell, who studied at the Chicago Art Institute and for several years traveled back and forth between the island and the United States, like many others, is representative of the cultural straddling that is so much a part of the migrant experience and brings so many different kinds of cultural explorations. His bright abstract expressionist paintings and landscape compositions are part of many US collections and those of numerous Latin American nations. In 1984, Roche Rabell was the first Puerto Rican to receive the Lincoln Medal from the governor of Illinois for his artistic contributions to that state.

Chicago-based Puerto Rican artist Bibiana Suárez is also a graduate of the Chicago Art Institute and a faculty member at DePaul University. Artist Juan Sánchez (1991) described Suárez's work as "a conflictive plebiscite of the mind" that "illuminates the cultural, social, and political friction of [her] spiritual, human, female, and Puerto Rican state of mind" (1–2). The artist herself has stated that her work attempts to create "a metaphorical sense of place, . . . not in Puerto Rico, not in Chicago, but my own island" (J. Sánchez 1991, 1).

In Orlando, Florida, artist Obed Gómez (obedart.com) is well known for capturing the exuberance of Puerto Rico's folkloric traditions. His colorful paintings have appeared on the covers of the city's Puerto Rican Day Parade brochure and *Orlando Arts Magazine.*

For some island Puerto Rican artists, New York and many other US localities are only stops made by the "airbus" that connects the island with the metropolis. It is difficult to fully understand their work without an awareness of this important dimension. Antonio Martorell is one of the most visible commuters, enriching stateside Puerto Rican communities with his impressive mixed-media installations and performances—often combining art, theater, and literary text. He frequently installs exhibits at colleges, galleries, and museums. His exhibition *Blanca Snow in Puerto Rico* (Snow White in Puerto Rico), held at New York's Hostos Community College Art Gallery in 1997, is one of his most impressive contributions to the community's cultural life. Moreover, together with theater director Rosa Luisa Márquez, Martorell has traveled to many US universities to engage students in the process of writing, staging, and acting in performances that rely on their own creativity and talent. One of his most memorable exhibits was the Centro-sponsored *Labor Exhibit* (2012), cocurated with Susana Torruella-Leval. It focused on the more than half a million Puerto Rican workers coming to the United States during the years of the Great Migration. At that exhibit both curators displayed a series of woodcuts illustrating the journey and gave a face to many of these laborers. Martorell's *Playa negra* (Black tar, 2010) woodcut series focused on the rooftop photos that migrants would send to their relatives back on the island and contrasts the images of prosperity that some migrants wanted to convey with the harsh realities of their working lives.

Popular Music

Mythifying of and yearning for the Puerto Rican homeland through creative literature is also manifested in some of the most popular songs written by composers and musicians, most notably those who at some point in their lives left the island to live in the United States, either for brief periods or longer stays. It is said that Puerto Ricans *llevan la música por dentro* (carry the music within them),[16] indicating the importance of this music in the sum of Puerto Rican cultural expression. Iconic songs such as Rafael Hernández's "Preciosa" (My precious homeland), Noel Estrada's "En Mi Viejo San Juan" (In my Old San Juan), and Bobby Capó's "Soñando con Puerto Rico" (Dreaming of Puerto Rico) are only a few of the best-known examples of the nostalgia, patriotic pride, and love for the homeland expressed by those Puerto Ricans finding themselves on distant shores.

Popular music undoubtedly represents an expressive form that has contributed significantly to propagating Puerto Rican cultural traditions, asserting a national consciousness within the diaspora, and generating the cultural vitality that connects island and stateside communities. From typical forms such as the *plena* (a working-class musical composition), the *bomba* (an oral recitation and folk dance of African origin), the *décima* (a peasant musical poetic composition), or the *aguinaldo* (a Christmas carol) to the romantic *bolero* (ballad) or the more upbeat and audacious dancing rhythms of salsa, pop rock, rap, hip-hop, and reggaetón, musical expressions are a vibrant part of Puerto Rican and Latino/a cultural and social life in the United States (Aparicio 1997; Quintero Rivera 1999; Flores 2000, 2009, 2016; J. Rivera 2003; Rivera, Marshal, and Pacini Hernández 2009; Rivera-Rideau 2015).

Folk music interpreter Manuel "El Canario" Jiménez first recorded and popularized island *plenas* in New York, alternating his musical craft with his regular trade as a merchant marine. In fact, many of the performers who are part of Puerto Rico's popular music hall of fame developed their careers off the island in other Latin American countries or within the various

Latino/a communities throughout the United States. Whether they traveled off the island on a temporary basis or had established residence in the United States, Puerto Rican and other Latino/a performers often shared the stage of the Teatro Hispano de Nueva York, the Teatro Puerto Rico, the Teatro San José, the Park Palace, and the famous Palladium Dance Hall. Harlem's celebrated Apollo Theater also opened its doors to some Puerto Rican and other Latino/a performers of this period.

Music was not only a form of entertainment. The creativity, visibility, and prominence of Puerto Rican performers were important to a community confronting a constant barrage of negative images in the press, movies, and other media (Glasser 1995; J. Santiago 1994). The songs and musical styles that emerged from the communities of the diaspora reflected a deep-rooted sense of Puerto Ricanness, connected to the island and also to the different urban barrios as part of that inexhaustible repertoire of survival strategies that migrants develop in the process of adapting to new, alienating environments.

Included among the best-known early figures in New York's musical circles were the talented performer-composers Rafael Hernández, Pedro Flores, and Bobby Capó. Hernández's Trío Borinquen and Cuarteto Victoria first performed some of his most memorable compositions in New York. The Puerto Rican homeland was central to his internationally known classic songs "Lamento Borincano" (Puerto Rican peasant's lament) and "Preciosa" (My precious homeland), both written in New York. Hernández's sister, Victoria, was a garment industry worker and piano teacher. Her musical inclinations led her to open Almacenes Hernández in 1927, the first major Puerto Rican–owned record store in the city (Glasser 1995).

Bobby Capó, Mirta Silva, and Pedro Ortiz Dávila (Davilita) performed at different times with Rafael Hernández's *cuarteto* before they achieved their own individual fame as composers and musical interpreters. Rafael Hernández lived in Mexico for many years and achieved continental fame. Outside his native Puerto Rico, Capó was well known in New York and Cuba. He was among the first Latino performers to host his own television show on a New York City station. Silva went on to become one of the most coveted performers in Cuba and lead singer of the famous Sonora Matancera Orchestra. After returning to Puerto Rico, Silva emerged as one of TV's favorite entertainers with her variety shows *Una hora contigo* (An hour with you) and *Tira y tápate* (Throw the rock and hide your hand). While living in New York, Davilita was a featured singer in composer Pedro Flores's New York musical ensembles. Years later, Davilita and Felipe "La Voz" Rodríguez became one of the most popular duos in New York and Puerto Rico. Raised in New York, singer Daniel Santos also made popular his unique singing style during this period. A fervent Nationalist, Santos also found a less repressive political environment away from the island.

The segregation prevalent in US society at the time caused some of the racial problems confronted by black Puerto Rican artists such as Hernández,

Davilita, and Santos. Before the 1960s civil rights laws barred such practices, dark-skinned performers were not only excluded from performing in some of the most popular white-only clubs but also were paid less than white or light-skinned Latinos/as (Glasser 1995).

Musicians such as Noro Morales, Tito Puente, and Tito Rodríguez were among the pioneers of the Big Band and Mambo Kings era of the 1940s and 1950s. Along with Cuba's Pérez Prado and Spain's Xavier Cugat, they entertained audiences in New York's celebrated Palladium Dance Hall. Morales's orchestra, which often alternated on the stage with Glenn Miller's, also performed on Broadway. Born in the United States to Puerto Rican parents, Tito Puente studied at Juilliard and soon became known for his musical experiments combining African American jazz with Latin rhythms. He was known as *el rey del timbal* (the king of the small drums) in a new genre labeled Latin jazz. Until his death in 2002, Tito Puente was one of the leading percussion artists and orchestra leaders in North America, with a musical career that spanned more than half a century. Tito Rodríguez and his Mambo Devils were among the first successful Puerto Rican musical groups to entertain US audiences in the late 1940s. Rodríguez came to New York, where his brother Johnny's trio had achieved popularity. In later years, Tito Rodríguez ventured into the popular bossa nova, but it was mostly his heartfelt style as a singer of romantic *boleros* that gained him fame in Venezuela, Argentina, and other countries.

In the late 1950s and 1960s, a new generation of stateside Puerto Rican and other Latino/a performers began to revolutionize the New York musical environment; their popularity extended to the island and other parts of Latin America. New York–born Charlie Palmieri, also a piano student at Juilliard, began to achieve recognition with his Orquesta Siboney in the early 1950s. In 1959, he joined Dominican flautist Johnny Pacheco and founded the musical group Charanga Duboney. Using a combination of the flute, violin, bass, and small drums, they invented the *pachanga* and *charanga* rhythms, which turned into dancing favorites for their stateside communities and their Caribbean countries of origin during the early 1960s. Another Puerto Rican *pachanguero*, Joe Quijano, started his own recording label, Cesta, and asked Charlie Palmieri to direct the production of the recordings of the Cesta All Stars, a label that included some of the most popular Latino/a performers of those years. Charlie Palmieri's brother, Eddie, also contributed to this new musical genre and to the Latin jazz genre. Although these performers made an impact on the musical world of Latinos/as during the 1950s and 1960s, they were not as successful in "crossing over" into the wider US market and climbing the Billboard charts as some of the more prominent performers achieving recognition after the 1990s (Flores 2016).

Born in Brooklyn of Puerto Rican parents, Ray Barreto was the first *pachanga* performer to "cross over" and make it onto Billboard's list of hits with his recording of the song "El watusi" (J. Santiago 1994). During the same period, José Calderón, better known as Joe Cuba, also achieved success with his famous Sexteto group for his combination of mambo and African American rhythm and blues to create the late-1960s boogaloo craze that revealed the marketing potential of Latino music (Flores 2000). Other Puerto Rican musicians, such as Johnny Colón, joined the popular musical vogue that blended Latin and African American rhythms. The *bugalú* was occasionally interpreted in English or bilingually. Ricardo "Richie" Ray, an accomplished US-born Puerto Rican pianist and Juilliard graduate, also started his career with this musical genre. He recruited another US-born Puerto Rican, Bobby Cruz, to become the lead singer in his orchestra, which had an extensive bilingual repertoire and achieved considerable popularity.

In 1964, Johnny Pacheco created the Fania recording label and opened the door for many other Latino/a performers to join the celebrated Fania All Stars, including Puerto Rican performers Bobby Valentín, Willie Colón, and Héctor Lavoe, Jewish American saxophonist Larry Harlow, and Cuban singer Celia Cruz, who was subsequently designated "Reina de la Salsa" (queen of salsa). Fania marketed the fusion of Afro-Caribbean rhythms with jazz, rock, and rhythm and blues as the salsa genre, creating an unbreakable transnational musical link between island and stateside Boricuas.[17] Salsa incorporated elements of the most popular Afro-Caribbean musical rhythms—*son*, mambo, *guaracha*, *pachanga*, *chachachá*, *son montuno*, and rumba. The coined term "salsa" reflected most accurately the spirit, vivaciousness, and *sabor* (flavor) that characterizes most of Latino music, and as a marketing label it unified the diverse musical rhythms and experiences of the various Caribbean diasporas in the United States.

Categorically, the Caribbean and other Latin American rhythms and genres have penetrated the US musical mainstream industry, as illustrated by the enormous success of many contemporary Latino/a performers practicing this genre, either in Spanish or bilingually. These hemispheric and global "musical migrations" (Aparicio and Jáquez 2003) have produced older and more recent waves of performers of "hybrid" musical content and styles. A leading salsa singer is Marc Anthony, known for several hit ballads and pop rock songs in English. His popularity in the United States has reached levels similar to those achieved by other Puerto Rican pop rock performers, such as Ricky Martin and Jennifer López. López, in particular, combined her musical and dancing talents with an acting career in film and television. Hollywood productions such as *Salsa* (1998) and *Dance with Me* (1999), the former featuring ex-Menudo member Robby "Draco" Rosa and the latter, Puerto Rican singer Chayanne and well-known African American performer Vanessa Williams, reflect the growing popularity of salsa and Latino music among US audiences since the 1990s.

Available studies on salsa music (Aparicio 1997; Quintero Rivera 1999) argue that aside from its entertainment value, this popular genre mirrors social, racial, and gender power relations among various sectors and between the sexes.[18] Cultural definition and affirmation are important components of this music. Songs such as "Color americano" (American color) by Willie Colón, "Buscando América" (Searching for America) by Panamanian singer Rubén Blades, "Latinos en Estados Unidos" (Latinos in the United States) by the late Cuban salsa diva Celia Cruz, and "Amor Latino" (Latino loving) by Columbian singer Carlos Vives are indicative of how interpreters and composers frequently use music as an instrument of social consciousness and as a means of proclaiming the panethnic sense of Latino/a identity that frequently transcends individual nationalities. "Color americano," a song written by Amílcar Boscán (1990, Sony International) and interpreted by Puerto Rican *salsero* Willie Colón, defines some of the basic elements of this identity:

> I have the honor
> of being Hispanic
> I have the Borincano flavor
> my dark-skin color
> almost brown
> is the pride of the
> Latino people, my man.
> (author's translation)

Some Puerto Rican folk singers of the genre called *la nueva trova* (the new folk song) also achieved popularity amid the social and political activism of the 1960s and 1970s. This music was performed at colleges and universities sponsored by community organizations and political demonstrations. Some performers frequently commuted between the island and the United States. One of the most popular, Roy Brown, recorded the album *Nueva Yol* (a common vernacular Spanish adaptation of "New York") in 1983. Earlier in his career, Brown, the son of a Puerto Rican mother and a North American father, had popularized the song "El negrito bonito" (The beautiful black man), which laments the harsh experiences and despair of a destitute black Puerto Rican migrant in New York City. Puerto Rican folk music influenced by African rhythms and traditions like the *plena* and the *bomba* has also inspired many interpreters, such as Los Pleneros de la 21, a group founded in 1983 by Juan Gutiérrez. Through their recordings and concert tours, this group has revitalized Afro–Puerto Rican traditional music within the diaspora.

Through the years, a wide diversity of popular musical expressions came out of the urban barrios. The most notable and commercially successful in the last two decades were rap, hip-hop, and reggaetón.[19] These provide off-beat ways of understanding the cultural, social, and racial interactions among Puerto Ricans and African Americans in the inner cities. Juan Flores (2000) noted the importance of rap: "Like other Latino groups, Puerto Ricans are using rap as a vehicle for affirming their history, language, and culture under conditions of rampant discrimination and exclusion" (137). In *New York*

Ricans from the Hip Hop Zone (2003), Raquel Rivera notes that despite the general undermining of Puerto Rican contributions to this genre, it shows their connection to and the influence of African American music and reaffirms Boricua African roots and their own racialized experiences. Unquestionably, the participation of Puerto Ricans in these musical styles adds to the many other forms of bilingual creative expression coming out of the urban barrios. Despite these genres' often sexist lyrics and foul language, the huge popularity of rap, hip-hop, and reggaetón allows their working-class social and political content to reach diverse musical audiences, almost as much as it reaches Latinos/as (Rivera, Marshall, and Pacini Hernández 2009). "Despacito" (Slowly) by Puerto Rican singer Luis Fonsi and rapper Daddy Yankee (also featuring pop star Justin Bieber), with its rhythmic feel-good dancing vibe that mixes Latin pop and rap and Spanish and English lyrics, became a number-one hit on the musical charts; it also achieved great popularity globally, even when most fans and listeners did not understand the meaning of the Spanish lyrics. It received the 2017 "Best Song of the Year" Latin Grammy Award.

Other popular Puerto Rican performers in these musical genres who have had an impact on both island and stateside communities are Vico C, Lisa M, Daddy Yankee, Tego Calderón, and, more recently, Taína Asili, to name only a few.

Asili's bilingual interpretation of the song "El no es mi presidente" (He is not my president), a song first introduced at the A Day Without Women March to Washington, DC, held on January 19, 2017, the day after Donald Trump's inauguration, is illustrative of the meaningful ways in which popular music can communicate social and political issues and conditions to multiple diverse contemporary audiences and still be marketable. In her music, a mix of Afro-Latin, reggae, and rock, protest lyrics convey the concerns of an Afro–Puerto Rican interpreter, in this instance, condemning what the new president represents: "El no es mi presidente / El no representa la voz de mi gente" (He is not my president / He does not represent my people's voice). The song also condemns his most blatantly racist and sexist policies and deplorable behavior: "Las vidas negras importan (blacks lives matter) / Ningún ser humano es illegal (no human being is illegal) / Basta la violencia sexual (enough of sexist violence)." Asili was one of many stateside Puerto Rican artists who brought together well-known and up-and-coming musicians to join her on her 2017 album *¡Viva Puerto Rico!* (Long live Puerto Rico!), recorded as a benefit compilation album by Latino/a artists, with proceeds going to Hurricane Maria relief efforts (www.mariafund.org).

Cultural Crossovers: Being a US Latino/a

In Puerto Rico, those who oppose statehood or independence frequently say that, because of its relationship with the United States, the island enjoys the best of two worlds (Benítez 1998). This statement assumes that the high levels of exposure to Anglo-American culture and the English language and to stateside publishers galleries, museums, editors, and art critics, together with the US citizenship status of Puerto Ricans, make it easier for some writers and artists to "cross over" into the US market. But for a long time that was not the case for the majority of Puerto Rican and Latino/a artists, writers, musicians, and performers.

Indeed, an increasing number of works by island writers are translated into English. Furthermore, writers such as Rosario Ferré (1938–2016), a native Spanish speaker and well-known author on the island and in other parts of the Spanish-speaking world, wrote two of her last novels, *The House on the Lagoon* (1995) and *Eccentric Neighborhoods* (1998), in English, and both were published by a prominent US publishing house. Prior to this incursion into the English-speaking market, some of her previous work had been translated from Spanish by others. However, the author rewrote these two novels for Spanish-speaking audiences and published them in 1997—a reversal of the pattern for most bilingual writers, especially since Ferré's first language was Spanish, not English, and after attaining her postsecondary education in the United States, she had been living in Puerto Rico for many years.

Before the publication of these novels, only a handful of first-generation Puerto Rican writers in the United States wrote in English. An early exception was Pedro Juan Labarthe in 1931, as noted in a previous section of this chapter. Stateside Puerto Rican writers of the 1940s and 1950s, first-generation migrants like Jesús Colón and Julia de Burgos, also wrote in English, although Spanish was their native language. While Burgos's English-language writing was limited to her last two poems, written shortly before her death, Colón wrote numerous columns in English for labor newspapers, such as the *Daily Worker* and *Mainstream*. Additionally he published a book of stories, *A Puerto Rican in New York and Other Sketches* (1961), which, despite his being a well-known community activist, was not known to most Puerto Ricans until it was rescued and published in a new 1982 edition by cultural studies scholar Juan Flores.

Around the globe, many important voices from nations that had endured the ravages of colonialism gained international recognition after their writings were translated into English. A similar statement could be made about stateside Puerto Rican writers and other artists trying to reach out to Spanish-speaking audiences in Puerto Rico and other countries. First-generation stateside Puerto Ricans who are Spanish speakers tend to write and publish mostly in that language. Those born or raised in the United States tend to write primarily in English, even when they are fully bilingual. Those whose primary language is English and who are less fluent in Spanish often mix and code-switch between the languages in what is commonly described as "Spanglish." This normal process allows them to explore new creative linguistic possibilities and communicative strategies with the written and spoken word. All in all, their skills and the deployment of the two languages and cultures they straddle are intrinsic to being Latino/a in the United States (see Acosta-Belén 1977; Valdes-Fallis 1978; Aparicio 1988; E. Morales 2002).

More frequently than ever before, the literary works of many US Puerto Rican and other Latino/a authors writing in English are being translated into Spanish and distributed and marketed throughout Latin America and Spain. Few of these authors do any creative writing directly in Spanish. This kind of bidirectional crossover writing is not yet the norm within Latin American or US literary traditions. Nonetheless, it is becoming quite common in the expanding field of US Latino/a literature, confronting both critics and readers with the perennial question of where to place these literary works. Are they part of US or Latin American literature, or will they eventually be regarded as belonging to both? The answer to that question does not change the fact that the increasing presence of Puerto Ricans and other Latinos/as in US society—and the transnational dynamics at work in the Americas and other parts of the world during the era of globalization—are producing new diasporic realities and cultural hybridity that shape cultural production, consumption, and marketability. These new realities also challenge conventional literary canons, models of immigrant assimilation, and cultural crossovers.

Crossovers in music and performance are illustrated by the unprecedented success of bilingual Puerto Rican musical performers Ricky Martin, Marc Anthony, Jennifer López, and Luis Fonsi, as well as other Latino/a performers, such as Gloria Estefan, Cristina Aguilera, Enrique Iglesias, Shakira, and Pitbull, to mention only a few. Their singing in both Spanish and English and the cultural hybridity revealed in their musical interpretations are more than just exotic marketing ploys to sell a product to the North American public. They signal how the people of Latin America and the Caribbean—Puerto Ricans included—are now making the spaces where they migrate their own, giving expression to the cultures they straddle, and making their presence felt beyond their respective communities. In referring to the Chicano/a presence in North America, writer Luis Valdez (n.d.) once stated, "We did not come, in fact, to the United States at all, the United States came to us." This statement could also be applied to Puerto Ricans, since the historic and socioeconomic circumstances of their migration were and are shaped to a large extent by the conditions created by US interventionist policies and economic and military power over their respective countries of origin.

Notes

1. "Autógrafo" (My autograph) was included in the collection *Mi libro de Cuba* (My book of Cuba), originally published in Havana in 1893. See Rodríguez de Tió (1968b), 1:317. English translation by José Nieto.

2. See the two-part article "La emigración puertorriqueña a E.U.," by Bernardo Vega, in *Liberación*, November 30 and December 14, 1946.

3. Both Jesús Colón and his brother Joaquín were targeted by the House Un-American Activities Committee (HUAC) of the US House of Representatives. Senator Joseph McCarthy instigated witch hunt hearings and interrogations against suspected communist subversives or sympathizers during the mid-1950s. Many individuals were investigated and subject to unsubstantiated accusations without due process. These hearings ruined the reputations of many individuals. This period is known as McCarthy era, and the word "McCarthyism" was coined to refer to these irresponsible practices and violations of US citizens' rights. Jesús Colón had a long record of writing for socialist and communist labor newspapers and being an American Labor Party member and a candidate. His brother Joaquín, however, did not share his political inclinations, which Jesús confirmed to the members of HUAC. Nonetheless, Joaquín was forced to retire from his federal job at New York City's central post office. See Joaquín Colón (2001).

4. Some of the best sources for the life and writings of Luisa Capetillo include Norma Valle Ferrer, *Luisa Capetillo: Historia de una mujer proscrita* (Río Piedras, PR: Editorial Cultural, 1990); Valle Ferrer (2008); and Julio Ramos, ed., *Amor y anarquía: Los escritos de Luisa Capetillo* (Río Piedras, PR: Ediciones Huracán, 1992). Also see the chapter "For the Sake of Love: Luisa Capetillo, Anarchy, and Boricua Literary History," in Sánchez González (2001), 16–41.

5. Franca de Armiño's play was not published until 1937, a year after the outbreak of the Spanish Civil War (1936–1939).

6. The terms "Neorican" and "Nuyorican" have been used since the 1970s to identify Puerto Ricans born or raised in the United States, although early on they carried some negative connotations. Traditionally, ethnic groups in US society have identified themselves by a hyphenated version of their national origin and the term "American" (e.g., Mexican-American, Cuban-American). However, historically, stateside Puerto Ricans have not been receptive to this form of identification, since they are US citizens by birth. Thus, as of yet, there is not a single generalized rubric used to distinguish Puerto Ricans living on the island or stateside. Acceptance of the term "Nuyorican" has been limited to a particular group of New York–based writers and artists. Considering that several other major US cities have large Puerto Rican communities, neologisms such as "Chicagorican" and "Orlandorican" are capturing the differences in geographic locations. The broader term "Diasporican" is being used more frequently in recent decades to refer to those Puerto Ricans living in the United States, but "Puerto Rican" and "Boricua" continue to be the most commonly used terms.

7. The word *asimilao* is a Spanish slang form of *asimilado* (assimilated). The English translation is: "assimilated? no way assimilated, / brother, I am "asimilao" / asi mi la o that's the truth / a part of me is asimilao."

8. The word *puertorra* is a colloquial way of referring to a Puerto Rican woman's nationality. Its spelling (*portorra*) in the verse of Esteves's poem is a mistake made by the author.

9. Translation of Mariposa Fernández's quoted verses: "no nací en Puerto Rico / Puerto Rico nació en mí" (I was not born in Puerto Rico / Puerto Rico was born in me).

10. The Spanish word *moreno* was commonly used in New York City to refer to an African American.

11. Although they share the same name, the poet Edwin Torres should not be confused with the Puerto Rican New York State Supreme Court judge and author of crime novels.

12. Among the Spanish translations of literary works by stateside Puerto Rican authors are the collection of poetry *Obituario puertorriqueño* by Pedro Pietri (San

Juan: Instituto de Cultura Puertorriqueña, 1977); the novels *Cuando era puertorriqueña* (New York: Vintage, 1994), *El sueño de América* (New York: Vintage, 1997), and *Casi una mujer* (New York: Vintage, 1999) by Esmeralda Santiago; the novel *Por estas calles bravas* by Piri Thomas (New York: Random House, 1998); and the novel *La línea del sol* (Río Piedras: Editorial Universidad de Puerto Rico, 1999) and collection of poetry and narrative *Bailando en silencio* (Houston, TX: Arte Público Press, 1997) by Judith Ortiz Cofer.

13. La Marketa was originally a produce market located in Spanish Harlem, similar to the typical Puerto Rican *plaza del mercado*. Today it is a place for typical Puerto Rican and other ethnic food vendors and for crafts stores.

14. Artist Juan Sánchez coined the term "Rican-constructions" for one of his exhibitions; it is also the title of one of his paintings.

15. The *De Debt/Decolonize* acrylic and collage on canvas was created for the Puerto Rico bundle installation debut of Occupy Museum's Debt Fair at the Whitney Biennial 2017 at the Whitney Museum of American Art. The installation was also on view at the Museo del Barrio (2017). The Spanish words above the map of Puerto Rico are lyrics from the *danza* "Verde luz" by Antonio Cabán Vale (El Topo).

16. In 1999, the title of the annual musical TV show (and released CD and video) sponsored by the Banco Popular de Puerto Rico was *Con la música por dentro* (San Juan: Banco Popular, 1999).

17. This period, known as the golden age of salsa music, is re-created in the documentary film *The Golden Age of Salsa Music with Larry Harlow*, dir. Orlando J. Guzman Colon (New York: Cinema Guild, 1998).

18. For many years Puerto Rico's media promoted a musical competition between *cocolos*, those who favored salsa music, and *rockeros*, those more adept at rock music. This separation in musical tastes paralleled a separation along class and racial lines. The *cocolos*, or *salseros*, were usually dark skinned and from the working class. See the documentary film *Cocolos y Rockeros*, dir. Ana María García (San Juan: Pandora Films, 1992).

19. The latter, a musical blend of Spanish-language hip-hop, Jamaican reggae, and other Caribbean beats, has been popularized throughout Latin America, North America, and Europe by several Puerto Rican performers like Daddy Yankee, Tego Calderón, Don Omar, Ivy Queen, Wisín y Yansel, and Calle 13. Rap trailblazers Vico C and Lisa M later became reggaetón rappers. Reggaetón originated in Puerto Rico in the late 1990s and has turned into one of the most popular and influential musical genres and dance styles.

9

The Colonial Quandary:
What Lies Ahead

Y así le grito al villano:
Yo sería borincano
Aunque naciera en la luna.
—Juan Antonio Corretjer,
"Boricua en la luna"

Puerto Rican migration is the bridge between two worlds—
inextricably linked and yet uniting and separating a people bound by language, culture, and birth right. Yet, what is the destiny of these migrants that long for a remembered past while demonstrating resiliency in the face of adversity in a new land? A massive number of Puerto Rican migrants made the ultimate sacrifice to leave their homeland in the 1950s and 1960s. While one might argue that they left the island in pursuit of economic opportunity abroad, it cannot be denied that their exodus was promoted and sponsored by policymakers on the island and in Washington, DC. Those that remained benefited as industrialization transformed the island and standards of living improved. In the 1970s, while facing the New York City debt crisis, many Puerto Ricans returned to the island—again, casualties of economic insecurity and deprivation. Even as they returned home to the land of their birth, some with their US-born offspring, they often faced prejudice and were stereotyped.

But at the dawn of the twenty-first century, Puerto Ricans in the United States could look back and celebrate the new communities they had participated in building. While no strangers to economic struggle, they could visualize a better future for their children and grandchildren. In sheer size alone, they now outnumbered their compatriots residing on the island. Their resiliency and cohesiveness allowed them to navigate mainstream society on their own terms—celebrating symbols of nationhood, language, culture, and the arts. After the twin catastrophes of economic recession and the impact of the 2017 hurricane on Puerto Rico, stateside communities have stepped up, raising funds and volunteering time and material to send to the island. They have taken in displaced family members and friends and made arrangements for the schooling of children and employment for adults. This outpouring of support portends well for the future of these communities as it highlights their continued cohesiveness in the face of adversity.

As we have shown throughout the various chapters of this book, telling the real stories of Puerto Rican migration to the United States unavoidably entails dealing with the unfettered and lasting US jurisdiction over Puerto Rico and the multiple effects of colonialism on the Puerto Rican people's ability to control their own destiny. The economic recession and debt crisis that began in 2007 has been magnified a decade later by the shattering effects of Hurricane Maria, and these two life-changing crises have traumatized Puerto Ricans, who now find their homeland beleaguered by unfathomable destruction, widespread desolation, and insurmountable fiscal insolvency.

At this writing, government officials still have no accounting of the number of lives lost during the storm and lingering aftereffects, but the human suffering is almost immeasurable. Additionally, the initial tepid and delayed emergency response of the US political leadership and the various federal agencies to Puerto Rico's alarming conditions exacerbates this situation. Besides the immense loss of billions of dollars in economic activity due to Hurricane Maria and the resulting prolonged state of emergency, early government estimates show that the island incurred around $90 billion in damage to its infrastructure; businesses and homeowners sustained extensive property losses; and the government needs about $21 billion just to keep running and providing regular services to citizens. It is mind-boggling that the US Congress and current administration cannot grasp or will not acknowledge the magnitude of the growing humanitarian crisis that is overturning and imperiling the lives of the US citizens of Puerto Rico and propelling them to migrate to the United States in massive numbers. The current New Millenium Migration estimates and projections for the period of 2017–2019 show that between 114,000 and 213,000 migrants will leave annually in the aftermath of Hurricane Maria and that Puerto Rico could lose up to half a million additional people during the indicated period (Meléndez and Hinojosa 2017).

Almost six months after Hurricane Maria hit the island, a CNN reporter noted that based on metrics from the response to this particular disaster, stories from some island residents, and opinions from a number of experts who study responses to hurricanes, Puerto Rico still "appears to be stuck between the "emergency" and "recovery" phases of disaster response for too many of its residents" (Sutter 2018). These residents see themselves as "the forgotten people," and countless citizens of this US territory still face shocking conditions. Federal agencies responding to the disaster (FEMA and the Army Corps of Engineers) blame the slow pace of restoring electrical power to all residents on "logistical problems" and the "remoteness" of an overseas island crossed by a central mountain range. While it is true that at least a third of its seventy-eight towns are located in these mountainous areas and most of the coastal towns also have rural sectors, Puerto Rico is only 100 miles long and 35 miles wide (3,500 square miles) in size and thus, slightly smaller than Long Island.

Considering the gravity of the present circumstances, government officials and experts believe that rebuilding costs could surpass the amount of the already accumulated bond debt. The chair of the Junta de Supervisión Fiscal (Financial Oversight and Management Board) and its executive director have warned the US Congress and bond fund investors of the unlikelihood of any forthcoming debt payments.

The ultimate control of the US Congress over the island and the resulting limitations it places on the ostensibly self-governing Commonwealth impede the insular government's ability to develop and implement economic solutions centered on protecting and improving the lives and well-being of Puerto Rican citizens. Moreover, because of the Donald Trump administration's contemptuous reactions to the emergency and post-hurricane conditions, now more than ever before, the present dire circumstances are forcing Puerto Ricans to reexamine their status as colonial subjects and the real implications of their lack of sovereignty, their second-class US citizenship, and the "separate and unequal" treatment they are receiving compared to other disaster victims in the continental United States. To make matters worse, the US tax reforms approved by Congress in late 2017 dealt another blow to the bankrupt island by treating Puerto Rico as a foreign country, rather than as part of the United States. The bill imposes a new 12.5 percent tax on Controlled Foreign Corporations on any income generated from licenses and patents, a provision that will be applied to US companies or subsidiaries currently located in Puerto Rico. By removing the previous tax breaks, many of these companies may relocate to other tax haven countries (Vicens 2017). Unavoidably, this panorama may also compel many island and stateside Puerto Ricans to renew and multiply their efforts to set a course toward decolonization.

Discussions in the past have immediately equated the notion of decolonization with independence on the grounds that in general Puerto Ricans tend to be very nationalistic, at least culturally, since that has not been proven to be the case politically. Paradoxically, the lack of electoral support for independence on the island also comes with a long history of anticolonial struggle and relentless political repression of independence groups and individuals joining them (see Churchill and Vander Wall 1990; Bosque Pérez and Colón Morera 1997; Nieves Falcón 2009; Denis 2015). But the sense of cultural nationalism is also evident in the collective spaces established by most of the stateside Puerto Rican communities. In addition, there is no compelling indication that the US Congress and general public are disposed to support statehood for Puerto Rico. Setting aside the current high levels of xenophobia, anti-immigration sentiment, and bigotry against populations of color in today's US society, statehood would entail the annexation of a new state that is culturally and linguistically different and now also fiscally bankrupt. Even if Congress would engage in a serious discussion about statehood for Puerto Rico, if requested by a majority of island Puerto Ricans, it is unlikely that it would accept the notion of a bilingual state joining the union, a case for which there is no precedent in US history. For instance, it took nearly sixty-five years from the conclusion of the Mexican-American War for New Mexico to be granted statehood in 1912. One reason for this long delay was that until 1900, the large territory lacked the minimum population of US citizens required for statehood. But another significant consideration was that New Mexico, one of the main territories in the Southwest, was known for its established and distinctive *nuevomexicano* cultural heritage rooted in the Spanish colonization of the region that started in 1598 (almost a decade before the Pilgrims arrived on North American shores in 1607). For over three centuries the territory developed distinct Spanish and later Mexican cultural attributes and traditions and maintained Spanish as the primary language of the non-Anglo settlers; its unmatched cultural vibrancy has been well documented (Gonzales-Berry and Maciel 2000; Meléndez 1997; Meyer 1996).[1]

Since even statehood supporters are unwilling to give up their culture and language, the viability of statehood for Puerto Rico in the current US political environment is most probably nil. Another compelling consideration, mostly ignored by Puerto Rican statehood supporters, is that Latinos/as, numbering an estimated 59 million in 2017, represent the largest population of color in the United States, and island Puerto Ricans would add an additional 3.4 million to the mix. As a state, Puerto Rico would have two senators, like the other fifty states, and a certain number of members in the US House of Representatives, depending on the size of the island's population at the time of incorporation, which would add to the number of stateside-elected Puerto Rican representatives in the US Congress.[2]

We have covered only a fraction of the intricate and lopsided relationship of domination and subordination between the two countries in order to establish a framework and set the parameters for understanding the historical evolution of the persisting patterns of Puerto Rican colonial migration to the United States and the manifold socioeconomic and political conditions and dynamics that account for the New Millennium Migration. As a whole, this book provides a nuanced portrait of the Puerto Rican presence in US society and of a stateside population that, since the 1970s, has continued to grow at an average rate of 34 percent each decade.

Since the 1898 invasion, the United States has repeatedly treated Puerto Rico as little more than "war booty," a territorial possession experiencing "benign benevolence" (Moynihan 1993) and subject to "an imperialism of neglect" (G. Lewis 1968). Given dismissive and negative federal government responses to requests from the island government seeking financial relief a few years ago through the same bankrupcy laws available to the fifty states of the union, and, subsequently, for hurricane disaster relief, Puerto Ricans are now being treated with "outright contempt" as "the other," less deserving US citizens.

Wrought by this uneven and unequal relationship, Puerto Rico remains one of the last vestiges of worldwide colonialism, once named "the oldest colony in the world" by a prominent island jurist (Trías Monge 1999a, 1999b). Another recognized scholar saw it as a nation still trapped "between the forces competing for power under the ruling colonial system and the forces opposing the system" (Maldonado-Denis 1972, 7).

There is no question that the island's daunting political limbo (Méndez 1997) is magnified by the inescapable fact that both Commonwealth and statehood supporters, currently representing about 95 percent of the island's electorate, continue to fiercely engage in political partisanship. Every four years they battle one another for control of Puerto Rico's local government and for their meager share of political influence over the US Congress and administration of the moment, while arrogantly dismissing the pro-independence minority that remains the primary locus of anticolonial struggle and resistance.[3]

Cultural nationalism, however, has continued to manifest itself quite vigorously among both island and stateside Puerto Ricans, regardless of their political sympathies or affiliations, and makes its presence known in multiple manifestations of Puerto Rican expressive cultures. Even during the decades of ruthless political repression exerted by federal and island government agencies against Puerto Rican Nationalists and other independence supporters (1930s–1970s), stateside communities provided a less oppressive and threatening space for the expression of cultural and political nationalism by individuals and community groups and organizations. This does not mean that they were exempt from FBI surveillance and infiltration during the most militant decades of the stateside Puerto Rican movement (1960s–1970s).

Whether their first language is Spanish or English or they were born in Puerto Rico or the United States, stateside Puerto Ricans have become an integral part of US society. They have done so without necessarily fully embracing white Anglo-American assimilation ideologies that often disparage ethnic and racial diversity and inclusiveness or developing into an internal political force to encourage statehood for Puerto Rico. Instead, Puerto Ricans are cultural navigators who continue to proudly nourish a separate and distinctive sense of Puerto Ricanness within the diaspora. Theirs is a complex hybrid, fluid, and deterritorialized diasporic colonial experience rooted in what it means to be Puerto Rican in different US locations but closely connected to Puerto Rico. Those Puerto Ricans who have made the United States their permanent home continue to contribute in multiple ways to this nation. Unlike other immigrant groups, as colonial migrants they have not been receptive to the hyphenated Puerto Rican–American identity that sociologist Jesuit priest Joseph P. Fitzpatrick used to describe them in the title of his "interpretative essay" *Puerto Rican–Americans: The Meaning of Migration to the Mainland* (1971). This book focused on the lives and experiences of the generation of Puerto Ricans born or raised in New York whose parents had arrived in the city during the years of the Great Migration. However, since then stateside Puerto Ricans and migration researchers have rarely used the hyphenated label—which is clearly redundant since all Puerto Ricans are US citizens.

The verses of the poem "Boricua en la luna" (Puerto Rican on the moon), which serve as the epigraph for this closing chapter, were written by Juan Antonio Corretjer (1908–1995),[4] regarded as Puerto Rico's most prominent male national poet and popularized on the island as well as in the diaspora by a song interpreted and recorded by Puerto Rican folk singer Roy Brown in 1987. The song and poem are now emblematic of the resilient spirit of Puerto Ricans in countering the injurious effects of their colonial condition. The melody was subsequently recorded in 1997 and reintroduced to younger generations of Puerto Ricans by the island's leading rock Latino group, Fiel a la Vega, so for most Puerto Ricans of all ages, it is a familiar classic folk song.

The verses of "Boricua en la luna" recount the migratory journey of a Puerto Rican couple to New York City, where they work tirelessly under exploitative conditions to make a living and where their son, the poetic voice, is born. Through his parents' migration experiences, he connects with his cultural roots and evokes a nostalgia for the homeland they left behind and that he can only imagine from their yearnings. Through this irrevocable bond and their hardships and diasporic existence, the poetic voice can symbolically establish a connection with the imagined island and emotively uphold who he is, where he comes from, his humble origins, and his own spirit of survival: "De una lágrima soy hijo / y soy hijo del sudor" (I am the child of a tear / the offspring of honest sweat). He defiantly affirms, "Como quimera en el canto / de un Puerto Rico de ensueño / y yo soy puertorriqueño sin ná, pero sin quebranto" (like some dream in song is spoken / on an isle in dreams I've been / for I am Puerto Rican / without a thing, but unbroken). The poem's closing verses convey the notion that no matter where Puerto Ricans happen to be, they will still be Puerto Rican, even if born on the moon: "Y así, le grito al villano / yo sería borincano / aunque naciera en la luna" (And, so, I shout to knave's din / I'd still be Puerto Rican / even if born on the moon) (poem's translation by Márquez 2007, 211–212).

Thus, whether the selected chapter epigraph expresses Puerto Ricans' strong attachment to their roots or a nationalistic zeal for the liberation of their island, these verses are a testament to cultural survival for a colonized Puerto Rican nation dispersed and disembedded from their territorial homeland by the colonial migration experience. The symbolic affirmation of Boricuaness in Corretjer's poem and the notion of being Boricua "even if born on the moon" also find expression in a long-standing Puerto Rican idiom, *mancha de plátano* (literally, the stain of the plantain), signifying the characteristic indelible nature of Puerto Ricanness.

As indicated in previous chapters, manifestations of nationalistic or patriotic sentiments in Puerto Rico were long considered "subversive" and largely attributed to independence supporters or the island's intellectual elite. Although these attitudes have changed to a certain degree among more recent generations of Puerto Ricans, the two major political parties on the island and their respective administrations still treat independence advocates as a marginal minority. Island Puerto Ricans are less aware that Puerto Rican communities in the United States have proven fertile ground for this cultural nationalism to manifest itself in different forms of cultural expression produced by both the elite and popular sectors. Expressions of Puerto Rican pride and Puerto Rico's liberation were an integral part of the stateside Puerto Rican movement of the civil rights and ethnic revitalization era, and some of its effects unquestionably spilled over into younger generations on the island. Symbols of *la puertorriqueñidad* (Puerto Ricanness), such as the Puerto Rican flag (suppressed on the island for decades), were in the late 1960s and early 1970s commonly displayed on hats, T-shirts, pins, and protest signs and banners by activists and other members of the stateside communities, regardless of their particular political-status views. In contrast, in Puerto Rico, during the same period, display of a stand-alone Puerto Rican flag was immediately associated with Nationalists and independence advocates. This gradually began to change in the 1950s and 1960s, influenced by the Commonwealth-sponsored cultural endeavors under Operación Serenidad, and in later decades when Puerto Rico's flag became a marketable and commercialized commodity among all sectors of the island population and lost most of its previous "subversive" affiliation (Dávila 1997). Any of the hundreds of thousands who attend the annual Puerto Rican Day Parade in New York City, watch it on TV, or see it in video clips and color photos cannot miss the surrounding sea of handheld Puerto Rican flags waved by multitudes of Puerto Ricans of all ages lining the parade's Fifth Avenue route.

The same stand-alone Puerto Rican flag has been on full display in Puerto Rico in dealing with the two life-changing crises that have transformed the present and future of all Puerto Ricans. First, the appointment of the Junta de Supervisión Fiscal to oversee matters related to Puerto Rico's debt crisis gave rise to the "black Puerto Rican flag," the result of an action taken by a group named Artistas Solidarixs y en Resistencia (Artists in Solidarity and Resistance), which changed to black and white the colors of the Puerto Rican flag mural painted on the door of a famous abandoned building in Old San

Juan.[5] The artists aimed to capture "a flag in mourning" after the US Congress passed the Puerto Rico Oversight, Management, and Economic Stability Act (PROMESA) and appointed the Junta without consulting the citizens of Puerto Rico or their local government. The black flag soon became a galvanizing symbol of protest, resistance, and civil disobedience against the imposed Junta and debt-holder predators. In a second instance, the Puerto Rican flag—with its original colors, including the correct shade of *azul celeste* (sky blue or light blue), which serves as background to the triangle that holds a lone white star in its center—is currently being displayed all over the hurricane-ravaged island to indicate the survival spirit and resilience of island Puerto Ricans despite their current circumstances.

Depleted arguments about who is an "authentic" or "genuine" Puerto Rican or about an alleged "pseudoethnicity" of stateside Puerto Ricans fed into Puerto Rico's long-standing fears of Americanization (Seda Bonilla 1972, 1977).[6] They provoked interesting debates in the past but, in the long run, fell short in analyses of both the "expressive and instrumental" (Ogbu 1990) functions that made Puerto Ricans born or raised in the United States define their own ways of "being" Puerto Rican. In other words, rather than interrogating who is a "true" or "real" Puerto Rican, we should ask, What are the different meanings and manifestations of being Puerto Rican on the island and within the communities that constitute the stateside diaspora? What are the contextual historical, ethnic, racial, social, and cultural factors that shape different identity constructions of Puerto Ricanness within the US and island contexts, and what function does identity play for marginalized and disempowered populations, such as Puerto Ricans, in their relationship to a white-dominated US society where racism, xenophobia, gender oppression, and white supremacy continue to rear their ugly heads? And lastly, at a time when Latinos/as are the largest minority group and demographic projections show that, by the middle of this century, the United States will become a majority population of color, what are the differences, including generational ones, and similarities in the ways island and stateside Puerto Ricans negotiate, construct, and assert their respective and complex identities in relation to their multiple locations—Puerto Rico, US society, the dispersed stateside communities, and the panethnic US Latino/a population?

Another interesting question that comes up regarding the sense of Puerto Ricanness of the diaspora relates to whether consciousness of nationality or ethnicity and racial difference translates into specific political preferences or affiliations regarding Puerto Rico's colonial status. Unfortunately, there has not been enough research to make reliable generalizations about how stateside Puerto Ricans would vote on a referendum on the political future of Puerto Rico that included the choices of statehood, independence, or enhanced status as a self-governing commonwealth or associated republic, or whether island officials would allow them to vote in such referendum without first establishing residency on the island. But more importantly, for the time being, this particular issue does not appear to be a central concern or political priority for the stateside communities. While Puerto Rico's colonial condition often filters into the agendas of stateside Puerto Rican grassroots and professional organizations, political and social movements, and cultural expressions, many other pressing local, state, and national issues and priorities within these communities, as well as other national concerns, take precedence over resolving the issue of Puerto Rico's colonial status. In the current environment, after the measures imposed by the US government due to Puerto Rico's debt crisis and the halfhearted official response to the widespread destruction caused by Hurricane Maria, it is highly unlikely that statehood is a viable alternative or even the subject of meaningful discussion among members of the US legislative and executive branches in the foreseeable future.

Most recent signals indicate that Congress and the current administration increasingly view Puerto Rico as an economic burden to the United States and are not confident (somewhat justifiably) that the island government can be transparent and efficient in handling federal funds allocated to the island. But in the improbable event that these views prompt an unrequested decision to grant independence to the island, such an action would not alter the US citizenship status of Puerto Ricans already living in the United States or born in Puerto Rico up to that point in time.

In a special issue of *Centro Journal* (2017), several scholars addressed the history and interpretations of the US citizenship of island Puerto Ricans and the legal changes that have occurred since the passage of the century-old Jones-Shafroth Act by the US Congress. Through analysis of the legal stipulations of the act and subsequent modifications, Venator-Santiago (2017) establishes that "today, being born in Puerto Rico is tantamount to being born in the United States" (13), as it conveys as a birthright US citizenship granted by the Nationality Act of 1940. On the other hand, Juan R. Torruella, a US federal judge, reminds us that in constitutional and legal terms island Puerto Rican residents do not share the same protections afforded to stateside US citizens. In the preface to the same special issue, Centro Director Edwin Meléndez reframes discussions that link the permanence of the US citizenship of island Puerto Ricans to statehood by provocatively arguing, "If indeed, Puerto Ricans have birthright U.S. citizenship, then it follows that U.S. citizenship cannot be taken from island-born Puerto Ricans residing in Puerto Rico or their children by an act of Congress even if their children are born after a change of political status to other than statehood. In this view, Puerto Rican U.S. citizenship is *permanent and irreversible*" (5) (our emphasis).

Regardless of the perennial political status and US citizenship debates on the island, one reality remains unchanged: there is a strong consciousness of ethnicity among stateside Puerto Ricans. The claim to "being Puerto Rican" and use of their unequal, underprivileged status to support their political and civil rights demands to share in the opportunities and privileges afforded to other US citizens serve as a powerful cohesive force. Ethnic mobilization as a political course of action has yielded some positive results for Puerto Ricans in increasing their political power and representation in cities like New York, Orlando, and Hartford, Connecticut (see Cruz 1998, 2000, 2017). It also has the potential for improving most recent voting participation rates in US elections, which are far from as high as they should be. Compared with the consistent high rates of electoral participation of island Puerto Ricans (around 2 million voters) for many prior decades, for the first time only 1.3 million voters (55.1 percent of registered voters) turned out for the 2016 gubernatorial election. The noticeable electoral decline reflects the resentment of many voters toward political partisanship and the collective failure of past government administrations of the two major parties to deal with the unrestrained borrowing and accumulation of debt that led to the current fiscal insolvency and austerity measures. Meanwhile, the degree to which the electoral participation and political power of stateside Puerto Ricans will surge or wane in future years as the proportion of US-born Puerto Ricans continues to surpass the population of migrant newcomers, or whether migrant newcomers will become engaged in US politics, is hard to predict at this time. But these will undoubtedly continue to be issues of interest to researchers and policymakers.

Island Puerto Ricans are presently at a crucial crossroads, facing two of the most difficult predicaments and challenges in the nation's history: rising from the ashes of financial insolvency and hurricane mayhem, and the challenges of rebuilding their devastated homeland. It is imperative that they envision new alternatives for sustainable economic reconstruction and development that are not focused on the needs and priorities of the United States. This means formulating plans for economic recovery outside the exhausted export-led industrial model that is totally dependent on US investment priorities and the availability of low-wage labor, tax exemptions, and physical facilities for attracting US companies to Puerto Rico. Some officials and economic experts have suggested a federally funded massive reconstruction project along the lines of the post–World War II Marshall Plan (European Recovery Program)—a US initiative that was key to rebuilding the economies and infrastructures of western European nations confounded by the ravages of war. However, it is unlikely that the current US Congress and administration would support a plan of such magnitude for Puerto Rico. This opens up opportunities to "imagine a Puerto Rico recovery designed by Puerto Ricans" (Yeampierre and Klein 2017) and for a sustained discussion on the various alternatives for decolonizing the island (Medina-Fuentes 2017).

The uncertainty of what lies ahead for Puerto Rico in recovering from its debt crisis and declared bankruptcy and the humanitarian despair and devastating damage left behind by Hurricane Maria will continue for many years, perhaps decades. But the added posthurricane fatalities and trauma will be part of the island's historical memory, retold to subsequent generations, just as previous ones heard numerous stories about the overwhelming destruction and human misery left behind by the Category 5 Hurricane San Felipe (1928) and the Category 4 Hurricane San Ciriaco (1899).

Commuter migration between the island and the colonial metropolis, which became part of the normal course of life for the Puerto Rican people throughout the twentieth century, is now becoming an ominous population exodus that could eventually turn into a brain drain that would deprive the island of the human capital and creative drive needed for its rebuilding. Moreover, the New Millennium Migration is producing a critical decline in indispensable tax revenues needed to ensure the most basic government services, meet pension obligations, and protect the general welfare of the population.

Migration allowed Operation Bootstrap to carry out its industrial modernization project, but its boom effect lasted for only a couple of decades. Since the 1990s, with the significant population growth of the Puerto Rican diaspora and of the US Latino population, along with the slight increase of stateside Puerto Ricans and other Latinos/as in the US Congress and in the governments of a few major cities, island officials are increasingly receptive to engaging stateside Puerto Ricans in more substantive discussion of particular issues related to the island. Puerto Ricans from both sides are finding common ground and have come together around issues of mutual concern. The diaspora played a prominent role in supporting the struggle to end the US Navy's bombing-training exercises on the island municipality of Vieques in the late 1990s and early 2000s, which enhanced the visibility, media coverage, and public outcry that eventually compelled the US government to relinquish its military control over this territory (see Barreto 2002; Acosta 2002; Ayala and Bolívar 2011). Numerous stateside Puerto Rican activists joined island Puerto Ricans in the civil disobedience campaigns in Vieques that received both international attention and more than the usual level of coverage from the US media, which publicized the many years of live-ammunition target training that had affected the quality of life and health of residents.

Some prominent stateside Puerto Ricans from the political, labor, intellectual, artistic, and sport sectors, along with grassroots activists of all social and political affiliations, participated in rallies and protests demanding cessation of the bombing and the US Navy's total withdrawal from the small island. Along with many island Puerto Ricans, they were arrested, often enduring physical humiliation and mistreatment by the military or

local police.[7] The grassroots activism from various sectors within and outside Puerto Rico and the combined efforts of Puerto Ricans and Latinos/as
serving in Congress all contributed to the navy's final withdrawal from
Vieques in 2003. Hence, "El Grito de Vieques" (The cry of Vieques; Acosta
2002) represents one of the longest and most sustained civil disobedience
campaigns in Puerto Rico's history and remains one of the best contemporary and most successful examples of the island and the diaspora coming
together in a common cause.

However, no cause in recent times has required critical intervention
and support from stateside Puerto Ricans like the current debt and hurricane crises, which, like the Vieques solidarity movement, are engaging the
support of all sectors of Puerto Rican society and the communities of the
diaspora. In general, unity stemming from single-issue movements tends
to wane after their main objectives are accomplished. This happened after
the US Navy's withdrawal from Vieques, despite the persistence of some
unresolved issues—notably the environmental cleanup of several areas of
the island heavily affected by decades of bombing and the high incidence
of cancer and other health problems among the population, linked to the
depleted-uranium ammunition used in the live-fire training exercises (Lugo-
Lugo 2011–2012).

The conflict over the US Navy's control of Vieques and its explicit disregard for the detrimental effects of the bombing on the environment and
the population's health made Puerto Ricans from all political sectors more
aware of the limitations of the current Commonwealth and their insular
government's constrained ability to make decisions to protect Puerto Rico's
territory and people. It had been a long time since Puerto Ricans felt so
explicitly targeted by the power and arrogance of the US government and
its military establishment. For many decades the majority of the island's
population had perceived the United States as a generous ally and valued
their US citizenship. But, in many ways, Vieques made clear that Puerto
Ricans were still no more than colonial subjects, and the human costs and
consequences of their lack of national sovereignty have been exposed and
ingrained in the Puerto Rican historical memory and public consciousness.

For stateside Puerto Ricans, their racialization and disenfranchisement in US society are major factors in the articulation of politicized and
often contested assertions of individual, collective, and panethnic identities—ranging from being Puerto Rican or Boricua, to being Nuyorican,
Chicagorican, Orlandorican, Diasporican, or any other term related to geographical location, to being part of a broader population of Latinos/as.
Claims to Puerto Ricanness provide members of the diaspora a shared
sense of identity and heritage, of who they are and where they come from,
empowering them to seek recognition and legitimacy and to struggle more
effectively against the forces of racism and inequality that they collectively

face. These counterhegemonic discourses are expressions of resistance to racialized ideologies that for centuries have eroded the self-esteem and dignity of populations of color and limit their access to the social and political power structures.

Although increased global migration is forcing the dominant industrialized countries, such as the United States, to come to grips with issues of diversity, inclusion, and tolerance, the expanding presence of immigrants and migrants also fuels anti-immigration backlash against Latinos/as and other groups of color from certain sectors of the white population that feel threatened by the country's changing demographics. The US Census has projected that by 2050 populations of color will represent over 50 percent of the total US population. The conservative takeover of the US political establishment that began in the 1980s is at a boiling point under the Trump administration, in which unhinged nativism and white supremacy seem intent on reversing some of the most meaningful liberal reforms of the 1960s and 1970s. These include voting rights, affirmative action, and safety net employment benefits and social programs. Additionally, some of the policies and actions of the current administration are an affront to civil liberties and threaten the health, financial, and environmental protections and well-being of the great majority of US citizens.

Puerto Rico cannot help but connect its lack of self-determination to the conditions that led it to become an island "adrift in debt" (Brown, Chan, Bates, and Huang 2017), engulfed in another mass migration cycle of undetermined magnitude and consequences. Almost three-quarters of a century ago, noted Puerto Rican intellectual Antonio S. Pedreira also used the pessimistic metaphor of a *barco a la deriva* (ship adrift) in his 1934 book *Insularismo* (Insularity) to describe the island and its people. He and other members of the Generation of the 1930s were trying to define their own Puerto Rican identity after more than three decades of the US colonial regime under the mantra of *¿Qué somos? ¿Cómo somos? ¿Y a dónde vamos?* (Who are we? What are we? Where are we going?). Since then subsequent generations of island and stateside Puerto Rican scholars and other sectors of these populations have come a long way in debunking Pedreira's insular vision (Flores 1979; J. A. Silén 1970, 1971) and reaching a better understanding of their mutual histories and the intricate nature and consequences of their colonial condition. One of the most obvious outcomes is migration.

A few decades ago, a prominent Puerto Rican demographer weighed in on the real implications of migration for the island: "An economy which depends on its ability to get rid of its excess population by means of migration cannot be expected to have great stability and finds itself on a very unsound base" (Vázquez Calzada 1979, 235). While we agree with his conclusion, we should add that both the island and US governments have a long record of complicity in viewing and relying on migration as an expedient means to avoid tackling some of the complex and contentious aspects of their unequal relationship.

It is now eminently apparent that the modern transformations introduced by Operation Bootstrap, celebrated by island and US officials and most Puerto Ricans at the time, revealed their shaky foundations in subsequent decades. The project showcased Puerto Rico as a model of industrial development, modernization, and democracy but also generated what was, until recent years, the largest population exodus in the island's history. Those of us who are the offspring of the Operation Bootstrap generation and experienced the transformation of Puerto Rico into an industrial modern society are now witnessing severe setbacks in its infrastructural progress and social gains caused by Hurricane Maria's destructive mayhem. Hazy memories of a "stricken land" and the wretched human landscape of the 1930s and 1940s are resurfacing. As then, Puerto Rico is now a nation in which the gap between the poor and the wealthy could not be more marked. Prior to the hurricane, almost half of the Puerto Rican population lived in poverty as defined by US standards. We cannot yet predict how high that rate will become in posthurricane years. We can say that the hurricane's fiercely destructive flooding, howling winds, and deadly mudslides affected the island's most vulnerable citizens—those living in humble wooden houses in the mountainous countryside, smaller municipalities, or the shantytowns of San Juan and elsewhere; a mass of workers subsisting on meager minimum wages or making a living through the informal economy, often relying on federally funded social programs to get *los cupones* (food stamps), housing subsidies, and health services to supplement their incomes. An overtaxed middle class, already strapped by government austerity measures, is facing the loss of productivity during the anticipated prolonged recovery; they lost their wages when schools, restaurants, other workplaces, and numerous small businesses closed or were destroyed. Many are defaulting on the mortgages of their destroyed or abandoned homes.

Most experts agree that in the early 1970s, all economic indicators began to expose the unstable foundation and volatility of Puerto Rico's capitalist economy, tarnishing the showcase image of earlier decades (Rivera-Batiz and Santiago 1996, 3). In 1996, Rivera-Batiz and Santiago pointed out the paradoxical nature of Puerto Rico's economic development vis-à-vis its fraught relationship with the United States. They referred to the many different constraints facing island government officials and policymakers, stemming from a combination of global factors, the federal government, and Puerto Rico's integration into the US economy. Most scholars agree with their view that one of the most obvious and persistent problems is that US needs and priorities are often at odds or work at cross-purposes with those of Puerto Rico. In assessing the general failures of Operation Bootstrap, Rivera-Batiz and Santiago (1996) concluded,

There is little question that the Puerto Rican government was an effective agent of economic change in Puerto Rico during the early years of Operation Bootstrap. The political consensus and social contract that allowed Operation Bootstrap to proceed were not without their costs and are unlikely to be repeated. And it might be argued that *it was the massive emigration of Puerto Ricans to the United States during the 1950s, more than any governmental policy, that allowed the increased standard of living on the island.* (163; emphasis added)

The correlation between Puerto Rico's colonial condition, the continuing commuter migration of Puerto Ricans, and their nomadic dispersion throughout the United States underscores the transnational and fluid nature of their migration trends and patterns. Moreover, it demonstrates the need for researchers to continue analyzing the many socioeconomic, political, and cultural implications and ramifications of the bidirectional exchanges between the two populations.

Fundamental paradigm shifts have taken place in Puerto Rican migration studies. First, scholars are more critical of interpretations of the migrant experience that portrayed working-class migrants as aimless, impoverished, or marginalized masses and denied agency to a people struggling to make a living in a foreign and often inhospitable environment. Confronting labor exploitation, class, ethnic, racial, and gender inequalities, and disempowering practices deeply ingrained in US society, and undergoing the adaptation process faced by most uprooted migrants, Puerto Ricans have striven to improve their individual status and that of their communities, hoping to build a more prosperous life in the United States.

Second, due to substantial changes in the socioeconomic status of stateside Puerto Rican in recent decades, their futures are neither engulfed in the uncertainty that characterized the 1970s nor entirely optimistic. Geographic dispersion across the United States to new and old destinations and higher rates of educational attainment are proving key factors in improving the overall status of the stateside communities. Some obvious problems still persist, but progress, measured in terms of socioeconomic indicators and social mobility, has been evident since the 1980s. Puerto Ricans are moving out of New York, and the city is no longer the place where the majority of them reside. Although most Puerto Ricans still reside in the Northeast and Midwest (New York, New Jersey, Connecticut, Pennsylvania, Massachusetts, and Illinois), growing communities are now found in Florida, Texas, and California.

Third, there are many differences in the socioeconomic conditions of Puerto Ricans and in the histories of their various stateside communities. Some of these communities are long established; others are relatively new. Some, largely those in the Northeast, still face serious problems of poverty and unemployment; other, more thriving communities are found in the southern and western regions of the United States. Additional differences in the overall status of Puerto Rican migrants relate to their educational and English-language skills and how long they have lived in the United States (see Santiago-Rivera and Santiago 1999). This is an important consideration, given the rapid pace of the New Millennium Migration and the large number of island-born Puerto Ricans coming to the United States.

Documenting the specific formations and evolution of the various stateside Puerto Rican communities calls for the meticulous hard work and insights of researchers from many fields. More meaningful comparative research is needed to enhance our understanding of the vast array of factors that account for differences and similarities among Puerto Ricans in their diverse geographic locations and contribute to a more nuanced portrait of their multifaceted and more complex migration experiences. Additional research is also needed about the actual commuter patterns of Puerto Ricans and about the different material reasons and personal motivations that account for this back-and-forth movement (Aranda 2006). After all, a significant portion of the diaspora is permanently settled in the United States, and considerable generational differences in their ties to Puerto Rico are to be expected.

Regardless of the above-mentioned differences, at the core of the Puerto Rican experience in the United States is a strong affirmation of cultural identity and a fervent sense of affiliation with Puerto Rico. To a lesser degree, there is also a panethnic identification with the shared experiences and struggles of other US Latinos/as. This latter identification is becoming increasingly important, since they are now the largest US population of color, and the census projects that their total population will continue growing in future decades, albeit at a slower pace than in the last three.

Literature, music, and the arts reflect the vitality of Puerto Rican cultural expressions. They are finding receptive audiences beyond the confines of the community and receiving growing recognition within the wider US society. Now that most of the old stereotypes and misconceptions of the past have been debunked, Puerto Rican scholars, activists, and other members of the community continue to labor tirelessly to improve the socioeconomic and political status of their compatriots. The invisibility and marginality of the past are gradually waning, and new generations of Puerto Ricans are growing up in the United States with more opportunities to learn about their heritage and develop a consciousness of the issues and obstacles impeding their socioeconomic and political progress.

The emotional, functional, and contextual dimensions behind the constructions of ethnic identities involve both agency and choice by the individuals and groups who define and negotiate these identities. In "Ode to the Diasporican" (2002), poet María Teresa "Mariposa" Fernández refers to being Boricua as a "state of mind," a "state of heart," and a "state of soul"—attributes shared by most Puerto Ricans everywhere—articulating the passionate ways in which many writers and artists of the diaspora define their Puerto

Ricanness. Thus, what it means to be Puerto Rican might have different meanings and expressions within the communities of the diaspora as compared to the island, but understanding these differences has the potential to bring all Puerto Ricans closer together in envisioning a path to decolonization, as well as in defining and advancing their respective social and political agendas and their claims for equal treatment and recognition of their productive labor in a US nation founded on the principles of equality and freedom.

Notes

1. The Amerindian Pueblo tribes in New Mexico were also Hispanicized to a certain degree when there was racial mixing with Spaniards, most notably after Santa Fe was founded (1610). At that time this territory was still part of the Viceroyalty of New Spain; it later became part of an independent Mexico in 1810 and was ultimately ceded to the United States in 1848.

2. If Puerto Rico becomes the fifty-first state of the Union, it will have two senators like other states in the US Congress and, depending on its population density, a few members in the House of Representatives. In 2017, Congress had five stateside Puerto Rican members (from New York, Chicago, Orlando, and Idaho). See Ryan Struyk, "Here Is What Would Happen to US Politics if Puerto Rico Became a State," *CNN Politics*, October 14, 2017, http://www.cnn.com/2017/10/14/politics/puerto-rico -state-congress-white-house/index.html.

3. Many status plebiscites and repeated attempts by different pro-Commonwealth and pro-statehood governors to persuade the US Congress to support reforms aimed at making Puerto Rico a more autonomous entity or a state never translated into responses for altering the status quo. For a detailed account of the long history of political status referenda or plebiscite bills introduced in the US Congress since the 1960s, see Juan Manuel García Passalacqua and Carlos Rivera Lugo, *Puerto Rico y los Estados Unidos: El proceso de consulta y negociación de 1989 y 1990*, 2 vols. (Río Piedras, PR: Editorial Universitaria, 1990, 1991); Marco Antonio Rigau and Juan Manuel García Passalacqua, *República asociada o libre asociación: Documentación de un debate* (San Juan: Editorial Atlántico, 1987); Carmen Gautier Mayoral, ed., *Poder y plebiscito: Puerto Rico en 1991* (Río Piedras, PR: Centro de Investigaciones Sociales, University of Puerto Rico, 1990). Also see the Elecciones en Puerto Rico/Elections in Puerto Rico website (http://electionspuertorico.org).

4. As indicated in Chapter 8, Corretjer had his own diasporic experiences in the United States. He and his nationalist comrades Pedro Albizu Campos and Clemente Soto Vélez spent five years as political prisoners in federal penal institutions. Not allowed to return to Puerto Rico after their release, they all settled in New York City. Corretjer lived there from 1942 to 1946, when he was able to return to the island. His newspaper *Pueblos hispanos* brings to light aspects of the lives and experiences of uprooted Puerto Ricans in New York City during the early years of the Great Migration.

5. The door flag mural is surrounded by several lithographic images of prominent Puerto Rican artists done by members of the collective Grabadores por Grabadores (Engravers by Engravers), creators of the original painting.

6. Debates about whether or not US Puerto Ricans should be considered "authentic" Puerto Ricans, especially if they did not speak Spanish, were partly fueled by the Hispanophilic tendencies of many island-based intellectuals critical of

the Americanization of Puerto Rico and fearful that stateside Puerto Ricans would only accelerate this process. Ironically, since the 1970s, Puerto Rican cultural nationalism has grown stronger both on the island and in the United States and is expressed more overtly than in earlier decades.

7. Among those arrested in civil disobedience demonstrations at the military training ground in Vieques were Puerto Rican members of Congress Luis Gutiérrez and Nydia Velázquez, New York State assemblyman Roberto Ramírez, African American community leader Reverend Al Sharpton, and environmental lawyer Robert F. Kennedy Jr. Several island political leaders and legislators were also arrested. In Washington, DC, Congressman José Serrano was arrested at a demonstration in front of the White House. US Puerto Rican performer, TV show host, and community activist Rosie Pérez was among those arrested in 2000 at a demonstration in front of the United Nations in support of the US Navy's withdrawal from Vieques.

Brief Chronology of
Puerto Rican History

ca. 2000 BC   Aboriginal groups from South America settle in the Antilles.

AD 1000   Taino indigenous culture develops in Puerto Rico.

1493   On November 19, during his second voyage to the New World, Christopher Columbus arrives at the island, which its indigenous Taino inhabitants call Boriquén. He renames it the Isla de San Juan Bautista.

1508   Spanish colonization begins under the command of Juan Ponce de León, appointed governor the following year. He establishes the first settlement, the Villa de Caparra. The administrative center is moved a year later near the island's largest port, given the name of Puerto Rico (meaning "rich port" in English). The names of the colony and its port are interchanged in subsequent years, with the island known as Puerto Rico and its port and capital as San Juan.

1510   The first sizeable shipment of enslaved West Africans is brought to Puerto Rico by the Spanish colonizers.

1511–1513   Major Taino rebellions against the Spaniards occur.

1521   A second settlement, the Villa de Sotomayor, is established in San Germán on the western part of the island to expand colonization.

1570   Construction begins of San Felipe del Morro, the island's largest fort, located at the entrance of San Juan Bay.

1586	The viceroyalty of Spain, located in Mexico City, provides what is known as the *situado mexicano* (Mexican budget subsidy) to support the island's colonial administration after extraction of its limited gold resources.
1595	The island is subject to an unsuccessful attack by the British under the command of Sir Francis Drake and his cousin Admiral John Hawkins.
1598	A second British attack takes place under the command of George Clifford, Earl of Cumberland. The British take over the city of San Juan and after a two-month siege are forced to leave due to the outbreak of a dysentery epidemic.
1625	A Dutch fleet, under the command of Balduino Enrico, attacks San Juan. The Dutch take the city but are forced to withdraw by Spanish troops. They pillage and burn the city before leaving.
1634–1638	San Juan, the administrative center of the colony, becomes a fortified walled city.
Mid-1600s	Puerto Rico, basically isolated from the European mercantilist trade circuit with the New World, relies on a contraband trade network largely controlled by the Dutch and by independent *corsarios* and buccaneers—privateers with access to vessels and suppliers of goods. This smuggling circuit lasts for over a century.
1765	The accession of the Bourbon dynasty to the Spanish Crown in 1759 brings modern reforms to the empire. Field Marshall Alejandro O'Reilly is sent to the island to assess its prospects for economic growth and starts a period of economic and administrative reforms aimed at making Puerto Rico a more profitable colony. The Spanish colonial government begins to promote immigration to the island through land grants and to end contraband trade. An expanding agricultural economy based on sugar and, to a lesser extent, coffee production also increases the traffic of enslaved Africans to the island.
1797	A British attack under the command of General Ralph Abercromby keeps the city of San Juan under siege for ten weeks, until Spanish troops and island creoles defeat the invaders.
1810	Ramón Power y Giralt becomes the first Puerto Rican delegate to represent the island in the Spanish Cortes.
1812	The Cortes de Cádiz in Spain approves the first Spanish constitution, and some liberal reforms are introduced in Puerto Rico for a brief period.

1815	Spain grants Puerto Rico the Real Cédula de Gracias (Royal Decree of Concessions), which introduces reforms to foster socioeconomic development, the opening of trade, immigration from other European countries, and some civil liberties.
1821–1848	Numerous rebellions of Puerto Rico's enslaved Africans take place, one of the largest in 1841.
1823	Spanish colonial officials on the island return to a policy of suppressing freedom of expression and the press in order to crush the independence sentiment that accounts for Spain's loss of most of its empire in the Americas. By the 1830s, Cuba, Puerto Rico, and the Dominican Republic are Spain's only colonies in the hemisphere.
1849	The *libretas de jornaleros* (workers' journals) system requiring certification of mandatory labor for agricultural workers is introduced.
1865	Antillean expatriates establish the Sociedad Republicana de Cuba y Puerto Rico in New York.
1867	Ramón Emeterio Betances and others found the Comité Revolucionario de Puerto Rico in New York City. This same year Betances releases his proclamation "Diez Mandamientos de los Hombres Libres" (Ten commandments of free men).
1868	On September 23, creoles proclaiming Puerto Rico's independence from Spain lead an armed revolt in the mountain town of Lares. This event is known as the Grito de Lares (Lares Revolt).
1869	A more liberal Spanish constitution brings reforms to Puerto Rico that allow creoles to create their own political parties and be represented in Spain.
	Eugenio María de Hostos arrives in New York City from Spain. He joins other Antillean separatists and becomes editor of the Spanish-language newspaper *La revolución*.
1870	The first political parties in Puerto Rico under the Spanish colonial regime are founded.
1873	With the birth of the First Republic in Spain, the enslavement of Africans and the *libreta de jornaleros* system are abolished in Puerto Rico.
1887	Román Baldorioty de Castro founds the Partido Autonomista Puertorriqueño to persuade Spain to grant self-government to Puerto Rico.

	The Spanish colonial governor implements the Componte regime—oppressive measures meant to discourage or punish autonomy or independence advocates on the island.
1889	Typographer Sotero Figueroa leaves the island for New York, where he joins the Antillean separatist movement and starts a printing press.
1891	Arturo Alfonso Schomburg and poet and journalist Francisco Gonzalo "Pachín" Marín arrive in New York and join the Antillean separatist movement. Marín revives his newspaper, *El postillón* (The courier), a year later to advocate for Antillean revolution against Spanish colonial rule.
1892	Cuban patriot José Martí founds the Partido Revolucionario Cubano in New York.
	The Club Borinquen, a separatist group of Puerto Rican male expatriates, the Club Las Dos Antillas for Puerto Rican and Cuban men, and the women's separatist group Club Mercedes Varona are founded in New York City.
	Separatist poet Lola Rodríguez de Tió and her journalist husband, Bonocio Tió, arrive in New York City, and she becomes a founding member of Club Mercedes Varona.
1895	José Martí leaves New York to join the rebels fighting the Spanish colonial government in Cuba and is killed in a skirmish with Spanish troops.
	The Sección de Puerto Rico of the Partido Revolucionario Cubano is founded in New York.
1897	Spain grants Puerto Rico a charter of autonomy.
	The women's separatist Club Hermanas de Rius Rivera is founded in New York by Lola Rodríguez de Tió, Inocencia Martínez (Sotero Figueroa's wife), and other women; members begin collecting medicines, clothing, and other donations to send to the rebel soldiers fighting in the Spanish-Cuban War.
1898	The February 21 explosion of the US naval vessel *Maine* at the Port of Havana leads to a declaration of war against Spain by the United States on April 21 and the invasion of Puerto Rico on July 25. The conflict is known as the Spanish-American War, Spanish-Cuban-American War, or the War of 1898.
	Sección members Julio J. Henna and Roberto H. Todd support the annexation of the island and assist the US government with its invasion plans.

The short-lived autonomist government headed by creole political leaders is disbanded, and Puerto Rico remains under US military rule.

1899 The Treaty of Paris, putting an end to the Spanish-Cuban-American War, is signed. Spain cedes the territories of Puerto Rico, the Philippines, and the Ladrones Islands (Guam) to the United States. Cuba is promised its independence but remains under US military rule until granted independence in 1902.

The Federación Libre de los Trabajadores is founded in Puerto Rico.

Hurricane San Ciriaco destroys the island's agriculture, including the coffee haciendas of the island's propertied class. It also brings devastation and numerous deaths to the peasant majority population of the island.

1900 The US Congress passes the Foraker Act to end military rule and implement a civil government in Puerto Rico, to be headed by a US-appointed governor and Executive Council.

Two new political parties, the Partido Federal (Federal Party) and the Partido Republicano (Republican Party), are founded in Puerto Rico.

1901 The US colonial government promotes migration of Puerto Rican agricultural contract workers to Hawaii.

1904 The Partido Unión Puertorriqueña (Unionistas), the party of the island's creole propertied class, is founded.

1912 The Club Puertorriqueño de San Francisco is established.

Feminist labor organizer and writer Luisa Capetillo travels to New York City and on to Tampa, Florida, in 1913 to organize tobacco workers.

1915 The Partido Socialista (Socialist Party), the political arm of the Federación Libre de los Trabajadores, is founded in Puerto Rico.

1916 *Tabaquero* (cigar roller) Bernardo Vega migrates to New York City.

1917 The US Congress passes the Jones-Shafroth Act, granting US citizenship to all Puerto Ricans born on the island.

Joaquín Colón López migrates from his hometown of Cayey to New York City.

1918   Jesús Colón, Joaquín's younger brother, migrates to New York City as a stowaway on a steamship. Along with many other Puerto Rican migrants to the city during those early years, he settles in the Navy Yard area of Brooklyn.

1920   The Jones Act, or Merchant Marine Act, known in Spanish as the *leyes de cabotaje*, restricts shipping trade to and from Puerto Rico to only US vessels and merchant marine workers.

1920   Puerto Ricans begin to settle in New York's East Harlem in large numbers. The neighborhood becomes known as Spanish Harlem or El Barrio.

1922   The Partido Nacionalista Puertorriqueño (Puerto Rican Nationalist Party) is founded in Puerto Rico.

             Bernardo Vega, Jesús Colón, Luis Muñoz Marín, and others found the Alianza Obrera (Workers' Alliance) in New York City to encourage workers to unionize.

             The founding of the Club Caborrojeño in the city marks the beginning of the hometown clubs established by migrants from different towns in Puerto Rico to promote social and cultural interactions and community networks.

1923   The Hermandad Puertorriqueña en América (Porto Rican Brotherhood of America) is founded in New York City to foster mutual aid and unity within the community.

1925   El Ateneo Obrero (Workers' Athenaeum) is established to give voice to the concerns of Puerto Ricans in New York City. Bernardo Vega and Jesús Colón are among its founding members.

1926   Riots break out in Harlem between old residents and newcomers to the neighborhood. Resentment over the growth of Puerto Rican– and Latino-owned businesses in a neighborhood at the time dominated by Jewish and Italian merchants contributes to the violence.

1927   Puerto Rican professionals found the Liga Puertorriqueña e Hispana (Puerto Rican and Hispanic League) in New York City to deal with community tensions and foster unity.

1928   Hurricane San Felipe, one of the strongest storms of the twentieth century, brings destruction to Puerto Rico. Its broad impact causes numerous deaths and devastates the agricultural economy, ruining local coffee and sugar cane planters.

1929   The Great Depression aggravates the island's dire conditions of poverty and unemployment.

| 1930 | Pedro Albizu Campos takes over the leadership of the Nationalist Party in Puerto Rico. |

| 1932 | The Coalición, a joining of forces of the workers' Socialist Party and the Republican Union Party, wins the legislative elections. Its support for statehood for Puerto Rico is counterbalanced by the increased activism of the Nationalist Party. |

| 1934 | New Deal policies are extended to the island; the Puerto Rico Reconstruction Administration and a younger generation of progressive politicians begin to make inroads in promoting socioeconomic reforms for a destitute and neglected US colonial territory. |
| | Puerto Rican policemen kill four Nationalist students in what is known as the Masacre de Río Piedras. |

| 1936 | Two Nationalists assassinate Colonel Francis Riggs, Puerto Rico's North American chief of police. Albizu Campos is arrested and sent to jail for conspiring to overthrow the US government in Puerto Rico. |
| | In New York, the Hispanic Section of the International Workers' Order (Sociedad Cervantes) is established under the leadership of Jesús Colón. |

| 1937 | Violence erupts when the police interfere with a Nationalist rally in the southern city of Ponce. Nineteen people, mostly Nationalists, die in the incident, known as the Masacre de Ponce. |
| | Lawyer Oscar Rivera García becomes the first Puerto Rican elected to the New York State Assembly. |

| 1938 | Luis Muñoz Marín founds the Partido Popular Democrático (PPD, Popular Democratic Party). |

| 1940 | The PPD wins enough votes to make Luis Muñoz Marín head of Puerto Rico's Senate. |
| | Puerto Rican poet Julia de Burgos arrives in New York. |

| 1941 | Rexford G. Tugwell, a member of President Franklin D. Roosevelt's liberal brain trust, is appointed to Puerto Rico's governorship. He becomes a supporter of the PPD's agenda to develop a plan for socioeconomic and political reforms for the island. |

| 1946 | President Harry S. Truman appoints Jesús T. Piñeiro as the island's first Puerto Rican governor since the beginning of the US occupation. |

1947   The landmark decision in *Méndez v. Westminster* makes seg-
             regation of Mexican children illegal in California schools.
             Among the case's plaintiffs are Gonzalo and Felicitas Méndez,
             a Mexican–Puerto Rican couple. The case becomes an impor-
             tant legal precedent for the *Brown v. Board of Education*
             (1954) decision banning school segregation in the United
             States.

1948   Luis Muñoz Marín becomes the first elected governor of
             Puerto Rico.

             The Migration Division is established with offices in San
             Juan and New York City to manage the Great Migration. It
             expanded to other US cities in later years.

1950   What becomes known as the Nationalist Revolt begins in the
             town of Jayuya and extends to other parts of the island.
             Nationalists perpetrate attacks on La Fortaleza, Governor
             Muñoz Marín's official residence, and on Blair House, in
             Washington, DC, temporary residence of President Harry S.
             Truman. Albizu Campos is arrested and sent back to prison.

1952   The constitution of the Estado Libre Asociado de Puerto
             Rico, or Commonwealth of Puerto Rico, is inaugurated.

1954   In Washington, DC, four Puerto Rican Nationalists enter the
             House of Representatives and open fire, wounding five mem-
             bers of the US Congress.

1956   Community leader Gilberto Gerena Valentín organizes the
             Congreso de los Pueblos (Council of Hometown Clubs). In
             later years, the Congreso plays a key role in initiating New
             York's annual Puerto Rican Day Parade.

1959   The first *Desfile Puertorriqueño* in New York marks the begin-
             ning of the Puerto Rican Day Parade tradition.

1961   Under the leadership of Antonia Pantoja, ASPIRA is founded
             in New York to promote the education of Puerto Rican youth.

1962   The Council of Spanish-Speaking Organizations, better known
             as the Concilio, is founded in Philadelphia and initiates the
             Puerto Rican Festival celebration two years later.

1963   An organized group of Puerto Rican activists participates in
             Martin Luther King Jr.'s historic March on Washington.

             The Council of Puerto Rican and Latino Community Organ-
             izations of the Lower East Side organizes the March for a
             Better Education to New York City Hall.

1965	Evelina López Antonetty founds United Bronx Parents, Inc., in the South Bronx to fight for community control of public schools and a more effective education.
1966	Division Street Riots in Chicago.
1967	The US Congress authorizes a political status plebiscite in Puerto Rico that gives an overwhelming victory to Commonwealth supporters.
1968	The PPD loses Puerto Rico's governorship after being in power for twenty years. Luis A. Ferré, an industrialist and a leader of the Partido Estadista Republicano (PER, Pro-Statehood Republican Party), who after having left the PER founded the Partido Nuevo Progresista (PNP, New Progressive Party) in 1967, becomes the first pro-statehood governor of Puerto Rico.

Inquilinos Boricuas en Acción (IBA) emerges in Boston to organize the South End Puerto Rican community against urban renewal displacement.

1969	The Young Lords, a Chicago street gang, turns into the Young Lords Organization to encourage grassroots civil rights and social justice activism among Puerto Ricans and other communities of color. A group of Puerto Rican students starts a New York chapter of the Young Lords and later becomes the Young Lords Party (1970).

Students at City College, CUNY, take over the institution to demand open admissions, the establishment of Puerto Rican studies, and other educational opportunities.

Taller Boricua is established in New York to promote the arts within the community and as a workshop for visiting artists to practice their craft.

1970	Herman Badillo becomes the first stateside Puerto Rican elected to the US House of Representatives.

The Museo del Barrio is established in East Harlem by a group of Puerto Rican artists.

1972	A group of Puerto Rican lawyers founds the Puerto Rican Legal Defense and Education Fund in New York.

The Nuyorican Poets Cafe opens on the Lower East Side.

PPD candidate Rafael Hernández Colón wins the governorship of Puerto Rico.

1973	Frank Bonilla establishes the Centro de Estudios Puertorriqueños at the City University of New York. One of the Centro's main activities is the creation of a library and archives to house documents about the migration experience.
1974	Taller Puertorriqueño is established in Philadelphia to promote the arts and Puerto Rican and Latino/a cultures in the region and to connect with other communities.
	Boricua College is established in New York.
1976	Villa Victoria, an IBA housing project, is completed in Boston.
	PNP candidate Carlos Romero Barceló wins the governorship of Puerto Rico.
1977	The National Puerto Rican Coalition emerges in Washington, DC.
	Humboldt Park Riots in Chicago.
1978	Robert García is elected to the US House of Representatives and serves until his resignation in 1990.
1980	Carlos Romero Barceló wins reelection by just a few thousand votes. It takes months before the election is finally certified.
1981	The National Congress for Puerto Rican Rights is established in the South Bronx.
1982	Angelo Falcón founds the Institute for Puerto Rican Policy in New York City.
1984	PPD candidate Rafael Hernández Colón returns to the governor's post.
1985	The Puerto Rican Action Committee of Connecticut in Hartford begins to play a major role in the political mobilization of the community.
1987	The Boricua Gay and Lesbian Forum is founded in New York City.
1988	Hernández Colón is reelected.
1989	The Department of Puerto Rican Community Affairs is founded in New York to replace the Migration Division.
1990	José Serrano from New York City is elected to the US House of Representatives.
1992	Luis Gutiérrez from Chicago and Nydia Velázquez from New York City are elected to the US House of Representatives. Velázquez is the first Puerto Rican woman elected to serve in Congress.

The Puerto Rican Studies Association is founded as a professional organization promoting research, teaching, and activism.

PNP candidate Pedro Roselló is elected governor of Puerto Rico.

1993 In his efforts to promote statehood for Puerto Rico, Governor Roselló holds a nonbinding political status referendum won by Commonwealth supporters.

1995 The Humboldt Park–Division Street Puerto Rican neighborhood in Chicago is officially named Paseo Boricua.

1996 Roselló is reelected to the governorship.

1999 Security guard David Sanes Rodríguez is killed by a stray bomb during air target practices at the US Navy base on the island of Vieques. This is the beginning of a movement to bring peace to the citizens of Vieques and force the navy to cease the bombings and leave the island.

2000 The Puerto Rican Heritage Society in Hawaii celebrates the centennial of the arrival of Puerto Rican contract workers and their families in Maui.

The Institute of Puerto Rican Arts and Culture is founded in Chicago's Humboldt Park and becomes the National Museum of Puerto Rican Arts and Culture in 2016.

The PPD candidate for Puerto Rico's governorship, Sila Calderón, becomes the first woman elected to the post.

2003 The US Navy withdraws from Vieques.

2004 The PPD candidate for the governorship, Aníbal Acevedo Vilá, formerly Puerto Rico's resident commissioner at the US Congress, is elected governor.

2008 PNP candidate Luis Fortuño is elected governor after representing the island as resident commissioner.

2012 PPD candidate Alejandro García Padilla is elected governor.

Carmen Yulín Cruz is elected mayor of San Juan, defeating the previous PNP incumbent, who occupied the position for twelve years.

2016 Puerto Rico defaults on its debt payments.

The US Congress passes the PROMESA Act, establishing the Junta de Supervisión Fiscal (Financial Oversight and Management Board) to oversee the process of restructuring Puerto Rico's debt and making debt payments to investors.

Darren Soto is elected to the US House of Representative to represent the Orlando-Kissimmee district in central Florida, where there is a large concentration of Puerto Rican residents.

2017   In early March, the Junta appoints Ukraine's former minister of finance, Natalie Jaresko, as executive director.

Barred from using traditional Chapter 9 bankruptcy protections, Puerto Rico declares a form of limited bankruptcy allowed under Title III of PROMESA on May 3.

On May 5, US Supreme Court chief justice John Roberts appoints Manhattan's US District Court judge Laura Taylor Swain to make any rulings related to Puerto Rico's bankruptcy case.

On September 6, Hurricane Irma, a powerful Category 5 storm, barely misses going over Puerto Rico, although it causes some flooding and loss of electric power in some areas.

On September 20, Hurricane Maria, a powerful Category 4 storm, makes landfall on the southwest coast of Puerto Rico and exits on the northwest coast. The strongest hurricane to hit the island in over a century, it causes unprecedented destruction, a prolonged island blackout, and precipitates high levels of mass migration to the United States.

Acronyms

ACS	American Community Survey
AFL	American Federation of Labor
CEREP	Centro de Estudios de la Realidad Puertorriqueña (Center for the Study of Puerto Rican Reality)
CPS	Current Population Survey
CUNY	City University of New York
DACA	Deferred Action for Childhood Arrivals
DIVEDCO	División de Educación de la Comunidad (Division of Community Education)
ELA	Estado Libre Asociado (Commonwealth of Puerto Rico)
FALN	Fuerzas Armadas de Liberación Nacional (Armed Forces for National Liberation)
FEMA	Federal Emergency Management Agency
FLT	Federación Libre de los Trabajadores de Puerto Rico (Free Federation of Puerto Rico's Workers)
HUAC	House Un-American Activities Committee
HYAA	Hispanic Young Adult Association
IBA	Inquilinos Boricuas en Acción (Boricua Tenants in Action)
ICP	Instituto de Cultura Puertorriqueña (Institute of Puerto Rican Culture)
IMF	International Monetary Fund
IPRP	Institute for Puerto Rican Policy
IPUMS	Integrated Public Use Microdata Series
LACS	Latin American, Caribbean, and US Latino Studies

315

MALDEF	Mexican American Legal Defense and Education Fund
MLN	Movimiento de Liberación Nacional (Movement for National Liberation)
MSA	metropolitan statistical areas
NACOPRW	National Conference of Puerto Rican Women
NCPRR	National Congress for Puerto Rican Rights
NILP	National Institute for Latino Policy
NMPRAC	National Museum of Puerto Rican Arts and Culture
NPRC	National Puerto Rican Coalition
PER	Partido Estadista Republicano (Pro-Statehood Republican Party)
PIP	Partido Independentista Puertorriqueño (Puerto Rican Independence Party)
PMSA	primary metropolitan statistical area
PN	Partido Nacionalista Puertorriqueño (Puerto Rican Nationalist Party)
PNP	Partido Nuevo Progresista (New Progressive Party)
PPD	Partido Popular Democrático (Popular Democratic Party)
PRACA	Puerto Rican Association for Community Affairs
PRC	Partido Revolucionario Cubano (Cuban Revolutionary Party)
PRCC	Puerto Rican Cultural Center
PRCDP	Puerto Rican Community Development Project
PREPA	Puerto Rico Electric Power Authority
PRERA	Puerto Rico Emergency Relief Administration
PRF	Puerto Rican Forum
PRFAA	Puerto Rican Federal Affairs Administration
PRFI	Puerto Rican Family Institute, Inc.
PRLDEF	Puerto Rican Legal Defense and Education Fund
PROMESA	Puerto Rico Oversight, Management, and Economic Stability Act
PRRA	Puerto Rico Reconstruction Administration
PRSA	Puerto Rican Studies Association
PS	Partido Socialista de Puerto Rico (Socialist Party of Puerto Rico)
PSP	Partido Socialista Puertorriqueño (Puerto Rican Socialist Party)
PUMS	Public Use Microdata Sample
SUNY	State University of New York

References

Abel, Jason R., and Richard Deitz. 2014. "The Causes and Consequences of Puerto Rico's Declining Population." *Current Issues in Economics and Finance* 20, no. 4. https://www.newyorkfed.org/medialibrary/media/research/current_issues/ci20-4.pdf.

Acevedo, Jeffrey. 2016. "Puerto Ricans Leaving Island for U.S. in Record Numbers." CNN, May 2. http://www.cnn.com/2016/05/02/americas/puerto-rico-exodus.

Acosta, Ivonne. 1987. *La mordaza: Puerto Rico, 1948–1957*. Río Piedras, PR: Editorial Edil.

———. 1993. *La palabra como delito: Los discursos por los que condenaron a Pedro Albizu Campos, 1948–1950*. Río Piedras, PR: Editorial Cultural.

———. 2002. *El Grito de Vieques y otros ensayos históricos (1990–1999)*. Río Piedras, PR: Editorial Cultural.

Acosta-Belén, Edna. 1977. "'Spanglish': A Case of Languages in Contact." In *New Directions in Second Language Learning, Teaching, and Bilingual Education*, edited by Heidi Dulay and Marina K. Burt, 151–158. Washington, DC: TESOL.

———. 1978. "The Literature of the Puerto Rican Minority in the United States." *Bilingual Review* 5, nos. 1–2: 107–115.

———. 1992a. "Beyond Island Boundaries: Ethnicity, Gender, and Cultural Revitalization in Nuyorican Literature." *Callaloo* 15, no. 4: 979–998.

———. 1992b. "Ideología colonialista y cultura nacional puertorriqueña." In *De palabra y obra en el Nuevo Mundo*, edited by Miguel León-Portilla, Miguel Gutiérez Estévez, Gary H. Gossen, and Jorge Klor de Alva, 463–498. Mexico, DF: Siglo Ventiuno.

———. 1993. "The Building of a Community: Puerto Rican Writers and Activists in New York City, 1890s–1960s." In *Recovering the US Hispanic Literary Heritage*, edited by Ramón Gutiérrez and Genaro Padilla, 179–195. Houston, TX: Arte Público Press.

———. 1999. "Hemispheric Remappings: Revisiting the Concept of *Nuestra América*." In *Identities on the Move: Transnational Processes in North America*

318 References

and the Caribbean Basin, edited by Liliana R. Goldin, 81–106. Austin: University of Texas Press.

———. 2009. *"Haciendo patria desde la metrópoli:* The Cultural Expressions of the Puerto Rican Diaspora." *Centro Journal* 29, no. 2: 49–83.

———, ed. 2011–2012. *The Legacies of Puerto Rican Cultural, Social, and Political Activism*. Special issue, *Latino(a) Research Review* 1–2.

———. 2013. "Reflections of a Scholar." In *A Mirror in My Own Backstage* by José Angel Figueroa, 1–2. New York: Red Sugarcane Press.

———. 2017. "Rediscovering Julia de Burgos: The People's Rebel Soul Poet." *Small Axe* 54: 188–202.

Acosta-Belén, Edna, Margarita Benítez, José E. Cruz, Yvonne González-Rodríguez, Clara E. Rodríguez, Carlos E. Santiago, Azara Santiago-Rivera, and Barbara R. Sjostrom. 2000. *"Adiós, Borinquen querida": The Puerto Rican Diaspora, Its History, and Contributions*. Albany, NY: CELAC and Comisión.

Acosta-Belén, Edna, and Virginia Sánchez Korrol, eds. 1993. *The Way It Was and Other Writings by Jesús Colón*. Houston, TX: Arte Público Press.

Acosta-Ponce, Carlos D. 2017. "In My Humble Opinion: My Review of Edgardo-Miranda-Rodríguez's *La Borinqueña*." *Educated Fanboy's Corner of Wisdom* (blog), September 7. https://carlosacostaponce.wordpress.com/2017/09/07/in-my-humble-opinion-my-review-of-edgardo-miranda-rodriguezs-la-borinquena.

Acuña, Rodolfo. 1972. *Occupied America: The Chicano's Struggle Toward Liberation*. San Francisco: Canfield Press.

Aim, James. 2006. "Assessing Puerto Rico's Fiscal Policies." In *The Economy of Puerto Rico: Restoring Growth*, edited by Susan M. Collins, Barry P. Bosworth, and Miguel A. Soto-Class, 319–398. San Juan, PR/Washington, DC: Center for the New Economy/Brookings Institution Press.

Alegría, Ricardo E. 1997. "An Introduction to Taíno Culture and History." In *Taíno: Pre-Columbian Art and Culture from the Caribbean*, edited by Fatima Bercht, Estrellita Brodsky, John Alan Farmer, and Dicey Taylor. New York: El Museo del Barrio, Monacelli Press.

Algarín, Miguel. 1978. *Mongo Affair*. New York: Nuyorican Press.

Algarín, Miguel, and Lois Griffith, eds. 1997. *Action: The Nuyorican Poets Cafe Theater Festival*. New York: Simon and Schuster.

Algarín, Miguel, and Bob Holman, eds. 1994. *Aloud: Voices from the Nuyorican Poets Cafe*. New York: H. Holt.

Algarín, Miguel, and Miguel Piñero, eds. 1975. *Nuyorican Poetry: An Anthology of Puerto Rican Words and Feelings*. New York: Morrow.

Alicea, John, and Carlos Velasquez. 2007. *50 Years of the Puerto Rican Day Parade*. New York: Galos.

Alvárez Nazario, Manuel. 1974. *El elemento afronegroide en el español de Puerto Rico*. San Juan: Instituto de Cultura Puertorriqueña.

———. 1977. *El influjo indígena en el español de Puerto Rico*. Río Piedras, PR: Editorial Universidad de Puerto Rico.

Anderson, Benedict. 1983. *Imagined Communities*. New York and London: Verso.

Anderson, Thomas F., and Marisel C. Moreno, eds. 2012. *Art at the Service of the People: Posters and Books from Puerto Rico's Division of Community Education (DIVEDCO)*. Notre Dame, IN: Snite Museum of Art, University of Notre Dame.

Aparicio, Frances. 1988. *"La vida es un Spanglish disparatero:* Bilingualism in Nuyorican Poetry." In *European Perspectives on Hispanic Literature of the United States*, edited by Geneviève Fabré, 147–160. Houston, TX: Arte Público Press.

———. 1997. *Listening to Salsa: Latin Popular Music and Puerto Rican Cultures.* Middletown, CT: Wesleyan University Press.

Aparicio, Frances, and Cándida F. Jáquez, eds. 2003. *Musical Migrations: Transnationalism and Cultural Hybridity in Latino/a America.* New York: Palgrave.

Aponte, Robert. 1990. "Definitions of the Underclass: A Critical Analysis." In *Sociology in America*, edited by Herbert J. Ganz, 117–137. Newbury Park, CA: Sage.

Aponte-Parés, Luis. 1995. "What's Yellow and White and Has Land Around It?" *Centro Bulletin* 7, no. 1: 8–19.

Aranda, Elizabeth. 2006. *Emotional Bridges to Puerto Rico: Migration, Return Migration, and the Struggles of Incorporation.* Lanham, MD: Rowman & Littlefield.

Armiño, Franca de. 1937. *Los hipócritas.* New York: Modernistic Editorial Publishing.

———. 2013. *Los hipócritas.* Edited by Nancy Bird Soto. San Juan: Editorial Tiempo Nuevo.

Arroyo, Rane. 1998. *Pale Ramón.* Cambridge, MA: Zoland Books.

———. 2005. *The Portable Famine.* Kansas City, MO: BkMk Press.

———. 2008. *Same-Sex Séances.* New Sins Press.

———. 2010. *Dancing at Funerals: Selected Plays.* Tokyo and Toronto: ahdada books.

Arroyo, William. 1986. "Lorain, Ohio: The Puerto Rican Experiment: A History Unexplored." In *Extended Roots: From Hawaii to New York*, edited by Oral History Task Force, 27–34. New York: Centro de Estudios Puertorriqueños.

Auffant Vázquez, Vivian. 2012. *La Liga de Patriotas Puertorriqueños de Eugenio María de Hostos.* San Juan: Publicaciones Gaviota.

Auletta, Ken. 1982. *The Underclass.* New York: Random House.

Ayala, César, and José L. Bolívar. 2011. *Battleship Vieques: From World War II to the Korean War.* Princeton, NJ: Markus Wiener Publishers.

Ayala, César J., and Rafael Bernabe. 2007. *Puerto Rico in the American Century: A History Since 1898.* Chapel Hill: University of North Carolina Press.

Baerga, María del Carmen. 2015. *Negociaciones de sangre: Dinámicas racializantes en el Puerto Rico decimonónico.* San Juan: Ediciones Callejón.

Baldwin, James. 1899. *Our New Possessions: Cuba, Puerto Rico, Hawaii, Philippines.* New York: American Book.

Barradas, Efraín. 1998. *Partes de un todo: Ensayos y notas sobre literatura puertorriqueña en los Estados Unidos.* Río Piedras: Editorial de la Universidad de Puerto Rico.

Barradas, Efraín, and Rafael Rodríguez, eds. 1980. *Herejes y mitificadores: Muestra de poesía puertorriqueña en los Estados Unidos.* Río Piedras, PR: Ediciones Huracán.

Barreto, Amílcar Antonio. 2002. *Vieques, the Navy, and Puerto Rican Politics.* Gainesville: University of Florida Press.

Barreto, Lefty. 1977. *Nobody's Hero.* New York: Signet.

Bean, Frank D., and Marta Tienda. 1987. *The Hispanic Population of the United States.* New York: Russell Sage Foundation.

Belpré, Pura. 1932. *Pérez and Martina: A Porto Rican Folk Tale.* New York: F. Warne.

———. 1946. *The Tiger and the Rabbit, and Other Tales.* Boston: Houghton Mifflin.

———. 1973. *Once in Puerto Rico.* New York: F. Warne.

Benítez, Marimar. 1988. "The Special Case of Puerto Rico." In *The Latin American Spirit: Art and Artists in the United States, 1920–1970*, edited by Luis R. Cancel, 72–105. New York: Bronx Museum for the Arts.

Benítez-Rojo, Antonio. 1992. *The Repeating Island: The Caribbean and the Postmodern Perspective*. Durham, NC: Duke University Press.

Bercht, Fatima. N.d. "Out of Focus Nuyoricans." El Puerto Rican Embassy. http://www.visiondoble.net/losblueprintsforanation/la-gallery.

Betances, Ramón Emeterio. 2008. *Obras completes*. Edited by Félix Ojeda Reyes and Paul Estrade. San Juan: Ediciones Puerto.

Betances, Samuel. 1972, 1973. "The Prejudice of Having No Prejudice in Puerto Rico." *Rican*, Part 1, 1.2, 41–54; Part 2, 1.3, 22–37.

Birson, Kurt. 2014. "Puerto Rican Migration and the Brain Drain Dilemma." In *Puerto Ricans at the Dawn of the New Millennium*, edited by Edwin Meléndez and Carlos Vargas-Ramos, 2–23. New York: Center for Puerto Rican Studies.

Blanco, Tomás. 1948. *El prejuicio racial en Puerto Rico*. San Juan: Biblioteca de Autores Puertorriqueños.

Blauner, Robert. 1972. *Racial Oppression in America*. New York: Harper and Row.

Bloch. Peter. 1978. *Painting and Sculpture of the Puerto Ricans*. New York: Plus Ultra.

Bonilla, Frank. 1974. "Beyond Survival: *Por qué seguiremos siendo puertorriqueños*." In *Puerto Rico and Puerto Ricans: Studies in History and Society*, edited by Adalberto López and James Petras, 438–469. New York: John Wiley and Sons.

Bonilla, Frank, and Ricardo Campos. 1986. *Industry and Idleness*. New York: Centro de Estudios Puertorriqueños.

Borjas, George J. 1985. "Assimilation, Changes in Cohort Quality and the Earnings of Immigrants." *Journal of Labor Economics* 3, no. 4: 463–489.

———. 1990. *Friends or Strangers: The Impact of Immigrants on the US Economy*. New York: Basic Books.

Borjas, George, and Marta Tienda, eds. 1985. *Hispanics in the US Economy*. Orlando, FL: Academic Press.

Bosque Pérez, Ramón, and José Javier Colón Morera. 1997. *Las carpetas. Persecución, política y derechos civiles en Puerto Rico*. Río Piedras, PR: CIPDC.

Boucher, Philip P. 1992. *Cannibal Encounters: Europeans and Island Caribs, 1492–1763*. Baltimore: Johns Hopkins University Press.

Boyce, William. 1914. *U.S. Colonies and Dependencies*. Chicago: Rand McNally.

Brown, Claude. 1965. *Manchild in the Promised Land*. New York: Macmillan.

Brown, Nick, Christine Chan, Daniel Bases, and Hang Huang. 2017. "Adrift in Debt." Reuters Graphics, June 29.

Brown, Wenzell. 1945. *Dynamite on Our Doorstep: Puerto Rican Paradox*. New York: Greenberg.

Bryan, William S., ed. 1899. *Our Islands and Their People, as Seen with Camera and Pencil*. St. Louis: Thompson Publishing.

Burgos, Julia de. 1997. *Song of the Simple Truth: The Complete Poems of Julia de Burgos*. Compiled and translated by Jack Agüeros. Willimantic, CT: Curbstone Press.

Caballero, Pedro. 1931. *Paca antillana*. New York: F. Mayans.

Cabán, Pedro. 1999. *Constructing a Colonial People: Puerto Rico in the United States, 1898–1932*. Boulder, CO: Westview.

———. 2005. "Puerto Rico Migration Division." In *The Oxford Encyclopedia of Latinos and Latinas in the United States*, edited by Suzanne Oboler and Deena González, 524–526. London: Oxford University Press.

———. 2009. "Puerto Rican Studies: Changing Islands of Knowledge." *Centro Journal* 21, no. 2: 257–281.

————. 2011–2012. "Critical Junctures and Puerto Rican Studies." *Latino(a) Research Review* 8, nos. 1–2: 25–41.

Cabranes, José A. 2015. "3 Main Reasons Why Puerto Rico Can't Declare Bankruptcy." *Washington Post*, July 22. http://www.businesinsider.com/3-main -reasons-why-puerto-rico-can't-declare-bankruptcy-2015-7.

Camacho Souza, Blase. 1982. *Boricua Hawaiiana: Puerto Ricans of Hawaii, Reflections of the Past and Mirrors of the Future: A Catalog.* Honolulu: Puerto Rican Heritage Society of Hawaii.

————. 1986. "Boricuas Hawaiianos." In *Extended Roots: From Hawaii to New York*, edited by Oral History Task Force, 7–18. New York: Centro de Estudios Puertorriqueños.

Capetillo, Luisa. [1911] 2004. *A Nation of Women: An Early Feminist Speaks Out/Mi opinión sobre las libertades, derechos y deberes de la mujer.* Edited by Félix Matos Rodríguez. Houston, TX: Arte Público Press.

————. [1916] 2009. *Absolute Equality: An Early Feminist Perspective/Influencia de las ideas modernas.* Translated by Lara Walker. Houston, TX: Arte Público Press.

Carr, Norma. 1989. "The Puerto Ricans of Hawaii, 1900–1958." Unpublished PhD diss., University of Hawaii.

Carr, Raymond. 1984. *Puerto Rico: A Colonial Experiment.* New York: Vintage Books.

Carrero, Jaime. 1964. *Jet neorriqueño.* San Germán, PR: Universidad Interamericana.

Casas, Bartolomé de las. [1552] 1992. *The Devastation of the Indies: A Brief Account.* Baltimore: Johns Hopkins University Press.

————. 1951. *Historia de las Indias.* Edited by Agustín Millares Carlo. 3 vols. Mexico City: Fondo de Cultura Económica.

Castro Arroyo, María de los Angeles. 1988. "De Salvador Brau hasta la 'novísima' historia: un replantamiento y una crítica. *Op. Cit. Revista del Centro de Investigaciones Históricas* 4: 9–55.

Centro de Estudios de la Realidad Puertorriqueña(CEREP) and Instituto de Cultura Puertorriqueña (ICP). 1992. *La tercera raíz: Presencia africana en Puerto Rico.* San Juan: CEREP and ICP.

Cervantes-Rodríguez, Margarita, and Amy Lutz. 2003. "Coloniality, Immigration, and the English-Spanish Asymmetry in the United States." *Nepantla* 4, no. 3: 523–550.

Chardón, Carlos. 1934. *Report of the Puerto Rico Policy Commission.* San Juan: Chardón Report.

Chávez, César. 2008. *An Organizer's Tale: Speeches.* Edited by Ilán Stavans. New York: Penguin Books.

Chávez, Linda. 1991. *Out of the Barrio: Toward a New Politics of Hispanic Assimilation.* New York: Basic Books.

Chenault, Lawrence R. 1938. *The Puerto Rican Migrant in New York City.* New York: Russell and Russell.

Chiswick, Barry R. 1978. "The Effect of Americanization on the Earnings of Foreign-Born Men." *Journal of Political Economy* 86, no. 5: 897–922.

Chiswick, Barry R., and Teresa A. Sullivan. 1995. "The New Immigrants." In *State of the Union: America in the 1990s.* Vol. 2: *Social Trends*, edited by Reynolds Farley, 211–270. New York: Russell Sage Foundation.

Church, A. M., ed. 1898. *Picturesque Cuba, Porto Rico, Hawaii, and the Philippines: A Photographic Panorama of Our New Possesions.* Springfield, OH: Mast, Crowell, and Kirkpatrick.

Churchill, Ward, and Jim Vander Wall. 1990. *The COINTELPRO Papers*. Boston: South End.

Cifre de Loubriel, Estela. 1964. *La inmigración a Puerto Rico durante el siglo XIX*. San Juan: Instituto de Cultura Puertorriqueña.

———. 1975. *La formación del pueblo puertorriqueño: La contribución de los catalanes, baleáricos y valencianos*. San Juan: Instituto de Cultura Puertorriqueña.

———. 1989. *La formación del pueblo puertorriqueño: La contribución de los gallegos, asturianos y santanderinos*. Río Piedras, PR: Editorial Universidad de Puerto Rico.

———. 1995. *La formación del pueblo puertorriqueño: La contribución de los isleño-canarios*. San Juan: Centro de Estudios Avanzados de Puerto Rico y el Caribe.

Cintrón Arbasetti, Joel. 2017. "A Storm More Severe." *Indypendent*, October 17. https://indypendent.org/2017/10/a-storm-more-severe.

City of New York. 1993. *Puerto Rican New Yorkers in 1990*. New York: Department of City Planning.

Cobas, José, and Jorge Duany. 1997. *Cubans in Puerto Rico: Ethnic Economy and Cultural Identity*. Gainesville: University of Florida Press.

Cockcroft, James. 1995. *The Hispanic Struggle for Social Justice*. New York: Franklin Watts.

Cohn, D'Vera, Eileen Patten, and Mark Hugo Lopez. 2014. "Puerto Rican Population Declines on Island, Grows on U.S. Mainland." Pew Research Center. http://www. pewhispanic.org/2014/08/11/puerto-rican-population-declines-on -island-grows-on-u-s-mainland.

Collazo, Sonia G., Camille L. Ryan, and Kurt J. Bauman. 2010. *Profile of the Puerto Rican Population in United States and Puerto Rico: 2008*. US Census Bureau: Housing and Household Economic Statistics Division. https://www.census.gov /contenUdam/Census/library/working-papers/201 0/demo/Collazo-ryan-bauman -paa2010-paper.pdf.

Colón, Jesús. [1961] 1982. *A Puerto Rican in New York and Other Sketches*. New York: International Publishers.

———. 2001. *"Lo que el pueblo me dice": Crónicas de la colonia puertorriqueña en Nueva York*. Edited by Edwin Karli Padilla Aponte. Houston, TX: Arte Público Press.

Colón López, Joaquín. 2002. *Pioneros puertorriqueños en Nueva York, 1917–1947*. Houston, TX: Arte Público Press.

Cruz, José E. 1998. *Identity and Power: Puerto Rican Politics and the Challenge of Ethnicity*. Philadelphia: Temple University Press.

———. 2000. *"Nosotros, puertorriqueños*: Contributions to Politics, Social Movements, and the Armed Forces." In *"Adiós, Borinquen querida": The Puerto Rican Diaspora, Its History, and Contributions*, edited by Edna Acosta-Belén, Margarita Benítez, José E. Cruz, Yvonne González-Rodríguez, Clara E. Rodríguez, Carlos E. Santiago, Azara Santiago-Rivera, and Barbara R. Sjostrom, 37–57. Albany, NY: CELAC and Comisión.

———. 2017. *Puerto Rican Identity: Political Development and Democracy in New York, 1960–1990*. Lanham, MD: Lexington Books.

Cruz, José, and Carlos E. Santiago. 2000. "The Changing Socioeconomic and Political Fortunes of Puerto Ricans in New York City, 1964–1990." Unpublished manuscript.

Cruz, Wilfredo. 2004. *Puerto Rican Chicago*. Charleston, SC: Arcadia Publishing.

Danziger, Sheldon, and P. Gottschalk. 1993. "Introduction." In *Uneven Tides: Rising Inequality in America*, edited by Sheldon Danziger and P. Gottschalk, 3–18. New York: Russell Sage Foundation.

Dávila, Arlene M. 1997. *Sponsored Identities: Cultural Politics in Puerto Rico*. Philadelphia: Temple University Press.

Dávila Santiago, Rubén. 1995. *Teatro obrero en Puerto Rico, 1900–1920: Antología*. Río Piedras, PR: Editorial Edil.

DeFreitas, Gregory. 1991. *Inequality at Work: Hispanics in the US Labor Force*. New York: Oxford University Press.

De Genova, Nicholas, and Ana Y. Ramos-Zayas. 2003. *Latino Crossings: Mexicans, Puerto Ricans, and Politics of Race and Citizenship*. New York: Routledge.

de Granda Gutiérrez, Germán. 1968. *Transculturación e interferencia lingüística en el Puerto Rico contemporáneo: 1898–1968*. Bogotá: Instituto Caro y Cuervo.

del Moral, Solsiree. 2013. *Negotiating Empire: The Cultural Politics of School in Puerto Rico, 1898–1952*. Madison: University of Wisconsin Press.

Denis, Nelson A. 2015. *War Against All Puerto Ricans: Revolution and Terror in America's Colony*. New York: Nation Books.

Des Verney Sinnette, Eleanor. 1989. *Arthur Alfonso Schomburg: Black Bibliographer and Collector*. Detroit, MI: New York Public Library and Wayne State University Press.

Díaz Carrión, Samuel. 2014. *Our Nuyorican Thing: The Birth of a Self-Made Identity*. New York: 2Leaf Press.

Díaz-Quiñones, Arcadio. 1993. *La memoria rota*. Río Piedras. PR: Ediciones Huracán.

Díaz Valcárcel, Emilio. 1978. *Harlem todos los días*. Río Piedras, PR: Ediciones Huracán.

———. 1993. *Hot Soles in Harlem*. Translated by Tanya T. Fayen. Pittsburgh: Latin American Literary Review Press.

Diffie, Bailey W., and Justine Whitfield Diffie. 1931. *Puerto Rico: A Broken Pledge*. New York: Vanguard Press.

Dinwiddie, William. 1899. *Puerto Rico: Its Conditions and Possibilities*. New York: Harper and Brothers.

Duany, Jorge. 2002. *The Puerto Rican Nation on the Move: Identities on the Island and in the United States*. Chapel Hill: University of North Carolina Press.

Duany, Jorge, and Félix Matos-Rodríguez. 2006. "Puerto Ricans in Orlando and Central Florida." New York: Center for Puerto Rican Studies.

Duany, Jorge, and Patricia Silver, eds. 2010. *Puerto Rican Florida*. Special issue, *Centro Journal* 21, no. 1.

Duffy Burnett, Christina, and Burke Marshall, eds. 2001. *Foreign in a Domestic Sense: Puerto Rico, American Expansion, and the Constitution*. Durham, NC: Duke University Press.

Dufoix, Stéphane. 2003. *Les diasporas*. Paris: Presses Universitaries de France.

———. 2008. *Diasporas*. Translated by William Rodarmor. Berkeley: University of California Press.

Emmanuelli Jiménez, Rolando, and Yasmín Colón Colón. 2017. "PROMESA": *Puerto Rico Oversight, Management and Economic Stability Act*. San Juan: Ediciones SITUM.

Enck-Wanzer, Darrel, and Iris Morales, eds. 2010. *The Young Lords: A Reader*. New York: New York University Press.

Espada, Martín. 1982. *The Immigrant Iceboy's Bolero*. Madison, WI: Ghost Pony Press.

————. 1990. *Rebellion Is the Circle of a Lover's Hand*. Willimantic, CT: Curbstone.

————. 1996. *Imagine the Angels of Bread*. New York: Norton.

————. 1998. *Zapata's Disciple*. Cambridge, MA: South End Press.

————. 2000. *A Mayan Astronomer in Hell's Kitchen*. New York: Norton.

Esquibel, Antonio, ed. 2001. *Message to Aztlán: Selected Writings of Rodolfo "Corky" Gonzales*. Houston, TX: Arte Público Press.

Estades Font, María Eugenia. 1988, *La presencia militar de Estados Unidos en Puerto Rico 1898–1918: Intereses estratégicos y dominación colonial*. Río Piedras, PR: Ediciones Huracán.

Estades, Rosa. 1980. "Symbolic Unity: The Puerto Rican Day Parade." In *Historical Perspectives on Puerto Rican Survival in the US*, edited by Clara Rodríguez, Virginia Sánchez Korrol, and José Alers, 97–106. New York: Puerto Rican Migration Consortium.

Esteves, Sandra María. 1980. *Yerba Buena*. New York: Greenfield Review Press.

————. 1984. *Tropical Rains: A Bilingual Downpour*. New York: African Caribbean Poetry Theater.

Falcón, Angelo. 2004. *Atlas of Stateside Puerto Ricans*. Washington, DC: Puerto Rican Federal Affairs Administration.

Falcón, Luis M., and Douglas T. Gurak. 1993. "Dimensions of the Hispanic Underclass in New York City." In *The Effects of Economic Restructuring on Latino Communities in the United States*, edited by Joan Moore and Raquel Rivera. Philadelphia: Temple University Press.

Farley, Reynolds. 1996. *The New American Reality*. New York: Russell Sage Foundation.

Federal Reserve Bank of New York. 2014. "An Update on the Competitiveness of Puerto Rico's Economy." https://www.newyorkfed.org/medialibrary/media /outreach-and-education/puerto-rico/2014/Puerto-Rico-Report-2014.pdf.

Fei, John, and Gustav Ranis. 1964. *Development of the Labor Surplus Economy: Theory and Policy*. Homewood, IL: Irwin Publishers.

Fernández, Lilia. 2012. *Brown in the City: Mexicans and Puerto Ricans in Postwar Chicago*. Chicago: University of Chicago Press.

Fernández, María Teresa. 1998. "Ode to the Diasporican." In *Resistance in Paradise: Rethinking 100 Years of U.S. Involvement in the Caribbean and the Pacific*, by Deborah Wei and Rachel Kamel, 78. Philadelphia: American Friends Service Committee.

Fernández, Mariposa. 2002. *Born Bronxeña: Poems on Identity, Love and Survival*. New York: Bronxeña Books.

————. 2016. *Ode to the Diasporican Boogaloo*. New York: SoundCloud.

Fernández, Ronald. 1987. *Los Macheteros: The Wells Fargo Robbery and the Violent Struggle for Puerto Rican Independence*. New York: Prentice Hall.

Fernández Méndez, Eugenio. 1972. *Art and Mythology of the Taino Indians of the Greater West Indies*. San Juan: Ediciones El Cemí.

Ferrao, Luis Angel. 1990. *Pedro Albizu Campos y el nacionalismo puertorriqueño*. Río Piedras, PR: Editorial Cultural.

Ferré, Rosario. 1995. *The House on the Lagoon*. New York: Farrar, Straus, and Giroux.

————. 1998. *Eccentric Neighborhoods*. New York: Farrar, Straus, and Giroux.

Figueroa, José Angel. 1973. *East 110th Street*. Detroit: Broadside Press.

————. 1981. *Noo Jork*. San Juan: Instituto de Cultura Puertorriqueña.

————. 2013. *A Mirror in My Own Backstage*. New York: Red Sugarcane Press.

————. 2015. *Un espejo en mi propio bastidor*. Translated by Alejandro Villalba. New York: Red Sugarcane Press.

Figueroa, Luis A. 2005. *Sugar, Slavery, and Freedom in Nineteenth-Century Puerto Rico*. Chapel Hill: University of North Carolina Press.

Figueroa, Sotero. 1892. "La verdad de la historia, I." *Patria*, March 19.

Fitzpatrick, Joseph. 1971. *Puerto Rican–Americans: The Meaning of Migration to the Mainland*. Upper Saddle River, NJ: Prentice Hall.

Flores, Juan. 1979. *Insularismo e ideología burguesa en Antonio S. Pedreira*. Habana: Casa de las Américas.

———. [1988] 1993. *Divided Borders: Essays on Puerto Rican Identity*. Houston, TX: Arte Público Press.

———. 2000. *From Bomba to Hip-Hop: Puerto Rican Culture and Latino Identity*. New York: Columbia University Press.

———. 2009. *The Diaspora Strikes Back: Caribeño Tales of Learning and Turning*. New York: Routledge.

———. 2016. *Salsa Rising: New York's Latin Music of the Sixties Generation*. New York: Oxford University Press.

Flores, Juan, and Pedro López Adorno, eds. 2015. *Pedro Pietri: Selected Poetry*. New York: City Lights Books.

Flores, William V., and Rina Benmayor, eds. 1997. *Latino Cultural Citizenship*. Boston: Beacon Press.

Foner, Eric. 1972. *The Spanish-Cuban-American War and the Birth of US Imperialism*. New York: Monthly Review Press.

Fonseca, Jay, and Leo Aldridge. 2017. "Puerto Ricans Are Going to Flee if President Trump Doesn't Fix Hurricane Relief." *Washington Post*, October 3.

Forbes-Lindsay, Charles H. 1906. *America's Insular Possessions*. Philadelphia: J. C. Winston.

Franqui-Rivera, Harry. 2017. "Why Puerto Ricans Did Not Receive U.S. Citizenship So They Could Fight in WWI." *Centro Voices*. May.

Freeland, Lucas. 2016. "The Financial Crisis in Puerto Rico: A Brief Report." Seattle, WA: Amazon Digital Services.

Friedrich, Carl J. 1965. Foreword to Charles T. Goodsell, *Administration of a Revolution*, vii–ix. Cambridge, MA: Harvard University Press.

Fuentes Ramírez, Ricardo R., ed. 2017. *Ensayos para una nueva economía: Desarrollo económico de Puerto Rico*. San Juan: Ediciones Callejón.

Galvin, Kevin. 1995. "Panel Wants Definition of Poverty Expanded." *Gazette*, May 1.

García, Gervasio. 1989. *Historia crítica, historia sin coartadas*. Río Piedras, PR: Ediciones Huracán.

———. 2000. "I Am the Other: Puerto Rico in the Eyes of North Americans." *Journal of American History* 86, no. 1: 33–64.

García, Gervasio, and Angel Quintero Rivera. 1982. *Desafío y solidaridad: Breve historia del movimiento obrero puertorriqueño*. Río Piedras, PR: Ediciones Huracán.

García, Mario T., ed. 2008. *A Dolores Huerta Reader*. Albuquerque: University of New Mexico Press.

García Passalacqua, Juan Manuel. 1996. *Los secretos del patriarca*. Río Piedras, PR: Editorial Cultural.

———. 1999. *Invadiendo al invasor: Puerto Rico y Estados Unidos en el siglo veintiuno*. Río Piedras, PR: Editorial Cultural.

Gautier Mayoral, Carmen, and María del Pilar Argüelles, eds. 1978. *Puerto Rico y la ONU*. Río Piedras, PR: Editorial Edil.

Géigel Polanco, Vicente. 1972. *La farsa del Estado Libre Asociado*. Río Piedras, PR: Editorial Edil.

Géliga-Vargas, Jocelyn A. 2011. "Afro–Puerto Rican Oral Histories: A Disruptive Collaboration." *Collaborative Anthropologies* 4: 90–118.

Géliga-Vargas, Jocelyn A., Irmaris Rosas Nazario, and Tania Delgado Hernández. 2007–2008. "Testimonios Afropuertorriqueños: Using Oral History to (Re)Write Race in Contemporary Puerto Rico." *Sargasso* 1: 115–130.

Gerena Valentín, Gilberto. 2013. *Gilberto Gerena Valentín: My Life as a Community Activist, Labor Organizer, and Progressive Politician in New York City*. Edited by Carlos Rodríguez-Fraticelli. New York: Centro Press.

———. 2013. *Soy Gilberto Gerena Valentín: Memorias de un puertorriqueño en Nueva York*. Edited by Carlos Rodríguez-Fraticelli. Translated by Andrew Herley. New York: Centro Press.

Girmay, Aracelis. 2007. *Teeth*. Willimantic, CT: Curbstone Press/Northwestern University Press.

———. 2011. *Kingdom Animalia*. Rochester, NY: BOA Editions.

———. 2016. *The Black Maria*. Rochester, NY: BOA Editions.

Glasser, Ruth. 1995. *My Music Is My Flag: Puerto Rican Musicians and Their New York Communities, 1917–1940*. Berkeley: University of California Press.

———. 1997. *Aquí me quedo: Puerto Ricans in Connecticut/Los puertorriqueños en Connecticut*. Middleton, CT: Connecticut Humanities Council.

———. 2005. "From 'Richport' to Bridgeport: Puerto Ricans in Connecticut." In *The Puerto Rican Diaspora: Historical Perspectives*, edited by Carmen T. Whalen and Víctor Vázquez-Hernández, 174–199. Philadelphia: Temple University Press.

Glazer, Nathan, and Daniel P. Moynihan. 1963. *Beyond the Melting Pot*. Cambridge, MA: MIT Press.

Gleason, Stephanie. 2017. "Puerto Rico's Bankruptcy Delayed, Moved to New York Following Hurricane Maria." *Street*, September 28. http://www.thestreet.com/story/14320965/1/puerto-rico-s-bankruptcy-delayed-moved-to-new-york-following-hurricane-maria.html.

Godreau, Isar. 2006. "Folkloric 'Others': Blanqueamiento and the Celebration of Blackness as an Exception in Puerto Rico." In *Globalization and Race: Transformations in the Cultural Production of Blackness*, edited by Kamari Maxine Clarke and Deborah Thomas, 171–187. Durham, NC: Duke University Press.

———. 2015. *Scripts of Blackness: Race, Cultural Nationalism, and U.S. Colonialism in Puerto Rico*. Urbana: University of Illinois Press.

Golder, Janine. 2011–2012. "Not Just a 'Boys Club': An Exploration of Female Voices in Nuyorican Literature." *Latino(a) Research Review* 8, nos. 1–2: 155–174.

Golubov, Nattie, ed. 2011. *Diasporas: Reflexiones teóricas*. Mexico: UNAM.

Gómez, Magdalena. 2004. *AmaXonica: Howls from the Left Side of My Body*. Longmeadow, MA: Rotary Records.

———. 2008. *Bemba y Chichón*. Longmeadow, MA: Rotary Records.

———. 2014. *Shameless Woman*. New York: Red Sugarcane Press.

Gómez, Magdalena, and María Luisa Arroyo, eds. 2012. *Bullying: Replies, Confesions, Rebuttals, and Catharsis*. New York: Skyhorse Publishing.

Gonzales-Berry, Erlinda, and David R. Maciel, eds. 2000. *The Contested Homeland: A Chicano History of New Mexico*. Albuquerque: University of New Mexico Press.

González, José Luis. 1950. *Paisa*. México: Fondo de Cultura Popular.

———. 1973. *En Nueva York y otras desgracias*. México: Siglo XXI.

———. 1980. *El país de cuatro pisos y otros ensayos*. Río Piedras, PR: Ediciones Huracán.

———. 1993. *Puerto Rico: The Four-Storeyed Country and Other Essays*. Translated by Gerard Guinness. Princeton, NJ: Markus Wiener Publishers.

González, Juan. [2000] 2011. *Harvest of Empire: A History of Latinos in America*. New York: Penguin Books.

Gonzales, Rodolfo "Corky." 2001. *Message to Aztlán: Selected Writings*. Houston, TX: Arte Público Press.

González García, María. 2014. *El negro y la negra libre: Puerto Rico 1800–1873: Su presencia y contribución a la identidad puertorriqueña*. San Juan: MGG Editorial.

González-Wippler, Migene. 1973. *Santería: African Magic in Latin America*. New York: Julien Press.

Goodsell, Charles T. 1965. *Administration of a Revolution*. Cambridge, MA: Harvard University Press.

Gustines, George Gene. 2018. "A Puerto Rican Hero Joins with Wonder Women and Others for Hurricane Relief." https://www.times.com/by/george-gene-gustines.

Gutiérrez, José Angel. 1999. *The Making of a Chicano Militant: Lessons from Crystal*. Madison: University of Wisconsin Press.

Gutiérrez, Luis. 2013. *Still Dreaming: My Journey from the Barrio to Capitol Hill*. New York: Norton.

Guzmán, Charlie "Isa." 2015. "Poetry Review, Urayoán Noel's *Buzzing Hemisphere/ Rumor hamisférico*." *Centro Voices*. https://centropr.hunter.cuny.edu/centrovoices /current-affairs/poetry-review-urayoán-noel's-"buzzing-hemisphererumor -hemisferico.

Guzmán, Pablo. 1998. "*La Vida Pura*: A Lord of the Barrio." In *The Puerto Rican Movement: Voices of the Diaspora*, edited by Andrés Torres and José E. Velázquez, 155–172. Philadelphia: Temple University Press.

Hall, Stuart. 1990. "Cultural Identity and Diaspora." In *Identity, Community, Culture, Difference*, edited by Jonathan Trutherford, 222–237. London: Lawrence and Wishart.

Handlin, Oscar. 1959. *The Newcomers: Negroes and Puerto Ricans in a Changing Metropolis*. Cambridge, MA: Harvard University Press.

Harrington, Michael. 1962. *The Other America: Poverty in the United States*. New York: Macmillan.

Haslip-Viera, Gabriel. [1996] 2017. "The Evolution of the Latino Community in New York City: Early Nineteenth Century to the Present." In *Latinos in New York: Communities in Transition*, edited by Gabriel Haslip-Viera and Sherrie L. Baver, 3–29. Notre Dame, IN: University of Notre Dame Press.

———. 1999. *Taino Revival: Critical Perspectives on Puerto Rican Identity and Cultural Politics*. New York: Centro de Estudios Puertorriqueños.

Haslip-Viera, Gabriel, and Sherrie L. Baver, eds. 1996. *Latinos in New York: Communities in Transition*. Notre Dame, IN: University of Notre Dame Press.

Hernández, Carmen Dolores. 1997. *Puerto Rican Voices in English: Interviews with Writers*. Westport, CT: Praeger.

Hernández, David, ed. 1977. *Nosotros: A Collection of Latino Poetry and Graphics from Chicago*. Special issue, *Revista Chicano-Riqueña* 5, no. 1.

Hernández, Pedro Juan. 2011–2012. "The Evolution of Centro's Archives of the Puerto Rican Diaspora, 1973–2012." *Latino(a) Research Review* 8, nos. 1–2: 85–100.

Hernández, Yasmín. 2018a. Yasmín Hernández Art. www.yasminhernandezart.com/about.

———. 2018b. "Soul Rebels, El Museo del Barrio." Yasmín Hernández Art. https:// www.yasminhernandezart.com/soul-rebels?lightbox=dataItem-iz21oepu.

Hernández Alvarez, José. [1967] 1976. *Return Migration to Puerto Rico*. Westport, CT: Greenwood Press.

Hernández Aquino, Luis. 1969. *Diccionario de voces indígenas de Puerto Rico*. Río Piedras, PR: Editorial Cultural.

Hernández Colón, Rafael. 1986. *La nueva tesis*. Río Piedras, PR: Editorial Edil.
———. 2014. *Estado Libre Asociado: Naturaleza y desarrollo*.
Hernández Cruz, Víctor. 1966. *Papo Got His Gun*. New York: Calle Once Publications.
———. 1969. *Snaps*. New York: Random House.
———. 1973. *Mainland*. New York: Random House.
———. 1976. *Tropicalization*. New York: Reed, Cannon and Johnson.
———. 1989. *Rhythm, Content, and Flavor*. Houston, TX: Arte Público Press.
———. 2006. *The Mountain in the Sea*. Minneapolis, MN: Coffee House Press.
———. 2017. *Beneath the Spanish*. Minneapolis, MN: Coffee House Press.
Hinojosa, Jennifer, and Carlos Vargas-Ramos. 2017. *2016 Almanac of Puerto Ricans in the United States*. New York: Centro Press.
Hispanic Federation. 2015. *Puerto Rico's Economic Crisis: Overview and Recommendations*. Washington, DC: Hispanic Federation.
History Task Force, Centro de Estudios Puertorriqueños. 1979. *Labor Migration Under Capitalism: The Puerto Rican Experience*. New York: Monthly Review Press.
———. 1982. *Sources for the Study of Puerto Rican Migration, 1879–1930*. New York: Centro.
Hobsbawm, Eric, and Terence Ranger, eds. 1983. *The Invention of Tradition*. New York: Cambridge University Press.
Horno-Delgado, Asunción, Eliana Ortega, Nina M. Scott, and Nancy Saporta Sternbach, eds. 1989. *Breaking Boundaries: Latina Writings and Critical Readings*. Amherst: University of Massachusetts Press.
Horwitz, Julius. 1960. *The Inhabitants*. Cleveland, OH: World Publishing.
House Committee on Natural Resources. 2017. "Bishop: PROMESA Oversight Board Needs New Tools to Ensure Puerto Rico's Recovery." November 7. www.naturalresources.house.com/documentsingle.aspx?DocumentID=403305.
Hulme, Peter. 1986. *Colonial Encounters: Europe and the Native Caribbean*. London: Methuen.
Ingalls, Robert P., and Louis Pérez Jr. 2003. *Tampa Cigar Workers*. Gainesville: University Press of Florida.
Jiménez de Wagenheim, Olga. 2005. "From Aguada to Dover: Puerto Ricans Rebuild Their World in Morris County, New Jersey, 1948 to 2000." In *The Puerto Rican Diaspora: Historical Perspectives*, edited by Carmen T. Whalen and Víctor Vázquez-Hernández, 106–127. Philadelphia: Temple University Press.
Jiménez-Muñoz, Gladys, and Kelvin Santiago. 1995. "Re/defining, Re/imagining Borders: The Artistic Production of Juan Sánchez." *Latino Review of Books* 1, no. 1: 16–25.
Jiménez Román, Miriam. 1999. "The Indians Are Coming! The Indians Are Coming! The Taíno and Puerto Rican Identity." In *Taíno Revival*, edited by Gabriel Haslip-Viera, 75–108. New York: Centro de Estudios Puertorriqueños.
Jiménez Román, Miriam, and Juan Flores, eds. 2010. *The Afro Latin@ Reader*. Durham, NC: Duke University Press.
Jorgenson, Dale W. 1961. "The Development of a Dual Economy." *Economic Journal* 71: 309–334.
Kanellos, Nicolás. 1990. *A History of Hispanic Theatre in the United States: Origins to 1940*. Austin: University of Texas Press.
———, ed. 2002. *Herencia: The Anthology of Hispanic Literature of the United States*. New York: Oxford.
———. 2011. *Hispanic Immigrant Literature: El Sueño del Retorno*. Austin: University of Texas Press.

Kanellos, Nicolás, and Helvetia Martell. 2000. *Hispanic Periodicals in the United States: Origins to 1960*. Houston, TX: Arte Público Press.

Kaske, Michelle. 2018. "Puerto Rico Could Cut Spending to the Bone—and Still Never Recover." https://www.bloomberg.com/news/articles/2018-03=15/greek -tragedy-redux-puerto-rico-embraces-risky-austerity-plan.

Katz, Michael. 1993. "The Urban 'Underclass' as a Metaphor of Social Transformation." In *The "Underclass" Debate: Views from History*, edited by Michael Katz, 3–26. Princeton, NJ: Princeton University Press.

Keegan, William F. 1992. *The People Who Discovered Columbus*. Gainesville: University Press of Florida.

Klein, Naomi. 2007. *The Shock Doctrine: The Rise of Disaster Capitalism*. New York: Picador.

Kolhatkar, Sheelah. 2017. "Profiting from Puerto Rico's Pain." *New Yorker*, November 6. www.thenewyorker.com/magazine/2017/11/06.

Koss, Joan Dee. 1965. "Puerto Ricans in Philadelphia: Migration and Accommodation." PhD diss.

Kroft, Steve. 2017. "Puerto Rico's Storm of Misery." *CBS News*, November 5. http://www.cbsnews.com/puerto-ricos-storm-of-misery.

La Fountain-Stokes, Lawrence. 2009. *Queer Ricans: Cultures and Sexualities in the Diaspora*. Minneapolis: University of Minnesota Press.

Labarthe, Pedro Juan. 1931. *Son of Two Nations: The Private Life of a Columbia Student*. New York: Carranza.

Laviera, Tato. 1979. *La Carreta Made a U-turn*. Gary, IN: Arte Público Press.

———. 1985. *AmeRícan*. Houston, TX: Arte Público Press.

Lemann, Nicholas. 1991. "The Other Underclass." *Atlantic Monthly*, December, 96–110.

Levins Morales, Aurora. 1998a. *Medicine Stories: History, Culture, and the Politics of Integrity*. Cambridge, MA: South End.

———.1998b. *Remedios*. Boston: Beacon.

Levins Morales, Aurora, and Rosario Morales. 1986. *Getting Home Alive*. Ithaca, NY: Firebrand Books.

Levy, Frank. 1977. "How Big Is the Underclass?" Working Paper 0090-1. Washington, DC: Urban Institute.

———. 1995. "Incomes and Income Inequality." In *State of the Union: America in the 1990s*, edited by Reynolds Farley, Vol. 1, 1–52. New York: Russell Sage Foundation.

Levy, Jacques E. 2007. *César Chávez: Autobiography of La Causa*. Minneapolis: University of Minnesota Press.

Lewis, Gordon K. 1963. *Puerto Rico: Freedom and Power in the Caribbean*. New York: Monthly Review Press.

———. 1968. *The Growth of the Modern West Indies*. New York: Monthly Review Press.

Lewis, Oscar. 1966. *La vida*. New York: Random House.

Lewis, W. Arthur. 1954. "Economic Development with Unlimited Supplies of Labor." *Manchester School* 22: 193–197.

Logan, John. 2002. *Hispanic Populations and Their Residential Patterns in the Metropolis*. Albany: Lewis Mumford Center for Comparative Urban and Regional Research, University at Albany, State University of New York. http://mumford1.dyndns.org/cen2000/HispanicPop/HspReportNew/page1.html.

López, Adalberto. 1974. "The Beginnings of Colonization: Puerto Rico, 1493–1800." In *Puerto Rico and Puerto Ricans: Studies in History and Society*, edited by Adalberto López and James Petras, 12–41. New York: John Wiley & Sons.

————. 1980. "The Puerto Rican Diaspora: A Survey." In *Puerto Rico and Puerto Ricans: Studies in History and Society*, edited by Adalberto López, 313–343. Rochester, VT: Schenkman Books.

López, Gustavo, and Jynnah Radford. 2017. "Facts on US Immigrants, 2015: Statistical Portrait of the Foreign-Born Population of the United States." Pew Research Center. *Hispanic Trends*. May 3. www.pewhispanic.org/2017/05/03/facts-on-u-s-immigrants/.

López, Iris. 2005. "Borinkis and Chop Suey: Puerto Rican Identity in Hawai'i, 1900 to 2000." In *The Puerto Rican Diaspora: Historical Perspectives*, edited by Carmen T. Whalen and Víctor Vázquez-Hernández, 43–67. Philadelphia: Temple University Press.

López, Iris, and David Forbes. 2001. "Borinki Identity in Hawai'i: Present and Future." *Centro Journal* 13, no. 1: 110–127.

López-Adorno, Pedro, ed. 1991. *Papiros de Babel: antología de la poesía puertorriqueña en Nueva York*. Río Piedras: Editorial de la Universidad de Puerto Rico.

López Mesa, Enrique. 2002. *La comunidad cubana de Nueva York: Siglo XIX*. Habana: Centro de Estudios Martianos.

López Tijerina, Reies. 2000. *They Called Me King Tiger: My Struggle for the Land and Our Rights*. Houston, TX: Arte Público Press.

Luis, William. 1997. *Dancing Between Two Cultures: Latino Caribbean Literature in the United States*. Nashville, TN: Vanderbilt University Press.

Lugo-Lugo, Carmen. 2011–2012. "An Island in Raw Skin: Vieques and the Transnational Activist Challenge to Puerto Rico's Colonial Invisibility." *Latino(a) Research Review* 8, nos. 1–2: 209–230.

Lynn, Laurence, and M. McGeary. 1990. *Inner City Poverty in the United States*. Washington, DC: National Academy Press.

Macarrón Larumbe, Alejandro. 2014. "Lessons from the European Demographic Winter for Puerto Rico." In *Puerto Ricans at the Dawn of the New Millennium*, edited by Edwin Meléndez and Carlos Vargas-Ramos, 210–234. New York: Center for Puerto Rican Studies.

Malaret, Augusto. 1955. *Vocabulario de Puerto Rico*. New York: Las Américas.

Maldonado, Alex W. 1997. *Teodoro Moscoso and Puerto Rico's Operation Bootstrap*. Gainesville: University of Florida Press.

Maldonado-Denis, Manuel. 1972. *Puerto Rico: A Socio-historic Interpretation*. New York: Random House.

————, ed. 1972. *La conciencia nacional puertorriqueña por Pedro Albizu Campos*. Mexico DF: Siglo XXI.

Marín, Francisco Gonzalo. 1997. "New York from Within: One Aspect of Its Bohemian Life." Translated by Lizabeth Paravisini-Gebert. In *The Latino Reader: From 1542 to the Present*, edited by Harold Augenbraum and Margarite Fernández Olmos, 108–111. New York: Houghton Mifflin.

————. 2002. "Nueva York por dentro: una faz de su vida bohemia." In *En otra voz*, edited by Nicolás Kanellos, 198–199. Houston, TX: Arte Público Press.

Marqués, René. [1951–1952] 1971. *La carreta*. San Juan: Editorial Cultural.

Márquez, Roberto, ed. 2007. *Puerto Rican Poetry: An Anthology from Aboriginal to Contemporary Times*. Amherst: University of Massachusetts Press.

Martínez, Soraida. N.d.a. "Verdadism, Paintings Juxtaposed with Written Social Commentaries Since 1992." Soraida. http://www.soraida.com/Credentials.htm.

————. N.d.b. "*Puerto Rican Stereotype: The Way You See Me Without Looking at Me*." Soraida. http://www.soraida.com/prs.htm.

Massey, Douglas. 1993. "Latinos, Poverty and the Underclass: A New Agenda for Research." *Hispanic Journal of Behavioral Sciences* 15, no. 4: 449–475.

Masud-Piloto, Félix M. 1988. *With Open Arms: The Evolution of Cuban Migration to the US, 1959–1995*. New York: Rowman & Littlefield.

Matos-Rodríguez, Félix V. 2005. "Saving the Parcela: A Short History of Boston's Puerto Rican Community." In *The Puerto Rican Diaspora: Historical Perspectives*, edited by Carmen T. Whalen and Víctor Vázquez-Hernández, 151–173. Philadelphia: Temple University Press.

Matos-Rodríguez, Félix V., and Pedro Juan Hernández. 2001. *Pioneros: Puerto Ricans in New York City, 1892–1948*. Charleston, SC: Arcadia Publishing.

McCaffrey, Katherine T. 2002. *Military Power and Popular Protest: The U.S. Navy in Vieques, Puerto Rico*. New Brunswick, NJ: Rutgers University Press.

Medina-Fuentes, José Nicolás. 2017. *La deuda odiosa y la descolonización de Puerto Rico*. San Juan: Publicaciones Libre Pensador.

Meléndez, A. Gabriel. 1997. *So All Is Not Lost: The Poetics of Print in Nuevomexicano Communities, 1834–1958*. Albuquerque: University of New Mexico Press.

Meléndez, Edgardo. 1996. *Puerto Rico en "Patria."* Río Piedras, PR: Editorial Edil.

———. 2013. "Citizenship and the Alien Exclusion in the Insular Cases: Puerto Rico in the Periphery of American Empire." *Centro Journal* 25, 106–145.

———. 2017. *Sponsored Migration: The State and Puerto Rican Postwar Migration to the United States*. Columbus: Ohio State University Press.

Meléndez, Edwin. 1993a. "Understanding Latino Poverty." *Sage Race Relations Abstracts* 18, no. 1: 3–43.

———. 1993b. "The Unsettled Relationship Between Puerto Rican Poverty and Migration." *Latino Studies Journal* (May).

———. 1993c. "*Los que se van, los que regresan*: Puerto Rican Migration to and from the United States, 1982–1988." Political Economy Working Paper Series no. 1, Centro de Estudios Puertorriqueños, New York.

———. 2017. "Preface: U.S. Citizenship in Puerto Rico: Over One Hundred Years of the Jones Act." *Centro Journal* 29, no. 1: 3–5.

Meléndez, Edwin, and Jennifer Hinojosa. 2017. "Estimates of Post–Hurricane Maria Exodus from Puerto Rico." Center for Puerto Rican Studies Research Brief, October.

Meléndez, Edwin, and Edgardo Meléndez, eds. 1993. *Colonial Dilemma: Critical Perspectives on Contemporary Puerto Rico*. Boston: South End Press.

Meléndez, Edwin, Clara Rodríguez, and Janis Barry Figueroa, eds. 1991. *Hispanics in the Labor Force: Issues and Policies*. New York: Plenum Press.

Meléndez, Edwin, and Carlos Vargas-Ramos. 2014. *Puerto Ricans at the Dawn of the New Millennium*. New York: Center for Puerto Rican Studies.

———, eds. 2017. *State of Puerto Ricans 2017*. New York: Centro Press.

Meléndez, Miguel "Mickey." [2003] 2005. *We Took the Streets: Fighting for Latino Rights with the Young Lords*. New Brunswick, NJ: Rutgers University Press.

Méndez, José L., ed. 1980. *La agresión cultural norteamericana en Puerto Rico*. Mexico: Editorial Grijalbo.

———. 1997. *Entre el limbo y el consenso: El dilema de Puerto Rico para el próximo siglo*. San Juan: Ediciones Milenio.

Meyer, Doris, 1996. *Speaking for Themselves: Neomexicano Cultural Identity and the Spanish Language Press, 1880–1920*. Albuquerque: University of New Mexico.

Mills, C. Wright, Clarence Senior, and Rose Goldsen. 1950. *The Puerto Rican Journey: New York's Newest Migrants*. New York: Russell & Russell.

Mintz, Sidney. 1974. *Caribbean Transformations*. Chicago: Aldine Publishing.

Miranda-Rodríguez, Edgardo. 2016. *La Borinqueña*. New York: Somos Arte.

Mohr, Nicholasa. 1973. *Nilda*. New York: Harper and Row.

————. 1975. *El Bronx Remembered*. New York: Harper and Row.

————. 1977. *In Nueva York*. New York: Dial Press.

————. 1979. *Felita*. New York: Dial Press.

————. 1985. *Rituals of Survival: A Woman's Portfolio*. Houston, TX: Arte Público Press.

————. 1986. *Going Home*. New York: Dial Books.

————. 1989. "Puerto Rican Writers in the US, Puerto Rican Writers in Puerto Rico: A Separation Beyond Language." In *Breaking Boundaries: Latina Writings and Critical Readings*, edited by Asunción Horno-Delgado, Eliana Ortega, Nina M. Scott, and Nancy Saporta Sternbach, 111–116. Amherst: University of Massachusetts Press.

————. 1995. *Growing Up in the Sanctuary of My Imagination*. New York: Julian Messner.

————. 1997. *A Matter of Pride and Other Stories*. Houston, TX: Arte Público Press.

Mohr, Nicholasa, and Antonio Martorell. 1995. *La canción del coquí y otros cuentos/The Song of el Coquí and Other Tales*. New York: Viking.

Moore, Joan, and Raquel Pinderhughes. 1993. *In the Barrios: Latinos and the Underclass Debate*. New York: Russell Sage Foundation.

Mora, Marie T., Alberto Dávila, and Havidán Rodríguez. 2016. "Education, Migration, and Earnings of Puerto Ricans on the Island and US Mainland: Impact, Outcomes, and Consequences of an Economic Crisis." *Migration Studies* 5, no. 2: 168–189.

Mora, Marie T., Alberto Dávila, and Havidán Rodríguez. 2017. *Population, Migration, and Socioeconomic Outcomes Among Island and Mainland Puerto Ricans*. Lanham, MD: Lexington Books.

Moraga, Cherríe, and Gloria Anzaldúa, eds. 1981. *This Bridge Called My Back: Writings by Radical Women of Color*. Watertown, MA: Persephone Press.

Morales, Ed. 1990. "Places in the Puerto Rican Heart Eddie Figueroa and the Nuyorican Imaginary." *Centro Voices*. https://centropr.hunter.cuny.edu/centrovoices/letras/places-puerto-rican-heart-eddie-figueroa-and-nuyorican-imaginary.

————. 2002. *Living in Spanglish: The Search for Latino Identity in America*. New York: St. Martin's Griffin.

Morales, Iris. 2016. *Through the Eyes of Rebel Women: The Young Lords, 1969–1976*. New York: Red Sugarcane Press.

Morales, Rebecca, and Frank Bonilla. 1993. *Latinos in a Changing US Economy: Comparative Perspectives on Growing Inequality*. Newberry Park, CA: Sage Publications.

Morales-Carrión, Arturo. 1971. *Puerto Rico and the Non-Hispanic Caribbean. A Study in the Decline of Spanish Exclusivism*. Río Piedras, PR: University of Puerto Rico.

Mormino, Gary R., and George E. Pozzetta. 1987. *The Immigrant World of Ybor City*. Urbana: University of Illinois Press.

Mörner, Magnus. 1967. *Race Mixture in the History of Latin America*. New York: Little, Brown.

Morris, Charles. 1899. *Our Island Empire: A Handbook of Cuba, Puerto Rico, Hawaii, and the Philippine Islands*. Philadelphia: J. P. Lippincott.

Moynihan, Daniel P. 1993. *Pandemonium: Ethnicity in International Politics*. New York: Oxford University Press.

Museo del Barrio. 1990. *Taller Alma Boricua 1969–1989*. New York: Museo del Barrio.

Museo del Barrio and Metropolitan Museum of Art. 1974. *The Art Heritage of Puerto Rico/La herencia artística de Puerto Rico*. New York: Metropolitan Museum of Art.

National Conference of Puerto Rican Women (NACOPRW). 1977. *Puerto Rican Women in the United States: Organizing for Change*. Washington, DC: NACOPRW.

National Congress for Puerto Rican Rights (NCPRR). 1996. "What Does NCPRR Do?" Columbia University, last updated May 14. http://www.columbia.edu /~rmg36/NCPRR.html.

National Puerto Rican Coalition (NPRC). 1999. *National Directory of Puerto Rican Elected Officials*. Washington, DC: NPRC.

Neely, F. Tennyson. 1898. *Neely's Panorama of Our New Possessions*. New York: Neely Publishing.

———. 1899a. *Neely's Color Photos of America's New Possessions*. New York: F. Tennyson Neely.

———. 1899b. *Neely's Photographs: Panoramic Views of Cuba, Porto Rico, Manila, and the Philippines*. New York: F. Tennyson Neely.

Negrón de Montilla, Aida. 1971. *Americanization in Puerto Rico and the Public School System*. Río Piedras, PR: Editorial Universitaria.

Negrón-Muntaner, Frances. 1994. *Brincando el charco*. New York: Women Make Movies (film).

Negrón-Muntaner, Frances, and Ramón Gosfroguel, eds. [1997] 2008. *Puerto Rican Jam: Rethinking Colonialism and Nationalism*. Minneapolis: University of Minnesota Press.

Nelson, Anne. 1986. *Murder Under Two Flags: The U.S., Puerto Rico, and the Cerro Maravilla Cover-Up*. Boston: Ticknor and Fields.

New York City Department of City Planning. 1993. *Socio-economic Profiles: A Portrait of New York City's Community Districts from the 1980 and 1990 Censuses*. New York: New York City Department of City Planning.

Nieves, Myrna, ed. 2012. *Breaking Ground: Anthology of Puerto Rican Women Writers in New York, 1980–2012/Abriendo caminos: Antología de escritoras puertorriqueñas en Nueva York 1980–2012*. New York: Editorial Campana.

Nieves Falcón, Pablo García Rodríguez, and Félix Ojeda Reyes. 1971. *Puerto Rico, grito y mordaza*. Río Piedras, PR: Ediciones Librería Internacional.

Nieves Falcón, Luis. 2009. *Un siglo de represión política en Puerto Rico, 1898–1998*. San Juan, PR: Ediciones Puerto.

Noble, David. 2002. *Death of a Nation: American Culture and the End of Exceptionalism*. Minneapolis: University of Minnesota Press.

Noel, Urayoán. 2005. *Kool Logic/La lógica kool*. Tempe, AZ: Bilingual Press/Editorial Bilingüe.

———. 2010. *Hi-Density Politics*. Buffalo, NY: BlazeVox Books.

———. 2014. *In Visible Movement: Nuyorican Poetry from the Sixties to Slam*. Iowa City: University of Iowa Press.

———. 2015. *Buzzing Hemisphere/Rumor hemisférico*. Tucson: University of Arizona Press.

Novas, Himilce. 1994. *Everything You Need to Know About Latino History*. New York: Penguin Group.

O'Neill, Gonzalo. 1922. *La indiana borinqueña*. New York: n.p.

———. 1923. *Moncho Reyes*. New York: Spanish-American Printing.

———. 1934. *Pabellón de Borinquen o bajo una sola bandera*. New York: Spanish-American Printing.

Ogbu, John. 1990. "Minority Status and Literacy in Comparative Perspective." *Daedalus* 119: 141–169.

Ojeda Reyes, Félix. 1992. *Peregrinos de la libertad*. Río Piedras, PR: Instituto de Estudios del Caribe.

———. 2001. *El desterrado de París: Biografía del Doctor Ramón Emeterio Betances (1827–1898)*. San Juan: Ediciones Puerto.

Ortiz, Altagracia, ed. 1996. *Puerto Rican Women and Work*. Philadelphia: Temple University Press.

Ortiz, Victoria, 1986. "Arthur Schomburg: A Biographic Essay." In *The Legacy of Arthur Alfonso Schomburg: A Celebration of the Past, a Vision for the Future*. New York: Schomburg Center for Black Culture.

Ortiz Cofer, Judith. 1987. *Terms of Survival*. Houston, TX: Arte Público Press.

———. 1989. *The Line of the Sun*. Athens: University of Georgia Press.

———. 1990. *Silent Dancing: Remembrances of a Puerto Rican Childhood*. Houston, TX: Arte Público Press.

———. 1993. *The Latin Deli*. 1993. Athens: University of Georgia Press.

———. 2000. *Woman in Front of the Sun: On Becoming a Writer*. Athens: University of Georgia Press.

———. 2015. *The Cruel Country*. Athens: University of Georgia Press.

Ortiz Guzmán, Angel, ed. 2006. *Hacia la Libre Asociación: El futuro*. San Juan: EMS Editores.

Padilla, Elena. 1958. *Up from Puerto Rico*. New York: Columbia University Press.

Padilla, Félix M. 1985. *Latino Ethnic Consciousness: The Case of Mexican Americans and Puerto Ricans in Chicago*. Notre Dame, IN: University of Notre Dame Press.

———. 1987. *Puerto Rican Chicago*. Notre Dame, IN: University of Notre Dame Press.

Pantoja, Antonia. 2002. *Memoir of a Visionary*. Houston, TX: Arte Público Press.

Pavlo, Walter. 2017. "Puerto Rico Debt Crisis: Lawsuit Claims UBS Scammed Island Residents." www.forbes.com/sites/walterpavlo/2017/11/02/puerto-rico-debt-crisis/lawsuit.

Pawel, Miriam. 2014. *The Crusades of César Chávez: A Biography*. New York: Bloomsbury Press.

Pedreira, Antonio. 1934. *Insularismo*. Madrid: Tipografía Artística.

Pedreira, Antonio S. [1941] 1969. *El periodismo en Puerto Rico*. San Juan: Instituto de Cultura Puertorriqueña.

Perdomo, Willie. 1996. *When a Nickel Costs a Dime*. New York: Norton.

———. 2002. *Postcards of El Barrio*. San Juan: Isla Negra Editores.

———. 2004. *Smoking Lovely*. New York: Rattapallax.

———. 2014. *The Essential Hits of Shorty Bon Bon: Poems*. New York: Penguin.

Pérez, Gina M. 2004. *The Near Northwest Side Story: Migration, Displacement and Puerto Rican Families*. Berkeley: University of California Press.

Pérez, Louis A. 1998. *The War of 1898: The United States and Cuba in History and Historiography*. Chapel Hill: University of North Carolina Press.

Pérez-Rosario, Vanessa. 2014. *Becoming Julia de Burgos: The Making of a Puerto Rican Icon*. Urbana: University of Illinois Press.

Picó, Fernando. 1990. *Historia general de Puerto Rico*. Río Piedras, PR: Ediciones Huracán.

Pietri, Pedro. 1973. *Puerto Rican Obituary*. New York: Monthly Review.

———. 1977. *Obituario puertorriqueño*. San Juan: Instituto de Cultura Puertorriqueña.

Piñero, Miguel. 1974. *Short Eyes*. New York: Hill and Wang.

———. 1980. *La Bodega Sold Dreams*. Houston, TX: Arte Público Press.

Poblete, Joanna. 2017. *Islanders in the Empire: Filipino and Puerto Rican Laborers in Hawai'i*. Urbana: University of Illinois Press.

Portes, Alejandro, and Rubén Rumbaut. 1996. *Immigrant America: A Portrait*. Berkeley: University of California Press.

Poyo, Gerald. 1989. *"With All, and for the Good of All": The Emergence of Popular Nationalism in the Cuban Communities of the United States, 1848–1898*. Durham, NC: Duke University Press.

Presser, H.B. 1980. "Puerto Rico: Recent Trends in Fertility and Sterilization." *Family Planning Perspectives* 12, no. 2: 102–106.

Proctor, Bernadette D., and Joseph Dalaker. 2002. *Poverty in the United States: 2001*. US Census Bureau, Current Population Reports, P60-219. Washington, DC: US Government Printing Office.

Puerto Rican Cultural Center (PRCC). N.d.a. "About." PRCC. http://www.prcc-chgo.org/about.

———. N.d.b. "Integrated PASEO." PRCC. http://www.prcc-chgo.org/integrated%20paseo.

Quintero Rivera, Angel. 1976a. *Conflictos de clases sociales en Puerto Rico*. Río Piedras, PR: Ediciones Huracán.

———. 1976b. *Worker's Struggle in Puerto Rico*. New York: Monthly Review Press.

———. 1980. "Notes on Puerto Rican National Development: Class and Nation in a Colonial Context." *Marxist Perspectives* 9, no. 3: 10–30.

———. 1988. *Patricios y plebeyos*. Río Piedras, PR: Ediciones Huracán.

———. 1999. *Salsa, sabor y control: Sociología de la música "tropical."* Mexico: Siglo Veintiuno Editores.

Ramírez, Yasmín. 2005. "Nuyorican Visionary: Jorge Soto and the Evolution of Afro-Taíno Aesthetic at Taller Boricua." *Centro Journal* 27, no. 2: 22–41.

Ramírez de Arellano, Arlene, and Conrad Seipp. 1983. *Colonialism, Catholicism, and Contraception: A History of Birth Control in Puerto Rico*. Chapel Hill: University of North Carolina Press.

Ramos, Juanita, ed. 1987. *Compañeras: Latina Lesbians*. New York: Latina Lesbian History Project.

Ramos-Zayas, Ana Y. 2003. *National Performances: The Politics of Class, Race, and Space in Puerto Rican Chicago*. Chicago: University of Chicago.

Ribero, Yeidy M. 2005. *Turning Out the Blackness: Race and Nation in the History of Puerto Rican Television*. Durham, NC: Duke University Press.

Rigau, Marco A., and Juan María García-Passalacqua. 1987. *República asociada y libre asociación: documentación de un debate*. San Juan: Editorial Atlántico.

Rivera, Carmen. 1994. *Julia*. In *Nuestro New York: An Anthology of Puerto Rican Plays*, edited by John V. Ambush, 133–178. New York: Penguin.

———. 2008. *La gringa*. New York: Samuel French.

———. 2014. *Julia de Burgos: Child of Water*. New York: Red Sugarcane Press.

Rivera, Carmen Haydée, and José L. Torres-Padilla, eds. 2008. *Writing Off the Hyphen: New Critical Perspectives on the Literature of the Puerto Rican Diaspora*. Seattle: University of Washington Press.

Rivera, Carmen S. 2002. *Kissing the Mango Tree: Puerto Rican Women Rewriting American Literature*. Houston, TX: Arte Público Press.

Rivera, Edward. 1982. *Family Installments: Memories of Growing Up Hispanic*. New York: Murrow.

Rivera, Eugenio. 2005. "La colonia de Lorain, Ohio." In *The Puerto Rican Diaspora: Historical Perspectives*, edited by Carmen T. Whalen and Víctor Vázquez-Hernández, 151–173. Philadelphia: Temple University Press.

Rivera, José. 1983. *The House of Ramón Iglesia*. New York: F. French.

———. 1994. *Marisol*. New York: Dramatists Play Service.

———. 2003. *References to Salvador Dalí Make Me Hot*. New York: Theatre Communications Group.

Rivera, Raquel Z. 2003. *New York Ricans from the Hip Hop Zone*. New York: Palgrave.

Rivera, Raquel Z., Wayne Marshall, and Deborah Pacini Hernández, eds. 2009. *Reggaetón*. Durham, NC: Duke University Press.

Rivera-Batiz, Francisco L. 1991. "The Effects of Literacy on the Earnings of Hispanics in the United States." In *Hispanics in the Labor Force: Issues and Policies*, edited by Edwin Meléndez, Clara Rodríguez, and Janis Barry Figueroa, 53–76. New York: Plenum Press.

———. 1992. "Quantitative Literacy and the Likelihood of Employment Among Young Adults." *Journal of Human Resources* (spring).

Rivera-Batiz, Francisco, and Carlos E. Santiago. 1994. *Puerto Ricans in the United States: A Changing Reality*. Washington, DC: National Puerto Rican Coalition.

———. 1996. *Island Paradox: Puerto Rico in the 1990s*. New York: Russell Sage Foundation.

Rivera-Rideau, Petra R. 2015. *Remixing Reggaetón: The Cultural Politics of Race in Puerto Rico*. Durham, NC: Duke University Press.

Rodríguez, Abraham. 1992. *The Boy Without a Flag: Tales of the South Bronx*. Minneapolis: Milkweed Editions.

———. 1993. *Spidertown*. New York: Hyperion.

———. 2001. *The Buddha Book*. New York: Picador.

———. 2008. *South by South Bronx*. New York: Akashic Books.

Rodríguez, Clara. 1974. *The Ethnic Queue in the US: The Case of Puerto Ricans*. San Francisco: R and E Research Associates.

———. 1989. *Puerto Ricans: Born in the USA*. Boston: Unwin Hyman.

———. 2000a. *Changing Race*. New York: New York University Press.

———. 2000b. "You've Come a Long Way Boricua! (Re)Viewing Our History in the Media." In *"Adiós, Borinquen querida": The Puerto Rican Diaspora, Its History, and Contributions*, edited by Edna Acosta-Belén, Margarita Benítez, José E. Cruz, Yvonne González-Rodríguez, Clara E. Rodríguez, Carlos E. Santiago, Azara Santiago-Rivera, and Barbara R. Sjostrom, 58–82. Albany, NY: CELAC and Comisión.

———. 2004. *Heroes, Lovers, and Others: The Story of Latinos in Hollywood*. Washington, DC: Smithsonian.

Rodríguez, Clara, and Edwin Meléndez. 1992. "Puerto Rican Poverty and Labor Markets." *Hispanic Journal of Behavioral Sciences* 14, no. 1: 4–15.

Rodríguez, Clara, Virginia Sánchez Korrol, and José Alers, eds. 1996. *Historical Survival of Puerto Ricans in the US*. 1996. Princeton, NJ: Markus Wiener.

Rodríguez Beruff, Jorge. 1988. *Política militar y dominación: Puerto Rico en el contexto hispanoamericano*. Río Piedras, PR: Ediciones Huracán.

Rodríguez Beruff, Jorge, and José L. Bolívar Fresneda. 2015. *Island at War: Puerto Rico in the Crucible of the Second World War*. Jackson: University Press of Mississippi.

Rodríguez de Tió, Lola. 1968a. "A Cuba." In *Obras completas*, 1:321. San Juan: Instituto de Cultura Puertorriqueña.

———. 1968b. *Obras completas*. 4 vols. San Juan: Instituto de Cultura Puertorriqueña.

Rodríguez-Silva, Ileana. 2012. *Silencing Race: Disentangling Blackness, Colonialism, and National Identities in Puerto Rico*. New York: Palgrave Macmillan.

Rogler, Lloyd. 1985. *Puerto Rican Families in New York City*. Maplewood, NJ: Waterfront Press.

Rogler, Lloyd, and August B. Hollingshead. 1961. "The Puerto Rican Spiritualist as a Psychiatrist." *American Journal of Sociology* 67, no. 1: 17–21.

Rosaldo, Renato. 1987. *Culture and Truth: The Remaking of Social Analysis*. Boston: Beacon.

Rosales, F. Arturo. 1997. *Chicano! The History of the Mexican American Civil Rights Movement*. Houston, TX: Arte Público Press.

Rosario Natal, Carmelo. 1983. *Éxodo puertorriqueño: Las emigraciones al Caribe y Hawaii: 1900–1915*. San Juan: n.p.

Rosenthal, Andrew. 2017. "Trump's Latest Outrage Against Puerto Rico." *New York Times*, October 12. https://nyti.ms/2kJXzoQ.

Rouse, Irving. 1992. *The Taínos: Rise and Decline of the People Who Greeted Columbus*. New Haven, CT: Yale University Press.

Rúa, Mérida M. 2012. *A Grounded Identidad: Making New Lives in Chicago's Puerto Rican Neighborhoods*. New York: Oxford University Press.

Sánchez, Juan. 1991. "The Metamorphosis/Search for the Island/Self and the Conflictive Plebiscite of the Mind." Catalogue of Exhibition *Bibiana Suárez: In Search of an Island*. Chicago: Sazama Gallery.

Sánchez, Luis Rafael. 1994. *La guagua aérea*. San Juan: Editorial Cultural.

Sánchez, María, and Anthony Stevens-Arroyo, eds. 1987. *Towards a Renaissance of Puerto Rican Studies*. New York: Atlantic Research.

Sánchez, Rita, and Sonia López, eds. 2017. *Chicana Tributes: Activist Women of the Civil Rights Movement*. San Diego: Montezuma Publishing.

Sánchez González, Lisa. 2001. *Boricua Literature: A Literary History of the Puerto Rican Literature*. New York: New York University Press.

———. 2013. *The Stories I Read to the Children: The Life and Writing of Pura Belpré, the Legendary Storyteller, Children's Author, and New York Public Librarian*. New York: Center for Puerto Rican Studies.

Sánchez Korrol, Virginia. [1983] 1994. *From Colonia to Community: The History of Puerto Ricans in New York City, 1917–1948*. Berkeley: University of California Press.

———. 2011–2012. "The Birth of an Institution: Multifaceted Prisms of PRSA's Early Years." *Latino(a) Research Review* 8, nos. 1–2: 60–72.

Sánchez Korrol, Virginia, and Pedro Juan Hernández. 2010. *Pioneros II: Puerto Ricans in New York City, 1948–1998*. Charleston, SC: Arcadia Publishing.

Sandoval-Sánchez, Alberto. 1992. "La identidad especular del allá y del acá: Nuestra propia imagen puertorriqueña en cuestión." *Centro Bulletin* 4, no. 2: 28–43.

Santiago, Carlos E. 1989. "The Dynamics of Minimum Wage Policy in Economic Development: A Multiple Time Series Approach." *Economic Development and Cultural Change* 38, no. 1: 1–30.

———. 1991. "Wage Policies, Employment, and Puerto Rican Migration." In *Hispanics in the Labor Force: Issues and Policies*, edited by Edwin Meléndez, Clara Rodríguez, and Janis Barry Figueroa, 225–245. New York: Plenum Press.

———. 1992. *Labor in the Puerto Rican Economy: Postwar Development and Stagnation*. New York: Praeger Publishers.

———. 1993. "The Migratory Impact of Minimum Wage Legislation: Puerto Rico, 1970–1987." *International Migration Review* 27, no. 4: 772–795.

Santiago, Carlos E., and Erik Thorbecke. 1988. "A Multisectoral Framework for the Analysis of Labor Mobility and Development in LDCs: An Application to Postwar Puerto Rico." *Economic Development and Cultural Change* 37, no. 1: 127–148.

Santiago, Esmeralda. 1993. *When I Was Puerto Rican*. Reading, MA: Addison-Wesley.

———. 1998. *Almost a Woman*. New York: Da Capo Press.

Santiago, Javier. 1994. *Nueva ola portoricensis*. San Juan: Editorial del Patio.

Santiago-Rivera, Azara L., and Carlos E. Santiago. 1999. "Puerto Rican Transnational Migration and Identity: Impact of English Language Acquisition on Length of Stay in the United States." In *Identities on the Move: Transnational Processes in North America and the Caribbean Basin*, edited by Liliana R. Goldin, 229–244. Austin: University of Texas Press.

Sassen, Saskia, 2014. *Expulsions: Brutality in the Global Capitalism*. Cambridge, MA: Harvard University Press.

Scarano, Francisco, ed. 1981. *Inmigración y clases sociales en el Puerto Rico del siglo XIX*. Río Piedras, PR: Ediciones Huracán.

———. 1984. *Sugar and Slavery in Puerto Rico: The Plantation Economy of Ponce, 1800–1850*. Madison: University of Wisconsin Press.

———. 1993. *Puerto Rico: Cinco siglos de historia*. San Juan: McGraw-Hill.

Schmidley, A. Dianne. 2001. *Profile of the Foreign-Born Population in the United States: 2000*. US Census Bureau. Current Population Reports. Series P23-206. Washington, DC: US Government Printing Office.

Seda Bonilla, Eduardo. 1972. *Requiem por una cultura*. Río Piedras, PR: Editorial Edil.

———. 1977. "Who Is a Puerto Rican? Problems of Socio-Cultural Identity in Puerto Rico." *Caribbean Studies* 17, nos. 1–2: 105–121.

Sen, Amartya K. 1966. "Peasants and Dualism with and Without Surplus Labor." *Journal of Political Economy* 64: 425–450.

Shaffer, Kirwin R. 2013. *Black Flag Boricuas: Anarchism, Antiauthoritarianism, and the Left in Puerto Rico, 1897–1921*. Urbana: University of Illinois Press.

Siegel, Arthur, Harold Orlans, and Loyal Greer. 1975. *Puerto Ricans in Philadelphia*. New York: Arno Press.

Silén, Iván, ed. 1983. *Los paraguas amarillos: Los poetas latinos en Nueva York*. Hanover, NH/Binghamton, NY: Ediciones del Norte/Bilingual Press.

Silén, Juan Angel. 1970. *Hacia una visión positiva del puertorriqueño*. Río Piedras, PR: Editorial Edil.

———. 1971. *We, the Puerto Rican People: A Story of Oppression and Resistance*. New York: Monthly Review Press.

———. 1976. *Pedro Albizu Campos*. Río Piedras, PR: Editorial Antillana.

———. 1996. *Nosotros solos: Pedro Albizu Campos y el nacionalismo irlandés*. Río Piedras, PR: Librería Norberto González.

Silva Gotay, Samuel. 1997. *Protestantismo y política en Puerto Rico 1898–1930*. Río Piedras, PR: Editorial de la Universidad de Puerto Rico.

Silvestrini, Blanca G., and María Dolores Luque de Sánchez. 1988. *Historia de Puerto Rico: Trayectoria de un pueblo*. San Juan: Editorial La Biblioteca.

Small, Mario Luis. 2004. *Villa Victoria: The Transformation of Social Capital in a Boston Barrio*. Chicago: University of Chicago Press.

Snite Museum of Art, University of Notre Dame. 2012. *Art and the Service of the People: Posters and Books from Puerto Rico's Division of Community Education (DIVEDCO), 1949–1989*. Notre Dame, IN: Snite Museum of Art.

Song-Ha Lee, Sonia. 2014. *Building a Latino Civil Rights Movement: Puerto Ricans, African Americans, and the Pursuit of Racial Justice in New York City*. Chapel Hill: University of North Carolina Press.

Soto, Pedro Juan. 1956. *Spiks*. México: Los Presentes.
———. 1973. *Spiks: Stories*. Translated by Victoria Ortiz. New York: Monthly Review Press.
———. 1962 . *Ardiente suelo, fría estación*. Río Piedras, PR: Ediciones Huracán.
———. 1973. *Hot Land, Cold Season*. New York: Dell.
Soto Vélez, Clemente. 1979. *La tierra prometida*. San Juan: Instituto de Cultura Puertorriqueña.
Sotomayor. Sonia. 2013a. *My Beloved World*. New York: Arthur A. Knopf.
———. 2013b. *Mi mundo adorado*. Translated by Eva Ibarzábal. New York: Vintage Group.
Stavans, Ilán. 2003. *Spanglish: The Making of a New American Language*. New York: HarperCollins.
———, ed. 2011. *The Norton Anthology of Latino Literature*. New York: Norton.
Sued-Badillo, Jalil. 1978. *Las caribes: Realidad o fábula*. Río Piedras, PR: Editorial Antillana.
———. 1979. *La mujer indígena y su sociedad*. Río Piedras, PR: Editorial Antillana.
Sued-Badillo, Jalil, and Angel López Cantos. 1986. *Puerto Rico negro*. Río Piedras, PR: Editorial Cultural.
Sullivan, Edward J., ed. 2010. *Nueva York 1613–1945*. New York: New York Historical Society and Scala Publishers.
Sutter, John D. 2018. "'We Are the Forgotten People': It's Been Almost Six Months Since Hurricane Maria, and Puerto Ricans Are Still Dying." https:/www.cnn .com/2018/03/15/politics/puerto-rico-six-month-deaths-sutter-invs/index.html.
Takaki, Ronald. [1993] 2008. *A Different Mirror: A History of Multicultural America*. New York: Back Bay Books.
Thomas, Lorrin. 2010. *Puerto Rican Citizen: The History and Political Identity in Twentieth-Century New York City*. Chicago: University of Chicago Press.
Thomas, Piri. 1967. *Down These Mean Streets*. New York: Knopf.
———. 1972. *Savior, Savior, Hold My Hand*. New York: Doubleday.
———. 1974. *Seven Long Times*. New York: Praeger.
Thompson, Lanny. 1995. *Nuestra isla y su gente: La construcción del "otro" puertorriqueño en Our Islands and Their People*. Río Piedras, PR: Centro de Investigaciones Sociales/Departamento de Historia, Universidad de Puerto Rico.
———. 2010. *Imperial Archipelago: Representation and Rule in the Insular Territories Under U.S. Dominion After 1998*. Honolulu: University of Hawaii Press.
Tienda, Marta. 1989. "Puerto Ricans and the Underclass Debate." *Annals of the American Academy of Political and Social Science* (January).
Tienda, Marta, and William Díaz. 1987. "Puerto Rican Circular Migration." *New York Times*, August 28.
Tienda, Marta, and L. Jensen. 1988. "Poverty and Minorities: A Quarter-Century Profile of Color and Socioeconomic Disadvantage." In *Divided Opportunities: Minorities, Poverty and Social Policy*, edited by G. Sandefur and Marta Tienda, 23–62. New York: Plenum Press.
Tió, Teresa. 2003. *El cartel en Puerto Rico*. Mexico: Pearson Educación.
Todd, Roberto H. 1939. *La invasión americana: Cómo surgió la idea de traer la guerra a Puerto Rico*. San Juan: Cantero Fernández.
Toro-Morn, Maura I. 2005. "Boricuas en Chicago: Gender and Class in the Migration and Settlement of Puerto Ricans." In *The Puerto Rican Diaspora: Historical Perspectives*, edited by Carmen T. Whalen and Víctor Vázquez-Hernández, 128–150. Philadelphia: Temple University Press.

Torre, Carlos, Hugo Rodríguez Vecchini, and William Burgos, eds. 1994. *The Commuter Nation: Perspectives on Puerto Rican Migration*. Río Piedras, PR: University of Puerto Rico Press.
Torres, Andrés. 1995. *Between Melting Pot and Mosaic: African Americans and Puerto Ricans in New York*. Philadelphia: Temple University Press.
———. 1998. "Introduction: Political Radicalism in the Diaspora—The Puerto Rican Experience." In *The Puerto Rican Movement: Voices of the Diaspora*, edited by Andrés Torres and José E. Velázquez, 1–24. Philadelphia: Temple University Press.
———. 2011–2012. "Puerto Rican Studies: Four Decades and Counting." *Latino(a) Research Review* 8, nos. 1–2: 9–24.
Torres, Andrés, and José E. Velázquez, eds. 1998. *The Puerto Rican Movement: Voices of the Diaspora*. Philadelphia: Temple University Press.
Torres, Edwin. 1975. *Carlito's Way*. New York: Saturday Review Press.
———. 1977. *Q&A*. New York: Dial Press.
Torres, Edwin. 1999. *Fractured Humorous*. New York: SUBpress.
———. 2001. *The All-Union Day of the Shock Worker*. New York: Roof Books.
———. 2010. *In the Function of External Circumstances*. New York: Nightboat Books.
———. 2014. *Ameriscopia*. Tucson: Camino del Sol, University of Arizona Press.
Torres Rivera, Alejandro. 1999. *Militarismo y descolonización: Puerto Rico ante el siglo 21*. San Juan: Congreso Nacional Hostosiano.
Torruella, Juan R. 2007. "The Insular Cases: The Establishment of a Regimen of Political Apartheid." *University of Pennsylavania Journal of International Law* 29, no. 2: 283–347.
Torruella Leval, Susana. 1998. "Los artistas puertorriqueños en los Estados Unidos: Solidaridad, resistencia, identidad." In *Puerto Rico: Arte e identidad*, edited by Hermandad de Artistas Gráficos de Puerto Rico, 371–402. Río Piedras, PR: Editorial Universidad de Puerto Rico.
Trelles, Miguel, and Juan Fernando Morales. 2013. *Posters on the Wall: Our Nuyorican Story*. New York: Center for Puerto Rican Studies, Hunter College.
Trías Monge, José. 1999a. *Puerto Rico: Las penas de la colonia más antigua del mundo*. Río Piedras, PR: Editorial Universidad de Puerto Rico.
———. 1999b. *Puerto Rico: The Trials of the Oldest Colony in the World*. New Haven, CT: Yale University Press.
Trigo, María de los Angeles. 2016. *The United States and the PROMESA to Puerto Rico: An Analysis of the Puerto Rico Oversight, Managements and Economic Stability Act*. San Juan: Author.
Tugwell, Rexford G. 1947. *The Stricken Land: The Story of Puerto Rico*. New York: Doubleday.
Turner, Faythe, ed. 1991. *Puerto Rican Writers at Home in the USA*. Seattle, WA: Open Hand Publishing.
Umpierre-Herrera, Luz María. 1987. *The Margarita Poems*. Bloomington, IN: Third Woman Press.
Underhill, Harold. 1961. "Puerto Rico: A Showcase of Democracy." *The Diplomat*. January 16, 36.
UN Human Rights Office of the High Commissioner. 2017. "Puerto Rico: Human Rights Concerns Mount in Absence of Adequate Emergency Response." October 20.www.ohchr.org/EN/NewsEvents/Pages/DisplayNews.aspx?NewsID=22326& LangID=E.
US Census Bureau. 2014. "Hispanic Roots: Breakdown of U.S. Hispanic Population, by Specific Origin: 2014." www.census.gov/popest/ and www.census.gov/acs.

————. 2003. *Annual Social and Economic (ASEC) Supplement, Current Population Survey (CPS)*. Washington, DC: Bureau of the Census.

US Commission on Civil Rights. 1976. *Puerto Ricans in the Continental United States: An Uncertain Future*. Washington, DC: The Commission.

US Department of Commerce. 1993. *1990 Census of Population and Housing Public Use Microdata Samples: Technical Documentation*. Washington, DC: Bureau of the Census.

US Department of Labor. 1903. *Report of the Commissioner of Labor on Hawaii, Bulletin of the Department of Labor*, No. 47.

Valdés, Vanessa K. 2017. *Diasporic Blackness: The Life and Times of Arturo Alfonso Schomburg*. Albany: State University of New York Press.

Valdes-Fallis, Guadalupe. 1978. *Code-Switching and the Classroom Teacher*. Washington, DC: Center for Applied Linguistics.

Valdez, Luis. N.d. https://www.goodreads.com/search?q=luis+valdez&search [source]=goodreads&search_type=quotes&tab=quotes.

Valle Ferrer, Norma, ed. 2008. *Luisa Capetillo: Obra completa: "Mi Patria es la Libertad."* San Juan/Cayey: Departamento del Trabajo y Recursos Humanos y Proyecto de Estudios de las Mujeres.

Vargas-Ramos, Carlos. 2017. *Race Front and Center: Perspectives on Race Among Puerto Ricans*. New York: Centro Press.

Vázquez Calzada, José L. 1973. "La esterilización femenina en Puerto Rico." *Revista de Ciencias Sociales* 17, no. 3: 281–308.

————. 1979. "Demographic Aspects of Migration." In *Labor Migration Under Capitalism: The Puerto Rican Experience*, edited by History Task Force, Centro de Estudios Puertorriqueños, 223–236. New York: Monthly Review Press.

————. 1988. *La población de Puerto Rico y su trayectoria histórica*. Río Piedras, PR: Universidad de Puerto Rico, Escuela de Salud Pública.

Vázquez-Hernández, Víctor. 2017. *Before the Wave: Puerto Ricans in Philadelphia, 1910–1945*. New York: Centro Press.

Vega, Bernardo. 1977. *Memorias de Bernardo Vega: Contribución a la historia de la comunidad puertorriqueña en Nueva York*. Edited by César Andreu Iglesias. Río Piedras, PR: Ediciones Huracán.

————. 1984. *Memoirs of Bernado Vega: A Contribution to the History of the Puerto Rican Community in New York*. Edited by César Andreu Iglesias. Translated by Juan Flores. New York: Monthly Review.

Vega, Ed. 1985. *The Comeback*. Houston, TX: Arte Público Press.

————. 1987. *Mendoza's Dreams*. 1987. Houston, TX: Arte Público Press.

————. 1991. *Casualty Report*. 1991. Houston, TX: Arte Público Press.

Vega Yunqué, Edgardo. 2004. *Lamentable Journey of Omaha Bigelow into the Impenetrable Loisaida Jungle*. New York: Overlook.

Velásquez, Alicea, and Carlos Velásquez. 2007. *Puerto Rican Day Parade*. New York: Galos.

Vélez Pizarro, Gustavo. 2015. *Puerto Rico's Debt Crisis: Challenges and Opportunities*. San Juan: Author.

Venator-Santiago, Charles R. 2017. "Today, Being Born in Puerto Rico Is Tantamount to Being Born in the United States." *Centro Journal* 29, no. 1: 13–15.

Venator-Santiago, Charles R., and Edgardo Meléndez, eds. 2017. *U.S. Citizenship in Puerto Rico: Over One Hundred Years After the Jones Act*. Special issue, *Centro Journal* 29, no. 1.

Vera-Rojas, María Teresa. 2010. "Polémicas feministas, puertorriqueñas y desconocidas: Clotilde Betances Yaeger, María Mas Pozo y sus 'charlas femeninas' en el Gráfico de Nueva York, 1929–1930." *Centro Journal* 22, no. 2: 4–32.

———. 2010–2011. "Alianzas transgresoras: Hispanismo, feminismo y cultura en *Artes y Letras.*" *Latino(a) Research Review* 8, nos. 1–2: 175–198.

Vicens, A. J. 2017. "The Final Republican Tax Bill Screws Over Puerto Rico." https://www.motherjones.com/politics/2017/12/the-final-republican-tax-bill-screws-over-puerto-rico/.

Wagenheim, Kal. 1975. *Survey of Puerto Ricans on the US Mainland in the 1970s.* New York: Praeger.

Walker, Ken L. 2010. "Out of My Own Way: An Interview with Edwin Torres." www.raintaxi.com/out-of-my-own-way-an-interview-with-edwin-torres/.

Wanzer-Serrano, Darrel. 2015. *The New York Young Lords and the Struggles for Liberation.* Philadelphia: Temple University Press.

War Department. 1902. *Annual Reports of the War Department, Report of the Military Governor of Porto Rico on Civil Affairs.* Washington, DC: Government Printing Office.

Whalen, Carmen T. 2001. *From Puerto Rico to Philadelphia: Puerto Rican Workers and Postwar Economies.* Philadelphia: Temple University Press.

———. 2006. *El Viaje: Puerto Ricans of Philadelphia.* Charleston, SC: Arcadia Publishing.

Whalen, Carmen T., and Víctor Vázquez-Hernández, eds. 2005. *The Puerto Rican Diaspora: Historical Perspectives.* Philadelphia: Temple University Press.

Wheeler, Major-General Joseph, and José de Olivares. 1899. *Our Islands and Their People as Seen with Camera and Pencil.* New York: N. D. Thompson Publishing.

White, Gillian B. 2016. "Puerto Rico's Problems Go Way Beyond Its Debt." *Atlantic*, July 1. https://www.theatlantic.com/business/archive/2016/07/puerto-rico-promesa-debt/489797.

White, Trumbull. 1898. *Our New Possessions.* Boston: Adams.

Wilson, William J., and Kathryn M. Neckerman. 1986. "Poverty and Family Structure: The Widening Gap Between Evidence and Public Policy Issues." In *Fighting Poverty: What Works and What Doesn't*, edited by S. Danziger and D. Weinberg, 232–259. Cambridge, MA: Harvard University Press.

Wilson, William Julius. 1987. *The Truly Disadvantaged: The Inner City, the Underclass, and Public Policy.* Chicago: University of Chicago Press.

Yeampierre, Elizabeth, and Naomi Kein. 2017. "Imagine Puerto Rico Recovery Designed by Puerto Ricans." *Intercept*, October 20. https://theintercept.com/2017/10/20/Puerto-rico-hurricane-debt-relief.

Young Lords Party and Michael Abramson. 1971. *Palante: The Young Lords Party.* Chicago: Haymarket Books.

———. 2011. *Palante: Voices and Photographs of the Young Lords, 1969–1971.* Chicago: Haymarket Books.

Zenón, Isabelo. 1974, 1975. *Narciso descubre su trasero: El negro en la cultura puertorriqueña.* 2 vols. Humacao, PR: Editorial Furidi.

Zimmerman, Marc. 2011. *Defending Our Own in the Cold: The Cultural Turns of Puerto Ricans.* Urbana: University of Illinois Press.

Index

Foraker Act of 1900, 8, 22*n*11, 65, 85, 124, 307
Ford Foundation, 184, 209
Forrest, Gerardo, 49–50, 53
Fortuño, Luis, 313
Foundation for Puerto Rico, 131
Fourteenth Amendment, 11
Fraga, Juan, 49
Franco, Francisco, 223
Free Federation of Puerto Rico's Workers. *See* Federación Libre de los Trabajadores de Puerto Rico
Freeland, Lucas, 138*n*3
Friends of Puerto Rico. *See* Los Amigos de Puerto Rico
Fuentes, Luis, 190
Fuerzas Armadas de Liberación Nacional (FALN, Armed Forces for National Liberation), 177, 178, 181
Fundación Comunitaria de Puerto Rico, 131

La gaceta del pueblo (The people's gazette), 220
García, Adrián, 267
García, Ana María, 89*n*16
García, Gervasio, 213*n*8
García, Robert, 186, 312
García Padilla, Alejandro, 123, 313
García-Ellín, Juan Carlos, 117*n*7
Gauguin, Paul, 263
GDP. *See* Gross domestic product
Gerena Valentín, Gilberto, 203, 310
Girmay, Aracelis, 248
Glazer, Nathan, 152
GNP. *See* Gross national product
Golder, Janine, 247
Goldsen, Rose, 66
Gómez, Magdalena, 247–248
Gómez, Obed, 274
González, José Luis, 31, 228
González, Juan, 180
Gottschalk, Peter, 140
Gráfico (newspaper), 222, 230, 231, 232
Graphic arts, 263–264
Great Depression, 4, 59, 64, 75–76, 308
Great Migration, 4, 6, 11, 59, 85, 87; in historical context, 91–99, 152–153, 172, 285; New Millennium and, 138*n*16; out-migration and, 126
Great Recession of 2007, 120–121, 138*n*1, 147, 166–167, 169*n*5

Greater Antilles, 26
Grito de Lares (Lares Revolt), 36, 48, 219, 223, 268, 305
Grito de Yara, 36, 48
Grosfoguel, Ramón, 252
Gross domestic product (GDP), 123
Gross national product (GNP), 121*fig*
Growing-up narratives, 252–256
Gruening, Ernest, 78, 81
Guabancex, 28, 41*n*5
Guagua aérea (airbus or flying bus), 14, 88, 153
Guarionex (Tapia y Rivera), 41*n*4
Guayama, 31
Guaynabo, 130
Guerrero, Amalia, 264
Guerrero, José, 269
Guevara, Ernesto "Che," 261
Gutiérrez, Juan, 279
Gutiérrez, Luis V., 185–186, 302*n*7, 312
Gutiérrez, Marina, 265
Guzmán, Charlie "Isa," 249

Hacendados, 37, 63
HACER. *See* Hispanic Women's Center
Haitians, 152
Hall, Stuart, 235–236
Harlem. *See* Spanish Harlem
Harlem Renaissance, 54, 231, 246
Harlow, Larry, 278
Hartford, Connecticut, 111, 113–115, 117*n*9, 162, 187
Harvest of Empire: A History of Latinos in America (González, J.), 180
Haslip-Viera, Gabriel, 28, 41*n*6, 208
Hatillo, 31
Hawaii, 68–71, 204, 244, 307, 313
Hawaii Sugar Planters' Association, 69
Hawkins, John, 304
Hay, John, 55
Head Start, 192
Health, 138*n*3, 185, 197
Henna, Julio J., 53, 306
Herencia: The Anthology of Hispanic Literature of the United States (Kanellos), 244
Heritage, 30–33, 70, 313
Hermandad Puertorriqueña en América (Porto Rican Brotherhood of America), 73, 308
Hernández, Carmen Dolores, 258

About the Book

Fully revised and expanded to reflect more than a decade of new developments and data, the second edition of this widely acclaimed book presents an up-to-date, comprehensive portrait of the second-largest Latino group in the United States.

Edna Acosta-Belén and Carlos Santiago trace the trajectory of the Puerto Rican experience from the early colonial period, through a series of waves of migration to the United States, to current cultural legacies and political and social challenges. Their work is an indispensable resource for anyone seeking to understand the history, contributions, and contemporary realities of the ever-growing Puerto Rican diaspora.

Edna Acosta-Belén is distinguished professor emerita of Latin American, Caribbean, and US Latino studies, and of women's, gender, and sexuality studies at the University at Albany, State University of New York. **Carlos E. Santiago** is commissioner of higher education for the state of Massachusetts; before joining the Department of Education, he was chancellor of the University of Wisconsin–Milwaukee and professor in the university's Department of Economics.